TOHOPEKA

TOHOPEKA

Rethinking the Creek War and the War of 1812

Edited by
Kathryn E. Holland Braund

A PEBBLE HILL BOOK
THE UNIVERSITY OF ALABAMA PRESS

Published by Pebble Hill, an imprint of the Caroline Marshall Draughon Center for the Arts and Humanities, College of Liberal Arts, Auburn University, and The University of Alabama Press

Manufactured in the United States of America

Typeface: ACaslon

∞
The paper on which this book is printed meets the minimum requirements of American National Standard for Information Sciences—Permanence of Paper for Printed Library Materials, ANSI Z39.48-1984.

Library of Congress Cataloging-in-Publication Data

Tohopeka : rethinking the Creek war and the war of 1812 / edited by Kathryn E. Holland Braund.
p. cm.
"A Pebble Hill Book."
ISBN 978-0-8173-5711-5 (pbk. : alk. paper) — ISBN 978-0-8173-8615-3 (electronic)
1. Creek War, 1813–1814. 2. Indians of North America—Wars—1812–1815. 3. Horseshoe Bend, Battle of, Ala., 1814. 4. United States—History—War of 1812. I. Braund, Kathryn E. Holland, 1955–
E83.813.T65 2012
973.5—dc23
2012005530

Cover image: Detail of map of the Battle of Horseshoe Bend by J. L. Holmes for Captain Leonard L. Tarrant of Winchester, Tennessee. The village of Tohopeka (Tehoopcau) is at the tip of the inside bend of the river. The main log fortification (Breast Works) are below, with Jackson's forces and artillery in front of them and red hatches (representing Red Stick Creeks defending the barricade) behind. Courtesy of the Alabama Department of Archives and History.

Cover design: Erin Kirk New

In remembrance of those who fought and died at Tohopeka

Contents

List of Illustrations ix

Foreword: A Deliberate Passion
Marianne Mills xi

Preface
Jay Lamar xv

Acknowledgments xvii

Introduction
Kathryn E. Holland Braund 1

1. Causalities and Consequences of the Creek War: A Modern Creek Perspective
Robert G. Thrower 10

2. Thinking outside the Circle: Tecumseh's 1811 Mission
Gregory Evans Dowd 30

3. "A Packet from Canada": Telling Conspiracy Stories on the 1813 Creek Frontier
Robert P. Collins 53

4. Red Sticks
Kathryn E. Holland Braund 84

5. Before Horseshoe: Andrew Jackson's Campaigns in the Creek War Prior to Horseshoe Bend
Tom Kanon 105

6. Cherokees in the Creek War: A Band of Brothers
Susan M. Abram 122

7. Horseshoe Bend: A Living Memorial
Ove Jensen 146

8. Fort Jackson and the Aftermath
Gregory A. Waselkov 158

9. "We Bleed Our Enemies in Such Cases to Give Them Their Senses": Americans' Unrelenting Wars on the Indians of the Trans-Appalachian West, 1810–1814
John E. Grenier 170

10. "Where All Behave Well": Fort Bowyer and the War on the Gulf, 1814–1815
David S. Heidler and Jeanne T. Heidler 182

11. Archaeology, Geography, and the Creek War in Alabama
Craig T. Sheldon Jr. 200

12. Digging Twice: Camps and Historical Sites Associated with the War of 1812 and the Creek War of 1813–1814
James W. Parker 232

Afterword: The Western Muscogee (Creek) Perspective
Ted Isham 247

Appendix 1: Current Preservation Status of Major Creek War/War of 1812 Sites in Alabama 249

Appendix 2: Known and Potential Archaeological Sites in Alabama 255

Bibliography 273

Contributors 301

Index 305

Illustrations

0.1. Battlefields and forts of the Creek War, adapted from "General Jackson's Campaign against the Creek Indians, 1813 & 1814" xiv

0.2. Detail of Captain Leonard Tarrant's map of the Battle of Horseshoe Bend xx–xxi

1.1. Map of Fort Mims and environs, 1813 19

1.2. Detail of Fort Mims map 20

2.1. Tecumseh 37

3.1. Burnt Corn Creek battlefield 72

4.1. Creek Indian weaponry 90

4.2. Head matron, Ribbon Dance, New Tulsa square ground, 1965 92

5.1. The Battle of Talladega 114–15

6.1. Detail from "For General Jackson's 1813–1815 Campaign against the Creek Indians" 131

6.2. Major Ridge 134

7.1. John Cheatham's battle map of Horseshoe Bend, March 27, 1814 150

7.2. Selocta, the son of Chinnabee, a Natchee (Natchez) Creek chief 152

7.3. Menawa, the military leader of Red Stick forces at Horseshoe Bend 154

7.4. Horseshoe Bend National Military Park 155

8.1. The Creek Nation following the Treaty of Fort Jackson 164

10.1. Oil portrait of General Andrew Jackson, ca. 1814 188

10.2. Map of Mobile Point and part of the bay and Dauphin Island 190–91
11.1. The Upper Creek country on the eve of the Creek War 202
11.2. Signs of war 215
12.1. Map of the war in South Alabama in 1813 and 1814 236–37
12.2. Military cap insignia from the Creek War and aftermath 241

Foreword

A Deliberate Passion: Creating and Commemorating the First National Park in Alabama

Marianne Mills

Horseshoe Bend is one of only four National Park Service units primarily focused on the period of the War of 1812. It is the only national park unit east of the Mississippi that commemorates a battle between US and American Indian forces. It is the site of the highest loss of American Indian life in a single battle in US history. And it was the first national park established in Alabama.

How does a place become a national park? Why are some places so precious to an entire nation that we hold them up as things that we want the world to know about us as a people? Creating a national park is not an easy process. Creating a new national park takes politics and it also takes people; so, passion and deliberate action.

There are four criteria for a national park. Each national park in our nation must be an outstanding example of a particular type of resource. A national park must possess exceptional value or quality in illustrating or interpreting themes of our nation's heritage. It must offer superlative opportunities for public recreation and enjoyment and/or scientific study. And every national park must retain a high degree of integrity as a true, accurate, and relatively unspoiled example of the resource. Today, there are nearly four hundred parks across the entire nation. National significance is a critical requirement for a national park. It must be considered suitable, which means that it has to represent a theme that is not currently represented in the national park system or by another agency. It has to be feasible, meaning it's practical and a big enough size for us to protect and want to invite the public into.

Each national park unit began with individuals who cared so deeply about a topic, an issue, or a place that they were willing to spend their time and sometimes even their money to set an area aside. In our case, the very first attempt was in 1907, when the Horseshoe Bend Battle Commission petitioned Congress to establish a military park. Had this happened, the park would have been one of the first fifteen units of the National Park System. But, instead, Congress merely awarded the group $5,000 to establish a monument, which we still have in the park today.

Time marched on, and in the 1940s, two very passionate people who loved history came together at a unique moment in time. Thomas Martin of Alabama Power Company and Judge C. J. Coley of Alexander City both wanted the Horseshoe Bend battlefield to be protected because there was the potential that the site would be flooded by the construction of Martin Dam. So these men worked tirelessly, knocking on doors, calling on their friends, and eventually they got the ear of Congress. In 1956, Congress told the state of Alabama that if it could acquire the land, then it would become a national park. So the process began. And in 1959, sufficient land was acquired so that the park was established. And so 2009 marks the fiftieth anniversary of Horseshoe Bend National Military Park.

Today, Horseshoe Bend is the second largest national park in Alabama, at 2,040 acres. The park not only includes the battle site but the site of a Creek village. It has four historic structures, including monuments and gravesites. We also have the remnants of Miller Covered Bridge. The park is abundant in natural resources as well, with 901 known plant species and 354 known animal species. We also have archaeological sites and museum collections. One hundred thousand people visit the park each year, and seventy thousand of them make use of park services. The park sponsors a series of special events and children's programs throughout the year.

Each park has to develop its purpose statement. In consultation with our partners, Horseshoe Bend (HOBE) developed these purpose statements:

- HOBE commemorates the Battle of Horseshoe Bend and the people in it.
- HOBE interprets the cultural relationship and conflicts leading to the Creek Indian War and its impacts on the Creek people.
- HOBE interprets the War of 1812 and the subsequent western expansion of the United States.
- HOBE interprets the role the battle played in the career of Andrew Jackson and the development of our nation.
- HOBE preserves the battlefield and associated landscapes that support native Alabama plants and wildlife.
- HOBE provides educational and recreational opportunities beyond compare that are compatible with those resources for enjoyment and inspiration for the visiting public.

We also have significance statements:

- The decisive battle led to the creation of the state of Alabama and the westward expansion of the United States.

- The events at Horseshoe Bend established the prominence of Andrew Jackson as a national hero and, ultimately, a political leader.
- The battle contributed to the forced emigration of most of the Creek people to Indian Territory (present-day Oklahoma).
- While the Revolutionary War gave definition to America as a nation, the War of 1812 began to give definition to the American identity as diverse people joined to fight for a new nation.
- Sites within the park provide a unique venue into interpretation of Creek Indian culture, the largest and most influential Indian nation in the Southeast in the late eighteenth and early nineteenth centuries.
- The victory at Horseshoe Bend gave leverage to the US negotiations during the 1814 Treaty of Ghent, which lead to a *status quo ante bellum* agreement, which means "let things return to the way they were before the war."

We have fundamental values, the things that all of us who work at the park hold dear:

- Horseshoe Bend contains the story of the power of individuals, like C. J. Coley and Thomas Martin, and the role of local communities, like Dadeville in Alexander City, in the establishment of a national park.
- We have natural beauty with clean air and night skies.
- We have converging ecosystems where the Blue Ridge meets the Piedmont physiographic region.
- We have a peaceful, modern setting that provides a point of contemplation on a very violent past.
- We offer opportunities for solitude, contemplation, and outdoor recreation.

So where is the passion today? We have a very exciting opportunity. The bicentennial of the Battle of Horseshoe Bend, in March 2014, is clearly significant and important. The bicentennial of the battle coincides with the centennial of the National Park Service. So there is a convergence of opportunities to promote our park, educate the public as to its national significance, and move forward with plans for the future. The newly organized Friends of Horseshoe Bend (http://www.friendsofhorseshoebend.org) will provide opportunities for everyone to become a supporter of the park. At Horseshoe Bend, we have the four *V*'s that we offer to every visitor: visit us often, visit us virtually (http://www.nps.gov/hobe/index.htm), volunteer at the park, and vote for any issues that are important to you that affect the park—stay passionate.

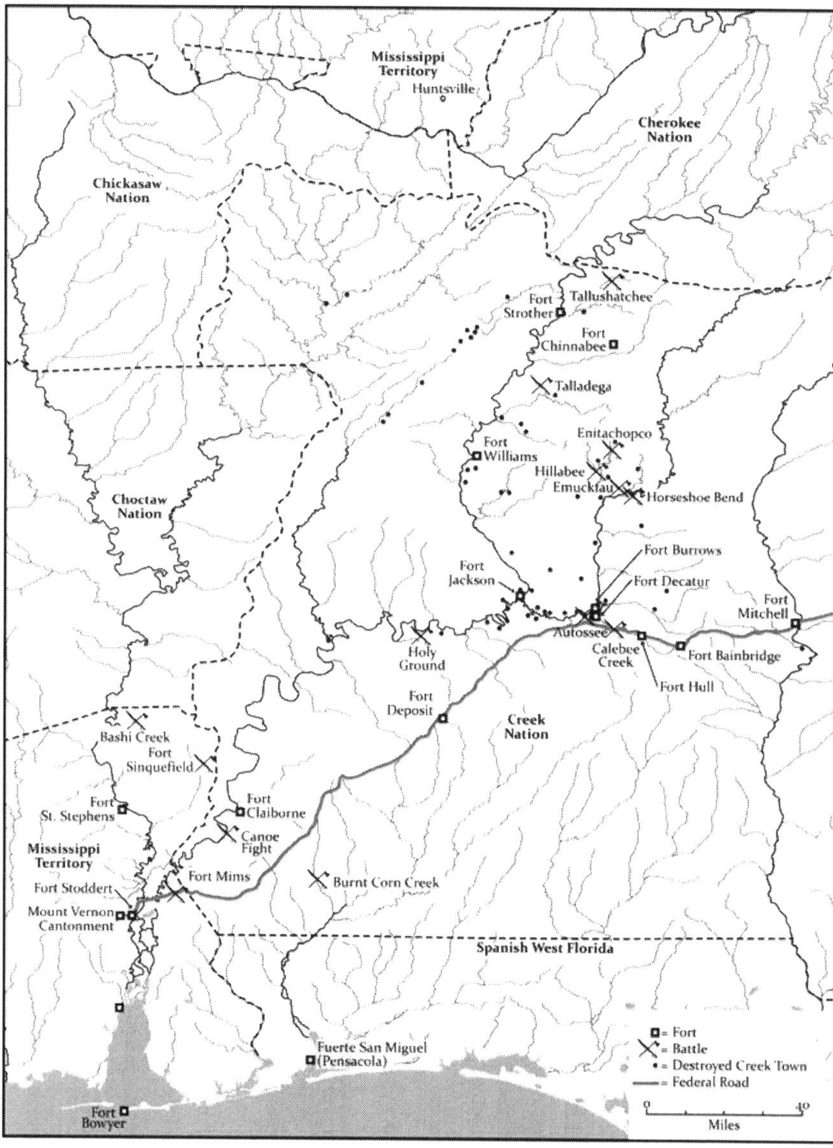

Battlefields and forts of the Creek War, adapted from "General Jackson's Campaign against the Creek Indians, 1813 & 1814," Record Group 77, CWMF, Misc. 11, 1813 and 1814, National Archives and Records Administration, Washington, D.C. Map by Sarah Mattics, Center for Archaeological Studies, University of South Alabama.

Preface

Jay Lamar

Almost two hundred years ago, the territory that would become Alabama was both ancient homeland and new frontier. In its forests and meadowlands, along its creeks and rivers, in its towns and forts and wilderness, a complex network of allegiances and agendas were playing out. In the early 1800s, the fabric of that network stretched and frayed as the Creek Civil War of 1813–1814 pitted a faction of the Creek Nation, known as the Red Sticks, against those Creeks who supported the Creek National Council. The war began in July 1813 as Red Stick rebels were returning to their towns with ammunition they had procured from the Spanish government in Pensacola. They were attacked near Burnt Corn Creek by Mississippi militia and settlers from the Tensaw area in a vain attempt to keep the ammunition from reaching the main body of disaffected warriors. The Red Sticks staged a retaliatory strike against a fortified settlement owned by Samuel Mims, which had become a gathering place for settlers who were protected by the Mississippi territorial militia. The attack on Fort Mims was a complete Red Stick victory, but the brutality of the assault, in which 250 people were killed, outraged the American public and "Remember Fort Mims" became a national battle cry. Against the backdrop of the American-British War of 1812, Americans, fearful that the Indians would ally with the British, quickly joined the war against the Red Sticks, turning the civil war into a military campaign designed to destroy Creek power. Assisted by Cherokee and Choctaw warriors, the allied forces devastated the Creek country, burning nearly every Creek town. The battles of the Red Sticks have become part of Alabama—and American—legend and include the famous Canoe Fight, the Battle of the Holy Ground, and, most significantly, the Battle of Tohopeka, or Horseshoe Bend, the final great battle of the war. There, an American army crushed Creek resistance and made a national hero of Andrew Jackson.

That is but the barest outline of this seminal event in Creek, southern, and national history. On May 22–23, 2009, the Caroline Marshall Draughon

Center for the Arts and Humanities, the engagement office for the Auburn University College of Liberal Arts, and the Horseshoe Bend National Military Park, with funding from the National Park Service, cosponsored a symposium on the Creek War and the War of 1812 in the South. Presenters representing a variety of perspectives and using a wide array of evidence and myriad approaches—from scrutiny of cultural and religious practices to literary and linguistic analysis, as well as new attention to material culture and documentary and archaeological records—filled in the details, added new information, disabused us of outdated interpretations, and urged us forward in discovery and discussion.

Gatherings such as the Creek War and War of 1812 symposium bring together scholars and the public to explore, learn about, and discuss issues and ideas that inform our understanding of who we are, where we've been, and where we are going. That is at the very heart of the Auburn University College of Liberal Arts' engagement mission. It is with great pleasure that we share with you and future readers the symposium proceedings gathered here. It will keep alive and even extend the intellectual exchange and excitement of discovery that are the cornerstones of meaningful outreach.

For their support of the symposium and this volume, we thank the wonderful people at Horseshoe Bend National Military Park. Marianne Mills, park director, and Ove Jensen, park ranger, were co-conspirators of the first order. We thank them especially for securing the grant from the National Park Service that funded the symposium. We also thank the Jule Collins Smith Museum of Fine Art and its director, Marilyn Laufer, and staff, Colleen Bourdeau and Mike Cortez, for offering assistance and space for the symposium. Managing everything from tables to technology, they were indispensable. A special thank you to the staff of the Caroline Marshall Draughon Center for the Arts and Humanities, especially Mark Wilson, Maiben Beard, Nancy Griggs, Dalton Hensley, and interns Cassity Holmes and Kate Winford, who worked tirelessly and with astounding organization to bring the symposium into being. Thanks also go to the dean of the College of Liberal Arts, Dr. Anna Gramberg, for her support of the symposium and this volume. Last but not least, I would be remiss if I didn't tell you that this gathering was the brainchild of Kathryn E. Holland Braund. Her academic expertise, her connections in the scholarly community, and her commitment to taking history to the people are a gift and a treasure to our college and university and to the state. Neither the symposium nor this book could have happened without her: both are a testimony to her deep commitment to preserving and sharing the history of our region and nation.

Acknowledgments

I would like to thank Ove Jensen, my friend and ally in this endeavor, for his vision and unwavering determination to bring historical scholarship and the public together. Ove's zeal and devotion to Horseshoe Bend National Military Park inspired me from the moment we first met and his continuing service to one of the Creek people's most revered sites warrants the respect of all who love historic places and admire the Creek people. Marianne Mills, who was superintendent of Horseshoe Bend National Military Park at the time of the symposium, spearheaded the funding effort from the National Park Service. She and Ove worked with Auburn University to make our Creek War and War of 1812 symposium a reality. I would also like to thank all the staff at Horseshoe Bend for their support and assistance. They are a collegial group of public historians who work tirelessly to promote and interpret one of the nation's most important battlefields. Thanks as well to Jay Lamar, who, as head of Auburn's Carolyn Marshall Draughon Center for the Arts and Humanities, is tireless in her efforts to bring scholars and the public together. The man responsible for most of the drudgery involved with making the symposium work, Mark Wilson, deserves special acknowledgment, not only for expert planning but for the good cheer with which the myriad tasks associated with the symposium planning were completed. I would also like to thank Dr. Charles Israel, chair of Auburn's History Department, for his support, encouragement, and assistance with the symposium. I would especially like to thank my fellow contributors for their collaboration on this project, as well as for the hard work their contributions represent. Special commendation is due to Sarah Mattics of the University of South Alabama, who worked with me to produce the maps for the volume. Many thanks are also due to Gregory A. Waselkov and Craig Sheldon for their assistance in numerous tasks associated with preparing illustrations, maps, and editing.

For permission to use images from their collections, I wish to acknowledge the assistance and support of the following individuals and their institutions: Meredith McLemore and Debbie Pendleton of the Alabama Department of Archives and History, Montgomery, Alabama; Hugh Alexander of the National Archives of the United Kingdom; Brett McWilliams for permission to use photographs of objects in his private collection; Frank White, executive director of the Alabama Historical Commission for permission to use a drawing of one of the objects in the AHC collections; Craig Sheldon for the use of his pen-and-ink sketch of artifacts; Lisa Haney of the Missouri Archaeological Society; Eric Seiferth of the Williams Research Center, Historic New Orleans Collection, New Orleans; and the National Park Service, Harpers Ferry Center.

Kathryn E. Holland Braund
Dadeville, Alabama

Battle of Horseshoe Bend, fought March 27, 1814. This map of the Horseshoe Bend in the Tallapoosa River was drawn by J. L. Holmes for Captain Leonard L. Tarrant of Winchester, Tennessee, who served with the West Tennessee Militia in the Creek War. The map depicts both the landscape and battle positions of Red Sticks, the Americans and their allies (with left corresponding to east; right to west; up to south; and down to north). **Surrounding Horseshoe Bend:** (top left) the "craggy hills" flanking the river; (bottom left) the Creek town of Nuyaka (Neuyorcau); (eastern riverbank) Coffee's cavalry brigade encircling the high ground around the river; (top right—above wavy line) the location that Cherokee Indians crossed the Tallapoosa River to attack; (top right—

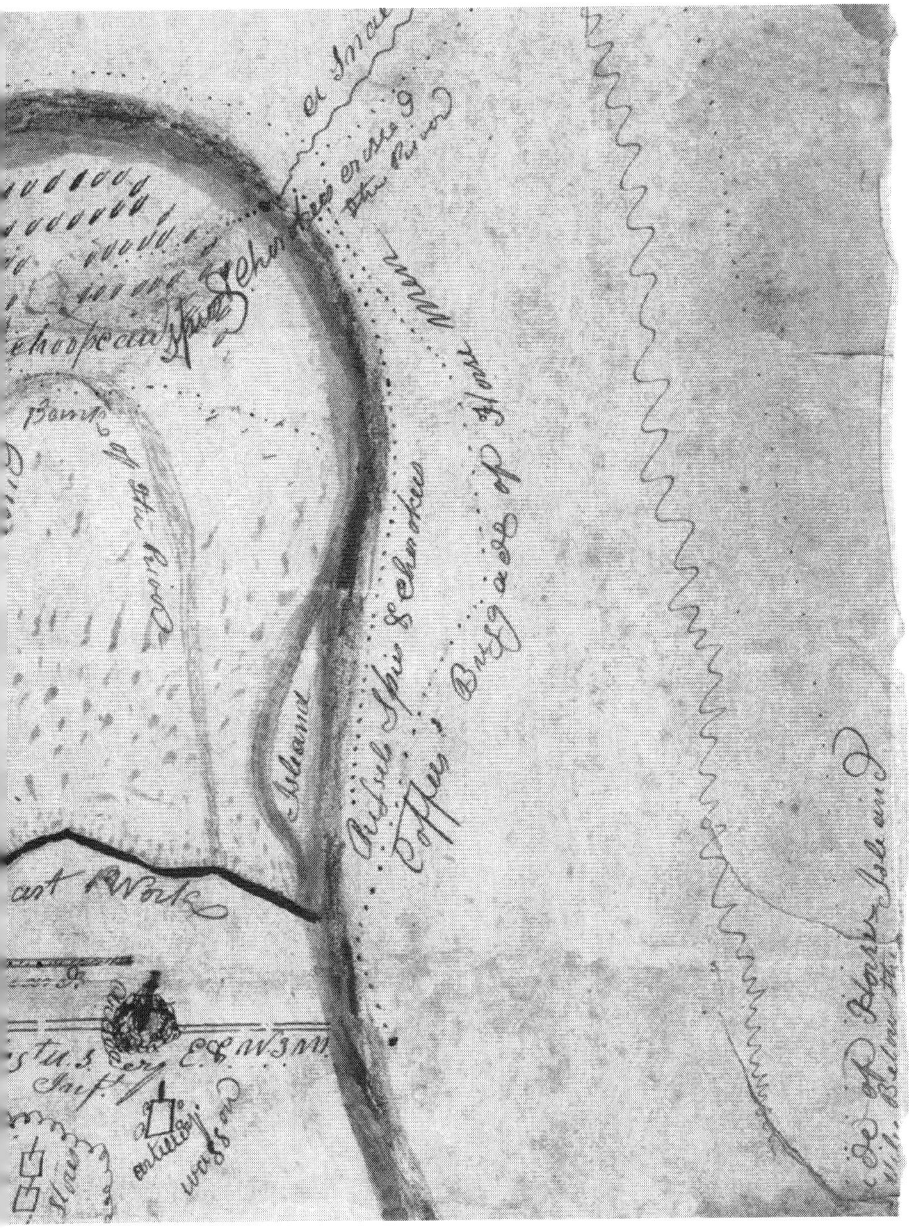

below wavy line) the location of Captain Russell's company (spies) and Cherokees; and (center right) the location at which Coffee's men crossed the river to complete their encirclement from the rear. **Inside Horseshoe Bend:** (south tip) the village of Tohopeka (Tehoopcau); (north of Tohopeka) Tohopeka's associated defense works behind the main log fortification across the bend (Breast Works); and (north of Breast Works) Jackson's forces, including the 39th US Infantry, East and West Tennessee militia units, the rear guard, and the artillery and baggage wagons. Map courtesy of the Alabama Department of Archives and History.

TONOPEKA

Introduction

Kathryn E. Holland Braund

As the corn was ripening in July 1813, the Creek people were engulfed by what Benjamin Hawkins termed a "rage of Frenzy."[1] Hawkins, who served as the United States' representative to the Creeks, might better have described it as a frenzy of rage, and a good deal of it was of his own making. Hawkins seemed oblivious to the intense strains that his efforts to transform Creek society and economy had imposed on the Creek psyche—not to mention the strains his relentless demands for land cessions, right-of-way, free navigation of rivers, and micromanagement of Creek internal affairs had wrought. Hawkins's efforts, known as the "plan of civilization," were meant to transform Indians from hunters to farmers and "reform" aspects of Indian culture to conform to American norms, particularly in regard to kinship practices and notions of property. Of course, the Creeks had always been farmers, but Hawkins envisioned a time when Creeks would abandon communal fields designed for basic subsistence and embrace private landholdings devoted to commercial agriculture. The plan was as broad as it was intrusive. It sought to transform Creek men into tillers of the soil, the traditional role of women. It denigrated clan membership and responsibilities and elevated the nuclear family, under the leadership of the dominant male, working on private land plots for profit. It meant new roles for women, who were to take up spinning and weaving. It encouraged citizens to abandon towns where communal values and hospitality were prized in return for rugged individualism and acquisitiveness in widely dispersed farmsteads, ranches, ferries, and taverns. It also meant, so the missionaries hoped, a conversion to Christianity. And it brought mounting pressures for the loosely organized government of the Creek towns, the National Council, to take on sweeping new responsibilities, including the very old problem of how to deal with demands for satisfaction by the United States when Creeks broke American laws or took American lives.[2]

While the Creek country roiled over these attempts at "reform," the world around it—both temporal and spiritual—churned with agitation and aggression. In the early fall of 1811, Tecumseh, a Shawnee diplomat and war leader, accompanied by sixteen other Shawnees and a number of Choctaws and Cherokees, visited the Creeks. No doubt, Tecumseh's message was grim, although Hawkins had a difficult time detailing exactly what the message was, for the Indian diplomats refused to speak freely in the presence of Americans. There is widespread agreement that he urged peaceful relations between all Indian peoples, warned of the rapacious American expansion, talked of the tensions in his homeland, and likely pointed to the cavalier way in which Americans demanded access through the Creek country and continued to encroach on Creek land and then claim it as their own. Most likely, he also invited widespread Creek participation in a pan-Indian alliance against US expansion.[3]

By June of 1812—less than a year after Tecumseh's visit—the United States was openly at war with the Shawnee and their British allies. As things went from bad to worse in the north for the Shawnee, things were not going well for the Creeks' Spanish neighbors in Florida either. By the spring of 1812, US citizens openly moved into the Mobile delta, claiming it was theirs under the terms of the Louisiana Purchase. The Spanish disputed the claim but didn't have the muscle to force them out and remained tenuously ensconced in Fort Charlotte. By April of 1813, General James Wilkinson seized Fort Charlotte, and the Spanish garrison evacuated to Pensacola. Meanwhile, American "patriots" from Georgia had invaded East Florida with a goal of extending US sovereignty there. Fighting between the Americans, whose ranks quickly included US regulars, and the Seminoles, who rightly viewed the action as hostile to their interests, continued through 1812 and well into 1813.[4]

The spectacle of Americans invading Spanish and Seminole territory likely did not surprise the Creek people, for their own lands had been subjected to American advances. And as they watched workers enlarge the Federal Road that ran through their territory over their objections and when told by Hawkins that Americans should now be allowed to travel freely down the Coosa River, it is hard to believe that a sense of foreboding did not engulf them. And, at some point, that foreboding turned to rage, particularly after the National Council, at Hawkins's insistence, had a number of Creek warriors executed for depredations and murders they had committed against Americans.

Hawkins himself recorded horrific "frenzy" as disagreement moved toward rage and, ultimately, erupted into civil war. Those he deemed "fanatics" were in open opposition to many of their chiefs, who had acquiesced to Hawkins's demands, profited from US annuity payments meant for tribal purposes, and were "friendly" to new economic opportunities for self-enrichment. To his superiors, Hawkins passed along accounts of "prophets" who, inspired by the Shawnee, claimed "magical powers" and called for attacks on leading Creek men and their families and for the destruction of property, particularly, livestock, spinning wheels, looms, and "everything received from the Americans."[5] As the Creek prophets danced and the stench of rotting livestock permeated the land, Creek warriors took up arms and the bloody business of self-destruction began in earnest.

Historians still debate on the precise causes and motivations of those who "raised the red stick of war" against their established leaders in the National Council, the "old Chiefs," as they were termed by the dissidents. The tensions introduced by the US civilization program and the growing resentment against the actions of the Creek National Council are frequently highlighted. Some scholars have focused on the growing disparity of wealth and political power in the Creek Nation, especially the tensions that existed between those of Creek and European ancestry who settled outside the boundaries of Creek town jurisdiction—particularly those who formed the nucleus of a thriving community in the Tensaw—and those who continued more traditional economic and social lifestyles in the Creek Nation proper.[6] The role of the native religion and the rise of a prophetic movement among the Creeks have also been the focus of much attention, as has the influence of Tecumseh in sparking the movement. Outside pressures, including US expansion, the changing economy, and the erosion of Creek power relative to surrounding American settlements, are all debated as scholars grapple to adequately describe and evaluate the key events that led to Creek civil war.[7]

The civil war quickly turned into another kind of war faster than most could comprehend what had happened. Americans immediately assumed that when the Creeks raised their symbolic war clubs, they would be aimed at them. And many welcomed the opportunity presented by the internal dispute and disarray as justification to invade the Creek country, humiliate the Creeks, and take even more of their land. The Creeks' civil war, almost from the beginning, became a US war against the Creeks.

The course of the Creek War is generally well known.[8] At Tuckabatchee, home to leading members of the National Council, insurgents laid siege to the town. A party of these Red Stick Creeks visited Spanish Pensacola, hoping to obtain assistance. They were attacked at Burnt Corn Creek by Mississippi territorial militia as they returned home. The attackers were at first successful and the dissidents fled, but as the poorly trained militia looted their packhorses, the insurgents regrouped and drove off their attackers. The surprise attack quickly led to retaliation, and the dissidents focused on the civilians and territorial militia "forted up" at the Samuel Mims plantation. Those at Fort Mims, hearing the rumors of war and attack, like many in the area, had gathered at hastily fortified sites for safety. Many of the inhabitants of the fort were of mixed Creek-European ancestry and, in fact, were closely related by clan and lineage to many of the attackers. Spurred on by a determination to revenge the attack at Burnt Corn, as well as by anger at the actions of the Tensaw community, Red Stick warriors quickly overwhelmed the poorly defended stockade, ultimately killing 250 of the occupants, including women and children, and took over 100 people into captivity. The captives included both those of mixed Indian ancestry as well as African Americans. The leader of the assault, William Weatherford, was closely related to many of those who had sought refuge at the fort. The overwhelming Creek victory, generally known as the Fort Mims Massacre, was viewed as an attack on US territory. The Creek civil war had become, in American eyes, a war against the United States, which was already at war with Britain. Following the attack on Fort Mims, the United States hastily organized a three-pronged invasion of the Creek country. Armies comprised mainly of territorial militia, from the Mississippi Territory, Georgia, and Tennessee, supplemented by regulars, were quickly raised and sent toward the heart of the perceived "rebellion" in the Upper Creek country.

But, at its core, the war was a civil war. At Tuckabatchee, as the insurgents grew in numbers, Big Warrior, the leader of the Creek National Council, had called for assistance from Georgia. With warriors from Coweta providing cover for the Tuckabatchees, most of the residents were able to escape, carrying what possessions they could. While the conflict raged, they took refuge near Coweta, the most important Creek town on the Chattahoochee River. Tuckabatchee was an "Upper Town," as those Creek towns along the Coosa, Tallapoosa, and Alabama Rivers are known. Coweta and other towns located on the Chattahoochee River were known as Lower Creek towns. These two major regional divisions (Upper and Lower) represented clusters of allied and related towns whose identity as "Creeks" had been forged in the distant past. With the evacuation of Big Warrior and other supporters of the National Council, the Upper Creek country was largely in the hands of insurgents, who were known as Red Sticks. While the Red Sticks found sympathizers among the Lower Creek towns, almost all the action of the Creek War came to be centered in Upper Creek country.

By late fall 1813, the American invasion of the Creek country was in full swing. The Creeks who stood behind the actions of the National Council—or at least did not support the actions of the Red Sticks—found themselves increasingly marginalized as "allies" of the larger force assembled to "humble" and "exterminate" the Red Sticks. Choctaws and Cherokees joined the expeditions into the Creek heartland as well. The first US victory came via the efforts of Tennessee's volunteers. Andrew Jackson's West Tennessee militia claimed its first sizable victory at the Creek town of Tallushatchee and then at Talladega, where the Tennessee forces assisted National Creeks who were besieged by Red Sticks there. Jackson's efforts ended the siege and resulted in the destruction of perhaps a third of the attacking Red Sticks. The Americans also waged a successful surprise attack on the Creek town of Hillabee, whose residents had already made known their intention not to support the Red Sticks.

Georgians managed to attack and destroy the Red Stick town of Autossee at the end of November. Mississippi troops lead by General Ferdinand Claiborne undertook several scouting expeditions and engaged in a number of minor engagements, including the Canoe Fight, in which a handful of Mississippi territorial volunteers and militia led by Sam Dale managed to overpower and kill a party of Creek Indians they spotted on a canoe on the Alabama River near the John Randon Plantation. In late December, the Mississippi troops, after an arduous effort, managed to reach the Red Stick encampment known as the Holy Ground and successfully destroyed it. Holy Ground, built on an inaccessible river bluff, was, as the name suggests, rumored to be safe from the attacks of Americans by a sacred barrier. But the defenders, led by William Weatherford, the mastermind of the attack on Fort Mims, also employed Creek warriors and armed African Americans to protect the town, which was successfully defended until the civilians there were evacuated. Americans looted and destroyed the town after the majority of the Red Sticks escaped, leaving its inhabitants—like most of the Creek people—homeless and hungry.

The effort against the Creeks resumed in early 1814, when Georgians and their Creek allies, primarily Yuchis under the command of Timpoochee Barnard, fought viciously at Calebee Creek. Following the battle, General John Floyd and the Georgians withdrew, leaving only Andrew Jackson's army in the field against the Creeks. Mobilizing an army of volunteer militia supplemented by the 6,000-man Thirty-Ninth US Infantry Regiment, Jackson moved his force toward the reported stronghold of the Abeika Creeks from the towns of Nuyaka, Okfuskee, Okchai, Eufaula, Fish Ponds, and Hillabee at a place called Tohopeka, a Muskogee word meaning "fence or fortification." After engagements at Emuckfau Creek and Enitachopco, Jackson's force of some 3,300 men, including 500 Cherokee and 100 National Creek warriors, reached the Horseshoe Bend on the Tallapoosa River on March 27, 1814. By the end of the day, the Red Stick defenders were almost completely destroyed. The battle was the most deadly in terms of Red Stick casualties in the war—857, according to Jackson's estimate. It secured Jackson's reputation as a ruthless and successful military leader, and proved to be the last major battle in the Creek War.

Jackson effectively ended the fighting phase of the war with the Treaty of Fort Jackson, which was signed on August 9, 1814, and stripped the Creek people of 21,086,793 million acres of land. With hundreds of dead warriors and many more civilians dead or nearly so from starvation and exposure, the Red Stick rebellion ended. Many leaders, including William Weatherford, surrendered and asked for mercy for their families. Many Creeks, particularly those from the Tallapoosa Creek towns along the lower reaches of the Tallapoosa River, abandoned their homeland permanently, seeking refuge in Florida. Some, including the young man who in adulthood was known as Osceola, continued the fight against US expansion in the later Seminole wars. Indeed, the First Seminole War is viewed by many as a mere continuation of the Creek War.[9]

While the war's outcome is undisputed, many misconceptions remain. Although it was a civil war, it was not a war between the Upper and Lower Creeks. While most Lower Creeks did oppose the Red Sticks, many Upper Creeks, including those in the important towns of Tuckabatchee and Nauchee, were targeted by Red Sticks and many Upper Creek towns were divided over the war. Nor, as some have suggested, was it a war between ethnic Muskogee Creeks and non-Muskogee components of the confederacy.[10] Indeed, the Nauchee (Natchez) town residents and many Yuchis fought with the Creeks who supported the National Council, while most of those from the Alabama towns joined the Red Stick movement along with the warriors from the Muskogee towns of the Abeika and Tallapoosa. Nor can it be entirely explained as a fight between those of "pure" and "mixed" racial ancestry. Many of the most famous Red Sticks, including Josiah Francis, Menawa, and William Weatherford, were of mixed race, while the leader of the National Council, Big Warrior of Tuckabatchee, was not.

The various chapters in this volume cannot, by their very nature, address all the complex issues associated with the cause and course of the Creek War, but they do reflect the research interests of symposium participants. Indeed, certain aspects of the conflict are almost completely missing, including the role of Creek women and African Americans in the war. Other aspects are only touched on tangentially, including the changing economic and social conditions in the Creek Nation, the nature of the prophetic movement, and the way in which the Creek War and Seminole wars are related. Rather, the chapters presented here relate a variety of new approaches and new questions, look at new sources, reassess old sources and conclusions, and, taken together, will allow both specialists and general readers to appreciate the complexities of the Creek War and the War of 1812 in Alabama as well as glean new insights. Especially important is the Creek voice. The volume begins with an overview of the conflict by Robert G. Thrower, the executive director of the Poarch Band Creek Nation's Calvin McGhee Cultural Authority and a descendant of members of the Creek Tensaw community. Drawn from wide reading in secondary and primary sources, Thrower's interpretation represents a nuanced view of a modern Creek Indian's assessment of the war and its historical coverage. Fittingly, the volume closes with a short essay by Ted Isham, who was the historic preservation officer for the Muscogee (Creek) Nation at the time of the symposium.

In their contributions, Gregory Evans Dowd and Robert P. Collins take on myths and rumors. Dowd reexamines the significance of Tecumseh's southern visit, including the role that the famous New Madrid earthquake played in events and the way in which intertribal diplomacy and alliance-building were continuations rather than innovations. Collins works to untangle the convoluted beginnings of the war and the manner in which rumor and fear propelled events. And both authors critically assess the standard sources and how they have been used—and misused—by historians since the beginning of the conflict. Cultural continuity is also a theme in my own essay on the origin and meaning of the term "Red Sticks," in which I explore both the weapon's history and the use of the moniker given to Creek dissidents, using documentary, pictorial, and anthropological evidence.

Three essays take a wide-angle approach to the Battle of Horseshoe Bend. Tom Kanon and Susan M. Abram focus on Jackson's campaign. In his essay, Kanon concentrates on Jackson's forces and battles prior to the engagement at the Horseshoe and explores the reasons that the Creek civil war was so quickly transformed into a US war against the Creeks. Abram explores the role of the Americans' Cherokee allies in the campaign and at Horseshoe Bend, where their actions hastened a US victory. Ove Jensen explores the battle itself through the unique perspective of place, in the way the site itself both shaped the battle and continues to shape our remembrance of the war.

The essays that follow range beyond Horseshoe Bend to explore events after the battle and the way in which the Creek campaign related to the War of 1812 along the Gulf Coast. In his essay, Gregory A. Waselkov explores the aftermath of Jackson's victory and the continuing Red Stick resistance as well as the war's lasting impact on the Creek Nation. John E. Grenier steps away from a southern focus in his essay to look at US aims and tactics and ties US actions in the South to those in the trans-Appalachian West during the same period. David S. Heidler and Jeanne T. Heidler examine events at Fort Bowyer and the complex way in which the Creek War affected the larger War of 1812 along the Gulf Coast.

Craig T. Sheldon Jr. and James W. Parker examine the role and usefulness of archaeology in understanding and uncovering new evidence about the war and those who fought it. Sheldon's emphasis is on the Creek side of the conflict, and he uses both documentary and archaeological evidence to discuss what a Creek war site would look like and how archaeological discoveries would add to our knowledge of Red Stick practices and, perhaps, their beliefs. Parker, on the other hand, concentrates on the camps, posts, and fortifications erected by the Americans, many of which have not been located or studied. His emphasis on the archaeology of an expeditionary force brings new clarity to the lives of the American soldiers during the conflict as well as the difficulties they encountered. Parker also includes two appendices, "Current Preservation Status of Major Creek War/War of 1812 Sites in Alabama" and "Known and Potential Archaeological Sites in Alabama," which readers might find useful. Both archaeologists, with their emphasis on the many places touched by the war, allow us to better understand the nature of the conflict.

The twelve essays in this volume, together with the foreword and afterword, represent refinements in the presentations made at the Creek War and War of 1812 symposium held in 2009. As superintendent Marianne Mills noted at the beginning of the symposium, national parks begin when an individual cares so deeply about a place that he or she is willing to spend considerable time and effort to see that the special place is set aside. People were passionate about the Horseshoe Bend battlefield long before it became a park in 1959 and had always recognized its significance as a site sacred to the history of the Creek people and a battlefield of national importance. And that passion continues since the area's incorporation into the National Park Service. Schoolchildren, locals interested in their own history, Creek Indians and those of Indian ancestry, living history participants, students, scholars, history buffs, and tourists all come to the park to learn about the battle. The park is a living memorial to those who fought and died there as well as a testament that history is important and that it ought to be accessible and engaging. In the spirit of the Horseshoe Bend National Military Park, it is our hope that this volume will not merely commemorate the fiftieth anniversary of the park's founding, but also disseminate scholarly findings to a variety of interested audiences and spur them to wider reading about the Creek Indians, their culture, and the Creek War. We hope as well that these chapters will inspire additional research and promote further study, interpretation, and preservation of other Creek Indian and Creek War sites in Alabama.

Notes

1. Benjamin Hawkins, *The Letters, Journals, and Writings of Benjamin Hawkins,* ed. by C. L. Grant, 2 vols. (Savannah, GA: Beehive Press, 1980), 2:651.

2. An excellent overview of Creek country during Hawkins's tenure is Robbie Ethridge, *Creek Country: The Creek Indians and Their World* (Chapel Hill: University of North Carolina Press, 2003). See also Angela Pulley Hudson, *Creeks, Paths, and Federal Roads: Indians, Settlers, and Slaves and the Making of the American South* (Chapel Hill: University of North Carolina Press, 2010).

3. John Sugden, "Tecumseh's Travels Revisited," *Indiana Magazine of History* 96 (June 2000): 151–68.

4. See James G. Cusick, *The Other War of 1812: The Patriot War and the American Invasion of Spanish East Florida* (Athens: University of Georgia Press, 2007).

5. Hawkins, *Letters, Journals, and Writings,* 2:651, 2:652.

6. Ibid., 2:757. See also Gregory A. Waselkov, *A Conquering Spirit: Fort Mims and the Redstick War of 1813–1814* (Tuscaloosa: University of Alabama Press, 2006); and Claudio Saunt, *A New Order of Things: Property, Power, and the Transformation of the Creek Indians, 1733–1816* (Cambridge: Cambridge University Press, 1999).

7. In *Sacred Revolt: The Muskogees' Struggle for a New World* (Boston: Beacon Press, 1991), Joel Martin interprets the Red Stick revolt as a religious revitalization movement. More recently, Alfred A. Cave places the Red Stick movement in the context of other Native American millenarian movements in his *Prophets of the Great Spirit: Native American Revitalization Movements in Eastern North America* (Lincoln: University of Nebraska Press, 2006).

8. The *Encyclopedia of Alabama,* an online resource, offers a variety of thoroughly researched articles related to the war and its participants by a variety of scholars, many of them contributors to the present volume. See http://www.encyclopediaofalabama.org/face/Home.jsp.

9. See David S. Heidler and Jeanne T. Heidler, *Old Hickory's War: Andrew Jackson and the Quest for Empire* (Baton Rouge: Louisiana State University Press, 2003).

10. J. Leitch Wright Jr., *Creeks and Seminoles: Destruction and Regeneration of the Muscogulge People* (Lincoln: University of Nebraska Press, 1986).

1
Causalities and Consequences of the Creek War

A Modern Creek Perspective

Robert G. Thrower

Prelude to Disaster: Division and Civil War

The Creek War of 1813–1814 began as a civil war between two factions within the Creek Confederacy. In the eighteenth and early nineteenth centuries, Euro-American influences and encroachments were producing profound changes in the culture of the Muskogee Creeks. Some Creeks, among these the ancestors of this author, migrated from Upper Creek towns along the Coosa/Tallapoosa confluence into the Tensaw region in the late 1700s. They assisted with the settlement of the Mississippi Territory, serving as guides, ferryboat operators, interpreters, and innkeepers. These people, whose descendants are today known as the Poarch Creek Indians, were among those known as the "Friendly Creek Indians" living in what is now southwest Alabama at the time of the Creek War.[1]

Anthropologists and historians have used terms such as "progressive" to describe those Creeks who embraced acculturation to American culture, and they have used "nativist" to identify those Creeks who held steadfastly to their traditional beliefs and lifestyles. The nativists grew increasingly adversarial toward the Americans and those Indian people perceived as "friendly" toward the US government. A growing rift between progressive and nativist Creeks evolved until the stage was set for the inevitability of civil war. For this author, it is both tragic and ironic that the same confederacy which had formed in reaction to Euro-American encroachments—the same confederacy that had managed to compromise and settle tribal differences and stood strong as a formidable union to be respected—divided and collapsed upon itself, primarily from internal problems that existed long before the war. It seems clear from the historic record that the outside pressures of the expanding US settlements and the tensions that resulted from the "civilization" program sponsored by the United States worked to divide the Creek people and led directly to war.

Roads to Ruin: Encroachment upon Tribal Lands

To understand the causalities of the Creek War, one must first examine the historical, political, and social changes that could produce a civil war within the Creek Confederacy. There are numerous scholarly theories of causality, some of which will be addressed throughout this work. The loss of tribal lands to non-Indian encroachment was certainly a precipitating factor for eventual armed conflict. Henry S. Halbert and T. S. Ball, two early historians of the conflict, saw encroachment of white pioneers into Creek territory (made possible through the establishment of a military road) as a primary cause for the Creek War. In fact, they specifically pointed to "the large and growing settlement of white pioneers along the Tombigbee and the Alabama rivers" as "the great exciting cause" of the war.[2]

The first road to ruin for the Creek Confederacy began with the establishment of a horse path intended to expedite postal deliveries between New Orleans and Washington, D.C. This postal route, the well-known Federal Road, would later be widened into a war road.[3]

The Creeks had only grudgingly granted permission for the establishment of the postal road. They raised strong opposition when the United States proposed the construction of the road that would link the Georgia frontier to the newly formed settlements in what is now Alabama. Tribal leaders were convinced that the Federal Road would provoke hostilities as whites traveled through Indian territory. Despite strong opposition from the Creeks, the United States proceeded with the conversion of the postal road into the military road in 1811, as war loomed with Great Britain and the United States foresaw the need to get soldiers to the Gulf Coast in the event of an attack. The Federal Road opened up access to wheeled vehicles, which led to increasing non-Indian traffic through Creek territory. The concerns of tribal leaders were quickly realized. The effects were clearly noticeable, and Benjamin Hawkins reported that, between October 1811 and March of the next year, 233 vehicles and 3,726 people had passed his Indian agency on the Flint River, heading west.[4] Further complications developed as many white settlers established permanent settlements along the borders of the Creek Nation. The Federal Road created a strong discontent among many of the nativist Creek warriors. Added to this discontent were the tensions resultant from non-Indian encroachments from many directions. As Frank L. Owsley Jr. wrote, "the Creeks found themselves facing the white man's frontier not only to the north and east but now to the west as well."[5]

Henry D. Southerland Jr. and Jerry E. Brown, who were among the first to study the Federal Road in detail, drew an insightful conclusion: "The overriding irony of the military road building is that, although it looked toward one war [War of 1812], it was the major cause" of the Creek War.[6]

A Potential Massacre Averted

The attack on the Upper Creek town of Tuckabatchee on July 22, 1813, by the Red Stick Creeks is frequently referenced as "the beginning of the Creek Civil War."[7]

But evidence of hostility among Creek factions existed long before the attack on Tuckabatchee. Consider an event that occurred in 1790, immortalized by Albert James Pickett in his early history of Alabama, concerning Sophia Durant, the sister of Alexander McGillivray. Pickett wrote:

> In the summer of 1790, while McGillivray was at New York, the Creeks threatened to descend upon the Tensaw settlers and put the whole of them to death. Mrs. Durant mounted a horse, with a negro woman upon another, and set out from Little River, camped out at night, and on the fourth day, arrived at the Hickory Ground, where she assembled the Chiefs, threatened them with vengeance of her brother upon his return, which caused the arrest of the ringleaders, and put a complete stop to their murderous intentions. Two weeks afterwards, this energetic and gifted woman was delivered of twins, at the Hickory Ground. One of them married James Bailey, who was killed at the fall of Fort Mims, in 1813.[8]

This account illustrates the severity of tensions already existent between the "progressive" Creeks of the Tensaw region and the Creeks of the more conservative Upper Creek towns. In the late 1700s, some sixteen families, the ancestors of the Poarch Creek Indians, migrated down from Upper Creek towns to settle in the Tensaw region. In the beginning, these migrations had occurred with the blessings of the Creek Nation. From this account, we can surmise that hostility had already developed between the inhabitants of the Creek towns and those settling in the Tensaw.

Benjamin Hawkins and the Plan of Civilization

A discussion of causalities of the Creek civil war would be remiss without an examination of the effects of the federal government's plan of civilization for the American Indian. R. S. Cotterill was among the first historians to identify the influence of Benjamin Hawkins as the principal cause of the Creek War. He wrote forcefully, "Creek War was, in its beginning at least, a civil war, having its cause neither in Tecumseh's visit in 1811 nor in the British seductions of 1812, but in a long-gathering dissatisfaction with the civilization program instituted by Hawkins and officially countenanced by the tribal government."[9]

Concerning the principal cause of civil war between the Upper and Lower Creeks, Benjamin W. Griffith Jr. repeated those sentiments in his work: "It is increasingly evident that the principal reason was the deep division between those who were acceding to Hawkins's attempts to acculturate them and those who were bitterly resisting."[10] As previously examined, contentions and profound cultural changes were sharply dividing nativist and progressive Creeks.

Enter now the work of Benjamin Hawkins, federal Indian agent, and the United States' plan to civilize the Indians. This plan served to intensify hostilities between the two opposing Creek groups. Complicating matters between the two groups was their extended history of intermarriages, treaties, and trading relationships. Hawkins's policy of assimilation is cited as a major cause of hostilities.[11]

Nativist Creeks rejected Hawkins and resisted the civilization plan. The resistance of nativists toward civilization efforts, particularly his economic reforms, was described in a letter from Benjamin Hawkins to the secretary of war in 1789: "'They told me they did not understand the plan, they could not work, they did not want ploughs, it did not comport with the ways of the red people, who were determined to persevere in the ways of their ancestors. They saw no necessity why the white people should change the ways of their ancestors.'"[12]

Conversely, the progressive Creeks were attracted to the plan of civilization and readily embraced it. From the perspective of this author, without Hawkins and the influences of the plan of civilization, Tecumseh's efforts would have had little traction for adoption by any of the Creeks. The divisions and consequences of the civilization plan produced a fertile environment for the introduction and growth of the Red Stick movement. As with General Andrew Jackson's eventual military involvement in the Creek War, Tecumseh found himself in opportune circumstances to promote his campaign among the Red Sticks.

Shifting Attitudes toward the Land

For the progressive Creeks, transformation of their culture shifted from traditional views of the land toward a more Euro-American perspective. Before Euro-American occupation and influences, the Creeks had no concept of private land ownership and did not measure their wealth in terms of that commodity.[13]

William Bartram noted in the late eighteenth century, "Every individual inhabitant or citizen has an equal right to the soil to hunt & range over this region except within the jurisdiction of each town or village."[14] Within Creek towns, families possessed individual plots but farmed them with a communal attitude. On the outer perimeters of the tribal towns, large fields were tended through the communal efforts of the Creek citizenry.

The acquisition and fencing of individual properties by progressive Creeks illustrates a profound departure from traditions of communal land ownership. Private land ownership had now become a visible indicator of material wealth for the progressive Creeks. By 1811, the concerns of nativist Creeks were growing as they had already lost millions of acres of access to hunting lands. These conditions led to the creation of a new vocabulary word in the Creek language, *ecunnaunuxulgee,* which translates as "people grasping after all [Native American] lands."[15]

Acculturation and Shifting Attitudes toward Material Wealth

Before the 1770s the deerskin trade did little to change the relationships between Creeks and their property. In accordance with their traditional roles, the men hunted as they had always done, and women continued to practice agriculture. With the deerskin trade, they participated in commercial exchange to secure some goods; but at that time, the market existed between them and the outside traders, not of their own kin.[16] James Adair noted the absence of material wealth among the Creek men in the eighteenth century, clarifying that: "Martial virtue, and not riches, is their invariable standard for preferment; for they neither esteem, nor despise any of their people one jot more or less, on account of riches or dress."[17]

Compared with their Euro-American neighbors, the Creeks possessed few material goods in the first half of the eighteenth century. The primary emphasis was upon community, not individuality. Selfishness was a concept unheard of, as one white trader married to a Creek woman discovered when she insisted on distributing all his trade goods freely to her kin.[18]

In 1765, a Creek leader named Mortar noted the growing dependency of Creeks upon the deerskin trade at a conference with the British and stated that it was "'absolutely necessary'" that the Creek people have foreign trade.[19] The effects of increasing reliance upon trade goods and material culture was observed by Bartram in the 1770s, who claimed, somewhat expansively and incorrectly, that the Creeks "were now entirely ignorant of any of the arts, whereby, to supply themselves with necessary clothing; they had almost forgotten how to make earthen Potts, & not one amongst them knew how to form a Stone Axe, or wooden Hough. All their dependence had rested upon the Traders, who supplied them with European Manufactures."[20]

As the deerskin trade flourished, Creeks were given access to an increasing variety of material goods. The cultural shift away from the traditional social dynamic of communalism and toward materialism and individual ownership increased the personal wealth of some Creeks. But at the same time, it further increased their dependence upon trade goods. Dependence upon the deerskin trade and the accumulation of material properties directly contributed to the demise of the white-tailed deer. The embracing of materialism and abandonment of traditional beliefs further weakened the confederacy and produced vulnerabilities that would be fully exploited by Euro-American forces.

Nativist Reactions: Curse of the Cattle

The acculturation of progressive Creeks accelerated hostilities between themselves and the nativist Creeks. The introduction of domestic animals, foremost among these cattle, proved to be both divisive and destructive. Not only did cattle disturb cornfields, they also competed with deer for cane and other food. Like horses, cattle soon became a source of wealth for some Creeks, and herds grew.[21]

As overhunting and encroachments by settlers and cattle combined to reduce hunting habitats, many Creeks blamed cattle for the sharp decline in white-tailed deer populations.[22] To make matters worse, the members of the Council of Safety in revolutionary Georgia recommended that payment to Indians should be made in cattle for their services. This purpose was stated: "'We are of the opinion this step would answer many valuable purposes. . .and would have a tendency not only of attaching them to our own interest from gratitude, but would also be a means of civilizing them, and by fixing the idea of property, would keep them honest and peaceable with us for fear of reprisals."[23] A disturbing and often overlooked aspect of the Red Stick movement was the slaughter of livestock. When Tecumseh visited the Creek Confederacy, he encouraged all Indians to destroy any connection with the whites, as well as the trade goods they had obtained from them. Among these goods, livestock were targeted, and as the movement gained momentum, the Red Sticks began the slaughter of all kinds of domesticated animals, all relatively new introductions into the Creek world. In many ways, they were the most visible symbol of the new economic pursuits prompted by the "civilization program."[24] Near the end of the Creek War, one American officer later reported that in his journey through the Creek nation, "'not a track of a cow or hog was to be seen in the Creek country.'"[25] As aggressions increased, the Red Sticks not only killed the livestock, but destroyed other items obtained from the Americans and abandoned their fields. The destruction of livestock and cornfields would ultimately work against the Red Sticks by depleting their future food reserves.[26]

Progressive Creeks were now the potential targets of Red Stick aggression and violence. With the Creek civil war already under way, Red Sticks from several Upper Creek towns made their way down to Spanish Pensacola to seek munitions and gunpowder. On their way back from Pensacola, at a place called Burnt Corn Creek, an incident occurred that further intensified the Creek civil war.

Burnt Corn: The Beginning of Sorrows

The Battle of Burnt Corn was an expression of Creek civil war and cannot be overlooked as a precipitating factor for the Fort Mims Massacre. From a modern Creek perspective, this conflict was the beginning of sorrows for the Creek Nation. It set in motion a chain of reactions that would ultimately lead to the tragedy at Fort Mims and the subsequent retaliation of US troops. History is full of "what ifs." One can only wonder how different history might be today if the Battle of Burnt Corn had not occurred. Certainly hostilities from the Red Sticks had occurred previously and threats of future ones were brewing. The intentions of the Red Sticks, traveling back from Pensacola with their supplies and munitions, were to focus attacks upon certain Upper Creek towns that had become more pro-American. Those plans would change abruptly following the attack upon the Red Sticks by both US militia and mixed-blood Creek militia from Tensaw. As an expression of the Creek civil war, Captain Dixon Bailey and his progressive Creek warriors from Tensaw joined up with Colonel James Caller's US militia forces to confront the Red Sticks at Burnt Corn. The Battle of Burnt Corn did not cause the Creek War, since the Indians were already bringing in arms with which to fight a war; however, it no doubt motivated many of those who were unaffected to join the hostiles.[27]

Fort Mims: The Beginning of the End

Despite significant and unanticipated casualties for the Red Sticks, Fort Mims was perceived as a victory for the Red Stick movement. Burnt Corn had already been declared a victory for the Red Sticks, and the success of the Fort Mims attack was further affirmation to the Red Sticks that they were capable of achieving future victories. As history affirms, their obedience and loyalty to the leadership of the Red Stick prophets would assure their eventual destruction. From a modern perspective, this author must agree with Owsley's broader interpretation of the Fort Mims event as a "catastrophe" for all Creeks. As Owsley noted,

> This event alone destroyed all possibility of good relations with the whites in Mississippi Territory. Immediately, there was a universal de-

> mand for the removal of all southern Indians. Had it not been for this disastrous massacre, it is possible that the Creeks and other southern Indians might have remained in the Southeast, where they more readily would have been assimilated into white society. Certainly they could have never held all or even most of their land, but with agriculture replacing hunting they would not have needed so much land. It should be remembered that these southern Indians have been largely assimilated in Oklahoma, a continuation of the process started before the removal. . . . Fort Mims must be viewed as even more of a catastrophe for the Indians when one considers that a large part of the fight was between pro-white and anti-white factions of the Creek Nation itself.[28]

Owsley's commentary emphasizes this as a civil war, and this affirms a modern Creek perspective. Fort Mims was, for our ancestors, the beginning of the end for both the Creek Confederacy and the Red Stick movement. It opened the door for American military intervention and became the ideal propaganda tool and rallying cry for vengeance by the incoming US troops. While Fort Mims has been historically perpetuated as a massacre of "white settlers" by "fierce Creek warriors," from the modern Creek perspective, Fort Mims was not only Creek Indians killing Creek citizens, but, in some cases, family killing family. To some degree, Halbert and Ball understood this when they called the Creek War a very "'personal' war."[29]

Regarding the initial attack upon Fort Mims, Gregory A. Waselkov insightfully noted "the considerable irony of white troops crying 'Indians' at the sight of the Redsticks when a formidable contingent of their own force consisted of Creek Indians of the Tensaw."[30] While there were non-Indians within the Fort Mims population, the Red Sticks were launching, foremost, an attack against the progressive Creeks within Fort Mims. The historian J. Leitch Wright Jr. pointed to internal ethnic and tribal divisions in the civil war and surmised that "many and probably most of the 'whites' who perished (or were made prisoners) in the stockade were Creeks of the pure Muskogee moiety who adopted much, if not all, of Hawkins's program of civilization."[31] Wright believed that "virtually all of the militia, women, and children at the fort were Creeks (or spouses of Creeks), though largely acculturated."[32] Claudio Saunt, too, repeated Benjamin Hawkins's assertion that the early battles of the war were largely between those intermarried Creeks he called "halfbreeds," who followed his acculturation plan, and those who did not.[33]

Fort Mims and Dixon Bailey

Why was Fort Mims selected as the target of Red Stick aggression? It is reasonable to hypothesize that, without the Battle of Burnt Corn, there would have been no Fort Mims Massacre. Certainly, the attack on Fort Mims was a direct retaliation for the aggressions directed toward the Red Sticks at Burnt Corn. And what motivated the second wave of attack on Fort Mims, which saw the premature departure of William Weatherford and the subsequent slaughter of remaining civilians there? Our oral traditions and tribal histories of the Poarch Creeks point directly to one primary occupant of Fort Mims, Captain Dixon Bailey. In his study of the attack on Fort Mims, Waselkov, who uses the term *métis* to describe the racially and culturally mixed Creek population at Tensaw, illuminated the primary motivation for the attack: "Modern scholars generally agree on the reason: the Tensaw métis led by Dixon Bailey had so far suffered few losses. These were the Creeks who stood against Peter McQueen's force at Burnt Corn Creek. These wayward Creeks had, from the Redstick perspective, willfully abandoned so many traditions, rejected the new religion, and now fought their own people alongside the whites."[34]

Concerning Bailey, Halbert and Ball wrote that one of the survivors of the massacre reported that William Weatherford, upon first entering Fort Mims, saw Bailey and shouted to him, "'Dixon Bailey, to-day one or both of us must die."[35] Later that afternoon, Dixon Bailey received a mortal wound attempting to escape the walls of Fort Mims. Waselkov recounted gruesome but revealing details of the last stage of the massacre that illustrate the Red Sticks' focused hatred, not only toward Dixon Bailey, but also toward other members of the Bailey family, including other Bailey siblings. He quotes an African slave who was captured by the Red Sticks but later escaped and told of his encounter with his captors: "'An Indian seeing him in the corner said come out, the Master of Breath has ordered us not to kill any but white people and half breeds. An Indian woman, who was in the house, was ordered out and to go home. Dixon Bailey's sister was asked what family she was of. She answered pointing to her brother [James], I am the sister of that great man you have murdered there, upon which they knocked her down, cut her open, and strewed her entrails around.'"[36]

Why were the Baileys so intensely hated by the Red Sticks? The hostilities between the Baileys and the Red Sticks had significant previous history long before the Fort Mims incident. During Benjamin Hawkins's early days among the Creeks, the Baileys themselves told Hawkins that they had been forced to move to Tensaw due to their free-ranging stock and that their fellow Creeks were "in the habit of destroying hogs or cattle whenever they trespass on the fields under cultivation.'"[37]

Nativist Creek attitudes toward the Baileys' encroaching cattle gave way to deeper jealousies that were largely economic in nature. With the Tensaw

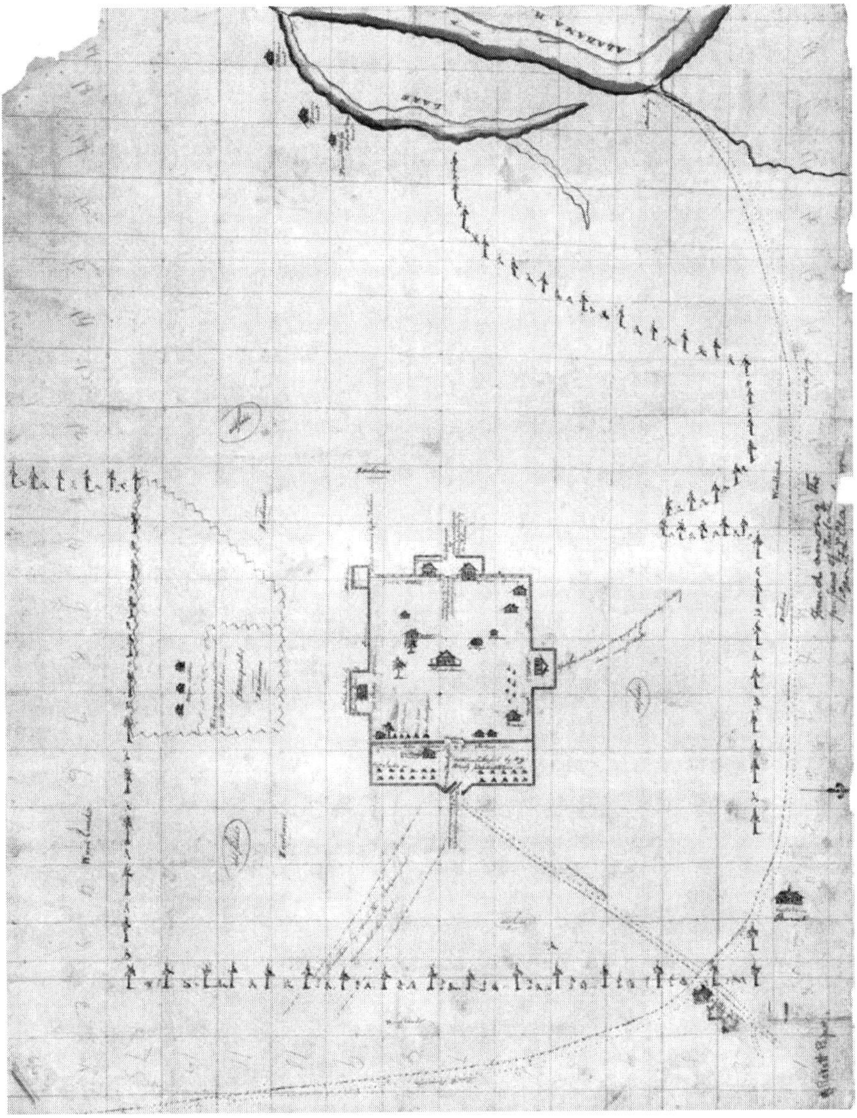

1.1. Map of Fort Mims and environs, 1813, owned by General Ferdinand Leigh Claiborne. Courtesy of the Alabama Department of Archives and History, Montgomery, Alabama.

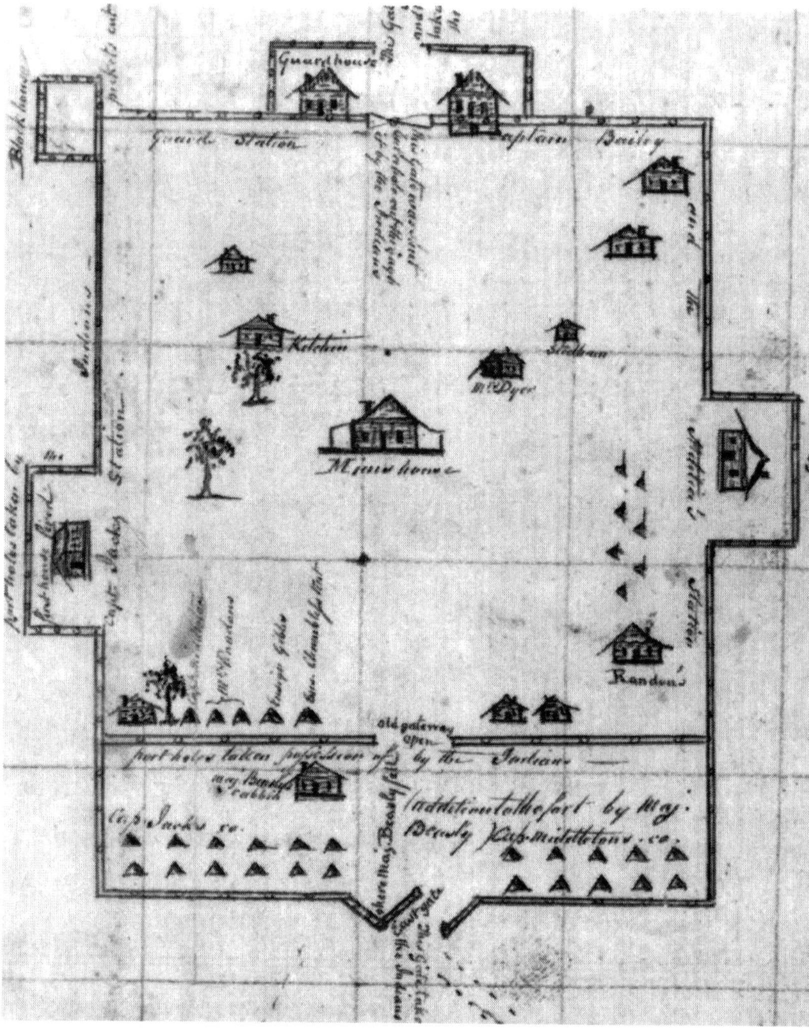

1.2. Detail of Fort Mims map. Courtesy of the Alabama Department of Archives and History, Montgomery, Alabama.

settlement's close proximity to Pensacola and Mobile, Tensaw Creeks such as Dixon Bailey were able to quickly establish themselves as a major competitor for trade within the Creek Nation. Originally, the Upper Creeks who had migrated down to the Tensaw settlement did so with the blessings of the Creek Nation. By 1809, the tensions within the Creek Nation were compounding, and again there were expressions of hostility toward Bailey and

and Linn McGhee, the ancestor of Lynn McGhee of the Poarch Creeks. According to Waselkov, Captain Sam Isaacs and a band of warriors from the town of Coosada visited the Tensaw in March 1809 "to levy taxes on the properties of the 'half breeds.'" Apparently, Isaacs demanded that Bailey pay a fee of one hundred dollars for the privilege of running a ferry across the Alabama River. Bailey and his ferry operator, Linn McGhee, both refused. As Waselkov observed, "Bailey rejected the implication that he and the other Tensaw métis were foreigners, subject to fees." He insisted that he had the same right as other Creeks to operate a ferry at that place.[38] Following this encounter, McGhee was assaulted and severely beaten by the Coosada warriors, who then proceeded to destroy Bailey's flatboat. Bailey and his mother, Mary, intervened, a skirmish ensued, and Isaacs and his men were overcome and humiliated.[39]

This historical record of escalating hostilities between the Bailey family and some Upper Creeks provides a microcosmic view of the tensions that were slowly pulling the Creek Confederacy apart. Ultimately, Dixon Bailey and his progressive Creek warriors from Tensaw would join Colonel Caller's US militia forces to confront the Red Sticks at the Battle of Burnt Corn. From the modern Creek perspective, the presence of Captain Bailey and his mixed-blood Creek militia at Burnt Corn was the primary reason Fort Mims was selected as the next target of Red Stick aggression. Fort Mims was a deliberate, retaliatory act on the part of the Red Sticks for the incident at Burnt Corn. At a more personal level, it was an act of revenge toward Dixon Bailey, his family, and his men.

The Creek War: An Exercise in Revenge and Brutality

Enter General Andrew Jackson, an opportunist who, unfortunately for all Creeks, was in the right position at the right time. News about the Fort Mims Massacre was the perfect propaganda tool for recruiting Americans to fight against the Red Sticks. Details of the massacre were exploited to the fullest extent. Wright wrote, "By word of mouth and through the press, grisly accounts circulated of how defenders were burned and hacked to death, babies cut out of live mothers' wombs, and infants' heads bashed against trees."[40] The attack on Fort Mims, from the white frontier perspective, was an unprovoked massacre of white settlers. With news of the massacre arriving in Nashville, Tennessee, on September 18, 1813, outraged citizenry called for a war "'to exterminate the Creek Nation and Abettors.'"[41] The myth of this incident as the massacre and butchery of hundreds of "white settlers" by "hostile Creek Indians" received full press throughout the United States. Casualty rates were inflated and the resultant paranoia and outrage of the

US public were catalyzed by this early publicity. Ironically, the misinformation concerning the ethnicity of victims and inflated casualty rates are still a problem in modern times. An examination and comparison of information on various historical markers at the present Fort Mims site will attest to the need for a revision of facts and interpretation. While the violence associated with Fort Mims was certainly brutal, it provided justification, in US eyes, for an equally brutal policy of retaliation and revenge. Certainly, a great opportunity was before Jackson, not only to avenge the "innocent" blood of the inhabitants of Fort Mims, but also to seize the chance to divide and, ultimately, to destroy the Creek Confederacy.

With the intervention of US forces, the Creek civil war was transformed into the Creek War of 1813. Armies moved against the Creeks from Mississippi and Georgia, burning and destroying Creek towns and engaging Red Sticks. But it is Jackson's campaign that captures our attention.

Retaliation at Tallushatchee

Euro-American historical accounts can certainly be biased, especially where American Indians have a role within that history. As we compare the tribal oral histories to the written historical records, we often observe that when the Indians "won," it was often called a "tragedy" and a "massacre." When the US troops won, it was often characterized as a "victory" and a "battle." Word came to General Andrew Jackson that a significant number of Red Stick warriors were camped in the Upper Creek town of Tallushatchee. Jackson responded by sending General John Coffee and his men to destroy the place. As a result, all of the Red Stick warriors were killed by the US forces in a relatively short period of time. Coffee was concerned over the fact that when his men ran into the Indians' houses, many women and children were slaughtered.[42] Jackson's official report of the Battle of Tallushatchee to Governor Willie Blount, dated November 4, 1813, reads, "'We have retaliated for the destruction of Fort Mims.'"[43] General Coffee's report on that same day reads, "'Not one of the warriors escaped to carry the news, a circumstance unknown heretofore.'"[44]

The Battle of Tallushatchee was the first major battle and victory for Jackson's campaign. The brutality of Jackson's troops did not go unnoticed. This attack, directed by Jackson and led by Coffee, would leave a lasting impression among some of their own men. Griffith wrote, "Not all of Coffee's men were exhilarated by this cold-blooded, systematic slaughter, which was to become the tactical model for subsequent operations against the Red Sticks. Lieutenant Richard Keith Call found the killing so horrible that it sickened him. 'We found as many as eight or ten bodies in a single cabin,' he wrote. 'Some of the cabins had taken fire, and half-consumed bodies were seen amidst the smoking ruins. In other instances dogs had torn and feasted on the mangled bodies of their masters. Heart sick I turned from the revolting scene."[45]

Tennessee frontier hero Davy Crockett was among the US forces assaulting the Red Sticks at Tallushatchee that day. Crockett later recalled that he had counted forty-six warriors running into a house for shelter: "We now shot them like dogs; and then set the house on fire, and burned it up with the forty-six warriors in it."[46]

The decimation of the village of Tallushatchee set a course of brutality which would characterize most of the US responses toward the nativist Creeks in the Creek War of 1813–1814. As Halbert and Ball revealed: "It was considered at first, a war upon the whites; it became, at length, and mainly, a war, almost of extermination, against the Indians."[47] Coffee reported that the Indians were primarily armed with bows and arrows. With all the men of Tallushatchee killed, it demonstrated to the US forces that they had a weaponry advantage and "it would be easy for the better armed Americans to annihilate the Indians."[48] The brutality at Tallushatchee also served as a powerful tool for psychological warfare, convincing undecided Creeks of the wisdom of allying themselves directly with Jackson's forces. Owsley observed that the battle "was the first of Jackson's engagements of total destruction. All the Indian men were killed and the town and crops were completely destroyed. Jackson's concept of fighting the Indians was total war, and his destruction of their food supply was probably as much a cause of the final defeat of the Creeks as any of their battle loses."[49]

"Fort Mims Was Again Avenged": The Hillabee Massacre

The Hillabee Massacre was one of the most serious blunders committed by US forces during the Creek War. The Hillabee Indians were in the process of negotiations with Jackson for surrender and terms of peace. While awaiting word from their messenger on what was hoped to be a favorable response from Jackson, General John Cocke ordered General James White to attack the Hillabee towns on November 18, 1813.[50] The unsuspecting Hillabees were caught by total surprise. Following the previous template of retribution forged at Tallushatchee, a massacre of the Hillabees took place. There was no reasonable way to define this as a battle. "'We lost not a drop of blood,'" White proudly reported to Cocke. Willis Brewer, an early Alabama historian, later noted, "'And Fort Mims was again avenged.'"[51] With this complete blunder on the part of both Cocke and White, the surviving Hillabees were outraged and blamed Jackson for the ensuing massacre. They would continue to fight with extreme vindictiveness against the US troops for the remainder of the war.

Tohopeka: The Battle of Horseshoe Bend

Tohopeka, the Battle of Horseshoe Bend, was the last major battle of the Creek War of 1813–1814. Halbert and Ball, in their account of the Creek War, detailed several incidents of brutality on the part of Jackson's troops; they wrote: "Before leaving Tohopeka, perhaps truth and justice require that another, a very unpleasant record should be made. It concerns the barbarity of some of Jackson's troops."[52] After the horrendous battle, the bodies of the dead were violated. One witness reported that "the party detailed to count the dead warriors found on the battle field of Tohopeka, so as to make no mistake in the count, cut off the tip of each dead Indian's nose so soon as the count was made."[53] Ms. Warren Wilbanks, an informant for Halbert and Ball, recalled that many of the Tennessee soldiers had cut long strips of skin from the bodies of dead Indians and with these made bridle reins.[54] Wilbanks also recalled a poignant incident involving the murder of an elderly noncombatant at Tohopeka: "When the Horse Shoe village was set on fire some of the soldiers noticed a very old Indian, a non-combatant, sitting on the ground, pounding corn in a mortar, as though unaware of the tumult and danger around him, and that a Tennessee barbarian, though called a soldier, deliberately shot him dead, assigning as his reason for doing so that he might be able to report when he got back home that he had killed an Indian."[55]

Another informant, Mr. Archibald McArthur, recalled an act of brutality against a young Indian boy: "In the heat of the fight a lost, bewildered, little Indian boy, five or six years of age, came among the soldiers, when one of them struck him on the head and killed him with the butt of his musket. When reproached by an officer for barbarity in killing so young a child, he replied, that the boy would have become an Indian some day."[56]

A similar sentiment of this legacy of brutality would be echoed many years later in Colorado in 1864. When asked for his justification for the massacre of numerous Indian children at the infamous Sand Creek Massacre, former Methodist minister and perpetrator Colonel John M. Chivington coolly replied, "'Nits make lice.'"[57]

Not since the deadly presence of Hernando de Soto had so many American Indians died in combat against non-Indians. Halbert and Ball surmised the brutality of the US forces with the following:

> Surely it was not needful, in avenging Fort Mims, as it was called, that the whites should imitate the barbarity of the Creeks. It is claimed that the truly brave are nearly always humane, but many a sacked city and a many a war-ravaged region can show that white soldiers may

equal in atrocity and barbarity and far exceed in the licentiousness the North American Indians. War at the best is ever terrible, and too many whites despise more or less what they call the inferior races of mankind. "Only an Indian" is a poor excuse for justifying a barbarity.[58]

Betrayal at Fort Jackson

From this author's perspective, General Andrew Jackson revealed his true nature in his attitudes and actions toward the Creek Indians that had allied with him at the conclusion of the Creek War. There was the assumption on the part of these Creeks that they would retain their tribal lands upon the defeat of the Red Sticks. One can only imagine the reaction of the Creeks who had fought against the Red Sticks upon their discovery that over twenty-one million acres of their land was about to be seized by Jackson through the Treaty of Fort Jackson. This acreage constituted more than one-half of the land area of the entire Creek Confederacy, and a considerable portion of this acreage came from the lands of the Creeks who had fought with Jackson.[59] The Creeks had already weakened and divided themselves through civil war, and now Jackson took the opportunity to subjugate and to conquer.

There were strong objections from the thirty-five chiefs who were assembled to sign the treaty. It is believed that only one of these chiefs had possibly been a Red Stick leader at some point within the conflict.[60] The chiefs made numerous speeches protesting the provisions of the treaty. To everyone present, the treaty was clearly unfair. Jackson was unmoved and presented his justification for the land seizures. He reflected back to the previous visitation and influences of Tecumseh. Jackson blamed the entire Creek Nation for tolerating Tecumseh's presence among them and for the subsequent rebellion and bloodshed that had followed. According to Jackson, they should have either seized Tecumseh and sent him as a prisoner to Jackson or killed him themselves. They had done neither, and now everyone would have to pay for the war.[61]

The Treaty of Fort Jackson was signed on August 9, 1814. In no way did it represent an agreement between the United States and the vanquished "enemy," the Red Stick Creeks. From a modern Creek perspective, it represented the beginning of numerous betrayals that Jackson would commit, not only toward his Creek Indian allies, but eventually toward his Cherokee and Choctaw allies as well. Though Jackson tolerated and used his Indian allies throughout the war, he certainly maintained a strong dislike toward his Creek allies. Owsley explains: "John H. Eaton, Jackson's friend and biographer, may have best explained Jackson's dislike of his Creek allies. According to Eaton, Jackson considered that the friendly Creeks had, when they joined his army, 'entered the ranks of the invading army' and were trying to exterminate their own people and destroy their own nation. This made them 'as traitors to their own country and justly deserving the severest punishment.'"[62]

The Treaty of Fort Jackson: Prelude to Removal

With the terms of the Treaty of Fort Jackson, one can surmise that Jackson had intentions far beyond that of payment for the war. The most tragic aspect of the Treaty of Fort Jackson was that it not only sought the destruction of the Creek Confederacy, but also foreshadowed the eventual removal of all southeastern tribes. Millions of acres of prime frontier land were opened for settlement by Americans. A westward expansion of the United States' boundaries would occur as new states joined the Union. Jackson, now perceived as the great war hero and politician, would rise in popularity to eventually obtain the presidency of the United States.[63] Then, in 1830, President Jackson would reveal his true intentions by evoking the Indian Removal Act, which created a shameful American tragedy, what this author describes as the "Trails of Tears," which would affect all southeastern Indian tribes. In 1832, the remaining lands of the Creek Nation were ceded to the United States and soon after, most of the Creek citizenry were removed to Indian Territory. The Creek Confederacy east of the Mississippi was obliterated.

Conclusion

On June 16, 1858, senatorial candidate Abraham Lincoln borrowed a biblical phrase in his speech to the Republican State Convention in Springfield, Illinois. With the steady growth of division and disunity within the nation, Lincoln reminded the people, "A house divided against itself cannot stand."[64]

When we examine the causalities and consequences of the Creek civil war and the Creek War of 1813–1814, we clearly see both the wisdom and the warning within that observation. Many of the darker aspects of human nature—disunity, hatred, revenge, and retaliation—all played their influential and deadly roles throughout this tragic story. While this chapter does not seek to pronounce historical judgments, one can find an abundance of accountability at all levels, both from Euro-American and Native American participation. Though divided by geography and, even still, at times, ideologies, the Muskogee Creek people of today have survived the overwhelming odds against them. Today, we progress forward into the future. We are still the "People of One Fire." Perhaps we can again find the strengths of agreement and unity for our future.

Notes

1. Anthony J. Paredes, "Federal Recognition and the Poarch Creek Indians," in *Indians of the Southeastern United States in the Late Twentieth Century,* ed. Anthony J. Paredes (Tuscaloosa: University of Alabama Press, 1992), 120.

2. H. S. Halbert and T. H. Ball, *The Creek War of 1813 and 1814,* ed. Frank L. Owsley Jr. (Tuscaloosa: University of Alabama Press, 1995), 38–39.

3. Henry DeLeon Southerland Jr. and Jerry Elijah Brown, *The Federal Road through Georgia, the Creek Nation, and Alabama, 1806–1836* (Tuscaloosa: University of Alabama Press, 1989), 21.

4. Southerland and Brown, *The Federal Road,* 39. For a more recent study of the road and its impact on the Creeks, see Angela Pulley Hudson's *Creek Paths and Federal Roads: Indians, Settlers, and Slaves and the Making of the American South* (Chapel Hill: University of North Carolina Press, 2010).

5. Frank Lawrence Owsley Jr., *Struggle for the Gulf Borderlands: The Creek War and the Battle of New Orleans, 1812–1815* (Gainesville: University Presses of Florida, 1981), 10.

6. Southerland and Brown, *The Federal Road,* 38.

7. Joel W. Martin, "The Creek Prophetic Movement," *Alabama Heritage,* no. 23 (Winter 1992): 13.

8. Albert James Pickett, *History of Alabama and Incidentally of Georgia and Mississippi, from the Earliest Period* (1851, repr., Birmingham: Webb Book, 1900), 419.

9. R. S. Cotterill, *The Southern Indians: The Story of the Civilized Tribes before Removal* (Norman: University of Oklahoma Press, 1987), 177.

10. Benjamin W. Griffith Jr., *McIntosh and Weatherford, Creek Indian Leaders* (Tuscaloosa: University of Alabama Press, 1988), 79.

11. Owsley, *Struggle for the Gulf Borderlands,* 11.

12. Quoted in Kathryn E. Holland Braund, *Deerskins and Duffels, Creek Indian Trade with Anglo-America, 1685–1815* (Lincoln: University of Nebraska Press, 1993), 185.

13. Claudio Saunt, *A New Order of Things: Property, Power, and the Transformation of the Creek Indians, 1773–1816* (Cambridge: Cambridge University Press, 1999), 40–42.

14. Gregory A. Waselkov and Kathryn E. Holland Braund, eds., *William Bartram on the Southeastern Indians* (Lincoln: University of Nebraska Press, 1995), 146.

15. Martin, "The Creek Prophetic Movement," 7.

16. Saunt, *A New Order of Things,* 42.

17. James Adair, *The History of the American Indians,* ed. and annotated by

Kathryn E. Holland Braund (1775; repr., Tuscaloosa: University of Alabama Press, 2005), 69.

18. Saunt, *A New Order of Things,* 43–44.

19. Quoted in Ibid., 43.

20. Waselkov and Braund, *William Bartram,* 195.

21. Saunt, *A New Order of Things,* 46–47; Robbie Ethridge, *The Creek Country: The Creek Indians and Their World* (Chapel Hill: University of North Carolina Press, 2003), 164–67.

22. Ibid.

23. Quoted in Saunt, *A New Order of Things,* 50.

24. Braund, *Deerskins and Duffels,* 186–87.

25. Quoted in Saunt, *A New Order of Things,* 257.

26. Joel W. Martin, *Sacred Revolt: The Muskogees' Struggle for a New World* (Boston: Beacon Press, 1991), 142.

27. Halbert and Ball, *The Creek War,* 342.

28. Owsley, *Struggle for the Gulf Borderlands,* 189–90.

29. Halbert and Ball, *The Creek War,* 340.

30. Gregory A. Waselkov, *A Conquering Spirit: Fort Mims and the Redstick War of 1813–1814* (Tuscaloosa: University of Alabama Press, 2006), 314, note 29.

31. J. Leitch Wright Jr., *Creeks and Seminoles: The Destruction and Regeneration of the Muscogulge People* (Lincoln and London: University of Nebraska Press, 1986), 173.

32. Ibid.

33. Saunt, *A New Order of Things,* 264.

34. Waselkov, *A Conquering Spirit,* 131–32.

35. Quoted in Halbert and Ball, *The Creek War,* 174.

36. Quoted in Waselkov, *A Conquering Spirit,* 132–33.

37. C. L. Grant, *Letters, Journals, and Writings of Benjamin Hawkins,* 2 vols. (Savannah, GA: Beehive Press, 1980), 1:28; Waselkov, *A Conquering Spirit,* 52.

38. Waselkov, *A Conquering Spirit,* 54.

39. Ibid.

40. Wright, *Creeks and Seminoles,* 173.

41. Michael Paul Rogin, *Fathers and Children: Andrew Jackson and the Subjugation of the American Indian* (New York: Alfred A. Knopf, 1975), 148.

42. Owsley, *Struggle for the Gulf Borderlands,* 65.

43. Halbert and Ball, *The Creek War,* 269.

44. Ibid.

45. Griffith, *McIntosh and Weatherford,* 119–20.

46. David Crockett, *A Narrative of the Life of David Crockett of the State of Tennessee* (Baltimore: Carey, Hart & Company, 1834), 88.

47. Halbert and Ball, *The Creek War,* 32.

48. Owsley, *Struggle for the Gulf Borderlands,* 65.
49. Halbert and Ball, *The Creek War,* xxvii, n. 44 (editor's notes).
50. Owsley, *Struggle for the Gulf Borderlands,* 67.
51. Halbert and Ball, *The Creek War,* 272.
52. Ibid., 276.
53. Ibid., 277.
54. Ibid., 276–77.
55. Ibid., 277.
56. Ibid.
57. Chivington, quoted in Winter Rabbit, "144th Anniversary of the Sand Creek Massacre of Nov. 29th, 1864," *Native American Netroots,* http://www.nativeamericannetroots.net/showDiary.do?diaryId=194 (accessed July 14, 2009).
58. Halbert and Ball, *The Creek War,* 277–78.
59. Owsley, *Struggle for the Gulf Borderlands,* 88.
60. Ibid., 91.
61. Ibid., 89.
62. Ibid.
63. Ibid., 194.
64. Abraham Lincoln, "House Divided Speech: June 16, 1858," *Abraham Lincoln Online,* http://showcase.netins.net/web/creative/lincoln/speeches/house.htm (accessed July 14, 2009).

2

Thinking outside the Circle

Tecumseh's 1811 Mission

Gregory Evans Dowd

According to long-standing conventions, challenged but not overthrown in the late twentieth century, Tecumseh's 1811 visit was a revolutionary departure from traditional tribal thinking, was that of a secular statesman who at some level stood apart from his brother's spiritual movement, and was echoed by earthquakes that proved decisive in gaining him support in Creek country. Let us think otherwise.

The intrepid Shawnee, aware that his people needed widespread alliances against the invaders from the East, went southward from his Ohio Valley homeland practically to the Gulf of Mexico. Something had to be done, he knew, about the invaders from the Atlantic who were claiming dominion over Indians and their lands in much of eastern North America. The Shawnee's name was well known to several military officers and numerous traders, but the name was not Tecumseh, and the year was not 1811. Tecumseh was not yet born; the year was 1764, and the name sits in the records as Charlot Kaské. Kaské, a Shawnee "beloved man," civil leader, and a close ally of, indeed a messenger for, the Ottawa Pontiac, was known among "all the nations for his Sense." He loved the French, or so he repeatedly said.[1] He spent most of Pontiac's War (from 1763 to 1766) in energetic but futile efforts to arouse France against Great Britain; he was more successful at rousing the Indians.[2]

Kaské, a native of Shawnee country on the Upper Ohio River, had spent time among the French villages of southern Illinois before boarding a convoy bound for New Orleans in early November 1764. His wife accompanied him.[3] His speech, recorded in New Orleans, indicates that this was at least his second visit to the city. He was speaking not just for himself, he said, but for forty-seven villages, each of which was marked on the great belt "of five branches" that he held in his hand.[4] Indians from the Lower Mississippi

River were also present. Kaské met diplomatic defeat among the French, who refused to assist him. But, when north of the Ohio River once more, he deployed his visit as a victory.[5]

Still carrying the large belt in March 1765, he uttered powerful words. Kaské predicted the revival of the French king and emphasized the coming of a vast French cargo to the north: "The french had made peace with them [the English, and] they were in a few months to begin the war again, but peace or war that they [the Indians] might depend on being well supplyd with arms and ammunition."[6] His actions, along with those of many others, stymied for over a year the British effort to gain control of the Illinois country, a thing they never really did.

Eleven years later, while a distant Congress debated independence in the spring of 1776, a party of militant Shawnees, Mohawks, and Ottawas, accompanied by a Cherokee interpreter, traveled seventy days to meet with Cherokees in the southern reaches of the Appalachian Mountains. A British agent was present, and he reported that toward the conclusion of the meetings, a Shawnee spoke for this northern Indian delegation to the Cherokee beloved town of Chota. Called by the British a renowned "French partisan," he could well have been Charlot Kaské. He unrolled a huge belt of wampum, nine feet by six inches, "strewed over with vermilion, red trade paint," perhaps the very belt noted in the records of 1764–1765. The Shawnees, he grimly recounted, "from being a great nation, were [now] reduced to a handful." Shawnees, like Cherokees, once "possessed lands almost to the seashore," and like them, all "red people who were once masters of the whole country [now] hardly possessed ground enough to stand on." The argument was not new in 1776: Indians shared great difficulties with the settler societies to the east and they could benefit from pan-Indian unity.

Like Kaské in Illinois, this speaker promised that "the French, who seemed long dead, were now alive again, that they had supplied them plentifully with ammunition, arms and provisions, and that they promised to assist them against the Virginians." He then ended his speech by reminding the Cherokees that they had accepted a Shawnee hatchet "six years ago [1770]." He urged the Cherokees to seize the hatchet and "use it immediately," and he declared his intention to "carry their talks through every nation to the southward."[7] When the Shawnee finished speaking, a leader of one Cherokee faction accepted the militant message, amid objections by others, including that Cherokee leader's own father. The Cherokees divided between those who sought pan-Indian action and those more established tribal leaders who sought to maintain peace.[8]

These episodes, and many like them, make clear that by the time of the

American Revolution, the idea of united Indian resistance to settler expansion had already taken hold among peoples from the Great Lakes to the Gulf of Mexico. These calls brought about no utopia, and they continued to elicit mixed responses in Indian communities; villages often divided from within while their militants united with members of other and often distant towns and peoples. The divisions did not bring civil war to the Cherokees in 1776 as they would to the Creeks in 1813, but they did weaken the Cherokees as warfare erupted with the new American states. A currency of militant religious ideas accompanied the calls for unity. The religious nativism of Pontiac's War in the 1760s is connected to this Shawnee's visit to the Cherokees in the 1770s. This Shawnee declared to the Cherokees that the Indians should receive aid from a greater power than France, for "their cause was just and . . . he hoped the Great Being who governs everything would favour their cause."[9]

It is safe to say that Tecumseh would have encountered such ideas as a child. He would have been, in 1776, anywhere from six to twelve years old—most authorities would say about eight—and most would agree that his Shawnee parents had lived for a time among the Creeks in what is now Alabama, returning to the Ohio country shortly before his birth. It is likely that he knew, in some detail, of the Creeks.

Shawnees continued to correspond with the southern peoples. In 1793, records indicate that a Shawnee named Red Pole went south in search of recruits to a vast alliance.[10] Four years before Tecumseh's tour of 1811, Indiana territorial governor William Henry Harrison had worried that Shawnee "war belts" had "been passing through all the Tribes from the Gulf of Florida to the Lakes." Harrison heard in 1810—a year before Tecumseh's famous tour—that Tenskwatawa was attempting to "raise the southern Indians, the Choctaws and the Creeks particularly," and Harrison added that "the Prophet's mother was a Creek."[11]

Tecumseh's trip southward in 1811 may have been, as one historian recently stated, "arguably the most impressive journey ever made on behalf of Indian unity."[12] But it was far from the only such trip by a Shawnee with a diplomatic mission. He was following in many footsteps.

Nor were Shawnees the only Indians who got around. There is good evidence of Cherokees and Creeks heading northward to participate in intertribal forms of resistance, especially from the American Revolution onward. Kathryn Braund has observed that the idea behind Tecumseh's mission was not, among the Creeks, "a new one; such talk had circulated among Creek councils since the mid-eighteenth century." She points to an effort in the 1770s among Creeks, Cherokees, Shawnees, and Delawares to mobilize against the English colonists. The Mortar of Okchai was, she observes, "the most prominent Creek to support the movement." The British were very concerned about the Mortar—his name is all over official Indian agency correspondence in the period.[13] And the activities he supported did not stop with his untimely death in the early 1770s. Indeed, even as Tecumseh was returning homeward in late 1811, Creeks were identified among the dead at the Battle of Tippecanoe, which marked the beginning, not the end, of the Indians' war of 1812.[14] William Henry Harrison, who commanded US forces at that battle, noted earlier in the year, even before Tecumseh's southern tour, that a "Muskoe" Indian had been killed in Vincennes by an Italian innkeeper.[15] By "Muskoe" he meant Creek. Observing the intertribal character of the "the Prophet's force" even earlier, in 1810, Harrison had included at Prophet's Town "20 or 30 Muskoes or Creeks."[16] And Creeks were not the only southern Indians at Tippecanoe. John Norton, who visited Shawnee villages in 1810, met a Cherokee who told him that many Cherokees lived at Prophet's Town.[17] Much earlier, even as the Shawnee Prophet had begun to preach in the early part of the decade, Cherokees sent messages to, and visited, the White River Valley of Indiana, where he then lived.[18]

Shawnees, Creeks, and Cherokees had many reasons to form alliances, not all of them hostile to the United States. These Indians increasingly hunted and met with relatives who had moved across the Mississippi River, where their migrations butted up against the expanding Osage dominion.[19] In 1804, Indian agent Benjamin Hawkins had been concerned about a growing Creek alliance against the Osage Indians, one that included Cherokees, Chickasaws, Choctaws, Delawares, and Shawnees. He heard that "they had united themselves against" the Osages. If peoples could discuss unity against the Osages, how much more difficult was it for them to discuss unity against the United States?[20]

Until relatively recently, historians interpreting such Indian efforts at unity in the age of revolution had to strain against a dominant organizational model that saw Indians as, above all else, tribal people. They had to make sense of a movement that was not tribal, that seemingly violated a core principle. Tribal peoples, such thinking had it, identified solely with their own and could not conceive of the advantages of unity. Only such geniuses as Tecumseh, and Pontiac before him, thrown up by nature like mutant DNA, rose above their peers to challenge the stolid minds of their tribes—people. Francis Parkman explained Pontiac as such a genius in his *The Conspiracy of Pontiac*. In that, he was following Pontiac's own English-speaking contemporaries, such as General Thomas Gage, who had toyed with the idea in the 1760s.[21] In 1810, William Henry Harrison called Tecumseh a genius, and the notion that Tecumseh's genius explained his movement was taken up by Harrison's partisan supporter, an early biographer of Tecumseh, Benjamin Drake.[22] Here is Harrison, writing as Tecumseh was on his southern tour:

> The implicit obedience and respect which the followers of Tecumseh pay to him, is really astonishing, and more than any other circumstance bespeaks him one of those uncommon geniuses which spring up occasionally to produce revolutions, and overturn the established order of things. If it were not for the vicinity of the United States, he would, perhaps, be the founder of an empire that would rival in glory Mexico or Peru. No difficulties deter him. For four years he has been in constant motion. You see him to-day on the Wabash, and in a short time hear of him on the shores of lake Erie or Michigan, or the banks of the Mississippi; and wherever he goes he makes an impression favorable to his purposes. He is now upon the last round to put a finishing stroke to his work. I hope, however, before his return that that part of the fabric which he considered complete, will be demolished, and even its foundations rooted up. Although the greater part of his followers are attracted to him from principle and affection, there are many others who follow him through fear; and he was scarcely a mile from town, before they indulged in the most virulent invectives against him. The Prophet is impudent and audacious, but is deficient in judgment, talents, and firmness.[23]

This tradition lived on through the twentieth century in works describing Tecumseh as a peculiar genius for conceiving a bold plan for Indian unity. Fairly typical is this military historian's statement: "Tecumseh realized what few Indians ever saw: only if all tribes made common cause could they hope to contain the United States."[24]

Long ago I argued that a broadly intertribal religious movement supported the efforts of both Pontiac and Tecumseh. Far from thinking outside the tribal circle, far from being geniuses rising above their tribally circumscribed peoples, these men, as I described them, were leading participants—with many others—in a widespread pan-Indian effort to regain for Indians control of their destinies, in this world and the next. The past generation of serious scholarship on Native Americans in the turbulent colonial and revolutionary eras offers another way of looking at the matter. It has taken the tribal circle, which for so long had defined scholarship on Native Americans, and thrown it out as the fixed, defining category of Native American identity. It has cast grave doubt upon the idea that the tribe or tribal identity determined human behavior.

Joshua Piker, in his recent history of the Creek town of Okfuskee, points out that "scholars have . . . become increasingly wary of referring to the Indians of early America as tribal peoples." He points to the "polyvocality and diversity" and the "fluid and ephemeral" character of "multitown associations." He opines, "Seventeenth- and eighteenth-century Indian life did not center on the tribe or the confederacy after all."[25] Piker follows Richard White, who points out in his award-winning *The Middle Ground* (1991) that "tribal identity, and the technicalities of kinship reckoning . . . did not dictate political behavior" in the turbulent world that gave birth to Tecumseh. White argues that identities were local and shifting and that larger claims to loyalty were often contingent and up for grabs.[26]

Even villages or towns could have remarkably multiethnic configurations. Tippecanoe, Greenville, and Horseshoe Bend (Tohopeka)—these centers of pan-Indian militancy obviously stand at one end of the spectrum as deliberate provocations to the emerging tribal governments. These three places were prophetic villages with clear nativistic intent, gathering militants from across a wide variety of villages and languages into single anti-American towns. They also had this in common: they grew in direct opposition to the US-recognized tribal leadership. Okfuskees who settled Tohopeka had, according to Piker, killed several of their headmen, those who had opposed the Red Sticks.[27] Similar events led to the Shawnee Prophet's towns to the north, first Greenville and then Tippecanoe, towns dedicated to the old intertribal vision.[28] There is a large history that demonstrates the gathering, for a time, of members of many different "tribes" into single villages at locations across eastern North America.

If tribes did not simply command human loyalties, if Indians saw themselves as parts of something larger and smaller than the tribal circle, we are also learning that the entities we have blithely called tribes have been, at least in the history of Indian North America after 1600, quite complicated social formations themselves. They competed with the rise of other large social formations, some of which lasted centuries and dominated large stretches of the continent, some of which existed with some European support, and in many of which Europeans played precious little direct role. Our bibliographies now include works describing how Ojibwes, Assiniboine, Cree, and Dakota peoples occasionally formed vast alliances in the northern Great Lakes and prairie West—a century before Tecumseh fought his first battle.[29] New scholarship on the Comanches on the southern Great Plains or Apaches in the Southwest indicates that they understood the power of gathering others into a kind of unity, even as Tecumseh grew from a boy to a man.[30] The history of Choctaws, and especially that of the Creeks, includes works describing gatherings of previously separate—and even linguistically diverse—peoples.

Strong forces, such as vast epidemics and widespread slave-raiding, did much to compel the consolidation of old ethnicities, some of them shattered, to borrow from Robbie Ethridge, into new social formations.[31] Whether or not we should refer to a Creek confederacy in the mid-eighteenth century or whether we should think instead of unstable multiethnic alliances of villages remains something of an open question, but almost no historians would speak of a generalized Creek tribe in 1750. This is not to deny the deep history or enduring presence of Creek or Muskogee peoples. Many scholars, Kathryn Braund among them, properly speak of a Muskogee or Creek Nation in the colonial era, and it is one composed of "different tribes speaking different languages or dialects." And even Piker himself, a strong proponent of the local, acknowledges the same thing as he points to shared "traits," "processes," "attributes," and "experiences" that "allow historians to discuss a shared Creek history." What we might say, then, is that the history of Indian peoples is as dynamic and complicated as that of, say, Britons or, a better example, Americans.[32]

Tecumseh may well have been a genius—but not because he invented the idea of Indian unity. Tecumseh did not struggle against ancient tribal loyalties or traditional intertribal hatreds; there was much that was not traditional about tribes and the ways they were constituted in 1811. Stressing Indian unity, Tecumseh did not think outside the tribal circle. Eastern North America had seen the rise of pan-Indian militancy since the middle of the eighteenth century, even as it saw the rise of larger multiethnic cultural formations that sometimes threatened to cohere as tribal nations or confederacies, such as the Muskogees. Pan-Indian militancy often competed, and sometimes competed violently, with the rise of the Indian tribal nation. This was especially true in 1811, and especially true among the Creeks. Fort Mims, where the word *heterogeneous* can be applied to both "Red Stick" assailants and "American" defenders, was one result. Horseshoe Bend was another.[33]

There is another way in which American legend and history have Tecumseh thinking outside the tribal circle; he is often portrayed as unconvinced by his brother's religious movement and even as hostile to his brother after some critical turning point. Sometimes he is viewed as having manipulated his brother from the start in order to win credulous Indians over to the cause of pan-Indianism. Sometimes he is viewed as having become exasperated by the Prophet, especially after the Battle of Tippecanoe, when, like an angry Zeus abusing Folly, he is reported to have seized his brother by the hair and shaken him, furious at the Prophet's starting of the war before the time was ripe.[34] Here, too, the conventional wisdom has seen Tecumseh as thinking outside of the Indian circle, urging a unity his followers could not compre-

2.1. Tecumseh. Engraving from Benson J. Lossing, *Pictorial Field-Book of the War of 1812*. The portrait was reputedly drawn from life by Pierre Le Dru. Courtesy of the Alabama Department of Archives and History, Montgomery, Alabama.

hend without deploying his allegedly foolish brother as a prophetic instrument.[35]

William Henry Harrison's own writings reveal another possibility. In July 1811, he saw Tecumseh as an heir to Pontiac: "Tecumseh has taken for his model the celebrated Pontiac and I am persuaded that he will bear a favourable comparison in every respect with that far-famed warrior."[36] There is nothing that upsets the conventional wisdom there. A year earlier, however, he had said something slightly different of Tenskwatawa, the Shawnee Prophet: "This fellow has boasted that he would follow the footsteps of the Great Pontiac."[37] Here, Harrison has the Shawnee Prophet himself, the religious leader, place himself in an Indian tradition of unity, and here Harrison was on target.

Literary historian Gordon Sayre has identified Tecumseh's story as fitting an emerging Anglo-American literary type: the Indian "tragic hero." Writings in this vein—histories, plays, poems, novels—both emphasized Tecumseh's "martial, republican virtues" and ridiculed his brother, the Prophet, whose "nativistic message, his persecution of rivals as witches, and then his fall from grace . . . all made him less appealing to sympathizers of the Indian cause."[38] To put it in a nutshell, we like to have our Tecumseh as a great statesman and our Tenskwatawa as a violent fanatic.

Stories of Tecumseh among the Creeks, however, provide many exceptions to this pattern. They diverge from the "tragic hero" motif, portraying Tecumseh much as his brother is more generally portrayed, as a false and dangerous prophet. In fact, in some accounts, he *is* his brother. Many of the records are, by the way, particularly bad as historical evidence, even worse than evidence for Tecumseh in the North.[39] Yet for all their weaknesses, they have strongly influenced scholarship. And they love earthquakes. I confess to loving these records for the way they treat Tecumseh as a holy warrior, for the way they think outside a circle of thought that defines Tecumseh as a tragic hero. But much as I run with that argument, I confess to concerns.

A distinguished body of writing, from such leading nineteenth-century experts on American Indians as Thomas L. McKenney through James Mooney, connects Tecumseh, the earthquakes of 1811–1812, and the Creek War of 1813–1814.[40] Frank Owsley Jr., writing in the early 1970s, sums up the by-then conventional wisdom: "By predicting the arrival of a comet in the sky and an earthquake which shook Tookabatchee, the Creek capital, Tecumseh was able to convince thousands of these Indians that they had angered their gods by following the ways of the white man. With this support and the encouragement of a group of prophets trained by Tecumseh, all of the hidden resentments of the conservative elements surfaced with fanatical enthusiasm."[41]

The idea that earthquakes were a major causal factor in the Red Stick War has proven to be irresistible. It is such a good story! American religion scholar Joel Martin and British historian John Sugden weave it into their scholarly works. Martin asks: "What led the Creeks to revolt. . . . ? Central to the Creek religious life were the native prophets, who appear to have gained increasing power in 1811 and 1812 based largely on the convergence of two remarkable events: first, the visit of Tecumseh . . . ; second, a series of tremendous earthquakes that shook much of North America and all of the Southeast. These two events, Creek prophets claimed, were related. According to the prophets, the earthquakes validated Tecumseh's anti-American message."[42] The earthquakes, then, rank with Tecumseh's visit as bringing on the Red Stick War.

John Sugden provides the most convincing reconstitution of Tecumseh's tour in the South. He is very precise on the difficulties scholars face in following the trip through Kentucky and Tennessee into the Choctaw country until reaching the Creek *talwa* at Tuckabatchee on September 19, 1811.[43] As he carefully points out, there is no direct record of the speech that Tecumseh gave at that place, or at any place on the southern mission. Yet with all this caution, Sugden moves onto the shaky ground. He notes, accurately, that a comet had become visible in the night skies toward the end of August. He claims that Tecumseh "seized upon" its appearance, "aluding to it as an omen that boded ill to his enemies." Napoleon, incidentally, had done the same thing with the same comet, or so it is said. Sugden's Creeks found it wonderfully revealing that Tecumseh's name meant "shooting star" and that the comet was at its "most brilliant" while the Shawnee was touring the Creek talwas. But comets are not like shooting stars. I have seen comets, most memorably Hale-Bopp in 1996–1997, and I have seen shooting stars, for example, a brilliant one over the Michigan farmland near the town of Dexter on the night of Barack Obama's inauguration, or, I could also say, the night someone last crashed into my car. They are not alike. The Great Comet of 1811 had a noteworthy tale that "forked," it hung in the sky for many weeks, and, indeed, it ranks only behind Hale-Bopp in terms of the length of its visibility. By contrast, a shooting star is a brief flash, and it is gone. "No Creek," Sugden judges, "could be blamed for believing that this man had truly been favored by the spirits."[44]

Then, Sugden accurately continues, beginning on December 16, 1811, the earthquakes came and occasionally rumbled through February 7, 1812. Says Sugden, curiously, "None were more astonished than Indian peoples." Tecumseh "had already armed them with an explanation," alleges Sugden, and the explanation was that the Great Spirit was angry with Indians for their lack of resistance to the United States and its ways of life. He says, with a notable passive construction, "Within months of the final quakes it was being reported that Tecumseh had actually predicted the event to the Creeks." This is a creative reading of the reports, as we shall soon see.[45]

Like Martin, Sugden refrains from claiming that Tecumseh actually predicted the quakes. But he sees it as a "fact" that enough "Creeks believed that he had done so" to influence the course of Creek history. We will soon see what kind of fact it is. Where Martin counts the earthquakes as one of two triggers of the Red Stick War, Sugden counts them as one of the three "linked factors" that brought on the conflict, for they "proved that [Tecumseh] was right."[46] The argument echoes that of Martin: "The resounding earth," Martin poetically insists, "had forcibly reminded the Muskogees of the fragility of This World and reconfirmed the awesome power of the Lower World."[47]

A few scholars have, quite reasonably and for a very long time, dismissed the idea that Tecumseh actually predicted the quakes. As early as the late nineteenth century, writers contemporary with James Mooney cast doubt upon records that suggested that Tecumseh had said anything about earthquakes.[48] And again, neither Martin nor Sugden states that Tecumseh actually predicted them. But they do count the quakes as one of two or three factors leading up to the war, lending critical, that is, historically important, millennial force to the movement for war; both scholars also tie the quakes to the visit of Tecumseh.[49]

Did the earthquakes count? How do they register on our causal scales? Did they matter much to the war? Creeks were already seismically divided long before Tecumseh's visit; his call for intertribal unity against both the United States and tribal leaders who cooperated with the United States resonated strongly on its own with an already growing militant faction. It is unclear that earthquakes persuaded anyone to join that faction. After all, the war broke out in the north at Tippecanoe among similarly divided Indian peoples before the first round of quakes, and, what is more, Creeks died in the November 1811 action. These deaths, and the retaliations they demanded, had a lot more to do with the war than did the shaking earth.

The ideas that tie Tecumseh to earthquakes and earthquakes to the war are more than romantic embellishment. They are, for one thing, markers of the remarkably different impression that Tecumseh made in the South than in the North. Tecumseh in the South is less a secular statesman or a tragic hero than he is, at best, an evangelistic advocate of Indian unity or, at worst, a false prophet. In the North, the conventional wisdom of the early nineteenth century and after has him as a secular, tragic hero, the genius who relied on his brother to convince Indians to join the movement for unity.

As portrayed in the South, Tecumseh is a zealot who relies on comets and earthquakes to gain sway among the Creeks.

Unstable evidence links earthquakes with the Creek War of 1813–1814. The earthquakes, centered in northeastern Arkansas, were indeed felt across the American interior—in Detroit, in Mobile Bay, even in Charleston. But from Creek country there is no good evidence that the tremors caused damage: no on-the-spot reports of a collapsed dwelling or an uprooted tree. In contrast to the lower-central Mississippi Valley, the quakes caused no flooding, landsliding, collapsing of riverbanks, or disinterment of buried matter in the Creek country. The leading historian of the earthquake sums it up: "A total area of over 1,000,000 square miles, or half that of the entire [lower 48] United States (today), was so disturbed that the vibrations could be felt without the aid of instruments." But houses around the talwas did not fall.[50]

If Creeks heard the ominous noises and felt the strange vibrations, and they probably did, did the vibrations and noises have a bearing on the war? Assuming that in all likelihood Creeks did know of the terrific scale of the quakes to their west and northwest, in what ways did the quakes contribute to the war? The evidence that they did is highly unreliable. Martin's evidence, for example, was all written well after the fact.[51] Sugden has relatively more contemporary evidence, but it is also poorly grounded. Sugden finds "the earliest reference to Tecumseh's prediction of the earthquake" to appear in a June 1812 gentlemen's magazine published in New York.[52] The article is by one Francis McHenry, and it is interestingly titled: "The Indian Prophet." The *Halcyon Luminary* apparently reproduced it from the Milledgeville *Georgia Journal.* On the trustworthiness of Mr. McHenry, we have an opinion by federal agent to the Creeks, Benjamin Hawkins:

> We experience some inconvenience from loose worthless characters traveling through this agency, and some, pretending to be scientific, misrepresenting everything they see, either from design, or from associating with persons who have fled from the restraints of civil society. You have a specimen of one of these travelers in the [Milledgeville] Georgia Journal of the 13th May, who signs himself Francis McHenry, answered in that of the 27th, by Timothy Barnard, public interpreter. This man passes himself sometimes as an Englishman, then a Virginian, and again a Scotchman.[53]

McHenry discusses an August 1811 declaration made in a Creek public square that a "lamp would appear in the west." The speaker claimed that should the Creeks not attend to the call for a "hostile attack upon the whites, . . .

the earth would, ere long, tremble to its center." McHenry wonders why there was not "a line published by our agent," Benjamin Hawkins, on the tremendous effect that this prediction was having on the Creeks. McHenry insists that the story of the prediction of the earthquake rests on very good authority, and he names some prominent figures who knew the Creeks well, from Alexander Cornells and Samuel Maniac (Moniac) to, perhaps most interestingly, a Mr. Stiggins in the Tensaw, whom, he says, "was present" at the prediction.[54]

Let's confront the reasons to be skeptical of this as a piece of reliable evidence linking Tecumseh to the earthquake. For one thing, it is, like much of the evidence upon which we have to rely, hearsay. He claims to have this from various traders and agents in the Creek country. There are, moreover, important errors. Tecumseh's name does not appear in the article; it is instead "the Prophet," presumably the Shawnee Prophet who tours the South. McHenry is not the only person to make this error. Next, the article dates the embassy to the Creeks as in August, not in September, when it actually took place. September would be very inconvenient to the author's argument because the comet was by then already very visible and nearing its most brilliant phase. The comet was, in comparison with most, quite spectacular. Visible to the naked eye when it came over the horizon in August, its luminosity peaked in October.[55] The article's main concern is with the Prophet's prediction of the comet among the Creeks: if the prediction had waited until September, it would not be a prediction, for the comet was already hanging brightly in the night sky. It was less noticeable in August. Finally, there is more to this, for the author is most interested in embellishing a peculiar scientific argument: that the comet caused the earthquakes. He suggests that the Prophet had spent an earlier part of his life in Quebec and Halifax (which is false) and that while there he had gained knowledge of astronomy, enough, at least, to know about the coming of the comet in 1811. This is odd, too, since this particular comet was unknown to astronomy until 1811. This is also another convenient error, for such an education among US enemies would make sense in 1812. In short, this article is very poor evidence that many Creeks in 1812 understood Tecumseh to have predicted earthquakes. The article's main argument is quite different, that the Shawnee Prophet knew the comet was coming, that he therefore knew the earthquakes were coming, and that this is how he deceived the Creeks. One must ask, How credulous were the Creeks, and how credulous are we?

There is a second early report from one year later, June 1813, that speaks of earthquakes. Published in Georgia, it is a report by Alexander Cornells, who writes of the Red Stick prophets among the Alabamas; they were predicting that "if any of the Indian towns refused their aids to the Prophets, they should be sunk by an earthquake." This item does put earthquakes into the mouths of the Red Sticks, but they are future and severe earthquakes, not the mild tremors felt in the Creek country in 1811 and early 1812. The article, too, says nothing of Tecumseh predicting quakes, though it does see him as the incendiary tool of Great Britain, and it says nothing of the Shawnee Prophet.[56] It does not list the earthquake as a primary cause of support for the Red Sticks. Tecumseh is not directly linked in any contemporary sources to the earthquakes, and the evidence for an indirect link is not strong.

Better evidence by religious missionaries and US agents suggests that a religious movement among the Cherokees gained some life from the shaking earth; but even here, there is room for doubt, for the earthquakes actually seem to have come more toward the end of the Cherokee movement than at its beginning. Puzzling too is this: while earthquakes seemingly compel Red Stick Creeks to war, they do not have that effect on Cherokees. Nor is Tecumseh connected to the earthquakes in these Cherokee reports.[57]

Let's assume for the moment that, after the quakes had sounded and vibrated in Creek country, the Red Sticks posited them as signs favorable to their movement. This is plausible, even likely, and it is thick in the subsequent lore. But not only must we still ask, Was this an important argument? We also have to ask, How important was it compared to all the other reasons Red Sticks might have had for attending to their prophets and for engaging in violence with their Creek opponents? Why do we, in the reading public, see Indians as being swayed, so to speak, by earthquakes? After all, no one, to my knowledge, has argued that US citizens saw the comet or the earthquakes as important causes of the American declaration of war on Great Britain in 1812, yet this is what is being alleged for Creek Indians and the United States. Gordon Sayre, in a recent book of literary analysis, suggests an answer. He posits, "The stereotype of Indian peoples as being in closer communication with the earth and heavens" has made the earthquakes so appealing to modern Americans. Sayre is onto something.[58]

Another line of thought among US citizens gave the earthquakes appeal: Christianity, especially familiarity with scripture. It is well known that the early nineteenth century was a time of evangelical growth in the United States, especially in the South. One of the most exciting sources for the idea that Tecumseh's prediction of the quakes galvanized the Red Sticks is the manuscript narrative of the Creek War by George Stiggins, who wrote a memoir and history in the 1830s or early 1840s. Stiggins, reporting from hearsay well after the fact, says that Tecumseh, when speaking in council, announced to the Creeks that once he became certain of victory against the Americans, he "would ascend to the top of a high mountain [in Indiana?] . . . and there he would whoop three unbounded loud whoops slap his hands together three times and raise his foot and stamp it on the earth three times . . . to make the whole earth tremble."[59] Then, confirming his predictions, the comet and the earthquake came, and "flying tales daily multiplied and were exaggerated in all parts of the nation."[60] We rely on Stiggins, in part, because he was affiliated by heritage with the Creeks; but note that he was, at age twenty-four or twenty-five in 1811, strongly hostile to and even appalled by the Red Sticks, whom he saw not only as irrational, but as sacrilegious and heretical. Stiggins, in orthodox Christian fashion, sees the age of true prophecy as having terminated with the advent of Christ and his genuine apostles; subsequent prophecies to those of scripture were heretical: "So the age and time of prophesy in the Creek nation," he writes, "preceded the light of reason and knowledge for a time, and many turned prophet which was a prelude to all the [Red Sticks'] mad and diabolical actions."[61] Stiggins views the Red Sticks primarily as false, even devilish, prophets.

Other later accounts of the Red Sticks evoke scripture more than history. J. F. H. Claiborne's imaginative record of Tecumseh's speech at Tuckabatchee remains influential in popular quarters, although Henry Sale Halbert and Timothy Horton Ball debunked the speech long ago.[62] Claiborne's rendition of Tecumseh's predictions is thick with scriptural resonance: the Shawnee would stamp his foot at Tippecanoe, and the "very earth shall shake." Biblically, Joel (2:10) announced, "The earth shall quake before them; the heavens shall tremble"; and he prophesied (3:16) that the Lord "shall roar" out of Zion "and the heavens and earth shall shake." Haggai made a prediction (2:6–9) in a verse some of us have sung in Handel's *Messiah:* "Yet once it is a little while, and I will shake the heavens, and the earth, and the sea, and the dry land; And I will shake all nations, and the desire of all nations shall come."[63]

The bogus transcripts that we have of Tecumseh's southern speeches are fanciful; they are more legend than history; they resonate more with the racial assumptions of Victorian Americans and with Christian notions of false prophecy than with the record; but they nonetheless contain a nugget of truth. In the few reports that actually date from the time of his visit, he is hardly the secular noble savage but is instead the leader of a religious movement hostile to the United States.[64] Andrew Jackson called him an "incendiary, the emissary of the Prophet."[65] Benjamin Hawkins, the federal superintendent of Indians in the region, and his Creek ally Alexander Cornells illustrate this tendency even more starkly: both men thought that Tecumseh was the famous Shawnee Prophet.[66] This may be, in part, because Tecumseh's mission was sacred, at least in his own terms.

So, let's think outside the circle. Rather than consider Tecumseh as a tragic genius originating a brilliantly creative idea of Indian unity against a stolid backdrop of tribalism, rather than seeing his idea as shining brilliantly like the 1811 comet against the deep tribal sky, it is more accurate to see the idea of pan-Indianism as developing over generations in competition with the idea of tribal or national confederacies. Both were notions with deep traditions by 1811, and both were dynamic developments. Both, in some measure, endure to this day. Both were in violent conflict during the War of 1812, when Shawnee fought Shawnee and Creek fought Creek. Tecumseh did not have to resort to charlatanry; he did not have to predict earthquakes or explain comets to convince many of the wisdom of united resistance. That wisdom was already a tradition. The idea of pan-Indian resistance to the United States resonated with old Creek ideas, much as with old Shawnee ideas, and Creek as well as Shawnee people had been discussing these ideas for generations among themselves and with one another. Neither Creeks nor Shawnees found the idea of pan-Indian organization to be in violation of their ancient tribal identities, for there was much about tribal identity that was not ancient, especially as that idea was being practiced by some of the leaders of their villages and towns. Only very weak evidence, greatly inflated by established assumptions about Native Americans and appealing to a Christian readership, has it that earthquakes played an important role in the Red Stick movement. As for the role of earthquakes in bringing on the war, it was insignificant. Neither Creeks nor Shawnees needed earthquakes to aggravate the social fault lines among them or to bring them into conflict with a very aggressive, imperial republic.

Scholars have long understood that the "tribe" too strongly configures our approaches to Native American social formations and historical activity. Tecumseh's journey southward, a repetition of earlier efforts at alliance building, contributed to the efforts of the Creek Red Sticks, who opposed the power not only of the United States but of a centralizing Creek National Council, which was itself a strengthening, developing, "tribal" entity that embraced multiple ethnicities. Both pan-Indian militancy and central tribal authority had contested histories lasting a lifetime before they collided during the Creek War and the War of 1812. Historians of the United States should be the last to be surprised by such contested histories, given the national history of US civil conflict. Indeed, Tecumseh's memory served different ends in the US North, where he became the brilliant Shawnee statesman and tragic hero, and the US South, where he became the prophetic anti-American zealot. It is hard to say that one is more accurate than the other. As historians and ethnohistorians, explicitly cautious about the shaky grounds provided by the biased written record of Native American history, we must equally attend to our own purposes as we consider such concepts as the tribe, the pan-Indian revolt, the statesman, and the prophet. As these fall from our lips and fingertips onto the turbulence that engulfed so many lives at Horseshoe Bend, we do well to wonder at their capacity to even contribute to an explanation for such a horror.

Notes

1. Lieutenant Robert Fraser to General Thomas Gage, Kaskaskia, May 15, 1765, Gage Papers, American Series, William Clements Library, University of Michigan, Ann Arbor (hereafter cited as WCL); see also Richard White, *The Middle Ground: Indians, Empires, and Republics in the Great Lakes Region, 1650–1815* (New York: Cambridge University Press, 1991), 300–305, 307.

2. De Neyon to Dabbadie, Dec. 1, 1763, *Collections of the Illinois State Historical Society* (hereafter cited as *CISHL*) 10:52–55; speech of the Shawnees to Monsieur de Neyon, Dec. 21, 1763, Gage Papers, WCL.

3. St. Ange to Dabbadie, Aug. 12, 1764, and Nov. 9, 1764, *CISHL,* 10:295, 354–57.

4. Journal of Dabbadie, Dec. 1764, *CISHL* 10:203; "Copy of a Speech made by the Shawnee Indian . . . ," *CISHL* 10:444; "Discours fait par le sauvage Chawanon," in Stuart to Gage, Mar. 19, 1765, Gage Papers, WCL.

5. Aubry à Gage, June 21, 1765, Gage Papers, WCL; "Speeches made by the Shawnee Chief . . . ," Feb. 24, 1765, and reply of M. Aubry, Feb. 24, 1765, *CISHL* 10:448, 452–53.

6. Robert Farmar to Gage, June 1, 1765, in Gage Papers, WCL, microfilm copy of selected documents at the Great Lakes–Ohio Valley Ethnohistory Archive, Indiana University, Bloomington.

7. Henry Stuart to John Stuart, Pensacola, August 25, 1776, in *Documents of the American Revolution,* ed. K. G. Davies (Shannon, Ireland: Irish University Press, 1976), 12:202–3 (hereafter cited as *DAR*). The previous paragraph relies on the same source. See also Colin G. Calloway, *The American Revolution in Indian Country: Crisis and Diversity in Native American Communities* (New York: Cambridge University Press, 1995), 194–95.

8. "Deposition of Charles Robertson, October 3, 1777," in *The Calendar of Virginia State Papers, 1652–1781,* ed. William P. Palmer (Richmond, 1875; repr., New York: Kraus Reprint Corp., 1968), 1:291–92; "Deposition of Thomas Houghton, October 3, 1777," ibid., 290; John P. Brown, *Old Frontiers: The Story of the Cherokee Indians from Earliest Times to the Date of Their Removal West, 1838* (Kingsport, TN: Southern Publishers, 1938), 4–13; and James P. Pate, "The Chickamauga: A Forgotten Segment of Indian Resistance on the Southern Frontier" (PhD diss., University of Mississippi, 1969), 53; *Pennsylvania Packet,* Aug. 13–27, 1776, Historical Society of Pennsylvania, Philadelphia, PA.

9. Henry Stuart to John Stuart, Pensacola, August 25, 1776, in *DAR* 12:202–3.

10. John Sugden, *Tecumseh: A Life* (New York: Henry Holt and Company, 1998), 238.

11. William Henry Harrison to Henry Dearborn, Vincennes, July 11, 1807, in *Governor's Messages and Letters of William Henry Harrison,* ed. Logan Esarey (Indianapolis: Indiana Historical Society, 1922) 1:224 (hereafter cited as *GMLWHH*); Harrison to Secretary of War, Vincennes, June 26, 1810, ibid., 1:434.

12. Sugden, *Tecumseh,* 236.

13. Kathryn E. Holland Braund, *Deerskins and Duffels: The Creek Indian Trade with Anglo-America, 1685–1815* (Lincoln: University of Nebraska Press, 1993), 150–51, 186.

14. Col. Matthew Elliott to Maj. General Brock, Amherstburg, July 12, 1812, in *Tecumseh: Fact and Fiction in Early Records,* ed. Carl F. Klink (1961; repr., Ottawa: Tecumseh Press, 1978), 102–4.

15. Harrison to War Department, June 6, 1811, in *Tecumseh,* ed. Klink, 82.

16. *GMLWHH,* 1:420.

17. John Norton, *The Journal of Major John Norton,* ed. Carl F. Klink and James J. Talman, Publications of the Champlain Society, vol. 46 (Toronto: Champlain Society, 1970), 175.

18. L. H. Gipson, ed., *Moravian Mission on White River* (Indianapolis: Indiana Historical Society, 1938), 297–98, 371, 521, 539.

19. Kathleen DuVal, *Native Ground: Indians and Colonists in the Heart of the Continent* (Philadelphia: University of Pennsylvania Press, 2006), 165.

20. Benjamin Hawkins, Tuckabatchee, journal, June 29, 1804, in *Letters of Benjamin Hawkins: 1796–1806,* Collections of the Georgia Historical Society (Savannah: Georgia Historical Society, 1916), 9:433.

21. For Pontiac as a genius, see General Thomas Gage to the Earl of Halifax, New York, April 14, 1764, in *Documents Relative to the Colonial History of the State of New York,* ed. E. B. O'Callahan et al., 15 vols. (Albany: Weed, Parsons and Company, 1853–1887), 7:619–20; Thomas Gage to William Johnson, New York, July 2, 1764, in *The Papers of Sir William Johnson,* ed. James Sullivan et al., 14 vols. (Albany: University of the State of New York, 1921–1965), 11:250; Francis Parkman, *The Conspiracy of Pontiac and the Indian War after the Conquest of Canada,* 6th ed., 2 vols. (1851; repr., Boston: Charles C. Little and James Brown, 1870) 1:183–86.

22. Reflecting on the ideas underpinning Tecumseh's movement, Glenn Tucker wrote in the 1950s that "such an amalgam could have been the product only of a mind rich in knowledge, firm in purpose and supple in understanding—the sort of mind that was disclosed in Tecumseh's speeches." Tucker, *Tecumseh: Vision of Glory* (Indianapolis: Bobbs Merrill, 1956), 93. New York Episcopalian bishop Henry Onderdonk noted in 1842 that Tecumseh's principles were "too profound

to be comprehended . . . by lawless savages. Tecumseh therefore, like Romulus and Mahomet before him, had recourse to the more solemn sanctions of religion" (Henry Onderdonk, "Life and Times of Tecumseh," manuscript in the collections of the US Library of Congress, 3).

23. Harrison to War Department, Aug. 7, 1811, excerpted in *Tecumseh,* ed. Klink, 89; Drake, in ibid., 56.

24. John K. Mahon, "British Strategy and Southern Indians: War of 1812," *Florida Historical Quarterly* 44 (1965–1966): 286.

25. Joshua Piker, *Okfuskee: A Creek Indian Town in Colonial America* (Cambridge, MA: Harvard University Press, 2004), 3.

26. White, *The Middle Ground,* 18. White writes that "the dissolution of some social units, the creation of others, all made the network of social and political loyalties . . . extremely complicated. In a given situation, people might very well have to choose between several competing social groups that had claims on their loyalty. As a result, in the historical record the simple categories of tribe, village, and clan sometimes hold and sometimes break down as people consciously evaluated their conflicting loyalties" (ibid., 20).

27. Piker, *Okfuskee,* 201–4.

28. More on its ethnic composition: Tohopeka had ties, as Joshua Piker has pointed out, to Okfuskee, but it also contained Red Sticks from across the Upper Creeks, Seminoles, and probably Shawnees.

29. Michael Witgen, "The Rituals of Possession: Native Identity and the Invention of Empire in Seventeenth-Century Western North America," *Ethnohistory* 54 (2007): 639–68.

30. Pekka Hämäläinen, *The Comanche Empire* (New Haven: Yale University Press, 2008), 23–25, 106, 348–49; Gary Clayton Anderson, *The Indian Southwest, 1580–1830: Ethnogenesis and Reinvention* (Norman: University of Oklahoma Press, 1999).

31. Steven C. Hahn, *The Invention of the Creek Nation, 1670–1763* (Lincoln: University of Nebraska Press, 2004); Robbie Ethridge, *Creek Country: The Creek Indians and Their World* (Chapel Hill: UNC Press, 2003), 22–31; Patricia Galloway, *Choctaw Genesis, 1500–1700* (Lincoln: University of Nebraska Press, 1995).

32. Braund, in *Deerskins and Duffels,* 4–6, reminds us of the enduring presence of Creeks throughout the period while acknowledging the vast changes. Marvin T. Smith, *Archaeology and Aboriginal Culture Change in the Interior Southeast: Depopulation during the Early Historic Period* (Gainesville: University Presses of Florida/Florida State Museum, 1987), esp. 135–37; Gregory A. Waselkov and John W. Cottier, "European Perceptions of Eastern Muskogean Ethnicity," in *Proceedings of the Tenth Meeting of the French Colonial Historical Society, April 12–14, 1984,* ed. Philip Boucher (Lanham, MD: University Presses of America, 1985), 194. Also quoted is Piker, *Okfuskee,* 6.

33. Gregory A. Waselkov, *A Conquering Spirit: Fort Mims and the Redstick War of 1813–1814* (Tuscaloosa: University of Alabama Press, 2006).

34. See virtually all biographies of Tecumseh; and Homer, *The Iliad,* book 19.

35. R. David Edmunds, perhaps the best Tecumseh and Tenskwatawa scholar, challenged these views in the 1980s; and he emphasized that the Prophet, not Tecumseh, led the movement until 1809. But he considered the vision of pan-Indian alliance to be extraordinary: "Tecumseh may have dreamed of a pan-Indian union, but most of his followers remained a tribal people. They still saw the world from a tribal perspective." Edmunds, *The Shawnee Prophet* (Lincoln: University of Nebraska Press, 1983), 189.

36. Harrison to Secretary of War, July 10, 1811, *GMLWHH,* 1:533.

37. June 10, 1810, *GMLWHH,* 1:425.

38. Gordon M. Sayre, *The Indian Chief as Tragic Hero: Native Resistance and the Literatures of America, from Moctezuma to Tecumseh* (Chapel Hill: UNC Press, 2005), 272, 275. This, in part, is explicitly following Richard White.

39. The northern versions of some of his speeches were at least recorded close in time to the telling—they still suffer from, for example, the fact that Tecumseh did not deliver his speeches in English and we cannot be sure of the translation. But in the South, all the renditions of his so-called speeches suffer that thick and typical problem of translation, and they were also written down and published considerably after the fact. They are essentially unreliable.

40. Thomas L. McKenney and James Hall, *History of the Indian Tribes of North America,* 3 vols. (1836–1844; repr., Totowa: Rowman and Littlefield, 1972), 1:94–95; James Mooney, in a classic work of American ethnography, follows McKenney:

> "Your blood is white. You have taken my talk . . . but you do not mean to fight. I know the reason. You do not believe the Great Spirit has sent me. You shall know. I leave Tuckhabatchee directly, and shall go straight to Detroit. When I arrive there, I will stamp on the ground with my foot and shake down every house in Tuckhabatchee." [Tecumseh leaves, and the Creeks count off sticks he had left them.] The morning they had fixed upon as the day of his arrival at last came. A mighty rumbling was heard—the Indians all ran out of their houses—the earth began to shake; when at last, sure enough, every house in Tuckhabatchee was shaken down. . . . The effect was electric . . . and many of the Indians took their rifles and prepared for war.

James Mooney, *The Ghost Dance and the Sioux Outbreak of 1890,* ed. Raymond J. DeMallie (1896; repr., Lincoln: University of Nebraska Press, 1991), 687; see also Thomas L. McKenney, *Memoirs: Official and personal, with sketches of travels among the Northern and Southern Indians, embracing a war excursion and descrip-*

tions of scenes along the Western borders (New York: Paine and Burgess, 1846), 162; and James L. Penick Jr., "I Will Stamp on the Ground with My Foot and Shake Down Every House," *American Heritage* 27 (1975): 86.

41. Frank Owsley Jr., "The Fort Mims Massacre," *Alabama Review* 24 (1971): 193.

42. Martin adds later that "violent earthquakes struck the southeastern United States, and support for Tecumseh's message increased dramatically." Joel Martin, "The Creek Prophetic Movement," *Alabama Heritage* 23 (1992): 4, 8; see also Joel Martin, *Sacred Revolt: The Muskogees' Struggle for a New World* (Boston: Beacon, 1991), 122–25.

43. Sugden, *Tecumseh,* 237–44.

44. Ibid., 246–47. For the reception of the comet in Europe, including the report on Bonaparte, see Frederick Burwick, "Continental Sciences: British and Continental Thresholds," in *A Concise Companion to the Romantic Age,* ed. Jon Klancher (Oxford, UK: Wiley-Blackwell, 2009), 174–75.

45. Sugden, *Tecumseh,* 250.

46. Ibid., 251.

47. Martin, *Sacred Revolt,* 124.

48. Henry Sale Halbert and Timothy Horton Ball, *The Creek War of 1813 and 1814* (Chicago: Donnohue and Henneberry, 1895), 72; Lewis S. Dean, "'Tecumseh's Prophesy': The Great New Madrid Earthquakes of 1811–1812 and 1843 in Alabama," *Alabama Review* 47 (1994): 163–64, 166–69. Dean doubts that Tecumseh predicted the earthquake. He does not question whether prophets used the earthquakes to advantage in drumming up support for war.

49. Halbert and Ball, *The Creek War,* 72.

50. Myron L. Fuller, *The New Madrid Earthquake* (1912; repr., Washington, DC: Government Printing Office, 1992), 8 (map), 17; Dean writes, "Probably a slight effect of the shocks were felt in Tuckabatchee (as well as throughout a large part of the Alabama area)" (Dean, "'Tecumseh's Prophesy,'" 166).

51. Martin, *Sacred Revolt,* 212–13.

52. Sugden, *Tecumseh,* 441, n. 11; Francis McHenry, "The Indian Prophet," *The Halcyon Luminary and Theological Repository* 1 (1812): 275–77.

53. Hawkins to William Eustis, Creek Agency, June 9, 1812, in *American State Papers, Indian Affairs,* ed. Walter Lowrie and Matthew St. Clair (Washington: Gales and Seaton, 1832–1861), vol.4, part 2, 812.

54. This may have been George Stiggins, but it may also have been his father, Joseph. In any case, while George Stiggins, writing in the 1830s or 1840s, claims to have it on good evidence that Tecumseh predicted the quakes, he does not claim to have been present at any of Tecumseh's speeches in 1811. See Theron A. Nuñez Jr., "Creek Nativism and the Creek War of 1813–1814," Part 2, *Ethnohistory* 5, no. 2 (Spring 1958): esp. 146–51 (this work is Stiggins's narrative from the Draper Manuscripts in a published form).

55. Burwick notes a variety of European opinions on the meaning of the comet: from portending victory or defeat to explaining the mental health of King George III (Burwick, "Continental Sciences," 174–75). The comet had not been predicted.

56. "Indian News," Dateline, Milledgeville, GA, June 30 [1813], includes, after an introduction, the "Report of A. Cornells to Hawkins, dated at Capt. Carr's, near Fort Hawkins, 22 June 1813," *The Enquirer,* Richmond, VA, July 13, 1813, 4, in *America's Historical Newspapers,* online with *NewsBank* through the University of Michigan Libraries.

57. For an account based on these records see William G. McLoughlin, "The Cherokee Ghost Dance Movement," in *The Cherokee Ghost Dance: Essays on the Southeastern Indians, 1789–1861,* ed. McLoughlin (Macon: Mercer, 1984), 114 (note the chronology), 126–27.

58. Henry Rowe Schoolcraft, writing from Michigan in 1820, fancifully linked the earthquakes with a North American war of resistance to settlers. Schoolcraft, who would soon emerge as one of America's leading experts on American Indians, features Indians in this poem only metaphorically. Here, instead of Indians, it is the ores of the earth who conspire to oppose the throngs of miners descending upon them. The earthquake is itself a war of resistance:

> And such heats were begat among metals and stones,
> That the cave filled with sulphur, and bellowed with groans;
> And the earth, as if grasped by omnipotent might,
> Quaked dreadful, and shook with the throes of affright;
> Deep northwardly rolled the electrical jar,
> Creating amazement, destruction, and war; . . .
> Every rock on our borders cracked, quivered, and shrunk,
> And Nackitosh tumbled, and New Madrid sunk.

H. R. Schoolcraft, *Transallegania; or, the Groans of Missouri* (New York: J. Seymour, 1820), 23; quoted in James L. Penick Jr., *The New Madrid Earthquakes* (1976; repr., Columbia: University of Missouri Press, 1981), 127.

59. George Stiggins, "A Historical Narration of the Genealogy Traditions and Downfall of the Ispocaga or Creek Indians," in *The Draper Manuscripts: Georgia, Alabama, and South Carolina Papers,* ed. Lyman Draper et al., microfilm (Madison: State Historical Society of Wisconsin, 1949), vol. 1, ser. V, no. 66:43.

60. Ibid., 42.

61. Stiggins, "Historical Narration," 66:45.

62. Halbert and Ball, *The Creek War,* 72; Henry S. Halbert, "Some Inaccuracies in Claiborne's History in Regard to Tecumseh," *Publications of the Mississippi Historical Society* 1 (1898): 101–3; Frank Lawrence Owsley Jr., *Struggle for the Gulf*

Borderlands: The Creek War and the Battle of New Orleans, 1812–1815 (Gainesville: University Presses of Florida, 1981), 11–14.

63. See also Ezekiel 38:20; John Francis Hamtramck Claiborne, *Life and Times of General Sam Dale, a Mississippi Partisan* (New York: Harper and Bros., 1860), 50–61. This particular version of the speech has long come in for criticism.

64. The Tecumseh of the South, then, is tied up with false prophecy and sacred revolt. To the North, it is not Tecumseh, but the Shawnee Prophet who deploys natural phenomena in support of his movement. The Prophet is said to have predicted an eclipse of the sun, taking up a challenge of William Henry Harrison's. And there was an eclipse in 1806; some have speculated that Tenskwatawa had learned of it from "teams of astronomers" who were then moving through the Midwest to observe the eclipse. No one has asked why Tenskwatawa was the only Indian to encounter these teams. The sources for the eclipse story are fanciful and untrustworthy, in any case, and all after the fact. See Edmunds, *Shawnee Prophet,* 48. Here, too, biblical references are abundant: Ezekiel 32:7, "I will cover the sun with a cloud, and the moon shall not give her light." See also Isaiah 13:10.

65. Jackson to Blount, Hermitage, June 5, 1812, *Papers of Andrew Jackson,* ed. Harold Moser and Sharon MacPherson (Knoxville: University of Tennessee Press, 1980–2002), 2:301.

66. Cornells to Hawkins, June 33, 1813, and Hawkins to General Armstrong, June 28, 1813, in *American State Papers,* ed. Lowrie and St. Clair, vol.4, part 2, 845–47.

3
"A Packet from Canada"

Telling Conspiracy Stories on the 1813 Creek Frontier

Robert P. Collins

The Creek War is commonly said to have begun with the Battle of Burnt Corn, a surprise attack by Mississippi territorial militia on a party of Red Stick Creeks that ended in an unexpected defeat of the attackers. The battle is conventionally understood to have raised Red Stick expectations of victory over the Americans and encouraged the August attacks on Fort Mims and Fort Sinquefield. For settlers, Burnt Corn is supposed to have caused either a general panic or a sobering awareness that they were now in a genuine Indian war.

But the American settlements near the Alabama, Tombigbee, and Mobile Rivers within the Mississippi Territory (in what is today south Alabama) were already in a panic-fueled state of chaos before the first Red Stick fired a shot at a settler. By the summer of 1813 this fear had become so acute that white, Indian, and "mixed-blood" settlers were abandoning their farms and "forting up" together in hastily erected blockhouses. One reason was certainly that the War of 1812, then entering its second year, had not gone well for US armies, and there were reasonable fears that a British fleet might appear at any time and land forces on the Gulf Coast, opening a new front on the vulnerable southern frontier. Any British troops could be expected to rendezvous with southern Indians and to issue a call for slaves to leave their masters and win their freedom by fighting for the king. Americans could not have known that it would take another year for the British government to mount any effective military action in the Gulf.[1]

But there was more than speculation about grand strategy informing the fears of settlers. They had seized onto a rumor of a conspiracy involving Britain and its northern Indian allies, the Spaniards in Florida, and, most alarming of all, the neighboring Creek Indians. Late in 1812 a few Creek Indians led by Little Warrior (Tvstvnvkuce) had traveled north to the "Indians of the lakes" residing at Prophet's Town. These Creeks were moved by Tenskwatawa's message of pan-Indian unity, spiritual renewal, and resistance to US expansion. In January 1813 Little Warrior's party joined Tecumseh's warriors at the Battle of River Raisin, a disastrous defeat for the Americans. Returning south, the Creeks heard a false rumor that their nation was already at war with the United States. They attacked and killed settler families on the Duck River in Tennessee, taking one captive.

This much is not in dispute. The rumor is that while still in the North, Little Warrior went on to Canada, where a British general gave him a "letter" or "packet" that, once presented to the Spanish governor of West Florida, would guarantee to the Indians a steady supply of guns and ammunition. These they were to use to attack Americans on the southern frontier.[2]

Historians' response to this story has generally been cagey. Such an assertion of authority by a British general over a Spanish official in a distant colony, especially while Spain remained neutral in the War of 1812, seems unlikely on its face. Nevertheless, the rumor appears in so many official documents, and was evidently so widely believed at the time, that it has perhaps seemed audacious to reject its veracity. Yet this is not a minor question. The rumor informs our understanding of the Red Stick mission to Pensacola to obtain war materiel from the Spanish authorities, July 20–23, 1813, as well as of the battle between Red Sticks and Mississippi militia on July 27 beside Burnt Corn Creek.

A closer examination of events in Pensacola preceding the Battle of Burnt Corn, as well as the general state of Anglo-Spanish relations in 1813, makes it difficult to sustain a belief in the physical existence of the "packet from Canada." While it is possible that some sort of document was given to Little Warrior by a British officer, it is most likely that the document, letter, or packet never existed except as a rumor that emerged during verbal retellings of the Creek warrior's exploits and violent death. It was, however, a rumor of historical significance. It appears to have been believed, or at least retold, by both US settlers and a significant number of Creeks. This was not the first time rumors had caused trouble in the region. Benjamin Hawkins, the US agent to the Creek Indians, complained in January 1813 of "foolish reports circulated . . . by idle worthless white people," while his assistant, the Creek Indian translator Alexander Cornells, worried about what he called "the lies that white people brought from Georgia"—from Georgia in particular—and the disturbing effect that these had on Creek leaders. "If there could be a stop put to these white liars, it would be a good thing," he wrote, "but I am afraid it will be our ruin."[3]

The Creek frontier had been a conflict zone for years, and the growing swarms of land-hungry Americans made it seem less and less likely that

Creek grievances would ever be redressed. White people had been encroaching on Creek land for generations, cutting timber, setting fires, and grazing cattle herds that fouled streams and destroyed canebrakes while competing with the Creeks' own cattle for rangeland. Whenever an Indian killed an American or stole horses, reprisals from the American side could be devastating, yet American outrages against Indians generally went unnoticed. The United States had cut a military road through the Creek Nation despite the objections of an overwhelming majority of Creeks, and Benjamin Hawkins, the US agent to the Creeks, spent much of his time in 1813 seeing to the building of bridges and ferries on this Federal Road. He also informed the Creek National Council that, like it or not, they must permit Tennesseeans to freely navigate the rivers that flowed past Creek towns and fields. The National Council had controversially assumed much of the authority that traditionally belonged with clans and towns, the two main sources of Creek identity. Yet the council was a poor protector, beholden to the demands of the United States government and the interests of a small class of wealthy Creeks. So for at least a brief period, many Creeks of diverse views were highly receptive to the cultural renewal and political revolution sought by Red Stick rebels.[4]

The rumor of the "packet from Canada" may have originated either among Creeks or Americans, in the Tensaw or Tennessee, on the Georgia frontier or in an Upper Creek town square. It may have been a deliberate fabrication or an unintentional distortion as news passed from person to person. However it started, the rumor spread quickly. The consistent effect of this rumor, no matter who repeated it or how sincerely they believed it, was to exaggerate the threat that Red Stick rebels posed to settlers and "Indian countrymen" in what is now south Alabama. In Tennessee and Georgia there was really no need for the rumor, as state leaders with their eyes on the Floridas and the Creek country already found it convenient to presume that Spain and the Indians were in league with Britain. What is more surprising is that the rumor was also repeated within the Creek Nation, both by the so-called friendly Indians, who adhered to the Creek National Council, and by their adversaries, the leaders of the Red Stick rebellion.

The first problem to consider is whether the packet from Canada actually existed. Nineteenth-century historians generally rested on the patriotic assumption that it did, or that at any rate British and Spanish "agents" had incited the Creeks to hostility. According to Pickett's *History of Alabama,* for instance, "the British fleet was seen off the coast, from which supplies, arms, ammunition and Indian emissaries were sent to Pensacola and other Spanish ports in Florida." American spies in Pensacola found "that the British agents were distributing to [the Indians] ample munitions of war."[5]

Other historians have concluded that Little Warrior received a document from a British officer, but that the Indians misunderstood the nature of the document. In Frank Owsley Jr.'s interpretation, "Little Warrior, the Creek chief who had gone to Canada with Tecumseh, had been given a letter . . . by the British officer who had entertained him. It was mistakenly assumed by the Indians that the letter was a request for the Spaniards to furnish the Indians with arms and ammunition." Owsley infers that the preceding West Florida governor, Mauricio de Zúñiga, had issued an invitation to the Creeks to come to Pensacola to receive arms, although he admits that Zúñiga denied doing so. In fact, nearly all of the actions taken by the Creek "hostile elements" are, in Owsley's reading, the result of promptings by white men—promptings that the "hostiles" frequently misunderstand. Although he finds considerable explanatory power in the "divided mind" of Gov. Mateo González Manrique and the diverse opinions among Spanish officialdom, Owsley consistently describes the Red Sticks as a mass of faceless men who are always of the same opinion and who, whenever they misunderstand a situation, are unanimous in their errors.[6]

This interpretation has a long pedigree. In the 1830s George Stiggins recorded a variant on the story of Little Warrior's packet, in which the illiterate Red Stick prophet Josiah Francis pretended to use magic to compose a letter in Spanish to González Manrique demanding arms. According to Stiggins, when the governor saw Francis's paper, he laughed and said it contained only meaningless marks. The incident, which supposedly occurred on a prior Red Stick visit to Pensacola, is difficult to reconcile with accounts of the July 1813 delegation. But the veracity of the story is probably beside the point. Stiggins told the story in order to mock the supposed ignorance and superstition of the prophets and their followers.[7]

To date, no historian has directly addressed the strong possibility that the British packet or document did not exist at all except as a rumor that emerged spontaneously after the death of Little Warrior. For reasons to be explored, the rumor was too useful not to be repeated, whether or not it was believed, by both Americans and Creeks.

Examined from a more remote historical perspective, the rumor is preposterous on its face. Even if Spain had been at open war with the United States, or had decided to wage covert war, it is difficult to believe that a British officer could have assumed the authority to requisition Spanish supplies to be used by Indians. The next problem is one of means. Pensacola and its starveling, chronically unpaid garrison could ill afford to supply anyone else. Setting aside the logistical difficulties, there is also the problem of trust. Although Britain and Spain had joined forces in the latest coalition against Napoleon, they were also traditional enemies that had been at war as recently as 1807. Six years later, Britain and Spain were allies, but never amigos. During the American Revolutionary War, Spain followed France in declaring war on Britain, then seized Pensacola, ending the twenty-year British reign over Florida. Fearing what Britain's domination of the seas might do to the Spanish Americas, Spain in 1796 renewed its treaty relations with France. This time the policy did not turn out well for Spain. France's new strongman, Napoleon Bonaparte, wheedled Louisiana away from Spain only to turn around and sell it to the Americans—a move that left the Floridas, especially West Florida, dangerously exposed. The British navy then dealt the Spanish a series of defeats, maintained a blockade on the crucial port of Cádiz, and twice occupied Buenos Aires, demonstrating to inhabitants of the future Argentine capital how incapable their viceroy was of defending them from invasion.[8]

In Pensacola, which remained in many ways an English, no less than a Spanish, town, the official hostility to Britain always had to be tempered with practical concerns. For instance, the provincial government had depended for years on a British firm, John Forbes and Company, to handle trade with the Indians.[9] In 1808 the Spanish relationship with Britain changed abruptly, after Napoleon forced King Ferdinand VII to abdicate in favor of Napoleon's brother, Joseph Bonaparte. All of Spain was soon in rebellion against French rule. Britain sent supplies, cash, and, finally, one hundred thousand troops to Spain to contest the French occupation. A turning point in the ensuing *guerra de guerrillas* came just after the United States declared war on Britain in June 1812. As the Tensaw settlements "forted up" against anticipated Indian attacks in the summer of 1813, news was arriving from Europe of the victory at Vittoria, in which Gen. Arthur Wellesley (now Viscount Wellington) and his Spanish allies had all but completed the reconquest of Spain.

From 1808 to the end of the War of 1812, the chaos at the pinnacle of Spanish government sent shocks throughout the empire. Authority devolved to officials at lower levels, and chains of command became confused. In 1810 the provisional government at Seville was overthrown by a second, more liberal government based at Cádiz, leaving colonial officials in a quandary. The Council of the Indies, which had at least nominally administered the Spanish Americas for three hundred years, was shut down in April 1812 and remained inactive for two years. The Spanish Empire in the New World was unraveling as South American revolutionaries proclaimed independence. Unofficially, Britain did what it could to encourage the process, allowing British merchants to violate the blockade that Spain tried to impose on the new South American states.[10]

Spain also had trouble with the expanding United States, especially in the

Florida provinces. American adventurers had been seeking for years to attach the Spanish Floridas by fair means or foul. American filibusters seized Baton Rouge and the westernmost portion of West Florida at a moment when the Spanish government was on the verge of anarchy. In April 1813 the Spanish garrison at Mobile had surrendered to a large American force accompanied by gunboats. Meanwhile, a former governor of Georgia was mixed up in a filibuster war in East Florida. Nevertheless, the Spanish government was determined to preserve friendly relations with the United States and to stay out of the War of 1812. And in Pensacola itself, Gov. González Manrique, like his predecessors, mostly bemoaned the province's poverty and vulnerability as he continually reminded his superiors that his soldiers and officials were going unpaid.[11]

Despite these facts, the rumor that Little Warrior had received a British promise of Spanish aid was too useful not to be believed, or at least repeated, by Creek Indians as well as Americans. For the Creek "old chiefs" devoted to maintaining friendship with the United States, the rumor underscored their sense of being a cohesive but outnumbered minority among their own people, and it added urgency to their appeals for internal unity, moderation from the neighboring state governors, and military assistance if needed from the US Army. For the Red Stick leadership, who were in the best position to know the truth or falsehood of the rumor, it served as a useful means of intimidating both the old chiefs and the American settlers. The Red Sticks do not seem to have had a single view on the best course for their rebellion to take, but some at least believed that it was best for their opponents to believe that the rebellion was part of a continental uprising that would humble the United States with the aid of Britain and Spain, two colonial powers that had formerly vied for the Creeks' trade and friendship. Repeating the rumor about Little Warrior, they must have thought, would frighten adversaries and impress prospective benefactors. These hopes were to be disappointed at Pensacola, where neither the Spanish governor nor the manager of the British-owned trading house responded to the Red Stick delegation entirely as expected.

In Tennessee and Georgia, as well as in Mississippi Territory, meanwhile, the rumor served to strengthen the case for further aggressive action against the Florida provinces. It also encouraged aggression against the Creek Nation, had any further encouragement been necessary. On July 20—the same day, as it happened, that the Red Stick delegation first arrived in Pensacola—Maj. Gen. Andrew Jackson released a broadsheet in Nashville encouraging enlistment for war against the Creeks. "The country to the South is inviting," he concluded. "Let us consolidate it as part of our Union."[12]

As for the settlers in the Alabama districts of the Mississippi Territory, the litany of danger from Indians was certainly not new. But as the non-Indian population of the Deep South increased, far surpassing the number of Indians and making inroads upon the Spanish Florida provinces, expressions of fear of danger from Indians and foreign agents did not subside. They increased. By 1813 the Tensaw and neighboring districts were in a panic that seems entirely out of proportion to the threat actually posed by Red Stick Creeks. Letters from that spring and summer asserted as fact that the whole Creek Nation had taken up the red war club against the white people and that British and Spanish agents were giving them weapons and supplies intended for the annihilation of the settlements. After interviewing early settlers of the region, historian Albert J. Pickett did not consider it hyperbole to state that in 1813 "everything foreboded the extermination of the Americans in Alabama, who were the most isolated and defenceless people imaginable."[13]

These fears were in spite of the Creek government's efforts to deter and punish violence by Creeks against Americans. Under terms of the Treaty of New York of 1790, the Creek National Council was obligated to bring to justice any Creek Indian who committed a crime against an American, and in the tense climate of 1812, the council's police force had been ruthless in tracking and killing the suspected murderers of two US travelers on the Federal Road. Little Warrior's party was also eliminated early in April for killing settler families in Tennessee. Violence on the frontier was endemic, and it is likely that some killings of both Americans and Indians left no trace in the documentary record. Yet the available evidence suggests that the Indians were bearing the brunt of violence in 1813, both because of civil war within the Creek Nation and because armed bands of settlers were attacking Indians who lived or worked in the Alabama districts.

Why then did the settlers manifest such great fear of Indian attack? Peter Silver has examined another historical case in which expressions of such fear have served to unify fractious settler groups and to justify deadly violence against neighboring Indians. During the Seven Years' War in western Pennsylvania, local political leaders parlayed the terror of Indian attacks and the threat of further violence into an "enraptured discourse of fear" that made it possible to unite mutually antagonistic settlers in coalitions. This "anti-Indian sublime" portrayed white people not as conquerors or a superior race, but as suffering victims of Indian savagery. Moreover, the Indians were almost always "co-bogeymen" who lacked the initiative to pose much of a danger except when they were supplied and directed by "a European villain of the moment." This emotionally compelling idea, according to Silver, "quickly proved all but unanswerable as political discourse." Even as settlers embarked on slaughtering Indians who had never posed a danger to them, the idea of the victimhood of white people prevailed, and support for anti-Indian violence became a test of loyalty.[14]

Like the Pennsylvania settlements studied by Silver, the Alabama districts, from the Tombigbee to the Mobile Rivers, were "a jittery, culturally competitive society" estranged even from the Natchez district, the other population center within the Mississippi Territory. The inhabitants were diverse, including French and Spanish creoles, and many a white settler had an Indian spouse or children. Most of the earliest English-speaking settlers had been Loyalists in the American Revolution, confronted since the late 1790s by an influx of new arrivals brimming over with the spirit of '76. Some of these new arrivals, in turn, brought with them rival affinities for their fellow Virginians, Carolinians, or Georgians from back East. The districts' proximity to the international border with Spain was opportune for men who wished to evade responsibility for breaking American laws. As trader George S. Gaines admitted, "good & honest men were rare, about that period" in and around the territorial capital of St. Stephens.[15]

The Mississippi territorial militia, charged with the protection of the frontier from threats to its security, was far more adept at brokering political power than at anticipating military challenges. Rank in the militia sometimes went with a seat in the territorial legislature, as it had for the commanding officer, Gen. Ferdinand L. Claiborne, and Col. James Caller, leader of the militia at the Battle of Burnt Corn. The logistical challenges of guarding a vast frontier were complicated by the parsimony of the legislature, which often balked at paying for ammunition or the costs of a mobilization. Officers' desire to maintain favor with the men, who also comprised the electorate, encouraged tolerance of citizens' reluctance to turn out for military exercises. The army's Thomas Flournoy, commander of the Seventh Military District, reprimanded Claiborne in 1813 for permitting lax discipline and allowing inactive officers to continue to draw pay and hold rank in the militia.[16]

Curiously enough, dread of Indian savagery went hand in hand with both poor preparedness and overconfidence. Under Caller's leadership, militia companies had often been called out to harass and murder Indians, prompting Judge Harry Toulmin to deride Caller and his associates as fanatics who "acted as if they were anxious to bring on an Indian war." On one occasion in 1812 he wrote, "A party of rangers have been sent out by Col. [Caller], without any occasion,—& whose avowed intention is to murder indians:—two companies of militia were ordered out by him on a groundless, idle rumour;—a party of indians were wantonly & without provocation fired upon by others,—and some peaceable Choctaws were almost beaten to death in Washin[gto]n County."[17]

Maj. Daniel Beasley, infamous for leaving the gate open at Fort Mims, was not exceptional in assuming that vigilance and attention to duty made little difference in an Indian fight. The militiamen who fought and fled at Burnt Corn Creek were typical of their peers. Col. Joseph Carson, a US Army officer attached to the territorial militia, expressed concern that the men were ill prepared for a conflict, but the men themselves displayed only eagerness for a fight and an appetite for military rank. On the morning before the Burnt Corn battle, Caller's small troop already had a colonel, four captains, and a large complement of lieutenants. Yet the men paused on their march to elect in addition a lieutenant colonel and four majors. As Pickett rather delicately observed, "This unusual number of field officers was made to satisfy military aspirations." In the Mississippi Territory, these were more or less identical to political aspirations.[18]

All of this suggests that the rhetoric of vulnerability served some purpose other than expressing a genuine fear of imminent annihilation. A politically charged "anti-Indian sublime" seems to have been flourishing on the Creek frontiers in the early 1800s. Years before Tecumseh's southern tour in 1811, letters and printed matter were already rich with portrayals of the Creek Indians as a hostile horde whose unique savagery had been set in motion by evil-intentioned white people, namely the British and Spanish. James Caller in 1807 linked the perceived vulnerability of the region's settlers to the prospect of glory for the United States. "Our population is small: we are surrounded, except on the Spanish side, by the most powerful tribes of Indians existing within the original limits of the United States. . . . Yet few as we are, we consider ourselves as an advanced guard, destined to defend the immense tract of valuable territory, which lies between the settlements on the Mobile and the state of Tennessee. We may *perish* at our posts; but we shall not *slumber* there."[19]

Peter Silver has found that the perceived threat of Indian attack was instrumental in forging a shared identity as "white people" out of disparate European ethnic groups and religious communities in mid-eighteenth-century Pennsylvania. But his model is not a perfect fit for the Creek frontier in the 1810s, where racial classifications were already well established. Many of the Mississippi Territory settlers were racially defined as "half-breeds," or as modern historians usually term them, mixed-bloods or, less frequently, *métis.* Both Indians and mixed-bloods could be classed as "friendly" or "hostile" based on their amity or enmity toward Americans. But if the fractious frontier was to unite to resist the perceived threat of annihilation by Indians, then its inhabitants needed a shared identity that described all of those who were in danger of becoming victims and who were resolved to fight back. That identity had to be available not only to whites, but to the numerous mixed-blood men who lived in or did business with the Alabama district settlements.[20]

A serviceable name for this identity is "Indian countryman," a term often used in memorial writings by and about settlers who fought in the Creek War. An Indian countryman was bicultural. He could be a white trader or planter who lived in the Creek Nation, more or less in accord with Creek mores. He could be a Creek Indian, usually but not always of mixed descent, who headed a plantation and owned slaves like a white man, or he could be a settler from the eastern states, or from Europe, who was on familiar terms with at least one or two Indians. His mother tongue might be English, Muskogee, French, or Spanish. References to Indian countrymen predate the War of 1812, and it would be absurd to argue that the concept was invented by a conspiracy of American expansionists. But as war gathered in 1813, the crucial fact about Indian countrymen became their perceived vulnerability to attack from hostile forces within the Creek Nation. Thus, the "anti-Indian sublime" in this region not only united fractious white settlers, but also established a context in which white and mixed-blood or bicultural people could collaborate against the perceived common enemy.[21]

This dynamic among the settlers must not have been apparent to the Red Stick strategists who led the mission to Pensacola. Otherwise, Peter McQueen and other spokesmen for the cause might not have exploited every opportunity to overstate the size, strength, achievements, and ambitions of their uprising. In other respects, the Red Stick spokesmen did tailor their message to the occasion. When appealing to the Spanish governor or an influential Briton, they stated their resolve to fight the United States, mentioned their lack of munitions and supplies, and inflated the number of warriors ready to take up arms. When speaking to potential adversaries within the Creek Nation, however, the Red Stick leaders spoke only of eliminating the "old chiefs" and then, perhaps, falling upon the nearest American settlements. They could not have realized that by claiming material support from Britain and Spain, they were not discouraging resistance but rather nourishing the unity and willingness of white settlers and Indian countrymen to act aggressively against them.

The rumor of Little Warrior's letter resonated in the Creek Nation and on its borders, but in Mobile and Pensacola, where the prospect of a British expedition seemed far more threatening than an Indian attack, the rumor never seems to have taken root. Yet it was to Pensacola and its Spanish government that the letter was supposed to be destined. So it is in Pensacola that the substance behind the rumor, if any, should be most discernible. It is highly suggestive that rumors of Little Warrior's British packet are not recorded in the official Spanish records or in any other surviving source from Pensacola. Absence of evidence does not prove that such a document was never mentioned, but it strongly suggests that, if mentioned at all, it was never taken seriously.

For Spanish colonial officials, West Florida was already all but a lost cause by the summer of 1813. It was not a question of whether the remnant of the province would fall to the Americans, only of when and how.

In the past, Spanish strategists had regarded friendly relations with the Indians as a means to help keep US expansion at bay without provoking open war. By the summer of 1813, though, with half of West Florida already in American hands, the time for Indian diplomacy seemed to have expired. A confidential report to González Manrique by his chief of engineers, Anastacio de Arango, on how to counter the threat from the Americans at Mobile recommended using only six Indians as spies in the Tensaw settlements, along with Spanish creole and Anglo-American agents. The report also recommended various ways to deploy regular and militia forces in case of an attack on Pensacola, but it made no recommendation for the recruitment or use of Indians as fighters.[22]

So it must have come as a shock to the governor when, only days after he forwarded Arango's report to Havana, some three hundred Indians arrived at Pensacola with a proposal to join in the war they assumed Spain was already fighting against the Americans.

The Red Sticks had made no secret of their journey to Pensacola. On the way, they had shot at a post rider, killing his horse and taking the mail with them. They burned the plantation of a wealthy Indian countryman, James Cornells, and took two captives, including Cornells's wife, Betsy Coulter.[23]

The party arrived at Pensacola on Tuesday, July 20, 1813, and held a meeting with Governor González Manrique the same day. According to González's official report, the delegation included twenty-four chiefs and three hundred warriors. The "principal chief"—presumably Peter McQueen, a Tallassee trader and one of the party's best-known men—told González that because the Americans continually sought to seize their lands, the Creeks had resolved to declare war upon them as allies of the Spanish and British. The Creeks, he continued, hoped to play an active part in the war, and to that end he requested weapons, munitions, provisions, and other articles they lacked.

González replied that he did not have the authority to make war on the Americans. Moreover, he had no weapons to give them, but he would give them powder, shot, provisions, and whatever else he could procure. The Creeks then departed, seeming to González (or so he reported) to be satisfied with his reply. The governor and the Creeks agreed to meet again at 11 a.m. Friday in the Plaza de Armas, where the government's gifts to the Indians would be publicly presented.[24]

Although González neglected to mention it in his report, the Creeks also offered him the US mail they had seized on the way to Pensacola. The governor, however, disappointed them by refusing to break the seal and open the mail, saying that he would forward the mail to Mobile if the Creeks did not object. They did object and decided to keep the mail themselves. Over the next four days some of the Indians opened the mail but left it behind when they departed Pensacola. González finally obtained it and forwarded it to a US Army officer in Mobile.[25]

On Wednesday morning, McQueen and five other Red Sticks met with González. This time they claimed that the entire Creek Nation was resolved to make war on the Americans, and their party had been "commissioned by the general government of the Nation" to request from the Spaniards the arms and munitions they lacked. The governor's lukewarm response had surprised and disappointed them. They had given their hand to the governor as a father and friend, McQueen said through the Spanish interpreter. In return the governor had given his hand but not his heart.

González replied by reiterating what he had said the day before, comparing himself to a "subordinate chief" who must obey his superiors. He also insisted that he truly had no weapons to give to the Indians. The six Creeks refused to accept that the governor lacked the authority to declare war. They replied with disdain that González had two tongues, using one to assure the Indians of his friendship and brotherhood while with the other he gave the same assurances to the Americans. González concluded the meeting with a promise to communicate their concerns to his superior, the captain-general in Havana.[26]

John Innerarity, manager of the Forbes and Company trading house, went to the governor's mansion to urge González not to give any munitions to the Indians, but found him already in conference with the six Creek delegates. Innerarity, whose company held claims for debts against the Creek Nation as well as a large number of individual Creek traders, had issued instructions to his employees not to give out any powder or lead under any circumstances. When the Creeks had departed, González summoned Innerarity, telling him that McQueen had demanded guns, swords, and twenty-five cases of gunpowder, with additional powder and shot to come from Forbes and Company. It was McQueen's view that the trading house had acquired its wealth and property from the Creek Nation, and the Nation now required some of it back. If the company refused, McQueen had concluded, then the governor should use compulsion. Otherwise, the Creeks would destroy the trading house and kill every Spaniard whom they found outside of the limits of West Florida.[27]

On the following morning the Creeks made their move on Forbes and Company, trying a variety of tactics to compel Innerarity to give them munitions. Accompanied by the parish priest and the governor's secretary, Francisco Gutiérrez de Arroyo, the Creeks arrived in force at the trading house and, in Innerarity's words, "squatted themselves on the galleries & stair case as thick as they could be strewed & in all their military attire." High Head Jim trembled and grimaced at Innerarity in a manner typical of Red Stick prophets. The performance was probably a signal to the prophet's followers that the British merchant was corrupt and untrustworthy.[28]

Innerarity seems to have surprised McQueen by knowing of the threats made against Forbes and Company at the previous day's meeting with the governor. The merchant succeeded in interrupting McQueen's speech with expressions of shock and dismay that the Creeks had so little regard for the company as to ask for gifts. Forbes and Company, he reminded them, had yet to receive some large cash payments that the national chiefs had solemnly promised to pay in order to discharge old trade debts. While Innerarity's choice of topic may well have inflamed his hearers' grievances against the Creek National Council, it also must have made clear to McQueen how little interest the firm had in destroying an institution that had promised to pay it tens of thousands of dollars. According to Innerarity, McQueen finally "had no other resource left but to deny all that the Gov[erno]r had informed [him]" about the delegation's animosity toward Forbes and Company.[29]

After this setback, McQueen and "another Chief attakulpie" launched their main argument for receiving munitions. Essentially repeating the case they had made before González, the two men claimed that nearly all the Indians from the Creek Nation to the Great Lakes were about to wage war on the United States at the command of the Great Spirit. Therefore, Forbes and Company had to choose sides by either giving ammunition and clothing to the delegation or being marked down as a friend of their enemies. Innerarity agreed to give the delegation some blankets, breechclouts, and salt, but no munitions. The Red Sticks parted from him with a great show of friendship, which Innerarity interpreted to mean that "they thought [this] was a beginning & that they could draw [him] on by degrees." The conference had lasted more than two hours.

Later that day the Red Sticks sought to reinforce their case by sending some Shawnee Indians to visit Innerarity, affirming that "all the Nations between the Missouri, the Mississippi & the Lakes had joined in the war except . . . the Cherokees, that they were all now like one fire, that they were determined to make the land clean of the Americans or to lose their lives." Seeking perhaps to appeal to Innerarity's patriotism, the Shawnees stressed their own friendship with the English and asked Innerarity to befriend "their Brothers, the Creeks," who had no one else to look to but the Spanish governor and the British trading house.[30]

At 11 a.m. Friday the Indians converged on the Plaza de Armas for the governor's gift-giving ceremony. Messengers were sent to Innerarity to send his presents to the square as well, and the merchant reluctantly complied, but stayed behind at the trading house. The governor had come up with one thousand pounds of gunpowder, a quantity of lead, more than forty barrels of provisions, as well as blankets, knives, and other articles, all of which were displayed in the square. Innerarity's gift consisted only of tobacco, beads, vermillion for face painting, three barrels of salt, and eight "Damaged Blankets." Several of the Red Sticks were enraged. Innerarity heard that "they set no bounds to their fury, scattered the Vermillion in the sand, flung the beads in the air and trampled upon the blankets." They then went to the trading house and, by Innerarity's account, "asked if I took them for Children or Warriors, expressed the utmost contempt for the present, & clamorously demanded ammunition."[31]

This time the Red Sticks who cornered Innerarity were not to be put off until the merchant had taken them to the storage loft of his store and shown them empty barrels that had contained gunpowder. The Indians were "quite incredulous," apparently unaware that for reasons of safety, Forbes and Company stored most of its powder outside the city at Fort Barrancas. His interrogators than demanded lead, without success. At last they settled on a demand for "plenty of blankets, Hatchets, Knives, Strouds etc." Picking up a theme from the Shawnees' rhetoric the day before, the Red Sticks asked Innerarity to inform his government of the number of Creek towns and warriors, figures that had also been given to González. "To all of this," Innerarity wrote, "I lent a deaf ear."[32]

In the Plaza de Armas, two Creek spokesmen approached the governor to state, through the interpreter, that if the governor's present was not increased, it would not be accepted. After González insisted he had no more to give, the spokesmen incited the Creeks to raise a war cry "in every direction." Some of the Creeks forced their way into the Forbes and Company tanyard, possibly to search for arms and munitions, and they stole several tools. Others singled out specific individuals to trouble, in particular, "one or two Americans" who lived under the protection of the Spanish government. It is probably at this point that some Creeks located the trader Zachariah McGirth and threatened to kill him, until a war leader known as Jim Boy promised to kill anyone who harmed McGirth. Peter McQueen led a small group back to the Forbes trading house to confront Innerarity once more. Accompanied by an interpreter, McQueen began what was probably a formal speech of censure in the Muskogee language.[33]

In the meantime, González had ordered drums sounded to call the garrison and militia to arms. A detachment of Spanish troops appeared in the yard of the trading house with drums rolling. The captain loudly announced in Spanish that Innerarity should relay the governor's order for McQueen and the other chiefs to "quit the town directly." Innerarity declined to translate, in order to avoid "irritat[ing] them any further," whereupon the captain drew his saber and approached McQueen while Alba, the Spanish interpreter, translated his order to leave the house. McQueen replied that he would leave when he finished speaking to Innerarity, "but [the captain] brandishing his Sabre in his face made him retire forcibly. McQueen now seemed quite submissive," Innerarity continued, "shook me by the hand, told me he was my friend, said that the Town had got alarmed for nothing, & that he nor none of the others intended to do any harm until they crossed the Spanish limits." With the Spanish garrison mobilized and manning the fort, McQueen and other Red Sticks returned to the square, which was now heavily guarded. In response to the Spanish troops, a body of young Red Stick warriors assembled on horseback at one end of the square. "The young men were loading their Carabines & seemed to [a]wait the event with a great deal of composure," Innerarity wrote, "until they saw the Artillery Men dragging the field pieces across the square, which seemed to appal [*sic*] them."[34]

At this critical juncture, Governor González stepped forward, surrounded by officers, and summoned McQueen to a parley. He upbraided McQueen and his companions, but to the exasperation of Innerarity and at least one Spanish officer, he did not threaten to punish them. Instead, he offered the same presents as before to the Red Sticks and asked Innerarity to increase his gift. Innerarity flatly refused, until several mutual friends joined in the governor's request.

Once peace was restored, some of the Creeks asked the governor's pardon for the unrest, calling it a "work of impetuous youth." Admitting the severity of the offense, they resorted to traditional diplomatic formulas, asking González to overlook it like a good father. McQueen and a larger group of chiefs visited Innerarity in the afternoon to express regret and renew their professions of friendship, and they listened patiently as the merchant rebuked them and complained that the governor had been too kind. After González and others persuaded Innerarity to give the Indians more goods, including some sugar and coffee, some of the Creeks seem to have given the credit to the governor, calling it a "new proof of [his] friendship and the generous heart of the Spaniards."[35]

The delegation's last day in Pensacola was not devoted solely to mending fences. McQueen and his party warned Innerarity to tell his brother James, in Mobile, to move his family out of the city, "for it was their intention to take Mobile at an appointed time." Innerarity privately dismissed the threat as "balder dash," yet he also feared that the Red Stick alliance was "very formidable" and growing in strength. If even the skeptical Innerarity conceded this much, it appears that the Red Sticks succeeded in conveying to Pensacolans an exaggerated idea of their movement's prospects. But this propaganda win did not bring as many material benefits as they had hoped for. Despite the US aggression at Mobile and the abiding threat to Pensacola, the Spaniards had refused to make common cause with the Creek rebels. Forbes and Company would stand by the Creek National Council for the sake of collecting its debts, if for no other reason. In terms of grand strategy, the Red Sticks' mission to Pensacola had been a disappointment.[36]

The size of the Red Stick delegation to Pensacola did not remain constant from day to day, and by the end of the week it had declined dramatically. Neither was the group entirely composed of Creeks. After turning down McQueen's demands, John Innerarity was lobbied by Shawnees. Choctaws were also concerned with the turn of events in Pensacola, and it is reasonable to expect that they sent observers who may have been numbered among the "*indios*" counted by the Spanish governor. González's estimate of the initial number of warriors, 300, is too round to be considered precise, but US spies also estimated the party's size at between 280 and 300 men. By Thursday, however, González expected that only 200 Indians would be on hand the following day to receive the government's gifts. As the governor and the trading house consistently refused to accede to the Red Sticks' requests, it seems that members of the delegation left, either to return to their homes or, as Owsley suggests, to try to bargain with private traders other than Forbes and Company. Innerarity believed that such transactions with "different people in Town" had brought the Creeks "some trifles." If US spy David Tạte's claim that the Creeks "had a plenty of money" was based on public opinion in Pensacola, then the Red Sticks probably had little success persuading acquaintances in town to give them additional gifts of any kind.[37]

Roughly 300 Indians appeared before the governor on July 20, but only 60 or fewer Creeks were present on July 27 at the Burnt Corn battlefield. Historians have accounted for this discrepancy in a variety of ways. Contemporary military sources insisted that Caller's militia faced the full complement of 300 Creeks, each of them well provided with Spanish arms and ammunition. Few historians have accepted this claim. Others have speculated that 300 Red Sticks left Pensacola, then divided into separate parties, only one of which was intercepted by the Mississippi militia. But this theory fails to explain why all three principal leaders of the delegation, representing Autauga, Tallassee, and the Alabama towns, were present at the Burnt Corn battlefield. It is far more likely, then, that the size of the Red Stick delegation diminished over the four days in Pensacola. Thomas Woodward's Creek informant, Jim Boy, stated "that he did not start with a hundred men, and all of those he did start with were not in the fight" at Burnt Corn. Jim Boy's claim makes better sense if it is understood to refer to the total number of men in the party that left Pensacola on July 23 or 24, not the number who had arrived on July 20.[38]

It is very difficult to determine today, as it must have been even in 1813, how many Creeks supported the Red Stick faction in its struggle against the Creek National Council. Dissatisfaction with the status quo was widespread, and there must have been a warm response to the pan-Indian message that Indians could improve the world by renouncing their own sins and seeking spiritual renewal. But it does not follow that a significant number of Creeks were willing to take up arms against the Americans. In exploring the dissension within the Creek Nation, it is vital to avoid the error of US frontiersmen, who postulated a neat division of "friendly" and "hostile" Indians animated mainly by their respective opinions of and relationships to white people. The Creeks' first priority was their own Nation and their fellow Indians.

Even the most militant Red Sticks placed the elimination of the "national" or "old" chiefs at the top of their agenda. Developments in the wider war between the United States and Britain gave them hope that this could be done and that heaven was on their side should they choose to do more than that. Statements by the Creek Nation's chief executive, Big Warrior, and by Hawkins's interpreter Alexander Cornells, suggest that the Red Sticks appeared to be a large movement with no leader, while the council chiefs and wealthy Indians were internally united but feared themselves greatly outnumbered. Probably a majority of Creeks were sympathetic to the Red Sticks, but only a relative few actually went to war against the "old chiefs." That was Alexander Cornells's verdict one month before Burnt Corn. Aside from the Alabamas, he wrote, "the towns of the Creeks who are said to have taken their talks, have not done it actively; their people are dancing their dances, but no man has moved to assist them."[39]

While some Red Sticks only wanted to see the principal chiefs turned over to them, others had much longer hit lists. One of the old chiefs, Cussetah Micco, reported some of the contradictory demands he had heard from Red Sticks or their friends. "The prophet's men," he wrote in July, only wanted the Nation to turn over the two principal chiefs, Big Warrior and Little Prince, along with Big Warrior's son Tuskenea. But he had also heard that the Red Sticks would "battle with all who take the white people's talk." The Red Stick movement was dedicated to purging the Creek Nation. Talk of falling upon the Tensaw settlements or capturing Mobile was secondary, and likely intended to overawe the Americans and West Floridians who heard of it.[40]

The contrasting experiences of two US generals who led detachments through the Creek Nation in 1813 may show evidence of the diverse sentiments among the Creeks, as well as the predilections of the respective commanders. Where Thomas Flournoy reported good order and a strong desire for peace within the Nation, James Wilkinson saw open hostility and evidence of imminent war. Probably each man experienced enough to support his own preconceptions about Creek hostility or the lack of it, while ignoring or slighting evidence to the contrary.[41]

There is no reason to think that all Red Sticks believed to the same extent in a revival of Indian spiritual power, much less that all of them agreed on a single course of action. The Coosada headman Tourculla, or Sam Isaacs, was among the first Creeks to become known as a prophet. Yet in 1813 Isaacs volunteered to help track down Little Warrior for killing families in Tennessee, an act that nearly cost him his life at the hands of other Red Sticks.[42]

There are signs of dissension among the Red Stick mission to Pensacola as well, including a quarrel, over the life of Zachariah McGirth, that escalated to the level of death threats. Disagreements, as well as disappointment with the stalled negotiations, may have contributed to the sharp decline in the delegation's numbers over four days.

John Innerarity's letter hints at another kind of dissension among the Red Sticks. When the prophet High Head Jim began "shaking" in Innerarity's presence, the merchant interpreted it as an attempt "to inspire terror" and took offense at it. "I was about ordering their shaker out of the house," Innerarity wrote, "but the interpreter told me not to pay any attention to him." There are three probable references for "the interpreter." It is possible that the governor's interpreter, Pedro de Alba, made the remark, but Innerarity mentions two other Spanish officials who were present, without naming Alba. Moreover, as a Spanish-English interpreter, Alba's services would have been unnecessary in a meeting between Innerarity and the Creeks. A more likely possibility is that the interpreter was an employee of Forbes and Company. In that case, Innerarity might be expected to refer to him by name, unless he thought it was a name his brother, to whom he was writing, would not have recognized.

A third possibility, and the most intriguing, is that "the Interpreter" was a member of the Red Stick party who had been designated to translate Muskogee or Alabama speeches into English. This seems likelier because Innerarity also refers to the "interpreter" as one of the few who accompanied McQueen to confront Innerarity on July 23 after the Red Sticks stormed out of the gift ceremony in the Plaza de Armas. Even so, the interpreter's advice "not to pay any attention to" the Red Stick prophet is ambiguous and may have meant that the significance of the prophet's actions was not for the Englishman to understand. No less plausibly, it may have signified that at least one supporter of the Red Stick cause was indifferent toward or critical of one of the prophets—and was unafraid to say so within the prophet's hearing.[43]

However discordant they had been while in town, the journey back to the Nation helped cure many of the Red Sticks of doubts and dissension. On July 27, three or four days' march from Pensacola, the band of no more than 60 men, including Peter McQueen, Josiah Francis, and High Head Jim, camped beside Burnt Corn Creek for their dinner. At about midday a troop of 180 militiamen burst out of the trees and attacked them. By mid-afternoon, however, James Caller's militia had entirely fled the field and dispersed, never to fight again as a unit. Although no more than 5 men had been killed and fewer than 15 were wounded, the militia fell apart.[44]

The battle was not the first time Caller had led a band of men to kill a smaller number of Indians, but it appears to have been the first time the Indians fought back rather than fleeing for their lives. Caller appears not to have been equal to the occasion. Whether or not he personally called a retreat and was among the first to flee, Caller did lose control of his men. After the battle he and another officer became lost in the woods for fifteen days until found by a search party.[45]

Such an unexpected outcome demanded an explanation, and the legend of Little Warrior and the British packet provided one ready-made. As General Claiborne wove the tale in letters to government officials, the brave if imperfectly commanded militia was driven from the field of Burnt Corn by a much larger force of hostile Indians. Caller and his officers tried but failed to rally the untrained soldiers, and a fraction of the force held out bravely before withdrawing. Moreover, the militia successfully confiscated part of a reputedly enormous cache of ammunition provided by the British and Spanish foes of the United States.[46]

Perhaps to shore up this account, three depositions were taken on August 1 and 2 in front of military witnesses, probably all three of them at the Mount Vernon cantonment. Each of the three recorded the testimony of a mixed-blood informant with confidential knowledge of the Red Sticks. James Cornells and Sam Manac (or Moniac) had purportedly encountered the Red Sticks at first hand. David Tate had spied on the recent Red Stick mission in Pensacola. All three were Indian countrymen, slave-holding planters, and, in Claiborne's words, "some of the most intelligent half Breeds." Their

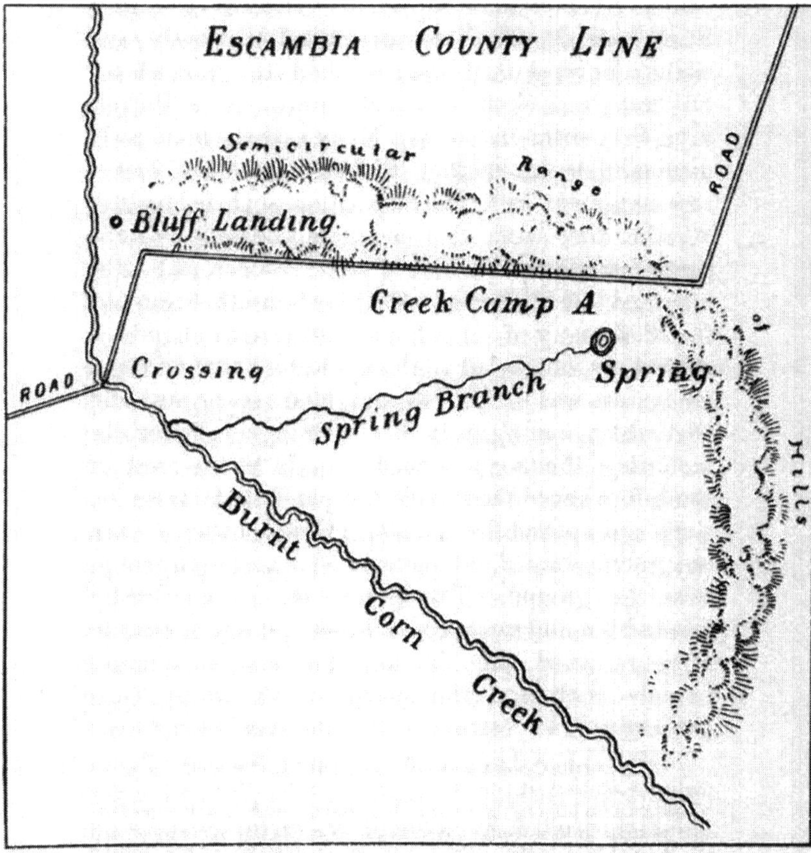

3.1. Burnt Corn Creek battlefield, according to Henry S. Halbert and Timothy H. Ball, *The Creek War of 1813–1814* (1895), 133.

loyalty was primarily to the US settlements rather than the Creek Nation, and they were among the strongest partisans for an aggressive policy toward the Red Sticks.[47]

James Cornells had the strongest reasons for antipathy toward the Red Sticks who had gone to Pensacola. On their way, the party had looted and burned his plantation, taking Cornells's wife, Betsy Coulter, and a man who lived on the plantation as captives. As the Red Sticks canvassed Pensacola for supplies, rumor had it that Betsy Coulter was traded to "Madame Baronne, a French lady, for a blanket."[48]

Cornells's deposition was taken by one A. L. Osborn, presumably 1st Lt. Audley L. Osborn, adjutant of the Mississippi Territorial Volunteers and one of the few professionally trained soldiers in the frontier militia. Of the three depositions, it offers the most extravagant account of Spanish arms supplies to the Creeks. After accompanying General Wilkinson through the Creek Nation in June and hearing threats from Indians who claimed to be friends of Great Britain, Cornells said he turned back through the Nation to find "Spanish Arms &c in the hands of the unfriendly Creeks, which they declare[d] they had received from the Spanish Gove[r]nor at Pensacola, from whom they could at all times receive as great supplies as they wished, on the authority of a letter from a British General in Canada, given to the Little Warrior, which letter when Little Warrior was killed was taken by McQueen a leading man of the unfriendly Creeks & carried to Pensacola."[49]

According to Cornells, then, the Spanish authorities had provided not only ammunition but weapons. The transaction had been completed in late June or early July, weeks before McQueen's Red Stick delegation first reached Pensacola. Yet McQueen is said to have been the one who delivered the "letter from a British General in Canada" that unlocked the limitless bounty of the Spanish governor's arsenal.

Cornells was not finished. Before crossing the Alabama River, he encountered "a free Negroes [*sic*]" carrying a message from Josiah Francis, the prophet, that "verry large supply (say forty horse loads of powder) & one barrel of flints with many guns . . . had been furnished on the North East side of the Bay of Pensacola," awaiting a Red Stick force to pick it up. What is more, a Red Stick party had already picked up "a considerable quantity of powder & other warlike stores obtained from the Spanish Governor by virtue of the order above mentioned," Little Warrior's letter from Canada. The account seems entirely fictitious. But for Tensaw settlers, who knew only that an American militia had been defeated by Indians, Cornells's sworn statement must have been compelling.[50]

Manac (or Moniac), the second of the three deponents, was also a wealthy Creek planter who, as Harry Toulmin remarked, had "certainly as much at stake as any man in the country." Although he was a brother-in-law of the prophet Josiah Francis, Manac was strongly opposed to his cause. Most of his relatives had joined the Red Sticks, and earlier in 1813 his own sister and brother had stolen cattle, horses, and slaves from his plantation. By his own account he was afraid to remain at his home near the Federal Road in the Creek Nation.[51]

Around July 11 or 12 the Red Stick party led by High Head Jim encamped at Manac's home, and Manac was brought before the Red Stick leader. What follows is the most famous description of the "shaking" rite practiced by Red Stick prophets. "He shook hands with me, and immediately began to tremble and jerk in every part of his frame, and the very calves of his legs would be convulsed, and he would get entirely out of breath with the agitation. This practice was introduced in May or June last by the Prophet Francis, who says that he was instructed by the Spirit."[52]

Manac purportedly won the prophet's confidence by making a false promise to "sell [his] property and buy ammunition, and join them." High Head Jim then confided the story of Little Warrior's letter. "He then told me that they were going down to Pensacola to get ammunition, and that they had got a letter from a British General which would enable them to receive ammunition from the Governor. That it had been given to the Little Warrior, and was saved by his Nephew when he was killed, and sent down to Francis."[53]

Manac's testimony differs from Cornells's in almost every particular except the existence of the British letter. The two even disagree on how the letter was transmitted after Little Warrior's death, with Cornells passing it to Peter McQueen and Manac passing it to Josiah Francis. Both men portray a pending transfer of a large quantity of ammunition from the Spanish government to the Creeks. For Cornells, the transfer was already under way in early July, while Manac describes a plan to arm every hostile Creek town with clockwork precision, followed by a coordinated attack on white settlements in Georgia, Tennessee, and throughout Mississippi Territory.

> High-Head told me that when they went back with their supply, another body of men would go down for another supply of ammunition, and that ten men would go out of each Town, and that they calculated on five horse loads for every Town. He said that they were to make a general attack on the American Settlements—that the Indians on the waters of the Coosa and Tallapoosa, and on the Black Warrior, were to attack the Settlements on the Tombigby and Alabama, particularly the Tensaw and Fork Settlements.—That the Creek Indians, bordering on the Cherokees, were to attack the people of Tennessee, and that the Seminoles and lower Creeks were to attack the Georgians.—That the Choctaws also had joined them and were to attack the Mississippi Settlements.—That the attack was to be made at the same time in all places where they got furnished with ammunition.[54]

Manac stated that his sister and other companions of the Red Stick chiefs were harshly treated and "very desirous to leave them, but could not." By listening to High Head Jim he learned that the war being waged in the Creek Nation "was to be against the whites and not between Indians themselves." Once they had overcome those Indians "who had taken the talk of the whites," the true nature of the conflict would be revealed. At that point, Manac implied, what had already been done to mixed-blood planters in the

Nation would be done to the property of whites: "They have destroyed a large quantity of my cattle, and burnt my houses on my river plantation, as well as those of James Cornells and Leonard McGee."[55]

Manac's deposition, as brief as it is, has long been part of the canon of southern history. Nineteenth-century historians often simply reproduced Manac's testimony word for word, including his error in dating the 1811 visit of Tecumseh to 1812.[56] His description of High Head Jim's shaking seems convincingly like eyewitness testimony, and his misdating of Tecumseh's visit is an understandable slip. Nevertheless, there are reasons to treat most of Manac's deposition skeptically. His motives for payback against the Red Sticks were as strong as James Cornells's, suggesting that parts of his testimony were wholly invented or skewed to make a compelling case for aggression. Assuming that Manac did not put words in High Head Jim's mouth, the prophet's motives for deceiving Manac must be considered. Despite his insincere promise to join the Red Sticks, High Head Jim most probably regarded Manac as an untrustworthy man who had been abandoned by his own kin. His shaking display was a sign to followers that he regarded Manac as corrupt. Why, then, would he confide in him? The answer, as Joel Martin has suggested, is that anything High Head Jim revealed to Manac was likely intended for the ears of the Red Sticks' enemies.[57]

David Tate, a half-brother of William Weatherford, was the third and final deponent. He said he had received news of the Red Stick mission to Pensacola from Sam Manac "on or about July 19," the day before the Red Sticks themselves arrived in Pensacola. Col. Joseph Carson commissioned Tate and two other men to spy on the Red Sticks in Pensacola. Tate returned after one day to file his report.[58]

Tate's claims, made before Judge Harry Toulmin, are considerably more modest than Cornells's or Manac's. Where the other two depositions describe a conspiracy against white settlers, Tate quotes González as intending to give the Red Sticks "a little ammunition" because "it had been customary" for prior governors to do this for Indian emissaries. Tate concluded that, far from giving the Red Sticks new weapons, the governor had not even fulfilled their request to have their old guns repaired, for as he said, "I have seen some gun locks which were taken from them in the late battle [of Burnt Corn] . . . and find them to be much out of repair." He also reported the governor's refusal to open the US mail captured by the Red Sticks, preferring to forward it to the Americans in Mobile, "as the Government of Spain & of the United States were on a friendly fooling [i.e., footing]." Tate's testimony also strikes a blow at Cornells's and Manac's assertions about Little Warrior's letter. Although the warrior's name is not mentioned, it is clear that the rumored "packet from Canada" is being referred to. "My friend also informed me that on the next day a letter was to be interpreted to the Indians which they had brought from a British general in Canada, & which they ellidged [i.e., alleged] contained a a [*sic*] request to the Governor to furnish them with arms and ammunition but that the Governor said it contained only a recommendation of them as friendly Indians."[59]

This passage presents evidence weakening the hypothesis that Little Warrior's British document never existed, suggesting instead that the document was simply a letter of recommendation that had been misinterpreted. It strains credulity, however, to believe that none of the Indians who allegedly handled the letter were able to either read it themselves or find someone else to read it, until the moment they presented it to González. By changing the fabled packet from Canada into a mere letter of introduction, perhaps Tate (or his informant) intended to explain away a rumor that had become too widely believed to simply reject as untrue.

The manuscript of Tate's deposition shows signs of having been amended while it was composed, possibly to address the objections of others who heard the testimony given. As both Manac and Tate were deposed on the same day, before the same judge, it is highly likely that each heard the other's testimony. Tate stated that on the evening of July 20 he asked his unnamed friend "whether the request of the Indians to be supplied with ammunition had been granted. He informed me that it had not and that he had remonstrated much against it." But this wording, which absolved González from conspiracy with the Creeks, was amended to read, "He informed me that it had not *been delivered* and that he had remonstrated much against it." The insertion left intact the claim of Cornells and Manac that the West Florida government had been a whole-hearted collaborator with hostile Indians.[60]

Tate concurred only partially with his fellow deponents in reporting that the Red Sticks planned to attack settlements on the Mobile and Tensaw, but not the Georgia and Tennessee frontiers. He attributed the information to a conversation with Betsy Coulter, James Cornells's captured wife. "She said that they were shy in co[nv]ersing before her.—but that they had told her expressly that they meant to destroy and plunder all the property of the half breeds and put them to death, and that she could could [*sic*] gather from them what she heard that they calculated on attacking the white people on these waters, within about 20 days; if they sacceeded [*sic*] in/prospering—ammunition." The last clause of this passage, which imposes a condition on the Red Stick plans, is incoherent, suggesting that it was composed under confused or contentious circumstances. The remainder of Tate's statement further undermines those of Cornells and Manac by first describing the governor's refusal to open the stolen US mail, then reporting John Innerarity's "slrictest injaction [i.e., strictest injunction] to persons in his employ not to sell any powder &c. to the Indians."[61]

As a wealthy Indian countryman, Tate's interests were essentially the same as Manac's and Cornells's, yet his version of events fails to conform to the "anti-Indian" narrative, in which diabolical foreigners were causing savage Indians to make war on blameless, vulnerable settlers. One reason for his dissent may be that, rather than suffering damages at the hands of Red Sticks, Tate may have been harmed by the militia's rush to intercept the Creek rebels. On the day before the Burnt Corn fight, Caller's volunteers rendezvoused with other volunteer companies at Tate's cow pens, probably causing damage to Tate's property. Tate was also the only deponent to have been commissioned to spy on behalf of the army, so he may have felt a sense of duty to refrain from sensationalizing his information. Nonetheless, Tate's deposition is open to question concerning the extent to which it represents the deponent's actual experiences. One flaw is Tate's reliance on the testimony of an unnamed friend whom he said "was intimate with the governor." The omission of the friend's name calls for an explanation, as Tate did not hide the identities of his other two informants, Betsy Coulter and John Innerarity. Also, Tate's admission that, because of prior threats from the Red Sticks, he "did not shew [him]self openly" during his one-day scout in Pensacola, suggests doubts about how he obtained his information.[62]

The rumor of Little Warrior's letter did not die out but gained new life from the events of the Creek War. We have seen how the letter helped explain away the US defeat at Burnt Corn, converting it into proof of Spanish conspiracy with the British and Indians. Even news of the Red Sticks' aggressive behavior in Pensacola was transformed, by the time Tennessee governor Willie Blount passed it on, into a "war dance" representing the shared determination of Indians, Spaniards, and Britons to invade the whole Southwest, including Tennessee and Georgia. Blount also embellished the rumor of Little Warrior's letter with details worthy of a Gothic novel. The Spanish governor, he wrote, had sent a "messenger" into Indian country to find Little Warrior's grave, "dig his body up, get the letter, and carry it to him." Like other versions of the rumor, Blount's report fails to explain why, if the Spanish were so determined to arm the Creek Indians, they had to wait for a British letter before doing it. Instead, the rumor functioned at an emotional level to justify Blount's vision of a campaign to eliminate "those deluded and turbulent Creeks" from their land, after which "each southern and western inhabitant will cultivate his own garden of Eden, and . . . import such comforts as he may think desirable" through ports that had once been Spanish. For those who aspired to destroy the Creek Nation, the rumor of Little Warrior's "packet from Canada" remained highly useful. For the Creeks themselves, however, whether "turbulent" or "friendly," the rumor's utility was soon exhausted.[63]

After their victory at Fort Mims, Josiah Francis and two other Red Stick leaders sent a letter to González reminding him of his promise to ask his superior for aid, promising an unbroken string of victories, and threatening to burn Mobile if González did not soon recover it himself from the Americans. González, having heard of two US defeats by Creek Indians in little over a month, did indeed suggest to his superior that he be given permission to supply the Indians. The new policy was approved by the Spanish government in December 1813, by which time Autossee and Eccanachaca (Holy Ground), two of the three principal Red Stick strongholds, were already in ruins. Even allowing for the scarcity of supplies in Pensacola, the Spanish policy change occurred too late to significantly affect the course of the Creek War.[64]

Late in the year, two letters from González to Red Stick leaders fell into American hands. Although the governor was restrained in his expressions of friendship and made no commitment to aid their cause, the very fact that a Spanish official had written to Red Stick chiefs sufficed for the Americans as proof positive of an Anglo-Spanish conspiracy. Claiborne saw to it that each of the letters was copied and distributed to his correspondents.[65]

If "history is written by the winners," then there is little wonder in the fact that the legend of Little Warrior's British letter has persisted in some form through nearly two centuries of southern historiography. Historians have seldom if ever embraced the story, or the accompanying ideological complex that Peter Silver has called the "anti-Indian sublime," as enthusiastically as settlers and Indian countrymen on the Creek frontier did. But a close look at this powerful rumor's surviving traces may help us recognize the imprint it has left on Creek historiography. Both Creeks and Americans sometimes said what they found convenient, not what they believed to be true—even when under oath.

Notes

1. "Alabama districts" is used as a term of convenience to refer to American settlements along the Alabama, Tombigbee, and Mobile Rivers and tributaries within the Mississippi Territory. The Tensaw district, lying along a tributary of the Mobile, was among the oldest and most extensive of these settlements. The Alabama districts included the Tensaw, Bigbee, and Forks neighborhoods, all of them relatively isolated from the few other population centers within the vast Mississippi Territory.

2. The province of West Florida had no governor during this period, but

the commandant of Pensacola was commonly addressed with the courtesy title of "governor." The commandant reported directly to the captain-general of Havana. Mateo González Manrique replaced Mauricio de Zúñiga as commandant in May 1813.

3. "Hawkins to Col. Monroe, 18 Jan 1813," in *American State Papers, Class II, Indian Affairs,* vol. 1, ed. Walter Lowrie (Washington, DC: Gales and Seaton, 1832–1834), 1:838 (hereafter cited as ASPIA). Also see Robbie Ethridge, *Creek Country: The Creek Indians and Their World* (Chapel Hill: University of North Carolina Press, 2003), 128–29.

4. Claudio Saunt, *A New Order of Things: Property, Power, and the Transformation of the Creek Indians, 1733–1816* (Cambridge: Cambridge University Press, 1999), 46–54, 90–108; Ethridge, *Creek Country,* 160–67; Henry DeLeon Southerland Jr. and Jerry Elijah Brown, *The Federal Road through Georgia, the Creek Nation, and Alabama, 1806–1836* (Tuscaloosa: University of Alabama Press, 1989), 34–36; "Hawkins to Armstrong, 26 Apr 1813," ASPIA, 1:840–41.

5. Albert James Pickett, *History of Alabama, and Incidentally of Georgia and Mississippi, from the Earliest Period* (Charleston: Walker & James, 1851), 521.

6. Frank L. Owsley Jr., *Struggle for the Gulf Borderlands: The Creek War and the Battle of New Orleans, 1812–1815* (Gainesville: University Presses of Florida, 1981), 25–26; also see Frank Lawrence Owsley Jr. and Gene A. Smith, *Filibusters and Expansionists: Jeffersonian Manifest Destiny, 1800–1821* (Tuscaloosa: University of Alabama Press, 1997), 97.

7. George Stiggins, "A Historical narration of the Genealogy traditions and downfall of the Ispocaga or Creek tribe of Indians, written by one of the tribe," in Theron A. Nuñez Jr., "Creek Nativism and the Creek War of 1813–1814, Part 2 (Stiggins Narrative, Continued)," *Ethnohistory* 5, no. 2 (Spring 1958): 151–52.

8. William S. Maltby, *The Rise and Fall of the Spanish Empire* (Basingstoke, Hamps.: Palgrave Macmillan, 2009), 164–70, 177.

9. The firm, initially Panton, Leslie & Co., operated under the name Forbes & Co. from 1803. William S. Coker and Thomas D. Watson, *Indian Traders of the Southeastern Spanish Borderlands: Panton, Leslie & Company and John Forbes & Company, 1783–1847* (Pensacola: University of West Florida Press, 1986).

10. H. M. Scott, *The Birth of a Great Power System, 1740–1815* (Harlow, England: Pearson Longman, 2005), 338–40.

11. *Nashville Clarion and Tennessee Gazette,* October 19, 1810, November 2, 1810; Owsley, *Struggle for the Gulf Borderlands,* 20–21, 23; Owsley and Smith, *Filibusters and Expansionists,* 93–94; H. S. Halbert and T. H. Ball, *The Creek War of 1813 and 1814* (Tuscaloosa: University of Alabama Press, 1995), 87, 107.

12. "Andrew Jackson to Tennessee Volunteers, 20 Jul 1813," printed proclamation, Andrew Jackson Papers, Library of Congress Manuscript Division.

13. "J. P. Kennedy to F. L. Claiborne, 24 July 1813," Letterbook F, J.H.C. Claiborne Papers, Mississippi Department of Archives and History, Jackson, MS (hereafter cited as Letterbook F); Pickett, *History of Alabama,* 521.

14. Peter Silver, *Our Savage Neighbors: How Indian War Transformed Early America* (New York: W. W. Norton, 2007), esp. xviii–xxiii, 316n7.

15. Silver, *Our Savage Neighbors,* xix; Halbert and Ball, *Creek War,* 29–30; James Caller, *The Declaration of the American citizens, on the Mobile, with relation to British aggressions* ([Wakefield, AL] September 1807), 2; George Strother Gaines, *The Reminiscences of George Strother Gaines, Pioneer and Statesman of Early Alabama and Mississippi, 1805–1843,* ed. James P. Pate (Tuscaloosa: University of Alabama Press, 1998), 131.

16. Mark Pitcavage, "Ropes of Sand: Territorial Militias, 1801–1812," *Journal of the Early Republic* 13 (Winter 1993): 482–92, 496–97; "Thomas Flournoy to F. L. Claiborne, 10 Aug 1813," in "Letters Relating to the Tragedy of Fort Mims: August–September, 1813," ed. James F. Doster, *Alabama Review* 14 (Oct. 1961): 274.

17. "Toulmin to John Graham, 5 Aug 1812," in *Territorial Papers of the United States,* vols. 5–6, *The Territory of Mississippi, 1798–1817,* ed. Edwin Clarence Carter (Washington, D.C.: GPO, 1937–38), 6:306–7.

18. "Joseph Carson to F. L. Claiborne, 29 July 1813," Miscellaneous correspondence, Tennessee State Library and Archives, Nashville, TN (hereafter cited as TSLA); Pickett, *History of Alabama,* 528.

19. Caller, *Declaration,* 3–4.

20. Theda Perdue, *Mixed-Blood Indians: Racial Construction in the Early South* (Athens: University of Georgia Press, 2003).

21. Ethridge, *Creek Country,* 77–79, 111–13; Andrew Frank, *Creeks and Southerners: Biculturalism on the Early American Frontier* (Lincoln: University of Nebraska Press, 2005). Ethridge sees "Indian countrymen" as a group distinct from other white and mixed-blood residents of the Creek Nation. Frank argues that race was not a significant factor in identity formation among either Creeks or Indian countrymen until the 1820s. A caveat: Because the term "Indian countryman" is specific to males, it implies that not only war, but politics, trade, and other facets of public life on the frontier were exclusively male domains. This assumption could be challenged even with regard to war.

22. "Arango to González (copy), 26 Jun 1813," enclosed in "González to Ruíz Apodaca, 9 Jul 1813," Archivo General de Indias, Papeles de Cuba (hereafter cited as AGI:PC), legajo 1794, no. 64. Translations from Spanish documents are the author's.

23. "H. Toulmin to F. L. Claiborne, [Aug. 12, 1813]," Letterbook F.

24. The list of presents given to the Indians is dated July 22, but information

in Innerarity's letters indicates that the ceremony in the Plaza de Armas must have occurred on July 23. "Mateo González Manrique to Juan Ruíz Apodaca, 23 Jul 1813," AGI:PC, legajo 1794, no. 94, 1418–19, 1421; "Mateo González Manrique a veinte y quatro jefes, 22 Jul 1813," AGI:PC, legajo 1794, part 17, no. 94, 1426; Elizabeth Howard West, ed., "A Prelude to the Creek War of 1813–1814, in a Letter of John Innerarity to James Innerarity," *Florida Historical Quarterly* 18 (1940): 249–53.

25. "Capt. J. B. Wilkinson to F. L. Claiborne, 11 August 1813," in West, "Prelude to the Creek War," 263.

26. González's interpreter in meetings with the Creeks was Pedro de Alba, who translated several English-language documents for the West Florida government. "Mateo González Manrique to Juan Ruíz Apodaca, 23 Jul 1813," AGI:PC, legajo 1794, no. 94, 1419–21.

27. West, "Prelude to the Creek War," 249–50.

28. Innerarity referred only to "their shaker," whom Elizabeth Howard West concluded must be either Josiah Francis or High Head Jim. But Francis, like Peter McQueen, was a trader with more than $500 in debts due to Forbes & Co. and was unlikely to be unknown to Innerarity. Francis was most likely present at this meeting but spoke little, or not at all. "List of Debts Due by the Traders and Factors," in "The Creek Nation, Debtor to John Forbes & Co., Successors to Panton, Leslie & Co.: A Journal of John Innerarity," ed. Marie Greenslade, *Florida Historical Quarterly* 9, no. 2 (October 1930): 86; West, "Prelude to the Creek War," 250–51.

29. West, "Prelude to the Creek War," 251–52.

30. Ibid., 252–53.

31. "Mateo González Manrique to Juan Ruíz Apodaca, 23 Jul 1813," 1421; "A veinte y quatro jefes, 22 July 1813," AGI:PC, legajo 1794, part 17, no. 94, 1426; Innerarity, quoted in West, "Prelude to the Creek War," 253–54.

32. Innerarity, quoted in West, "Prelude to the Creek War," 253–54; "A veinte y quatro jefes, 22 July 1813," AGI:PC legajo 1794, part 17, no. 94, 1426.

33. Thomas S. Woodward believed that Jim Boy was another name for High Head Jim, but it is more likely that Woodward conflated the two men. "Mateo González Manrique to Juan Ruíz Apodaca, 23 Jul 1813," 1421–22; West, "Prelude to the Creek War," 254; Halbert and Ball, *Creek War*, 128–29.

34. "Mateo González Manrique to Juan Ruíz Apodaca, 23 Jul 1813," 1422; Innerarity, quoted in West, "Prelude to the Creek War," 255.

35. "Mateo González Manrique to Juan Ruíz Apodaca, 23 Jul 1813," 1422–23; West, "Prelude to the Creek War," 255–56.

36. West, "Prelude to the Creek War," 257–58.

37. "Mateo González Manrique to Juan Ruíz Apodaca, 23 Jul 1813," 1418; "J. P.

Kennedy to F. L. Claiborne, July 24, 1813," Letterbook F; "Joseph Carson to F. L. Claiborne, July 29, 1813," TSLA; West, "Prelude to the Creek War," 253, 256; Tate deposition, Letterbook F; Owsley, *Struggle for the Gulf Borderlands*, 26.

38. Historian-poet A. B. Meek raised the number of Red Sticks at Burnt Corn to 350, but he also increased Caller's 180 men to 300. Halbert and Ball suggest that "only a part of the force, mainly under the command of Jim Boy," left Pensacola, "while the greater party, from some cause, tarried a while longer in Pensacola." Alexander Beaufort Meek, *The Red Eagle: A Poem of the South* (New York and Mobile: D. Appleton, S. H. Goetzel, 1855), 105; Alexander Beaufort Meek, "Massacre at Fort Mims," in *Romantic Passages in Southwestern History* (New York: S. H. Goetzel, 1857), 244–45; Halbert and Ball, *Creek War*, 128; Thomas S. Woodward, *Woodward's Reminiscences of the Creek, or Muscogee Indians, Contained in Letters to Friends in Georgia and Alabama* (Montgomery, AL: Barrett & Wimbish, 1859), 97–98.

39. "Treaty of Fort Jackson, 10 August 1812," "Reply of Big Warrior," and "Report of Alexander Cornells," all June 22, 1813, ASPIA, I:846.

40. "Cussetah Micco to B. Hawkins, 10 Jul 1813," ASPIA, 1:849; "James Curnels deposition" and "The deposition of David Tate's of lawful age," Letterbook F; "The Deposition of Samuel Manac, of lawful age, a Warrior of the Creek Nation," in Halbert and Ball, *Creek War*, 91–93; West, "Prelude to the Creek War," 257. A manuscript copy of the Manac deposition is available at the Alabama Department of Archives and History, Montgomery, AL (SPR 26).

41. "Thomas Flournoy to David B. Mitchell, 26 Apr 1813," Telamon Cuyler Collection, Hargrett Library, University of Georgia, Athens, GA; "James Wilkinson to Harry Toulmin, [25] June 1813," quoted in Halbert and Ball, *Creek War*, 88–90.

42. Gregory A. Waselkov, *A Conquering Spirit: Fort Mims and the Redstick War of 1813–1814* (Tuscaloosa: University of Alabama Press, 2006), 54, 83, 89, 299n42.

43. Innerarity at another point in his letter mentions "the Spanish Interpreter," presumably Pedro de Alba. I am suggesting that the Creek "interpreter" went to the trading house with McQueen, and Alba, "the Spanish Interpreter," arrived soon afterward with the Spanish detachment. West, "Prelude to the Creek War," 251, 254, 255.

44. Pickett, *History of Alabama*, 523–25; Stiggins, "Historical narration," 54; Woodward, *Woodward's Reminiscences*, 86, 97–98; Halbert and Ball, *Creek War*, 134–40.

45. "F. L. Claiborne to Majors Bailey, Tait, and Moniac, 31 Jul 1813" and "James Wilkinson to F. L. Claiborne, 4 Aug. 1813," Letterbook F.

46. "F. L. Claiborne to J. W. Bowyer, 9 August 1813," "F. L. Claiborne to D. Holmes, 12 August 1813," "F. L. Claiborne to Governor of Georgia, 14 August 1813," and "F. L. Claiborne to Benjamin Hawkins, 14 August 1813," Letterbook F.

47. "F. L. Claiborne to Gov. of Ga., 14 Aug 1813," Letterbook F; Waselkov, *Conquering Spirit,* 89.

48. Curnels deposition, Letterbook F; Halbert and Ball, *Creek War,* 126.

49. Waselkov, *Conquering Spirit,* 336n23, 346n162; Curnels deposition, Letterbook F.

50. Curnels deposition, Letterbook F.

51. "H. Toulmin to F. L. Claiborne, [12 Aug 1813]," Letterbook F; Halbert and Ball, *Creek War,* 91.

52. Manac, quoted in Halbert and Ball, *Creek War,* 91–92.

53. Ibid., 92.

54. Ibid.

55. Ibid., 93.

56. For transcriptions (and revisions) of Manac's deposition, see, for example, John W. Monette, *History of the Discovery and Settlement of the Mississippi Valley* (New York: Harper & Brothers, 1848), 2:394–95; J. F. H. Claiborne, *Life and Times of Gen. Sam Dale, the Mississippi Partisan* (New York: Harper & Brothers, 1860), 69–71; Halbert and Ball, *Creek War,* 91–93. Halbert and Ball correct Manac's erroneous date for Tecumseh's visit.

57. Joel Martin, *Sacred Revolt: The Muskogees' Struggle for a New World* (Boston: Beacon Press, 1991), 220n7.

58. Tate deposition; Waselkov, *Conquering Spirit,* 93–94; Halbert and Ball, *Creek War,* 127.

59. Tate deposition.

60. Ibid.

61. Ibid.

62. Ibid.; Halbert and Ball, *Creek War,* 130, 141–42.

63. "Willie Blount to Brigadier General Thomas Flournoy, Nashville, October 15, 1813," ASPIA,1:855–57.

64. "Josiah Francis, the Old King, Old Interpreter, and Mougceweihche to Gov. González Manrique," AGI:PC, legajo 221b, 335–36; Owsley, *Struggle for the Gulf Borderlands,* 9.

65. "Manrique to Gentlemen, 29 Sept 1813" (4 copies), "Manrique to My Friend and Brother, 15 Nov 1813" (2 copies), both in Letterbook F; "Manrique to My Friend and Brother, 15 Nov 1813," SPR21, Alabama Department of Archives and History, Montgomery, AL.

4
Red Sticks

Kathryn E. Holland Braund

In July 1813, Creek agent Benjamin Hawkins sent a talk to the Creek Indians, whom he feared were aggrieved to the point of war, noting, "I hear you are preparing yourselves for war. I hear you have taken part with the prophets. . . . I hear you have begun the war dance, made your war clubs, and are for war with the white people." These "fanatical" Creek chiefs, as Hawkins termed them, are best known to us as the Red Sticks.[1] These insurgents rose up in opposition to the policies of the Creek National Council, and many were motivated by a religious prophetic movement that called for a rejection of the cultural, economic, and political reformation then taking place and espoused by the US government. This chapter will explore why these insurgents were called Red Sticks and what it meant to be a Red Stick, as well as the origin, meaning, and use of the implement itself.[2]

For generations, Creek scholars and others have posited that "red sticks" were merely the small bundles of cane used as time-keeping devices by the Creeks. Perhaps the first to make this connection was Thomas L. McKenney, whose multivolume *History of the Indian Tribes of North America* was originally published in the late 1830s. McKenney explained,

> [So] that no mistake might happen in regard to the day on which the Indians were to strike, he prepared bundles of sticks—each bundle containing the number of sticks corresponding to the number of days that were to intervene between the day on which they were received, and the day of the general onset. The Indian practice is, to throw away a stick every morning—they make, therefore, no mistake in the time. These sticks Tecumthé caused to be painted red. It was from this circumstance that, in the former Seminole war, these Indians were called "Red Sticks."[3]

H. S. Halbert and T. H. Ball, in their still influential *The Creek War of 1813 and 1814,* originally published in 1895, drawing on McKenney's work, wrote of Tecumseh's purported visit to the Seminoles: "It is reported that he gave them a bundle of prepared sticks, painted red, each stick to represent a day, according to the number of days to elapse before he wished them to enter on the war path, one of which they were to throw away each day that there might be no mistake; and this is said to have been the origin of the term 'Red Sticks' as applied to the hostile Indians."[4] And over the last century or so, generations of scholars have quoted Halbert and Ball and perpetuated the notion that this practice, commonly known as "broken days," is the source of the terms "Red Sticks" and "Red Stick War." The latest to perpetuate this origin is the recently released *Handbook of North American Indians: Southeast,* a long-awaited and supposedly definitive reference volume for southeastern Indians. The author of the entry "Creek Confederacy before Removal" wrote, "Because they were known to use this traditional device [the broken days], the militants in the Creek War of 1813–1814 were called by White people, Red Sticks, and the war itself, the Red Stick War."[5]

Tecumseh's biographer, John Sugden, likewise settles for the "broken days" explanation. Sugden concludes that Tecumseh probably didn't use "broken days" but that "once the Creek War of 1813 was underway the red sticks were circulated and gave the hostiles their name."[6] Sugden dismisses the notion that a Shawnee medicine wand carried by Tecumseh could be the source of the term. Tecumseh's "wand" was a medicine stick bedecked with feathers. George Catlin's later painting of Tecumseh's brother, the Prophet, shows him holding such an implement. The Shawnee medicine wand or stick neither looks like nor has the same ritual purpose as a Creek war club.[7]

Most references since Halbert and Ball's, Walker's included, drop the association with Tecumseh for the origin of the broken days. For, indeed, the use of bundled sticks for counting time was a traditional practice among all the Indians of the Southeast. Such sticks were made from cane and were generally known as "broken days" since the sticks were either thrown away or broken and destroyed at the beginning of each day to mark the passage of time.[8]

Among the many writers to describe the use of time-keeping sticks was Louis LeClerk Milfort, who resided for a time among the Creeks in the late eighteenth century and claimed to have participated in many war rituals. According to Milfort, when a town's head warrior determined on war, he sent to clan war chiefs in the town a war club "accompanied by a certain number of sticks which serve to inform the warriors who carry them into the different districts of the nation, of the day on which they are to be at the general meeting and of the number of young men who must march."[9] James

Adair, in his *History of the American Indians,* relates that the sticks were not only red, but frequently "notched" and "square."[10] George Stiggins, a Creek of mixed ancestry who later wrote a history of the conflict, reported that "the broken days is a bundle of broken parts of twigs about four inches long every piece for one day tied carefully in a bundle one of the sticks is thrown away at sun rise every day to the last which is the day appointed."[11]

It is also appropriate to note that Indians used these sticks for all occasions when it was necessary to synchronize time, such as to meet for a ball play or conference of leaders from many towns. On those occasions, obviously, the sticks would not have been painted red.[12]

Halbert and Ball, although they repeated McKenney's "broken days" account, also prefaced their account with it "is said," which careless readers have ignored. For later in their work, these two careful scholars assert the real reason the term was employed: "The hostile Creeks were often called 'Red Sticks,' because their war-clubs were invariably painted red. 'Red Stick' was considered an honorable appellation, and as such it will occasionally be used in this work. 'Red Stick War' is the name by which the War of 1813 is still known among the Creeks of the Indian Territory."[13] Their source for this information is easy to ascertain, for they lift their language straight from a note by Albert J. Pickett in his *History of Alabama* (1851): "The Indian war-party were often called the "Red Sticks," because their war-clubs were invariably painted red."[14]

Although historians have dithered over the issue, the extant documentary record makes it very clear that the Red Sticks were so named because of their war clubs. A number of sources claim that the war club was first introduced to the Creeks by the Shawnee. In writing about Sam Dale, of the Canoe Fight fame, his biographer claimed that during Tecumseh's visit among the Creeks, "Every weapon but the war-club—then first introduced among the Creeks—had been laid aside."[15] Halbert also wrote that the war club "was introduced, or revived, by Tecumseh."[16] But Tecumseh did not introduce the war club among the Creeks, and neither did it become the sole weapon of the insurgents.

The War Club in Creek Cosmology

In June 1735, Chekelli Mico and a number of other Creek headmen from both Upper Creek and Lower Creek towns recited the creation account of their people for the newly arrived Georgians. According to these men, in the beginning the Muscogee people came out of the "Mouth of the Ground" and began their journey eastward toward the Sun. Their story recounts the difficulties they encountered and the manner in which the people found assistance from the Earth in the form of beneficial plants, ceremonies, and helpful beings. The legend, delivered orally, was translated into English by

Georgia officials and recorded on a buffalo skin. We can be sure that much was left out, as the scribes condensed it, but the surviving narrative reveals that the war club entered Creek life during this creation journey: "That at the Hill there was a Stick which was very uneasy and made a Noise and they could not tell how to pacifye it that they took a Motherless child and push'd it at the Stick killed the Child therefore they took the Stick and Carry it with them when they go to Warr And the Stick was like the Wooden Tomihawk which they use to this day and of the Same Sort of Wood."[17]

This "stick" is a war club. The Muskogee term for the club is *atássa.*[18] Like many others, George Stiggins so strongly associated war clubs with militants inspired by Tecumseh that he erroneously believed that the term was of Shawnee origin.[19] But *atássa* is a Muskogean term and the name of a leading Tallapoosa Creek town. During the eighteenth century, visitors noted a massive pillar of pine, some forty feet high, at the Creek town of Autossee. Such symbolic war poles, which were painted red during times of war, could be found in many Creek towns, usually those specifically designated as war or "red" towns. It was here that war captives were ritually tortured and burned to death and where scalps were displayed.[20] John Swanton reported that Creek elders in post-removal period recalled that these posts were "said to have been in the shape of war clubs (atasa)."[21]

Eighteenth-century documents reveal that raising a red stick or club was a metaphor for declaring war. For example, in the opening phases of the American Revolution, the Creek war chief Emisteseguo promised the British, "If the red warriors to the northward would hold a red stick against the Virginians there, I would hold one against them here."[22] And at the end of a war, the red sticks were buried, as happened in 1776 when the leading warriors of the Creeks and Choctaws met in Pensacola and ritually surrendered their symbols of war to John Stuart, the British superintendent of Indian Affairs, who had mediated the peace. Stuart wrote:

> Both parties appointed to meet in the street before my door; each party had a white flag as an emblem of peace and were highly painted. They halted about 300 yards distance from each other, their principal chiefs singing the peace song and waving eagles' tails and swans' wings over their heads. Then they began to advance slowly when at a signal given a number of young men sallied out from each party and made a sham fight in the space between them. At last both parties met, and after saluting each other joined hands in my presence. Their chiefs then came into my house and delivered into my hands two war clubs painted red as the last ceremony of laying down their arms, which I promised to bury very deep in the earth, and made them a short congratulatory speech upon the occasion.[23]

The symbolism of war sticks and war poles was universal across the South, as were symbols of peace: white feathers and peace pipes. For example, in the 1740s, a leading Chickasaw headman was accused of sending "runners to the other Nations with a painted War Stick" to rouse them against the English. The plot fizzled, but the action is positive proof that Creeks and other southern tribes did not need an introduction to the symbol of war from a Shawnee.[24]

But the war club—or red stick—was more than a symbol. Indeed, it was an important weapon in the warriors' repertoire, which by the eighteenth century included "guns, darts, clubs, and tomohawks."[25] Thus, from the beginning of time through the historic period, the Creek people possessed war poles and war clubs—red war poles and clubs. Red, the symbolic color of blood and aggression, was the color of war. White, as in those eagle tails and swan wings, symbolized peace and purity.[26]

Manufacture and Appearance

Although war clubs had been in use by the Creeks since time immemorial, there is always the possibility that there was something distinctive about those used in 1813. Contemporary sources, however, do not indicate any break in the pattern of production or appearance of war clubs by the Creeks. The general lack of precise descriptions by contemporaries would seem to argue that they were no different than those usually employed by Creek warriors. One of the earliest descriptions of the clubs used in the Red Stick War comes from an epic poem by Lewis Sewall, published in 1833, which defined "Red-Sticks" as "a kind of war club, about two feet long, thick and heavy at one end, in which was fixed a sharp piece of sharp iron or bone; with which they struck their captives with great violence on the head and speedily put an end to their existence. They were painted red, hence the term 'Red-sticks.'"[27] Halbert, the famed early Alabama historian already quoted, addressed the question specifically in an essay on Red Sticks in 1884. He obtained information from "an aged man . . . who had passed much of his early life among the Creeks." The informant had been a member of the burial party that visited Fort Mims and recalled "that among the debris strewn around that ruined fortress were great numbers of red sticks." This unnamed informant's information is worth quoting in detail. He noted that the clubs or sticks were "exclusively" produced from "winter hackleberry and the white oak runner" since those woods are "exceedingly hard and tough." Halbert wrote:

> The warrior would select a bush having a single, large, bending root. He cut his stick about three feet long, leaving about seven inches to the root, or club end. After stripping off the bark, he began about two inches from the end of the root, and beveled down two sides of the

> bend to a sharp edge, about five inches long, so that this beveled part bore some resemblance to the curving blade of a hatchet. After this, the stick was thoroughly seasoned over a fire, the warrior giving an additional hardness to the sharp edge of the bend by rubbing over it as much tallow as the heated wood would absorb. The stick was then painted red, with the exception of the club end, which part of the warrior expected to dye red in the blood of an enemy. The paint generally used was made of a soft, red stone, found in different portions of Alabama, but sometimes use was made of the red juice of the pokeberry, and the puccoon root. The stick received several coats of the paint. After the last coat had become dry, a hole was then bored through the handle, about five inches from the end, and a strong loop of buckskin or deer's sinew was fastened therein. The red stick was now complete and ready for service. In using the weapon, which was always wielded in one hand, the wrist of the warrior was inserted in the loop, so that, if in any manner the stick should be knocked out of the owner's grip, he could easily regain his hold, as he would find it hanging by the loop from his wrist. In action, the warrior always smote his victim on the head with the sharp edge of the bend, a single stroke not unfrequently causing death. The red stick in addition to gun, bow and arrow, was used by the Creeks during the entire war.[28]

Other sources mention "a sapling which grew from the sides of a river bank and which curved upward toward the light; clubs made of such wood were obviously of great strength and elasticity."[29]

The production of this essential war tool was suffused in symbolic and spiritual meaning, from the red color to the use of puccoon (*Sanguinaria canadensis* L.), commonly known as bloodroot, a powerful emetic, which was also taken as medicine by warriors.[30]

William Bonar, a Carolina spy whose 1757 map of the Creek towns is adorned with a montage of Creek war tools, provides virtually the only depiction of Creek war clubs from the historic period. In addition to a pipe tomahawk, hatchets, musket, quiver with arrows, powder horn, sword, and drum, he drew two war clubs: a ball type and gunstock type.[31] These, however, seem to be generalized depictions of clubs. Another frequently cited image of a historic Creek club was drawn in 1732 by an anonymous Frenchman and depicts an unusual, notched club, the design of which is repeated on poles supporting a council house.[32]

Clubs are striking weapons, designed for close combat. In his study of Mississippian war clubs, Wayne Van Horne noted many design variations, including clubs with mallet-type heads, those with a cutting edge, and those with inset projections. Van Horne identified the Creek *atássa* as a sword-

4.1. Creek Indian weaponry, including a ball-head club and a gunstock club (*lower right*), both with embedded blades or points. From William Bonar, "A Draught of the Creek Nation, May 1757." CO700/Carolina21. Courtesy of the National Archives of the United Kingdom.

form club that, in his words, "resembled a broadsword that was one to three feet in length and was shaped like a European broadsword, or falchion, without a hilt."[33] He noted that this type of club was the most popular in the protohistoric period and was "perhaps the most technologically sophisticated." Clubs enlarged "the arc of the swing," resulting in "a higher velocity and increased force upon impact."[34]

Men into Warriors

The first contact that young men had with a club was during the ceremony when they received their war names. Stiggins related that this occurred at the Busk, or Green Corn Ceremony:

> In the process of the festival at night mostly in intervals for rest the young men are divested of their given name that they had from in-

> fancy, and invested with what is called a war name which name they go and are known by the rest of their life it is done thus, previously to the ceremony of naming it is intimated to the young man that is to be named by one of the Kings or Warriors for either can give names the name that he is thereafter to assume and go by, when the time arrives for the ceremony one of the Kings or Warriors rises from his seat and calls the name in a shrill long tone of voice, at the call the young man rises and picks up the war club or mallet called by them *attussa* and goes forth to him, when he informs the new man that he is now named as other men and he now can assume the manners and customs of other men he then puts a feather in his head, when that is done the new dubbed man, raises his war club above his head starts a long whoop and runs round in a circle to where he started and when he stops he cries youh youh, from that he is ever after a man with a name.[35]

The Busk was and continues to be the main ceremonial event of the Creek annual cycle. Ostensibly the celebration of the new year's corn crop and a period of devoted religious ritual and introspection, the Busk also featured the rites associated with war. Young men received their war name, war dances that featured mock battles were performed, and the red stick of war, painted white, was carried by two matrons in the Ribbon Dance, performed by women. John Swanton, who reported extensive observations on twentieth-century Creek practices, opined that the war clubs carried by the women were likely adorned with enemy scalps in earlier times. He wrote, "I suspect that this dance was an attempt to represent war as a protective institution and to thank the being or beings who preside over human destiny for having so well defended them against assaults of the—as usual—perfidious foe."[36]

In the early 1880s, Creek leaders Legus F. Perryman and Pleasant Porter were questioned about the ritual and related that at the Busk, women danced the "Red War Dance, the War Dance, the Paint-Up Dance ('to paint up for war')." This activity was preceded by "another long speech . . . telling of their wars, of their great warriors, and of their great deeds, in order to encourage the young men to become great warriors and leaders. If a war was on foot the warriors would be ready to set out, being now purified." Women "had boards made in the shape of tomahawks, painted red, and decorated with black and white feathers, and they shook them as they danced."[37]

A man's association with a war club continued until death. Creek warriors who died at home were buried "in a sitting posture, and they [were] furnished with a musket, powder and ball, a hatchet, pipe, some tobacco, a club,

4.2. Head matron, Ribbon Dance, New Tulsa square ground, 1965, carrying a ceremonial war club into the square ground. From James H. Howard, *The Southeastern Ceremonial Complex and Its Interpretation,* Memoir No. 6 of the Missouri Archaeological Society (Stillwater: Oklahoma State University, 1968). Courtesy of the Missouri Archaeological Society.

a bow and arrows, a looking glass, some vermillion [war paint] and other trinkets, in order to come well provided in the world of spirits."[38]

Louis LeClerk Milfort related that when the war chief of a town decided to declare war to avenge insults by an enemy, he painted a war club red—but only part of it—and displayed it to the town. This, he recorded in his memoirs, "signified that a part of the nation, that is to say, the young men, must hold themselves in readiness to march; for if the club had been painted red all over, the entire nation should have had to keep ready, which happened only in the most unusual cases." I take this to mean that a partially painted club called on the young men of a particularly town—or perhaps even a particular lineage—to avenge an insult. Milfort's entire Creek "nation" at war would have been most unusual, indeed, and most likely means all the towns of a particular component—for example, the Abeika or Tallapoosa towns. But, as during the Creek-Choctaw war of the 1760s, it might have meant all the warriors of the Upper Creek towns were engaged in conflict. Milfort also wrote that the particular style in which each chief painted his club was loaded with meaning, including the number of warriors called on to participate.[39]

Milfort asserted that in his day—the 1790s—the "Indians have entirely abandoned these weapons, but they have preserved the club as a symbol of war only, and have replaced it in battle with the tomahawk or small hatchet."[40] But in the religious and cultural revivalism of the early nineteenth century, conservative Creeks, the militant Red Sticks, revived the symbolism and use of their ancient weapon—if indeed it had ever really been abandoned.

Writing about the Creeks of his own day, who had lived through the Creek War, Stiggins noted that Creek warriors went "into action with their guns on their shoulders their knife and tomahawk hanging to their side and war club stuck in their belt." Stiggins also recorded that "a war club is shaped like a small gun about two foot long and at the curve near where the lock would be is a three square piece of iron or steele with a sharp edge drove in to leave a projection of about two inches." John Reid and John Henry Eaton, in their biography of Andrew Jackson, offered much the same description of war clubs from the era: "Instruments used by the Indian tribes, on commencing hostilities; and which, when painted red, they consider a declaration of war. They are formed of a stick, about eighteen inches in length, with a strong piece of sharp iron affixed at the end; and in appearance resemble a hatchet. They use them principally in pursuit, and after they have been able to introduce confusion into the ranks of an enemy."[41]

The club, modern Creek informants would recall, was "an implement like a combined hatchet and knife, which could either be retained in the hand or thrown."[42] The modern version, still used in Green Corn rituals into the twentieth century, is smaller and closely resembles a large knife.[43]

At the scene of battle, Creek warriors frequently left a war club. One such reference dates from March 1766, when Creek warriors encountered a Choctaw near their border, scalped him, and left a "War stick" by his body.[44] This visible war token testified to the desire of combatants to identify themselves, to prove their retaliation for past injustice, and claim bragging rights for victory.

The war club was the warrior's weapon of choice in other matters as well. Cuckold warriors used clubs to mete out punishment to their wives and their paramours. William Bartram recounted such an instance: "About a dozen young Indian fellows, conducted by their chief (the injured husband) having provided and armed themselves with knotty cudgels of green Hickory, which they concealed under their mantles, . . . [the offender] was instantly surrounded, knocked down, and then stripped to his skin, and beaten with their knotty bludgeons."[45] John Pope, who toured the Creek country in the 1790s, confirmed that the clubs for beating adulterers were of hickory, recording that injured husbands "repair to a Thicket, and supply themselves with *Hickory* Clubs."[46] Stiggins simply called them "large sticks."[47]

How these "knotty bludgeons" and hickory clubs and sticks differed in construction from war clubs is impossible to say. And whether there was a difference—as Pope's testimony that the clubs were newly made implies—is likewise unknown.

Thus, as civil war erupted in 1813, it was natural for Creek warriors enraged at the actions of the Creek National Council to turn to their long-established war rituals and weapons. At the beginning of the Creek civil war, many observers noted that the Shawnee visitors introduced a new dance among the Creeks, the "Dance of the Lakes." As Alfred Cave has written, this dance—like other Indian dances—was a "highly charged invocation of sacred power."[48] Samuel Moniac, a Creek warrior who opposed the Red Sticks and ought to be a reliable source, reported that "it was not till about Christmas that any of our people began to dance the war dance. The Muscogees have not been used to dance before war, but after. At that time about 40 of our people began this northern custom."[49]

Many historians have pointed to this as evidence of Shawnee influence among the Creeks—particularly their war dance. Perhaps Moniac had not danced prior to war, but the historical record is replete with examples of just the opposite. The most telling comes from Moniac's contemporary, George Stiggins, himself a Creek of mixed ancestry, who, like Moniac, opposed the Red Stick Creeks. According to Stiggins, "[Once the Creeks] conclude that the cause of Collision is of so glaring a nature as to admit of no compromise or palliation, of nothing but the blood of the Enemy, it is a positive declaration of war." The chiefs' decision was

> announced to the assembled body of the chiefs and warriors by the orator explaining to them and the assembly the reason why they are justified in a declaration of war, before they make a descent on their enemy, on a day appointed they assemble at their town house square in complete armor, all stript and painted red, black and white as they go into action, with the guns on their shoulders, their knives and tomahawks hanging to their sides and war clubs stuck in their belts. . . . [then the war chief] raises the sacred war whoop and begins to sing and dance.[50]

Joel Martin, in his study *Sacred Revolt,* has written that much of the appeal of the Dance of the Lakes was because it was "not a native Muskogean dance. . . . Because it was an 'import,' this dance satisfied the rebels' needs for a radically new and unfamiliar dance. . . . [T]he dance was a war dance."[51] But we do not know precisely how the Dance of the Lake differed from Creek war dances for there are no precise descriptions of the dances undertaken by Creeks as they took up their red sticks in 1813 or in earlier periods. In any case, dancing prior to warfare was a very familiar ritual practice to Creek warriors, as was the adoption of dances from other tribes.

The Creek war dance was literally a call to arms and invoked spiritual or supernatural aid in the quest to avenge blood and defend the people or their land. The ceremony, which included an oration or declaration of justification, sanctioned the taking of enemy life and called for solidarity and commitment by the town and its warriors. The Creek war dance and painting of war colors figuratively and literally transformed peaceful husbands and fathers into life-taking men of war. Stiggins is not alone in his description of the Creek insurgents as "red painted men." The Creek term used by the Creeks, *ecatecvlke,* to describe the insurgents literally means "those who make themselves red."[52] We have come to know the Creek insurgents of 1813 as Red Sticks, but they are not unique among Creek warriors in either ritual preparation or war practice.

One of the first mentions of war clubs from the Creek War period comes in July 1813, after leading accommodationist chiefs of the Creek National Council had sanctioned the execution of those responsible for depredations on the Duck and Ohio Rivers. The result was a call to arms against these chiefs for ordering the executions, and some Creeks took up the red stick of war against members of the National Council, some of whom took refuge at the Creek town of Tuckabatchee. As they prepared to attack, Hawkins reported to his superior that "the nation generally are badly armed and much reliance placed by the opposition on their bows, arrows, war clubs and magic."[53] It is wrong to suppose that the insurgents turned to traditional weapons because they lacked guns, for they did not, and Hawkins noted this fact in the report of a skirmish between Autossee and Tuckabatchee warriors.[54]

In his talk to the militants on July 6, 1813, Hawkins related: "I hear you have begun the war dance, made your war clubs, and are for war with the white people. What is this for?"[55] Whatever their motivation and intent, it seems clear that these Creeks called upon the ancient and honorable symbol—the war club—to indicate their intent against those Hawkins termed "the besieged."[56] To spread their message, the Red Sticks also sent "red arrows & war clubs" to various towns, particularly those of the Lower Creeks.[57] The Creek prophet Josiah Francis informed the Spanish governor of Pensacola, "The spirit above [had directed them] to take the war club in hand . . . [and the] whole creek nation is united and taken up the red stick."[58]

Red clubs were much in evidence at Fort Mims. Major Daniel Beasley was among the first to fall, and Albert J. Pickett informed his readers that the Red Sticks "felled him [Beasley] to the earth with their clubs and tomahawks." Dixon Bailey's son Ralph, who was turned over to Red Sticks by Bailey's slave Tom, was dispatched by a war club. According to Pickett, the attackers "dashed out his brains with war-clubs." Pickett's account, based on both documentary sources from the times and the reminiscences of survivors, claimed that when William Weatherford attempted to restrain the warriors, he was threatened by "many clubs . . . raised over his head."[59] And as Halbert reported, the burial party dispatched to Fort Mims after the assault found many red sticks littering the ground.

Regarding the attack on Mims, Stiggins wrote that the prophet Paddy Walsh instructed the warriors to "throw down their fire arms . . . [in favor of their] war clubs and scalping knives."[60] Actually, Creek warriors relied on the war club to kill at close range, but they did not eschew other weapons, including rifles, or neglect defensive works such as the barricade at Tohopeka.

Soon after Mims, members of the Kemball and James families were "dispatched" with war clubs by warriors under Josiah Francis, as were many other settlers in lower Tensaw. Jeremiah Austill was "felled" with a war club during the Canoe Fight.[61] Subsequent accounts have Austill taking the war club and using it—successfully—against his opponent.[62]

In a report on the state of the war party in September 1813, Benjamin Hawkins noted that the warriors of Kialigee had "taken the war club & danced the prophet's dances."[63] James Tait described the horror of the battle at Autossee, when Americans and their Creek allies stormed the Red Stick village. Tait's description of one elderly defender of the town, who he identified as the "Old Tallissee king," provides a rare glimpse into how a Creek warrior wielded his war club. Tait related that the warrior "mounted a horse from whence he encouraged his warriors by frequent waivings of his war club, himself firing upon us, at intervals with his rifle." His efforts were ended by US artillery when "a cannon was directed towards him—charged with grapeshot, one of which took effect in the neck of the brave old king; the club no longer felt the grasp of its war-like possessor."[64]

As the war front broadened in August 1814, reports came in from Pulaski County, Georgia, of attacks by Creek warriors: "Three Indians arouse out of the corn and one of them fired" on John Rabun "and wounded him severely in the back" and shoulder. The warriors left a "red stick" behind, then proceeded to two other houses, which they plundered and relieved of possessions.[65]

And so the reports of war clubs or sticks continued throughout the conflict. One of the most instructive reports of just how Red Sticks used their clubs—in combination with their rifles and scalping knives—comes from the pension record of Jesse Webb, who was one of the Tennesseans who assaulted the barricade at Tohopeka. Among the first to scale the barricade, he was first wounded by a bullet in

> the fleshy part of the right arm which occasioned a considerable loss of blood the second wound a bullet in my left groin which ranged back and Lodged and since my return home was cut out with a knife the third bullet in the right breast which glanced coming out under my Arm my fourth was from the blow of a club which split my breast bone and laid me prostrate with the earth at the same moment an Indian mounted me to take a trophy from my head but was fortunately prevented [by] a fellow soldier bayoneting him in the attack.[66]

The repeated and frequent use of war clubs by insurgent Creeks led Benjamin Hawkins to refer to them by that title: Red Clubs. Whether the hefty object looked more like a club or a stick is of little consequence. They were one and the same.[67]

And the insurgents were not the only ones to employ them, for the Creek establishment behaved as traditional Creek warriors when engaged in action with their US allies. Prior to battle, like their Red Stick opponents, they painted themselves in war colors. James Tait watched as his Creek allies "blacked themselves, their faces, at some burnt lightwood stumps and logs" before they took the field against the Red Sticks.[68] Like the Red Sticks, the Creek Indians who opposed them used war clubs and bows and arrows. Indeed, the Americans saw to it that their Creek allies were poorly supplied with guns, and as a result these Creeks were forced to rely heavily on traditional weapons.[69] So similar in appearance and manner did the various Creek combatants appear that very early in the war, Creeks wishing to distance themselves from the militants were already wearing "something white about their heads."[70] As Tennesseans marched south in late 1813, they were already aware that their allies would "either have white plumes in their hair, or a deers tail." Anticipating the need for such distinguishing marks, Jackson's Cherokee allies requested that the army provide "3 or 400 Deers tails" as they would be hard to procure south of the Tennessee River.[71]

The problem of what to call the insurgents and what to call their Creek opponents puzzled contemporaries. In fact, for much of 1813, Hawkins frequently referred to the "opposition" as "Fanatical Chiefs."[72] Only as the war progressed did he adopt the sobriquet "Red Clubs" or "Red Club Men." Andrew Jackson employed a variety of terms to describe the combatants, usually falling back to the military standards of "friendly" and "hostile" Indians or, for the insurgents, "the enemy." One reference to "Red Sticks" is particularly instructive. In a letter of March 2, 1814, to Thomas Pinckney, Andrew Jackson reported that a Creek woman brought into their camp stated that "she had been taken prisoner by the red sticks and had made her escape." This Creek woman had been a prisoner of those who had taken up the red stick of war. The context would suggest that it was the Creek woman who used the term "Red Sticks," for it was highly unusual for Jackson, who seemed to have employed the term only when quoting Creek reports.[73] Thus, Red Sticks was the logical name the insurgents gave themselves—or were so dubbed by their Creek brethren who faced their wrath and their war clubs. After the war, it was necessary for Creek leaders to distance themselves from the Red Stick faction that brought on the war of 1813. Those who fought as Red Sticks were universally maligned for their role in bringing on the war. But the war club and its associated ritual of painting for war never lost their symbolism or utility for Creek warriors.

In the Creek War of 1836, Thomas McKenney used the same language: "The warriors, without a single exception, painted themselves for war."[74] After removal, the custom of painting for war continued. John Mix Stanley was surprised when leading Creek headman Opotheleyaholo arrived to have his portrait painted "in the manner in which he paints himself when going to war." The painter noted, "It was with difficulty that he was afterwards induced to wash his face, and sit for a portrait which his friends would be able to recognize."[75] Another of Stanley's subjects was Tomathly Micco (Little King), the principal chief of the Upper Creeks after removal. He was "painted in the attitude of holding a red stick, which is invariably carried by him, during the ceremonies of the busk or green-corn dance. It is emblematical of red-stick or late Creek war."[76] Stanley's conclusion that the war club was "emblematical" of the late Creek war is incorrect since Creek warriors carried the red stick as their symbolic weapon long before the war of 1813. But his remarks do point to continuity as well as the legacy of the war, which literally colored the memory and meaning of the atássa.

In time, Red Stick again became an honorable appellation. Today, in the Muscogee Creek Nation, the organization that honors modern Creek combat veterans is known as the Red Stick Society. Muscogee Creek war veterans have served in various branches of the US armed forces in the two world wars, Korea, Vietnam, Kuwait, and Afghanistan. Fittingly, their website features two of the Creek Nation's most noted warriors, William Weatherford and Menawa, both Red Stick veterans of the great civil war that split the Creek Nation in 1813.

Notes

1. Benjamin Hawkins, *The Letters, Journals, and Writings of Benjamin Hawkins,* ed. C. L. Grant, 2 vols. (Savannah, GA: Beehive Press, 1980): 2:647.

2. The term "White Sticks" has been employed in recent years to refer to the opponents of the Red Sticks. That term was not used historically and has no basis in fact.

3. According to McKenney, Tecumseh presented Big Warrior with "a bundle of sticks—gave a piece of wampum and a war-hatchet" during his visit to Tuckabatchee. Thomas L. McKenney and James Hall, *History of the Indian Tribes of North America, with Biographical Sketches and Anecdotes of the Principal Chiefs. Embellished with One Hundred and Twenty Portraits, from the Indian Gallery in the Department of War, at Washington,* 2 vols. (1836–44, Repr. Kent, OH: Volair Ltd., 1978), 1:61–62.

4. Henry Sale Halbert and Timothy Horton Ball, *The Creek War of 1813 and 1814* (Chicago: Donnohue and Henneberry, 1895), 65.

5. Willard B. Walker, "Creek Confederacy before Removal," in *Southeast*, ed. Raymond D. Fogelson, vol. 14 of *Handbook of American Indians,* ed. William C. Sturtevant, 385–86.

6. John Sugden, "Early Pan-Indianism: Tecumseh's Tour of the Indian Country, 1811–1812," *American Indian Quarterly* 10 (Fall 1986): 288–89 (quotation on 289).

7. Ibid. See "Extract from a Journal Written in the Creek Nation of Indians," *National Intelligencer,* September 5, 1818. The journal writer reported that Tecumseh "carried with him a red stick, to which he attached certain mystical properties, and the acceptance of which was considered as the joining of his party." See George Catlin, *Letters and Notes on the Manners, Customs, and Condition of the North American Indians,* 2 vols. (London, 1841), 2:117.

8. James H. Howard and Willie Lena, *Oklahoma Seminoles: Medicines, Magic, and Religion* (Norman: University of Oklahoma press, 1984), 239.

9. Louis Milfort, *Memoirs; or a Quick Glance at My Various Travels and My Sojourn in the Creek Nation,* ed. and trans. Ben C. McCary (Kennesaw, GA: Continental Book Co., 1959), 148.

10. James Adair, *History of the American Indians,* ed. and annotated by Kathryn E. Holland Braund (London: Edward and Charles Dilly, 1775; repr., Tuscaloosa: University of Alabama Press, 2005), 124.

11. George Stiggins, "A Historical narration of the Genealogy traditions and downfall of the Ispocaga or Creek tribe of Indians, written by one of the tribe," 60, Lyman Draper Manuscript Collection, vol. 1, series 5: Georgia, Alabama, and South Carolina Papers, Wisconsin Historical Society, Madison, Wisconsin.

12. For example, in 1772, British agent David Taitt was notified of a meeting of Upper Creek chiefs by the receipt of "fourteen pieces of cane." "David Taitt's Journal to and through the Upper Creek Nation," in *Documents of the American Revolution, 1770–1783,* ed. Kenneth G. Davies, 20 vols. (Dublin, Ireland: Irish University Press, 1972–79), 5:258 (hereafter cited as Davies, *DAR*).

13. Halbert and Ball, *Creek War,* 134.

14. Albert James Pickett, *History of Alabama, and Incidentally of Georgia and Mississippi, from the Earliest Period* (Birmingham, AL: Birmingham Book and Magazine Co., 1962), 580.

15. J. F. H. Claiborne, *Life and Times of Gen. Sam Dale, The Mississippi Partisan* (New York: Harper & Brothers, 1860), 53–54.

16. H. S. Halbert, "The Creek Red Stick," *Alabama Historical Reporter* 2 (May 1884): n.p. No doubt, he based this conclusion on Claiborne's history.

17. Rodney M. Baine, "The Myth of the Creek Pictograph," *Atlanta History* 32 (Summer 1988): 48.

18. Albert S. Gatchet, *A Migration Legend of the Creek Indians, with a Linguistic, Historic and Ethnographic Introduction,* vol. 1, *Brinton's Library of Aboriginal Literature,* no. 4 (Philadelphia: D. G. Brinton, 1884), 128.

19. Stiggins, "A Historical narration," 12. Stiggins's mother's family were Natchez Creeks. It is unclear if he actually spoke Muscogee.

20. Gregory A. Waselkov and Kathryn E. Holland Braund, eds., *William Bartram on the Southeastern Indians* (Lincoln: University of Nebraska Press, 1995), 106, 154. In 1784, Samuel Butler noted "a Lightwood poste 8 feet high with a head to it which appeard to have been in the ground for Upwards of a hundred years" near Shoulderbone Creek. Samuel Edward Butler, "Diary of Samuel Edward Butler, 1784–1786," MS 432, Hargrett Library, University of Georgia, Athens, GA; Adair, *History of the American Indians,* 383–84, and see 195 and 215 for a description of war poles raised by Chickasaw warriors. These were located at the home of the warrior, rather than the town center.

21. John R. Swanton, *Social Organization and Social Usages of the Indians of the Creek Confederacy,* Bureau of American Ethnology Bulletin no. 42 (Washington, DC: Government Printing Office, 1928; repr., New York: Johnson Reprint Co., 1970), 437.

22. Emisteseguo to John Stuart, November 19, 2776, in Kenneth G. Davies, ed., *Documents of the American Revolution, 1770–1783,* 20 vols. (Dublin, Ireland: Irish University Press, 1972–79), 12:250.

23. John Stuart to Lord George Germain, October 26, 1776, Davies, *DAR,* 12:239.

24. Wilbur R. Jacobs, ed., *The Appalachian Indian Frontier: The Edmond Atkin Report and Plan of 1755* (Lincoln: University of Nebraska Press, 1967), 46.

25. Adair, *History,* 321.

26. In *A Sacred Path: The Way of the Muscogee Creeks* (Los Angeles: UCLA American Indian Studies Center, 2001), Jean Chaudhuri and Joyotpaul Chaudhuri label this red and white duality as "red stick" and "white stick." While their discussion of the characteristics of the red and white divisions essentially comport with other sources, they are alone in employing the term "stick" to denote these essential divisions. In historic Creek practice, as Gregory A. Waselkov has observed, "Not only does the phrase 'White Sticks' lack historical legitimacy, it violates the logic of traditional Creek color symbolism. The Creeks of the eighteenth and early nineteenth centuries did frequently oppose red and white to symbolize, roughly speaking, war and peace. But the idea of 'White Stick,' referring either to a war club—an atássa, the emblematic symbol of war—painted white for peace or to a peaceful warrior, makes no sense in Creek cultural context." Gregory A. Waselkov, *A Conquering Spirit: Fort Mims and the Redstick War of 1813–1814* (Tuscaloosa: University of Alabama Press, 2006), 299n40.

27. Lewis Sewall, *The Miscellaneous Poems of Lewis Sewall* (Mobile, AL, 1833), 27.

28. Halbert, "The Creek Red Stick," np.

29. Colin F. Taylor, *Native American Weapons* (Norman: University of Oklahoma Press, 2001), 22.

30. Although it was dried and reduced to power and used as a coloring and dye, its primary use was as an emetic. Virgil J. Vogel, *American Indian Medicine* (Norman: University of Oklahoma Press, 1970), 354.

31. William Bonar, "A Draught of the Creek Nation, made in 1757 by William Bonar," Great Britain National Archives [Public Record Office], London and Kew, C0700/Carolina 21, Kew, England; for a discussion of war club typology, see Theodore Brasser, "War Clubs," *American Indian Tradition* 7 (1961): 77–83.

32. "Caban de Conseille," Département des cartes et des plans, DE DD 2987 (8816) B, Bibliothèque nationale de France, Paris.

33. Wayne Van Horne, "The Warclub: Weapon and Symbol in Southeastern Indian Societies" (PhD diss., University of Georgia, 1993), 65.

34. Ibid., 67 and 61.

35. Stiggins, "A Historical narration," 27.

36. John R. Swanton, *Modern Square Grounds of the Creek Indians,* Smithsonian Miscellaneous Collections, vol. 85, no. 8 (Washington, DC: Smithsonian Institution, 1931), 45–46. See also James H. Howard, *The Southeastern Ceremonial Complex and Its Interpretation,* Memoir of the Missouri Archaeological Society, no. 6 (Stillwater: Oklahoma State University, 1968), 74–78. For descriptions of war symbolism and ritual during the Busk, see John Howard Payne and Ethan Allen Hitchcock, *A Traveler in Indian Territory: The Journal of Ethan Allen Hitchcock,* ed. Grant Foreman (Norman: University of Oklahoma Press, 1996), 133–36.

37. J.N.B. Hewitt, "Notes of the Creek Indians," *Smithsonian Institution Bureau of American Ethnology, Bulletin 123* (1939): 152–53. Personal communication from Jack B. Martin to the author, August 17, 2005, regarding Mary Haas's field notes on Creek term for Red Sticks.

38. Bernard Romans, *A Concise Natural History of East and West Florida,* ed. Kathryn E. Holland Braund (New York, 1775; repr., Tuscaloosa: University of Alabama Press, 1999), 148.

39. Milfort, *Memoirs,* 147.

40. Ibid., 148.

41. Stiggins, "A Historical narration," 35; John Reid and John Henry Eaton, *The Life of Andrew Jackson,* ed. Frank L. Owsley Jr. (Tuscaloosa: University of Alabama Press, 1976), 29.

42. Swanton, *Social Organization,* 406.

43. See also Howard and Lena, *Oklahoma Seminoles,* 119, 145.

44. Dunbar Rowland, ed., *Mississippi Provincial Archives, English Dominion, 1763–1766: Letters and Enclosures to the Secretary of State from Major Robert Farmar and Governor George Johnstone,* vol. 1 (Nashville: Brandon Printing Co., 1911), 524.

45. Waselkov and Braund, *William Bartram on the Southeastern Indians,* 101.

46. John Pope, *A Tour through the Southern and Western Territories of the United States of North-America,* facsimile reproduction of the 1792 edition, Bicentennial Floridiana Facsimile Series (Gainesville: University Presses of Florida, 1979), 56.

47. Stiggins, "A Historical narration," 22.

48. Alfred A. Cave, *Prophets of the Great Spirit: Native American Revitalization Movements in Eastern North America* (Lincoln: University of Nebraska Press, 2006), 68.

49. Samuel Manac, Deposition, August 2, 1813, SPR 26, Alabama Department of Archives and History, Montgomery, AL.

50. Stiggins, "A Historical narration," 35. Stiggins wrote, "The national council is convened." In earlier times, it was the town councils who decided for war. And, obviously, during the Red Stick uprising, this was also the case.

51. Joel W. Martin, *Sacred Revolt: The Muskogees' Struggle for a New World* (Boston: Beacon Press, 1991), 71.

52. Communication from Jack B. Martin, August 17, 2005.

53. Hawkins, *Letters, Journals, and Writings,* 2:645.

54. Ibid.

55. Ibid., 2:647.

56. Ibid., 2:648.

57. Ibid., 2:650.

58. He also notes, "As the power we received was to fight the americans . . . [we] went against a garrison at tennisau and he put the garrison in flames." Josiah Francis and the Old Interpreter et al. to Governor of Pensacola, August 1813, Papeles de Cuba Legajo 221B, 335, microfilm reel 311, P. K. Yonge Library, University of Florida, Gainesville.

59. Pickett, *History,* 533, 536, 537.

60. Stiggins, "A Historical narration," 66.

61. Pickett, *History,* 546, 565.

62. Halbert and Ball, *Creek War,* 234.

63. "State of the War Party in September 1813," John Howard Payne Papers, vol. 10, Newberry Library, Chicago, IL. This copy of Hawkins's report does not list him as the author.

64. Peter A. Brannon, ed., "Journal of James A. Tait for the Year 1813," *Georgia Historical Quarterly* 8 (1924): 235. Tait relates that there were two "kings" killed; and later, a pipe belonging to the "Old Talesee, or tame king," who was reported to be dead, was forwarded to the governor of Georgia. John Floyd to Peter Early, December 12, 1813, Floyd Papers, Georgia Department of Archives and History, Morrow, GA. However, the ninety-five-year-old Tallassee King died as a prisoner at Fort Jackson and was buried there. Joseph Graham to Major General Pinckney, June 14, 1814, Joseph Graham Papers, 1780–1836, North Carolina State Archives, Raleigh, NC.

65. Allen Tooke to Peter Early, with copies of affidavits, Aug. 6, 1814, Document TCC426, Southeastern Native American Documents, 1730–1842, Galileo: Digital Library of Georgia Database, http://metis.galib.uga.edu/ssp/cgi-bin/tei-natamer-idx.pl?sessionid=c9cfda05-4ac8831b95-7227&type=doc&tei2id=TCC426 (accessed Sept. 20, 2003).

66. Jesse Webb, Veteran's Pension file, Invalid File 317, Records of the Veterans Administration, Record Group 15, National Archives and Record Administration, Washington, DC.

67. Information collected by Christian Limbaugh and Alexander Cornlees from the Wolf Warrior, June 14, 1814, Doc. TCC874; and Benjamin Hawkins to Peter Earley, June 15, 1814, Doc. TCC875, both in Southeastern Native American Documents, 1730–1842, Galileo: Digital Library of Georgia Database (ac-

cessed Sept. 20, 2003). For reference to Red clubs, see Hawkins, *Letters, Journals, and Writings,* 2:660, 668, 671, 672, 675, 676, 683, 685, 692.

68. Brannon, "Journal of James A. Tait," 8:235.

69. Thomas S. Woodward, *Woodward's Reminiscences of the Creek or Muscogee Indians,* American Old West Edition (Montgomery, AL: Barrett and Wimbish, 1859; repr., Mobile, AL: Southern University Press, 1965), 89.

70. Governor Mitchell reported that Georgia militia in Jones County had "reported their orders were to kill every Indian they saw who had not something white about their heads." And Creek headmen had informed the Georgians of "the mark by which the prophets' party may be known." Georgia governor David Mitchell did not indicate what that mark was, but we might suppose it was a specially painted war club. Hawkins, *Letters, Journals, and Writings,* 2:660.

71. Andrew Jackson, *The Papers of Andrew Jackson,* ed. Harold D. Moser and et al., 7 vols. (Knoxville: University of Tennessee Press, 1980–2007), 2:434.

72. Hawkins, *Letters, Journals, and Writings,* 2:647.

73. Jackson, *Papers of Andrew Jackson,* 3:36. For example, when reporting the account of one of his Creek spies, he employed the term in a letter to John Coffee. See John Spencer Bassett, *Correspondence of Andrew Jackson,* 7 vols., Carnegie Institute of Washington series, no. 371, Papers of the Department of Historical Resources (Washington, DC: Carnegie Institute of Washington, 1926–35), 1:378–79.

74. McKenney and Hall, *History of the Indian Tribes,* 1:290.

75. John Mix Stanley, *Portraits of North American Indians, with Sketches of Scenery. Painted by J. M. Stanley, Deposited with the Smithsonian Institution* (Washington, DC: Smithsonian Institution, 1852), 9–10.

76. Ibid., 12.

5
Before Horseshoe

Andrew Jackson's Campaigns in the Creek War Prior to Horseshoe Bend

Tom Kanon

An anxious Andrew Jackson, writing hurriedly to his wife from Fort Strother in early March 1814, told her he was "buried in preparations for a movement from this place," a movement he promised would "put a speedy end to the Creek war." "As soon as it is done," he vowed, "I shall without delay return to your arms."[1] Absent from his beloved Rachel for more than five months, Jackson was in the midst of planning an assault on the Creek Nation to hopefully bring an end to a war his fellow Tennesseans thought would never have lasted so long. On March 27, 1814, Jackson's army of Tennessee volunteers and militia, US regular forces, and a contingency of Cherokee Indians conducted a crushing blow on the Creeks at their fortified village on the banks of the Tallapoosa River. Approximately nine hundred Creek warriors perished on that fateful day, making it the most devastating combat loss for Native Americans in North American history.[2]

This chapter traces the activities of the Tennessee army from the time the state declared war on the Creek Nation in September 1813 until the climactic battle at Horseshoe Bend in March 1814. In the six months preceding that battle, Andrew Jackson and his army crisscrossed the hilly landscape of what is now northern Alabama, torching abandoned Indian villages, destroying Indian crops, and killing as many Red Stick Creeks as they could find. In reality, fighting Creek Indians became the least of Jackson's worries. This chapter, therefore, concentrates less on Tennessee's military engagements than it does the extenuating circumstances surrounding Jackson's efforts to bring the Creek Nation to its knees.

An analysis of Jackson's campaigns in the Creek War prior to Horseshoe Bend reveals a litany of stumbling blocks the Tennessee commander had to overcome during his quest to eliminate the Indian "threat" in the old Southwest. An extreme shortage of supplies, an uncompromising and unknown terrain, a disgruntled and undisciplined army whose fervor for war never matched his, political detractors at home, and constant physical pain vexed Jackson throughout most of the Creek War.

In regard to the last-mentioned obstacle, historians should not be too quick in dismissing the fact that Jackson suffered from severe diarrhea and dysentery throughout the war, not to mention a bullet he carried in his left arm from a gunshot received during a fracas in Nashville prior to embarking on the campaign.[3] One can only conjecture how these physical ailments must have affected Jackson's judgment and personality—a personality already known for its irascibility and touchiness. On the other hand, one must admire Andrew Jackson for his ability to perform as ably as he did in the field. No one pushed himself harder than Jackson to defeat his foes—in this case, the warring faction of the Creek Indians.

Jackson's aggressiveness is emblematic of his fellow westerners' attitude toward Indian-settler relations in the Southwest in the early nineteenth century. The animosity between Indians and Anglo-Americans escalated after the Revolutionary War when white settlers began pushing at the boundaries of the Indian nations. Depredations by both sides resulted in a retaliatory state of affairs steeped in violence.

In Tennessee, the desire to obtain navigational rights of exportable rivers to the Gulf of Mexico accentuated the clamor for Indian land. So important was this goal that Governor John Sevier told the state legislature in 1801 it would be "impossible that the state of Tennessee can long exist in any degree of credit and political respectability" without access to Alabama's river systems.[4] An editorial from a Nashville newspaper, written on the eve of the War of 1812, described the Creek territory as "extremely beautiful and finely watered with excellent springs and navigable rivers." Indeed, when Jackson issued his general orders to the Tennessee militia in July 1813—*before* the declaration of war against the Creeks—he offered his troops this incentive for the possible elimination of the Muscogee Nation: "The country to the South is inviting. Let us consolidate it as part of our Union. The soil which now lies waste and uncultivated, may be controverted [*sic*] into rich harvest fields, to supply the wants of millions."[5] Ironically, then, the very elements that made the Muscogees a prosperous nation—an invaluable river system and "inviting" soil—also led to their eventual demise.

Rock-strewn mountains and rugged hills punctuated the terrain traversed by Jackson's army advancing into Creek territory. The Tennesseans, mostly on foot, had to endure the adversity of marching through unfamiliar ground absent of roads or even wide trails. Getting supplies to an army on the move in this setting became a logistical nightmare. Furthermore, inclement weather dampened the spirits of a starving army that often slept on the cold, rain-soaked ground. Devoid of tents for the most part, the Tennessee army of the early Creek campaigns had little in the way of camp equipment, save some blankets and rudimentary utensils. Food shortages, disagreeable marches, and a total lack of any "comforts" no doubt played a major role in troop morale as the war slowly progressed.

Despite these deterrents, Tennesseans pressed on toward the Creek Nation with a determination to stem the tide of what they perceived as an Indian menace to white civilization. Weaned on a legacy of Indian cruelty and barbarity, Tennesseans were not surprised with the increasing reports of isolated Indian depredations occurring on the frontier in the first decade of the nineteenth century. Westerners regarded such incidents as evidence of Indians failing to cope with ongoing attempts by white officials to "civilize" the tribes. After all, so the frontier population believed, marauding Indians were merely being *Indians.*

Yet, nothing prepared the white populace of the Southwest for the sheer dread created by the mass destruction at Fort Mims—a situation made worse by the ensuing panic and wild rumors hatched by inflammatory reports of the slaughter. The news of the calamity quickly spread northward into Tennessee, where forebodings of Indian attacks had already reached a fever pitch the previous year. One Tennessean in Giles County recalled a minor panic in the spring of 1812 when the militia was called out in the neighboring counties in response to an erroneous report that Creek warriors destroyed the town of Huntsville and killed fifty families in Giles County. In nearby Maury County, men were in a state of hysteria and women in tears as they assembled in the town of Columbia for safety only to find the report had been a false alarm.[6] The murder of several settlers near the mouth of the Duck River in May 1812 and the subsequent abduction of a white woman named Martha Crawley led to a state of emergency in West Tennessee after it was assumed a band of Creek warriors was responsible for the act. Reaction to the incident was swift, but frustrating, as the perpetrators safely made their way back to the Creek homeland with their female prisoner in tow. The pressure put on the Creeks by white officials seeking vengeance on the responsible individuals fanned the flames of political discontent within the Creek Nation and in no small way led to the outbreak of a Creek civil war. For Tennesseans, the Martha Crawley incident was a too-familiar reminder of the type of border warfare they thought ended more than a decade earlier. Clearly it was time for *something* to be done about the Creek Indians.[7]

On September 24, 1813, the Tennessee General Assembly passed an act "to repel the invasion of the state of Tennessee by the Creek Indians, and to afford relief to the Citizens of the Mississippi Territory and other purposes." The legislation authorized the governor to organize up to 3,500 men to be paid by an acquired loan of $300,000 (hopefully to be repaid by the federal government).[8] The wording of the act is intriguing in the sense that the resolution implied a defensive, rather than an offensive, action. War was declared to "repel" a Creek incursion; yet, a massive army enlisted for an invasion of the Creek homeland. Thus, as far as Tennessee was concerned, the so-called Creek War officially began.

In fact, the movement against the Creeks had its roots earlier than the legislative reaction to the Mims disaster. Secretary of War John Armstrong, concerned with reports of civil unrest within the Creek Nation, instructed Tennessee governor Willie Blount in July 1813 to call out 1,500 troops from the state for a possible operation against the Creeks. Armstrong indicated the Tennessee contingency would be united with a like number of Georgia troops. A month later, Blount informed Jackson, major general of the West Tennessee Militia, of Armstrong's communication, adding that perhaps 5,000 Tennessee troops might be mustered in order to "repel" any sort of Creek invasion. Jackson agreed with Blount's estimate for a 5,000-man force from Tennessee, hoping to combine it with a brigade from Georgia and the Third US Infantry Regiment, stationed in the Southwest.[9]

Headstrong, volatile, and argumentative, the forty-six-year-old Jackson had a checkered history of scandal and violence acerbated by a vaulting ambition and a steely determination to win at all costs. Despite being bedridden by grievous wounds acquired through a recent "duel" that was more like a barroom brawl, a zealous Jackson grabbed his saber, donned his military garb, and raced to the rendezvous point to embark on a mission in which he aspired to fulfill his quest for martial glory.

Within days of the state legislature's act, Jackson wrote to his military counterpart in East Tennessee, Major General John Cocke, warning "that the whole war party of the Creeks [was] in motion" and advised Cocke that only through "rapidity of movement alone can success be calculated against Indians." Jackson also wanted to know when Cocke would be able to mobilize his division and when supplies from East Tennessee could be expected.[10] Jackson's relationship with Cocke would deteriorate as the war went on chiefly due to the latter's own desire for military fame coupled with the ongoing rivalry between the two sections of the state. In fact, the contention between the generals eventually escalated to court martial proceedings against Cocke for supposed subversive activities designed to hamper Jackson's success on the battlefield.[11]

The inability of the two sections of the Tennessee forces to join as one fighting force during the conflict was indicative of the failure of the overall military strategy involved in the Creek War. The plan, as devised by the commander of the Sixth US Military District, General Thomas Pinckney, revolved around the theory that the volunteers of Tennessee and Georgia would work in tandem with the militia of the Mississippi Territory and elements of the US Regular Army. In reality, the lack of consolidation between these units caused one historian of the war to quip, "About the best that can be said for the cooperation existing among these armies is that they did not fight each other."[12] Historians may debate whether the Creek War would have come to a successful conclusion much sooner than it did if the various US armies had been able to coordinate their efforts in a tighter and timelier fashion. There were still the difficult questions of supplies and transportation, not to mention the fierce and fanatical determination of the Red Sticks.

As in practically every war, enthusiasm to participate in the Creek conflict was highest at the onset. A Nashville newspaper applauded Tennessee's volunteerism with a prediction that the state would easily raise four thousand to five thousand men. When the call came for Tennessee volunteers in late September 1813, so many men in Maury County offered their services to fight that officials had to resort to a lottery to determine which ones had the honor to take the field. Still smarting from the aftermath of Fort Mims, Tennesseans flocked to the mustering grounds intent on inflicting punishment on the Creeks. In Franklin County, one settler volunteered for service, recalling, "My countrymen had been murdered, and I knew that the next thing would be, that the Indians would be scalping the women and children all about there, if we didn't put a stop to it." That settler, David Crockett, signed up for a tour of duty, despite his wife's protests, recalling, "My dander was up, and nothing but war could bring it right again."[13] Crockett's remarks, in addition to revealing the volunteer spirit of Tennesseans in the fall of 1813, are telling in a number of ways. First, he points the finger of blame squarely at "Indians" rather than the Creeks specifically. This lack of distinction between tribal nations and the lumping of all Native Americans as simply "Indians" was commonplace on the American frontier, leading to unfair stereotypes of aborigines diverse in their language, customs, and culture. Second, Crockett insisted that the only way to assuage his "dander" was to go to war—a reflection of the frustration many Americans felt toward the plodding and unsuccessful "civilization" process conducted by the federal government when dealing with western Native Americans.

In any event, Tennesseans seemed ready, willing, and able to fight—at least on the surface. Behind the façade of enthusiasm, however, lay a cold fact: Tennessee volunteers, for the most part, were ill prepared (psychologically and physically) for the discipline of army life and the rigors of a harsh military campaign. "There had been no war among us for so long," admitted Crockett, "that but few, who were not too old to bear arms, knew any thing about the business."[14] To make matters worse, there were often simply no arms to bear. The myth of the pioneer who never went anywhere without his trusty musket or rifle and could shoot a squirrel between the eyes at a range of a hundred yards has masked the reality that many settlers in the early 1800s did not have suitable arms or, if they did, were not very proficient in their use. In many instances during the Creek War, the state either purchased or confiscated weapons from the civilian population to furnish the military, despite the militia law that required a soldier to bring his own rifle or musket as part of his basic equipment.

The dilemma of obtaining and transporting supplies plagued most of Jackson's campaign into Creek territory. Jackson, in a November 1813 letter to Secretary of War Armstrong, claimed the war against the Creeks could have been terminated in a few weeks "had [he] not been compelled by the want of supplies."[15] Samuel Bains, a sergeant in the First Regiment of Tennessee Volunteer Infantry, lamented to his wife that he was "much weakened by want of provision." Writing from Fort Deposit in November 1813, Bains complained that his company had lived on less than half-rations for the past two weeks or more.[16] Jackson's aide, John Reid, wrote in late October 1813: "I speak seriously when I declare, I expect we shall soon have to eat our horses."[17]

The absence of food supplies in the Creek campaign was symptomatic of the quartermaster situation throughout the War of 1812. Although the government established a Quartermaster's Department in March 1812, rations were supplied through a contract system overseen by the secretary of war and not under the jurisdiction of the quartermaster. Jackson once referred to contractors as "the greatest curse to an army." Because of the reliance on private firms and the lack of quality control, even when the quantity of supplies was sufficient, the quality was often subpar.[18]

The supply shortages experienced in the Creek War often equated to bad-tempered troops. Trouble began after the army returned to Fort Strother from the battle at Talladega (fought November 9, 1813) only to find a camp absent of provisions. The men had been on low rations for the past three weeks, and for the three days before their return to Strother they had no food at all. As the rigors of the campaign wore on, desertions became epidemic—forty or fifty at a time deserting at night—according to one recruit.[19]

Disciplining raw, untrained troops was another issue facing Jackson. Discontent surfaced among the troops almost from the beginning of the campaign. Courts-martial proceedings became a common occurrence, with charges ranging from firing a gun within camp, disrespecting an officer, or sleeping on duty to desertion and mutiny. The punishments meted out to those convicted of these crimes included riding the "wooden horse" with ten-pound weights suspended on each leg; hanging by one arm with a sharp pin under each foot to rest on; wearing a shirt inside out with "desertion" marked on the back; and, in extreme instances, the death penalty. Death sentences were routinely commuted by the commanding officer except in mid-March 1814 when Jackson ordered a young soldier named John Woods to be executed for mutiny. The ramifications of this act would haunt Jackson during his quest for political office a decade later.[20]

Mutinous conduct fomented as the result of enlistment disputes between the men and officers of Jackson's army and Old Hickory. While many of the militia felt their enlistment period to be over by December 1813, Jackson insisted it was several months later. The ensuing discontentment came to a head on December 10 (the date the enlistment period was to expire) when Jackson had the volunteers, serving under different enlistment terms, line up outside Fort Strother to disarm the militia accused of mutiny and desertion. Looking into a loaded cannon aimed at them, the militiamen were "persuaded" to remain a few more days until the arrival of reinforcements. Curiously, Jackson never blamed the men themselves for their mutinous conduct, pointing the finger instead at the officers for inciting the men.[21]

In between the frustrations of providing for famished troops and contending with mutinous behavior, Jackson had to fight a fierce contingency of Red Stick warriors. Always outmanned and outgunned, the Creeks waged a valiant but useless struggle. Modern archaeological findings at Creek War battle sites—including musket balls, gun parts, gunflints, arrow points—reveal the Red Sticks utilized a variety of weapons. Guns were the preferred weapon, but obtaining ammunition was always a problem, as well as the repair of disabled muskets and rifles. Warriors would fire their weapons as long as the ammunition lasted and then quickly resort to the bow and arrow. Creek warriors, facing overwhelming firepower from the Americans, augmented by the use of artillery, had an estimated 1,600 deaths during the war.[22]

The Tennessee army participated in five battles prior to engagement at Horseshoe Bend, with Andrew Jackson in personal command at three of the clashes. Mustering the majority of his forces at Fayetteville, Tennessee, in early October 1813, Jackson advanced his troops into the Creek Nation via Huntsville, the last "civilized" outpost in northern Mississippi Territory. General John Coffee's cavalry, acting as an advance unit for Jackson, burned a few abandoned Creek villages along the Black Warrior River; but a frustrated Coffee wrote on October 24 that he was convinced "the Indians will never meet us in action. . . . [T]hey will certainly desert their country before us."[23]

While Coffee was desperately looking for Red Sticks to fight, Jackson marched his army to the southernmost point of the Tennessee River, where he erected Fort Deposit. While waiting for much-needed supplies there, Jackson received reports of a considerable body of Indians in the vicinity of Ten Islands on the Coosa River (in present-day St. Clair County, Alabama). In late October Jackson set out for this area, arriving on November 3, and commenced building a stockade dubbed Fort Strother, which would serve as a base of operations during most of the Creek campaign. Jackson's initial march into Creek territory became a portent of things to come: it proved almost impossible to move the baggage wagons across the hazardous mountains; and food rations became dangerously low during the march.

At the nearby Creek town of Tallushatchee, Coffee finally located some Indians to fight. Jackson ordered Coffee to destroy the town, and on the morning of November 3 Coffee's troops (numbering about nine hundred mounted gunmen) encircled the village. Two companies were detached from this circle to lure the Red Stick warriors into the open. The Creeks fell into the trap and came out to attack the Americans. Before they realized their mistake, the Creeks were shot down in a short period of time as they attempted to retreat back into their village. Coffee's men then systematically went through the village, going from house to house, killing any warriors (as well as some women and children) they uncovered. The Creek dead amounted to about two hundred while Coffee's losses were five killed and forty-one wounded.[24]

David Crockett, one of the participants of the battle, witnessed a Creek woman kill a soldier with a bow and arrow—the first man he ever saw killed that way—and then watched revenging soldiers fire on the woman with "at least twenty balls blown through her." Crockett summed up what happened at Tallushatchee in his now-famous statement: "We shot them like dogs." Crockett recounted another chilling incident. "I recollect seeing a boy who was shot down near the house," Crockett later wrote in his autobiography. "His arm and thigh was broken, and he was so near the burning house that the grease was stewing out of him." Jackson's aide, John Reid, visited the battlefield the next day and wrote in his journal: "Most of the dead bodies I saw were parched up by the burning of the houses over them after they were killed." A shocked Reid came within sight of four or five wounded Indian women and recalled, "But I could not feel in my heart to go up to them." Coffee, elated by his success, wrote his wife on November 4: "Our men are in excellent spirits—we shall very soon finish the work of destruction of those wretches and return home."[25]

The destruction was just beginning. Several days later, while waiting for much-needed supplies and a rendezvous with the East Tennessee troops at Fort Strother, Jackson received a plea from the "friendly" Creek village at

Talladega, which was besieged by Red Sticks. Seizing the opportunity to destroy a large hostile force, Jackson marched his army of two thousand men and encamped about six miles from Talladega on the evening of November 8. The next morning, Jackson encircled the town and the one thousand Red Sticks about to assault it. It was a sound plan, but, in advancing his troops forward for the attack, a large gap formed between the rear of the right wing of the cavalry and a brigade of militia. The Indians discovered the opening and made their escape, but not before the Tennesseans had killed about three hundred of them. US losses amounted to fifteen killed and about eighty-five wounded. Jackson buried his dead in a mass grave and made his way back to Fort Strother, where a skeleton force waited in anticipation of reinforcements from East Tennessee.[26]

In early November 1813 Brigadier General James White attempted to rendezvous his East Tennessee troops with Jackson's army at Fort Strother. He sought help from his commanding general, John Cocke, who had his own idea about "glories in the field." Per Cocke's orders, White's forces (consisting of one thousand men) marched to the Upper Creek town of Little Okfuskee and burned the deserted village. White then proceeded to destroy two more Creek villages emptied by a fleeing population. On the night of November 17 the army came within several miles of a Hillabee village; and, at daylight the next day, White ordered a surprise attack on the surrounded town, killing about sixty warriors and capturing hundreds more. The surprise was total and no American lives were lost. The four hundred Cherokees attached to White's army did most, if not all, of the actual fighting. Unbeknownst to White, the Hillabees had sued for peace and were negotiating with Jackson for terms of surrender when the assault by the East Tennesseans occurred.[27]

Meanwhile, Jackson was literally in a winter of discontent as his "mutinous" troops began to desert him in droves, fully convinced they had served their prescribed terms of enlistment. As the new year of 1814 began, a bitter but determined John Coffee vowed to his wife that he would never leave his post or his friend Jackson. "All those who have left the service will one day see their error," Coffee sternly predicted. Another loyal Jackson aide, Colonel William Carroll, returned to Tennessee to drum up an army so that Jackson would not have to give up the Creek campaign—a retreat some advised as necessary, considering the circumstances. After the exasperating experience of dealing with his own disgruntled troops, Coffee had little confidence in the nine hundred sixty-day recruits Carroll managed to assemble. "They are clamorous and I fear will not do much good," Coffee wrote. They would quickly be put to the test.[28]

The new recruits arrived at Fort Strother in mid-January 1814 and Jackson

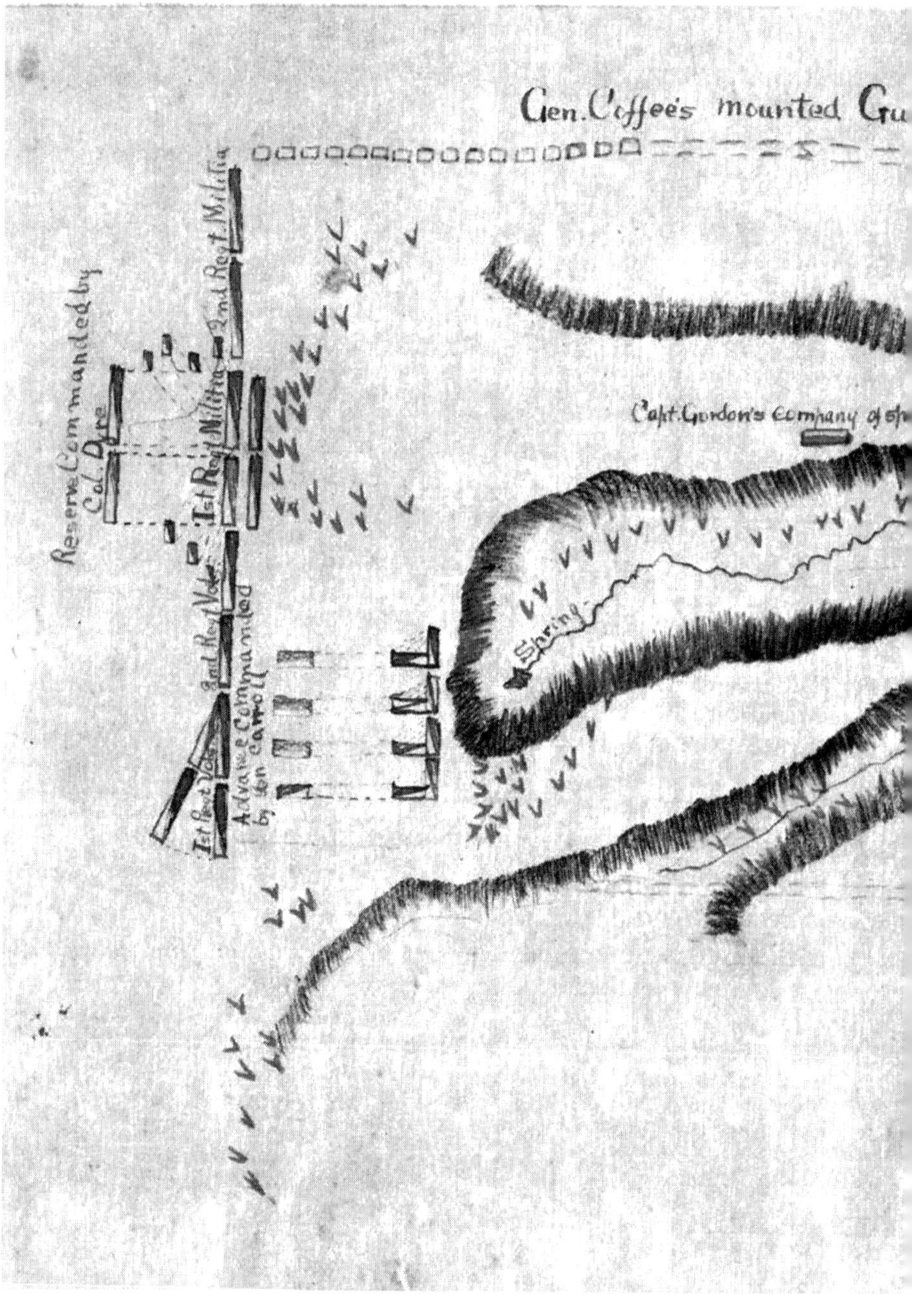

5.1. The Battle of Talladega. Courtesy of the Alabama Department of Archives and History, Montgomery, Alabama.

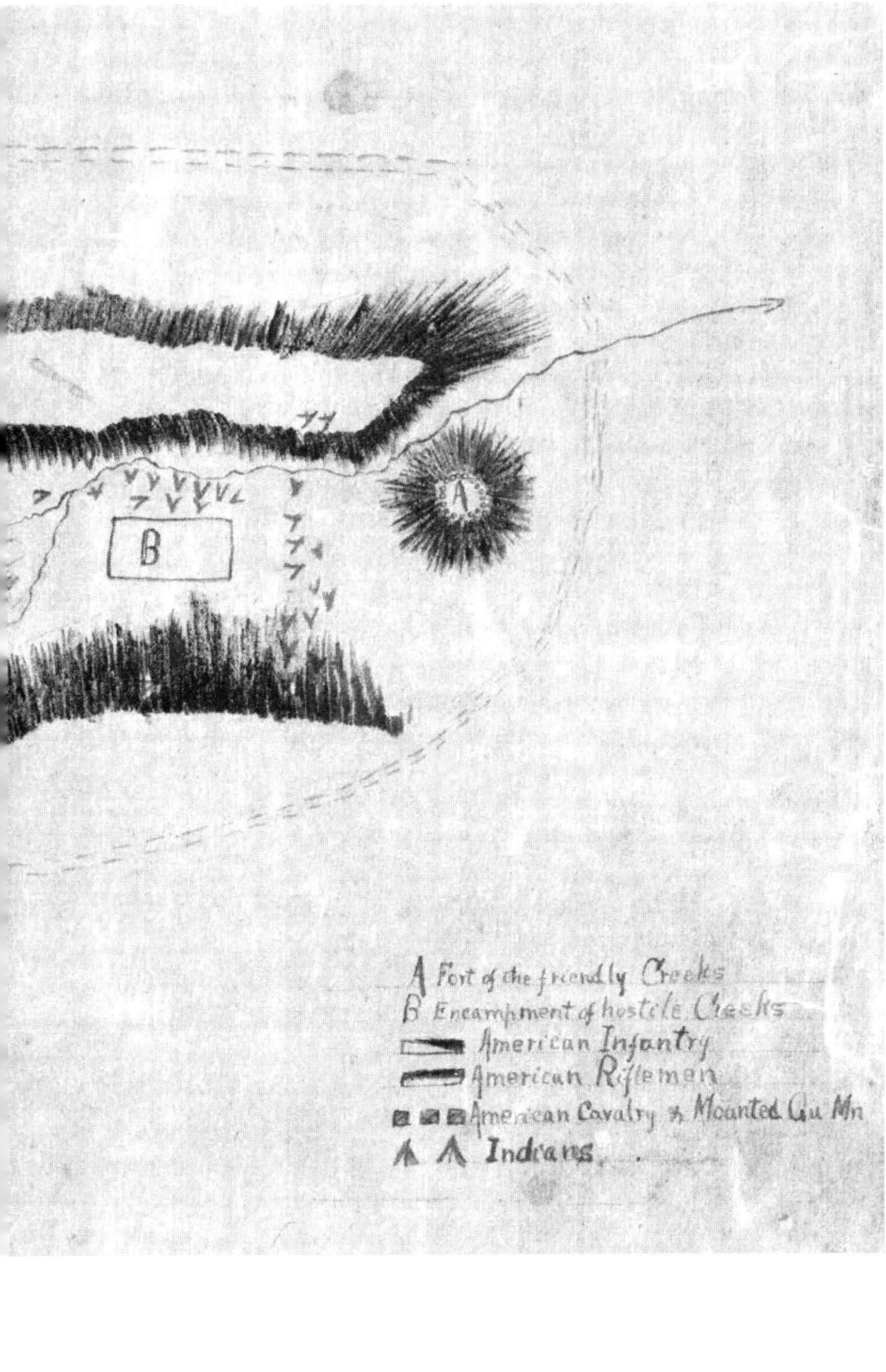
A
B
A Fort of the friendly Creeks
B Encampment of hostile Creeks
American Infantry
American Riflemen
American Cavalry & Mounted Gu Mn
Indians

lost no time in taking the offensive into the heart of Creek country. On January 22 and 24, the Tennesseans clashed with the Creeks at Emuckfau and Enitachopco, respectively. Jackson set up a fortified camp at the mouth of Emuckfau Creek on the Tallapoosa River and, in the dawning hours of January 22, the Red Sticks furiously charged the earthworks. Jackson wrote that his raw troops met the Creeks' "bold & ferocious attack with firmness and undaunted resolution." Jackson's barricade was nearly breached, but the Indian assault failed, and the Red Sticks fled with the Cherokees and friendly Creeks hot in pursuit. Jackson ordered General Coffee to take four hundred men and an additional three hundred friendly Indians to seek out the Red Stick encampment and destroy it, but Coffee returned, indicating the hostile camp was too well fortified (this, of course, was the breastworks at Horseshoe Bend). Shortly after Coffee's return, the Creek Red Sticks conducted a second charge on Jackson's right flank, which turned out to be a feint for a major assault on the left. Again, Jackson quickly responded to the threat, and his men staved off what might have been a disaster. In the process, between forty to fifty Creeks were killed while American losses amounted to four killed and several wounded, including Coffee, who received a slight wound, and Major Alexander Donelson (Coffee's brother-in-law and Jackson's nephew), who died in combat.[29]

Short on men and supplies, Jackson opted not to force the issue by attacking the Indian camp at Horseshoe Bend. Instead, he began a slow march back toward Fort Strother, keenly aware he was being followed by Red Sticks eager to pounce on the straggling army. On the morning of January 24, while crossing Enitachopco Creek, the assault Jackson anticipated occurred, and Jackson actually "felt rejoiced" at the opportunity to destroy the enemy. Smug satisfaction quickly turned to stark horror when Jackson saw his rear guard break ranks, "throwing every thing into confusion." Trying to rally his panic-stricken troops, Jackson nearly broke his left arm, still suffering from former wounds, while drawing his sword. The day was saved, according to Jackson, by his "little Spartan band" of artillerists, commanded by Lieutenant Robert Armstrong, who valiantly dragged their artillery piece in the face of heavy enemy fire to the top of a rise in order to pour out a tremendous volley of fire against the oncoming Red Sticks. Their initial assault broken, the Creeks retreated with the Americans in pursuit for more than two miles. Jackson claimed the Creeks lost upwards of two hundred men in this action and that more would have been killed had it not been for "the cowardly conduct" of two of his officers (Colonels Nicholas Perkins and John Stump). "They ought to be shot," Jackson sneered. Just as in the case of the December "mutiny," Jackson was quick to blame the officers rather than the men, for he believed officers "shew [*sic*] the example."[30]

As his wounded army limped back to Fort Strother, Jackson must have been painfully aware that the past few days had been a close call. The near disasters at Emuckfaw and Enitachopco, coupled with the frustration of dealing with malcontented troops and never-ending supply shortages, must have hardened Jackson's resolve to renew the Creek War under more favorable circumstances. First, a new army would be formed without a hint of enlistment debate. Second, discipline needed to be rigorously enforced and augmented by the addition of trained US regular troops. Finally, a steady source of supplies and a sure means of obtaining them would have to be initiated. Only when these elements were in place would Jackson make his final move against the Creeks. Beginning in February 1814, Jackson set the wheels in motion to accomplish these goals.

Having experienced the exasperation of conveying supplies via wagons only, Jackson opted to incorporate water transportation to ensure a more satisfactory supply system. To support this plan, boats were built and wagon roads were constructed. With the help of Governor Blount's call for 5,000 militia troops, Jackson began to assemble and train a new army. Oddly enough, he now had *too* many troops on hand. He trimmed the number by adopting a rigid discipline policy designed to diminish his oversized army by driving his troops to desertion. Jackson welcomed the addition of the Thirty-Ninth US Infantry, which helped fill the ranks and aided in maintaining a strong discipline. By the time of the Horseshoe Bend campaign, Jackson's army amounted to 3,500 troops, including a contingency of Cherokee and friendly Creeks. All the ingredients were in place for a decisive conquest at Horseshoe Bend.[31]

Despite the sometimes awkward triumphs sustained by the Tennesseans, Jackson's popularity rose within the military community and the nation at large. Victories, no matter what the circumstances, were still victories, and the nation looked to the South for encouragement when there was little else to shout about during the War of 1812. Even as early as mid-November 1813, newspapers in the Mississippi Territory were touting "Jackson and his band of heroes." "No more need our citizens flee to the woods and hiding places for refuge from the fell tomahawk of the savage," proclaimed the *Washington (Mississippi Territory) Republican* in its November 17, 1813 issue.[32]

Not everyone was as enthusiastic as the newspapers of the day. John Sevier, a longtime political and personal foe of Jackson's, was critical of Old Hickory's military prowess. "He neither knows how to march, encamp, fortify or fight an army," Sevier complained, "and the longer he is at it, the less confidence will his men have in him."[33] On another occasion Sevier wrote, "I am sure there have been men and time enough to have destroyed two such nations," regarding the length of time it was taking to rebuke the Creeks.[34]

Ironically, Sevier wrote this statement on March 27, 1814—the day Jackson won his brutal victory at Horseshoe Bend.

The initial campaign against the Creeks in late 1813 and early 1814 taught Jackson lessons he would retain throughout the War of 1812. Numerical superiority in men and arms was only half the equation in the formula for defeating the enemy. A reliable system of obtaining adequate supplies—coupled with a disciplined army whose fighting spirit was not hampered by enlistment squabbles—was an essential factor on the field of combat. The experience of leading mixed forces of militia, volunteers, regular army, and Indians served Jackson well by the time he got to New Orleans in late 1814, where he successfully commanded a similar polyglot army.

It is difficult to assess Andrew Jackson's incentives for fighting the Creek War. That Jackson was a glory-seeker cannot be denied, but his motivations were more complex than that. He often drove his men as hard as he fought Indians. He distrusted most Indians, hated the British and Spanish, and had the inclination to completely destroy all opposition. The scandals and duels in which he participated may have been a reflection of the violent frontier that shaped his character.[35] Certainly, the long tradition of border warfare between Anglo-Americans and Indians played a crucial role in the way both sides reacted to one another. For many Tennesseans the Creek War was an overdue chastening of Indians based on years of ferocious depredations supposedly instigated by the British or Spanish on innocent settlers. And, from a practical point of view, a war against the Creeks offered an opportunity to acquire the much-coveted lands held by the Indians. For the Muscogee Nation, the Creek War represented the final breakdown of their traditional social structure and initiated the process of eventual removal from their cherished homelands.

Notes

1. Avery O. Craven, ed., "Letters of Andrew Jackson," *Huntington Library Bulletin* No. 3 (February 1933): 116.

2. For a detailed account of this battle, see Thomas Kanon, "'A Slow, Laborious Slaughter': The Battle of Horseshoe Bend," *Tennessee Historical Quarterly* 58 (Spring 1999): 2–15. It should be noted that Jackson's army at Horseshoe Bend included approximately one hundred "friendly" Creek warriors.

3. For more on Jackson's ailments during the war, see Ludwig M. Deppisch, "Andrew Jackson and American Medical Practice: Old Hickory and His Physicians," *Tennessee Historical Quarterly* 62 (Summer 2003): 131–51. The bullet in Jackson's left arm remained there until 1832, when it was surgically removed.

4. Robert H. White, ed., *Messages of the Governors of Tennessee,* vol. 1, *1796–1821* (Nashville: Tennessee Historical Commission, 1952), 98–99.

5. *Nashville Democratic Clarion and Tennessee Gazette,* June 10, 1812, and July 27, 1813.

6. Memoirs of James Norman Smith, 1789–1860, 4 vols., University of Texas Library, Austin, 2:3–8.

7. For an analysis of the impact of the Martha Crawley incident, see Tom Kanon, "The Kidnapping of Martha Crawley and Settler-Indian Relations Prior to the War of 1812," *Tennessee Historical Quarterly* 64 (Spring 2005): 3–23. What was once designated as "West Tennessee" is now referred to as "Middle Tennessee," the western geographical part of the state then being considered Indian territory.

8. *Acts Passed at the First Session of the Tenth General Assembly of the State of Tennessee* (Nashville: T. G. Bradford, 1813), 3–4. Militia laws required that, with some exceptions, all free white males between the ages of eighteen and forty-five had to belong to the state militia. The Tennessee General Assembly's act of September 1813 called for volunteers based on precedents set by previous volunteer acts of the federal government authorizing the president to call upon the states for volunteers in a national emergency. In this case, however, Tennessee called out its troops without the sanction of the federal government. Money-conscious state officials breathed a sigh of relief when President James Madison approved the measure later that year.

9. Armstrong to Blount, July 13, 1813; and Blount to Jackson, August 14, 1813, both in John Spencer Bassett, ed., *Correspondence of Andrew Jackson,* 6 vols. (Washington, DC: Carnegie Institution of Washington, 1926–1935), 1:315–17; Jackson to Blount, July 31, 1813, in *The Papers of Andrew Jackson,* vol. 2: *1804–1813,* ed. Harold D. Moser and Sharon Macpherson (Knoxville: University of Tennessee Press, 1984), 416–17. Secretary of War Armstrong had, in fact, already suggested 1,500 troops from Tennessee combined with 1,500 from Georgia and the Third US Infantry.

10. Jackson to Cocke, September 28, 1813, quoted in *Library of Congress Acquisitions: Manuscript Division* (Washington, DC: Library of Congress, 1991), 7–8.

11. For more on the feud between Jackson and Cocke, as well as the rivalry between East and West Tennessee, see my article, "'Glories in the Field': John Cocke vs. Andrew Jackson during the War of 1812," *Journal of East Tennessee History* 71 (1999): 47–65.

12. Arthur H. Hall, "The Red Stick War: Creek Indian Affairs during the War of 1812," *Chronicles of Oklahoma* 12 (September 1934): 282.

13. Memoirs of James Norman Smith, 2:15–16; David Crockett, *A Narrative of the Life of David Crockett, of the State of Tennessee* (Philadelphia: E. L. Carey and A. Hart, 1834), 72–73. For a review of Tennessee's martial spirit prior to the War of 1812, see William A. Walker Jr., "Martial Sons: Tennessee Enthusiasm for the War of 1812," *Tennessee Historical Quarterly* 20 (March 1961): 20–37.

14. Crockett, *Narrative of the Life of David Crockett,* 71.

15. Jackson to Armstrong, November 20, 1813, in Bassett, *Correspondence of Andrew Jackson,* 1:356. Also see Jackson to Willie Blount, December 26, 1813, ibid., 409–11; and Jackson to Armstrong, December 30, 1813, ibid., 424–25.

16. "Samuel Bains Letter," *Alabama Historical Quarterly* 19 (Fall/Winter 1957): 405.

17. John Reid to William B. Lewis, October 24, 1813, Tennessee Historical Society Miscellaneous Files, 1688–1951, Tennessee Historical Society, Nashville, Box 9, Folder L-48 ½.

18. For more on the Quartermaster Corps in the War of 1812, see Erna Risch, *Quartermaster Support of the Army: A History of the Corps, 1775–1939* (Washington, DC: Center of Military History—United States Army, 1989), chapter 5. Jackson quote is taken from a letter to T. A. Smith, October 4, 1815, Andrew Jackson Papers, 3rd Series, Library of Congress, Washington, DC.

19. *The Self Vindication of Colonel William Martin, Against Certain Charges and Aspersions Made Against Him by Gen. Andrew Jackson and Others, in Relation to Sundry Transactions in the Campaign Against the Creek Indians. In the Year 1813* (Nashville: John S. Simpson, 1829), 27; "Samuel Bains Letter," 406.

20. "Proceedings of Courts-Martial in the Creek War," *American Historical Magazine* 6 (July 1901): 251–59. For the execution of John Woods, see Robert V. Remini, *Andrew Jackson and the Course of the American Empire* (New York: Harper & Row, 1977), 211–12. At the time, the Woods execution did not carry the weight that it did later on; in fact, newspapers such as the *Nashville Clarion* barely remarked on it. See the March 22, 1814, issue, for instance.

21. *Self Vindication of Colonel William Martin,* 16–19. The genesis of the dispute stemmed from the February 6, 1812, act of the federal government that required one year's service of the militia unless discharged sooner by the president or secretary of war. Tennesseans who enlisted in December 1812, part of the ill-fated Natchez Expedition, were affected by this act. Ending their service in April 1813, Jackson insisted the men were "dismissed," not "discharged," and they were still eligible for four or five months more service.

22. Gregory A. Waselkov and Brian M. Wood, "The Creek War of 1813–1814: Effects of Creek Society and Settlement Pattern," *Journal of Alabama Archaeology* 32 (June 1986): 16. Creek casualty figures are taken from Russell Thornton, *American Indian Holocaust and Survival: A Population History since 1492* (Norman: University of Oklahoma Press, 1987), 104. These figures, by the way, do not specify if women and children are included. Furthermore, I believe Thorton's estimate to be a very conservative one.

23. John Coffee to Mary Coffee, October 24, 1813, in John H. DeWitt, ed., "Letters of General John Coffee to His Wife, 1813–1815," *Tennessee Historical Magazine* 2 (December 1916): 275–76. Coffee (1772–1833) was a land speculator

and close friend of Jackson's who fought in all of the campaigns in the Creek War and the War of 1812. He was married to Mary Donelson, a relative of Rachel Jackson.

24. Frank Lawrence Owsley Jr., *Struggle for the Gulf Borderlands: The Creek War and the Battle of New Orleans, 1812–1815* (Gainesville: University Presses of Florida, 1981), 64–65.

25. Crockett, *Narrative of the Life of David Crockett,* 88–89; Journal of John Reid, Tennessee State Library and Archives, Nashville (hereafter cited as TSLA); John Coffee to Mary Coffee, November 4, 1813, in "Letters of General John Coffee," ed. DeWitt, 276–77.

26. Jackson to Willie Blount, November 15, 1813, in *Correspondence of Andrew Jackson,* ed. Bassett, 1:348–50.

27. James White to John Cocke, November 24, 1813, reprinted in *Nashville Whig* (December 21, 1813). Jackson sent a message to General Cocke about the peace agreement with the Hillabees on November 18—the very day Cocke's army attacked the village. Had the two armies of East and West Tennessee been in closer contact, Cocke would have known of the Hillabees' offer of peace sooner. As it was, the Hillabees felt betrayed and thereafter determined to fight to the death. See Owsley, *Struggle for the Gulf Borderlands,* 67.

28. John Coffee to Mary Coffee, January 8, 1814, in "Letters of General John Coffee," ed. DeWitt, 280.

29. Andrew Jackson to Rachel Jackson, January 28, 1814, in *The Papers of Andrew Jackson,* vol. 3: *1814–1815,* ed. Harold D. Moser, David R. Hoth, Sharon Macpherson, and John H. Reinbold (Knoxville: University of Tennessee Press, 1991), 17–19.

30. Ibid., 19–21.

31. Owsley, *Struggle for the Gulf Borderlands,* 76–79.

32. Cited in *Biographical and Historical Memoirs of Mississippi: Embracing an Authentic and Comprehensive Account of the Chief Events in the History of the State and a Record of the Lives of Many of the Most Worthy and Illustrious Families and Individuals,* 2 vols. (Chicago: Goodspeed Publishing Co., 1891), 1:136.

33. John Sevier to George Washington Sevier, February 20, 1814, John Sevier Papers, Calvin M. McClung Historical Collection, Knoxville, TN.

34. John Sevier to Walter King, March 27, 1814, John Sevier Papers, 1752–1838, Box 1, Folder 5, TSLA.

35. For a brief analysis of the complexity of Jackson's character, see David S. Heidler and Jeanne T. Heidler, *Old Hickory's War: Andrew Jackson and the Quest for Empire* (Mechanicsburg, PA: Stackpole Books, 1996), 16–19.

6
Cherokees in the Creek War

A Band of Brothers

Susan M. Abram

In July 1813, civil war erupted among the Creeks, southern neighbors of the Cherokees. A disaffected faction labeled as the Red Sticks opposed the increasing US influence in the Creek National Council and its usurpation of clan authority. Although the Cherokees had often considered the Creeks as enemies, many had fought together as allies during the Chickamauga War against white intrusion into eastern Tennessee during the revolutionary era. And both nations could claim members of mixed Cherokee-Creek descent, especially in the towns along their common boundary. Thus, there was much to bind the tribes together. But Cherokee leaders feared that the Creek hostilities might threaten their own citizens who lived near the Creek border. Some Creek families sought and received refuge in nearby Cherokee towns, but this act of kindness left Cherokees feeling even more vulnerable to Red Stick attacks.[1] Due to the persuasive encouragement of the older, seasoned warriors in their thirties and forties, the elder Cherokee leaders finally opted to join the National Creeks, Chickasaws, Choctaws, and the United States to put down the Red Stick Creek rebellion.[2]

In late September 1813, the US government officially requested Cherokee assistance in the war against the Creeks through Indian agent Return J. Meigs. Forty-six-year-old Charles Hicks, who had previously served as Cherokee interpreter to Meigs, relayed the message to the Cherokee Council. Prominent headman John Walker, whose son had married the daughter of Meigs, replied for the Cherokee Council that the Cherokees might supply five hundred to seven hundred men. Meigs, serving also as an agent for the War Department, commissioned Walker as a first major on October 7, 1813. Cherokees began to leave their homes to muster into the service of the United States under Andrew Jackson, commander of the volunteer Tennessee troops.[3]

Cherokee warriors mustered into service for a period of three months, beginning on October 7, 1813. Each company included a first and second lieutenant, an ensign, a first, second, third, and fourth sergeant, and a first, second, third, and fourth corporal. To avoid any misidentification with the enemy, Jackson ordered, "Our freinds [*sic*] shall wear white plumes in their hair, or Deer's tails."[4]

Meigs, insisting that a white officer lead the Cherokees, appointed thirty-nine-year-old Gideon Morgan, Walker's white son-in-law, to become the general in charge of the Cherokee regiment of approximately six hundred men, divided into seven companies. Jackson insisted that Principal Chief Path Killer receive a commission as colonel even though his age kept him from field duty. Other prominent Cherokee headmen, such as Richard Brown, likewise received the rank of colonel, while John Lowry became a lieutenant colonel.[5]

Even though Meigs was confident that the Cherokees were trustworthy allies, he feared repercussions from neighboring whites over this decision. Many Americans at this time had misgivings about the value or loyalty of Indian allies. Yet Meigs painstakingly determined that "the Cherokees would be of great value" and lobbied and received equal pay for comparable rank for enlisted Cherokees.[6]

Unbeknownst to the Cherokees, Meigs believed that this gesture let them "feel themselves under control," though in reality he felt that the government must "keep them dependent." He surmised, therefore, that this act would "flatter their pride to be considered in some degree on a footing with our troops." Though he supported their service, Meigs felt that the Cherokees owed their current welfare and even their very existence to the United States, it having taken "them by the hand & made them human beings."[7] Like Meigs, many Jeffersonian Republicans believed that Native Americans depended upon the federal Indian policy's civilization plan to "save" the Indians from themselves.

The Cherokees never heard these negative sentiments or questions of their loyalty in any official capacity. As a large group of Cherokees mustered into service at the Cherokee Agency on October 29, 1813, Meigs addressed the gathering, saying, "We are a band of Brothers in this war acting in a common cause."[8] Of course, the Cherokees took this statement to mean that they would be on equal footing with the rest of the American troops.

By early October 1813, in anticipation of moving against the Red Sticks, General James White, part of General John Cocke's eastern Tennessee army, erected Fort Armstrong, or "Camp Coocey," on the Coosa River above Turkey Town and near the present Alabama-Georgia border.[9] This fort also served as a base for building boats for the transportation of supplies down the Coosa into Creek territory.[10] Jackson had contractors constantly looking for provisions for the troops, especially after gleaning what he could from the area's Cherokees. Wagons transported supplies gathered at Camp Ross, today's Chattanooga, to Fort Armstrong. The fort, near the junction of the Coosa and Chattooga Rivers, was named for then-secretary of war John Armstrong. Jackson hoped that this military presence would discourage Red Stick incursions against Cherokee towns and provide some security to Cherokee families whose traditional defenders were leaving to become part of his army. At various times, Cherokees garrisoned the fort along with some of White's men.[11]

By early October, preliminary intelligence gathering indicated that a considerable force of Red Sticks had gathered near Ten Islands on the Coosa River while two other forces were also assembling. There were reports that the enemy had erected "forts made of brush with earth thrown over them" but suffered from a paucity of provisions, having destroyed livestock throughout the Creek Nation.[12] Reports of gathering Red Sticks were soon confirmed when Walker received an urgent message from Path Killer asking him to bring warriors to the aid of Turkey Town, which supposedly was the next military target of the Red Sticks. Two hundred Cherokee men, along with some national or allied Creeks, arrived after a forced march, but an attack never came.[13]

The Cherokees remained in a state of alert, however, fearing a Red Stick attack at any time. Scouts indicated that they had found signs of twenty-eight Red Stick campfires not far from Turkey Town. Jackson attempted to assuage their anxiety by boldly stating, "The hostile Creeks will never attack you before they have a brush with me; & that brush I think will put them out of the humors of fighting again for a considerable time."[14]

Beginning in October, Path Killer and Jackson sent groups of scouts or spies to reconnoiter the enemy's positions.[15] Even before receiving his commission as a colonel, Richard Brown, who lived about twenty-five miles from Ditto's Landing on the Tennessee River, and around twenty of his men served as "pilots and spies." Jackson believed "that much dependence can be placed on this man and his party."[16] Colonel Coffee also sent Major John H. Gibson and David Crockett to lead a scouting party. The group separated with orders to meet at a rendezvous point. Crockett's party arranged for the Cherokee Jack Thompson to guide them further. In the tradition of Cherokee war scouts, Thompson was to "holler like an owl" when he came near their camp. After the other party did not show, Crockett made his way to the house of a man named Radcliff, a white man who was married to a Creek woman. Radcliff informed him of "painted warriors" crossing the Coosa River and heading toward Fort Strother, which Jackson had established on the Coosa River at Ten Islands to serve as a base of operations and supply depot.[17] Coffee doubled the guard after the major, who had just returned, confirmed Crockett's report.

Coffee and approximately seven hundred Tennessee cavalrymen from the Second Regiment of Volunteer Mounted Riflemen, along with some Cherokee warriors, searched for hostile towns down the Black Warrior River for ten days in early October 1813. It was from this area that a Mrs. Crawley, a captive taken at the Duck River massacre, had escaped.[18] At three towns, Coffee confiscated three hundred bushels of direly needed corn before setting the abandoned structures ablaze, except for some at the confluence of the Sipsey and Mulberry Forks. Late in the month, Colonel Robert Dyer with two hundred Tennessee Volunteer Mounted Gunmen attacked Littafuchee on Canoe Creek, taking twenty-nine prisoners after destroying the town.[19]

By the beginning of November, the allied Creek chief William McIntosh arrived at the Cherokee town of Hightower with the news that the Red Sticks were preparing for an assault. About twenty Cherokees under Major John Walker had assembled,[20] and, as Jackson's army reached Turkey Town, these Cherokee warriors joined them. Jackson had captured two Creeks who told him of the Red Sticks gathering at Tallushatchee, some twenty-five miles south of Turkey Town. Jackson decided it was time to make a preemptive strike.

On the morning of November 3, Jackson dispatched Coffee, now a brigadier general, and his 900 men to encircle the hostile party, and the subsequent fierce engagement ended in the defeat of the Red Sticks. Cherokee Colonel Richard Brown and seventeen of his men participated "with great bravery in the action."[21] The troops razed the town's cabins, burning alive those who had sought refuge inside. All total, the Red Sticks lost 186 warriors, as well as 84 taken prisoner.[22]

The vast number of the Cherokee regiment under Morgan arrived too late to participate in the fighting. They did, however, gather twenty wounded Red Sticks and took them to Turkey Town. Jackson informed Lowry that the government might demand their return as well as the horses and saddles the warriors had confiscated after the battle. The next day soldiers swept the area looking for any food to add to their scanty provisions. Apparently, some found and ravenously ate potatoes that had actually baked in the very fires that had consumed the trapped Red Sticks.[23] Walker reported that he and his fellow warriors did participate in the destruction of the Red Sticks, recalling that their "situation looked dismal to see, Women & Children slaughtered with their fathers."[24] The troops left the bodies of their dead enemies to the dogs.

From Fort Strother at Ten Islands, the group next moved toward the besieged Lashley's Fort. There 160 National Creek families from the town of Talladega, about thirty miles further to the south, had sought refuge and sent requests for assistance to Jackson. On November 9, Jackson's troop of 1,200 infantry and 800 cavalrymen attempted with some success to encircle the Red Sticks and killed approximately 290 of the enemy. The need to care for the wounded, compounded by a shortage of rations and an absence of forage for the horses, forced the Americans and their allies to retreat.[25]

Though the Cherokees were part of Jackson's larger army, it remained common for them to act individually or in small groups without specific orders. As in earlier times, if no chance to achieve martial success presented itself, the Cherokee warriors made their own opportunities. Captain Jacob Hartsell, assigned to the Second Regiment stationed at Fort Armstrong, recorded in his journal that on November 15, "Cherokees brought in Six prisoners . . . from the Seeder [Cedar] townes," located on a small tributary of the Coosa River in present-day Talladega County, Alabama. Four days later, Colonel Richard Brown met with Jackson to discuss these prisoners and relayed that Generals White and Cocke had told him to dispense of them as he saw fit. Brown informed Jackson that his men had "shot and Tomahocked in a crewel maner [*sic*]" two captives before scalping and killing them. In fact, one of the enemy warriors suffered through three scalpings "cause the[y] said he kil[l]ed three white men in his time."[26] Though some prisoners escaped, the Cherokees adamantly insisted on claiming the remaining three.

Due to the heavy losses at Tallushatchee and Talladega, the Red Sticks from the Creek Hillabee towns sued Jackson for peace, and he accepted. Tragically, at least four Cherokee companies, acting on orders from Cocke and White, were not aware of the Hillabee surrender. These warriors, along with some of General White's troops, marched from Fort Armstrong on November 12 and engaged the surprised Hillabees on November 18. Cherokees killed over 60 warriors and took 250 women and children captive "without the loss of [Cherokee] Blood" and arrived back from the expedition on November 22.[27]

In a letter to Meigs, Colonel Morgan expressed pride in his Cherokee charges and he related that he felt their action at Hillabee had proven their worth as soldiers as well as their attachment to their US allies. Morgan, who proudly boasted that the Cherokees acted with the utmost "cool, deliberate bravery," especially touted forty-seven-year-old Lieutenant Colonel John Lowry's bravery when "six of the enemy fell beneath his sword."[28] He gave additional accolades to Captain David McNair and his scouts and concluded, "In fact, should I attempt to do justice to each person, it would be the shortest method to furnish the muster roll of the Regiment."[29] Of course, this battle soon became known as a massacre since it was virtually one-sided. Even Jackson later observed, "Mr. Ross and a Cherokee who were there, tell me there was only one gun fired by the enemy."[30] This adds credence to the fact that future acts of surrender did not seem an option for other Red Sticks, who most likely believed that Jackson had deliberately ordered the massacre of the Hillabee warriors after their capitulation.

Three Cherokee officers, Major John Walker, Captain Alexander Saunders, and Lieutenant Ridge missed the action due to their orders to mount an elevation to prevent any enemy retreat. Not to be left out of the action, they were led by Walker, with a few others, to a nearby town six miles away, where they killed three Red Sticks and captured forty women and children. When the warriors "dispersed in pursuit of plunder," eighteen armed Red Sticks confronted Walker, who on his own convinced them to surrender.[31]

On November 21, Cherokees captured a Red Stick scout who the American commander at Fort Armstrong allowed "to punish In the[i]r one [own, *sic*] way." The Cherokee warriors cut off the clubbed extension of his hair and then struck his head with their tomahawks. They next scalped him, stripped him, placed a rope around his neck, and then stabbed him to death. Before the enemy warrior died, the Cherokee warriors paraded him before the "Shee Coocys [Coosa women] and Children" until "all the women cryed and made Everey kind of noise."[32] The warriors soon escorted the captive women and children to their new families in Cherokee territory, who would determine whether to adopt or enslave them.

In addition to Jackson's Tennessee and Cherokee troops, soldiers from Georgia and Mississippi Territory were also at work against the Red Sticks through the end of 1813. Georgia troops led by General John Floyd successfully attacked Autossee on November 29 but then returned to Georgia. On December 16 and 17, 1813, Floyd's troops destroyed the hastily abandoned Red Stick towns of Nuyaka and Mad Dog's Village near a great bend of the Tallapoosa River. Reconnaissance revealed that a large body of the enemy occupied the opposite side of the river, but the troops retreated because recent downpours had so swollen the river and for want of provisions. Other towns they "contemplated burning" but did not included Tuckabatchee, Tallassee, and Emuckfau.[33] Floyd, along with Creek forces under William McIntosh, again took the field in January 1814, but the Red Sticks forced his retreat at the Battle of Calebee. Troops from the Mississippi Territory under General Ferdinand Claiborne, aided by 150 Choctaws, hit the heart of the Red Stick movement by successfully destroying Holy Ground, or Eccanachaca, on December 23, 1813. Once again short troop enlistments and supply shortages forced the Americans to retreat from Creek country.[34]

Determinedly, Jackson sought to gather supplies and men for a late winter campaign. Beginning in October at Lookout Mountain Town in present-day northwest Georgia, Lieutenant Colonel Lowry's men had suffered from the bitterness of a cold fall and asked Meigs to procure blankets and coats. Meigs was forced to draw $3,362 from public funds to arm the Cherokees and provide some winter clothing "to enable them to take the field to co-operate with the American troops against the Common enemy."[35] Yet Jackson stubbornly strained Cherokee resources by insisting on commandeering all available meat, corn, and meal from them in order to provision his army. That left little to supply Cherokee family needs throughout the rest of the winter.

Many Cherokee men had answered the call to arms but owned no guns. Some of the Cherokee military leaders now requested that Meigs provide ammunition or authorize the newly promoted Major Ridge to supply some at the government's expense. On January 14, 1814, Jackson authorized Adjutant General Robert Searcey to provide forty-five Cherokee warriors with powder and lead. In addition, they complained that they needed blankets and clothing, yet the cost for supplying these items was deducted from the tribal annuity.[36] They also sought that the government furnish a gunsmith so that they could better "stand with our white brothers," but Meigs denied their request.[37]

The families of the Cherokee warriors suffered that winter too. Meigs noted that many were "on the point of starving for the want of corn . . . and [were] intirely [*sic*] destitute of Bread" as a "consequence of the Troops having consumed all their corn when on their way to fort Strother." At least forty families had to relocate. One of the Cherokee Ross brothers begged for government aid, lamenting, "Humanity speaks loudly in favour of those distressed Cherokees who has resided on the road or within reach of the Army." Others applied to Meigs for the same reason, reminding him, "All our young Warriers [*sic*] is Starting of[f] to War with Generall Jackson Armey [*sic*] and our Women and Children will be in Great Suffering." Cocke confirmed this, noting, "Cattle are scarce among the Cherokees," and he would "despair of getting a considerable number from them."[38]

The warriors had become so "destitute of warm cloathing" that Morgan sought two hundred blankets for his men before they left for the March expeditions into Red Stick territory.[39] Jackson, however, had other ideas and asked Morgan to save the government the expense of provisioning the Cherokees, hoping they could instead get their supplies and thirty days of rations from Lewis Ross in Chattanooga.[40] By early March, Jackson would lack meat rations, and the possibility of securing any more from the Cherokees was out of the question, having thoroughly exhausted their resources.

Jackson constantly experienced difficulty in maintaining troops and sufficient provisions, factors that plagued the Americans throughout the war. Short militia enlistments and incompetent contractors resulted in the hit-and-run tactics of the Americans almost from start to finish. Faced with this paucity of provisions, Jackson sent Coffee and his cavalry away to Huntsville to find forage for their horses.

Insisting that they had fulfilled their terms of enlistment and facing the cold and hunger of remaining in the field, the vast majority of East Tennessee militiamen left Jackson. They proceeded to destroy Cherokee property and terrorize Cherokee families along their way home. Soldiers stole horses, clothing, and personal items, burned fences, and slaughtered livestock, often while threatening their victims at gun or knifepoint.[41] The white troops apparently were not the only threat to the Cherokee home front. Jackson informed Lowry to treat those Creeks "who have lately come into your nation, & whom you suspect to be unfriendly & acting as spies," with all dispatch, even putting them to death if deemed necessary.[42]

Throughout late winter, many Cherokee warriors nonetheless remained active with Fort Armstrong as their base of operations. Though Jackson furloughed many Cherokees home, most chose to stay close in the Wills Valley area. One Cherokee detachment worked with Lieutenant Colonel William Snodgrass's Second Regiment East Tennessee Volunteer Militia from mid-January into February at Fort Armstrong to secure supply and communication lines.[43]

Fort Armstrong was no more than a hastily constructed "small fort built of poles which a strong man could pull up." Nevertheless, the Cherokees had established a square ground with four structures that opened in the front where the "chiefs set agreeable to Rank, [and] in these houses are deposted [*sic*] their relics, & scalps."[44] Nearby, they built a functional, traditional council house. Also during this time, approximately fifteen men remained on guard near Path Killer's residence in Turkey Town. Some of these warriors/soldiers had fought at the recent Battles of Tallushatchee and Nuyaka and so were seasoned veterans.[45]

Anticipating an active campaign, the Cherokees now sent for the warriors from the Valley Towns.[46] Cherokees began to set out for Fort Armstrong to await Morgan's arrival. While Jackson prepared to mount a new offensive, Lowry and a few of his men returned from a twenty-day scouting mission and reported that they had killed two Red Stick spies and "took one Negro" spy sent from the Eufaula towns.[47] Morgan attempted to hold the Cherokees under Lowry in check until the next campaign. Meigs hoped that the five hundred expected Cherokee troops could organize into regular corps under Richard Brown, John Lowry, and John Walker. He felt that to commission them as officers would solidify the military alliance. He cautioned, however, that they would still need to be "guided by our Councils."[48]

Lowry, James Brown, and Ridge agreed to meet Morgan at Fort Armstrong on January 20, 1814. From there, Morgan informed Meigs that several Cherokees were "determined to an excurtion [*sic*] into the Creek nation"; and though he beseeched them to wait, "nothing Could Remove their Stubborn determination."[49] One group left Fort Strother to chase a small Red Stick raiding party, which had stolen slaves from a nearby Creek town.[50] Walker and his men did not join Morgan, who left for Ross's in hopes of procuring more desperately needed blankets. Most opted to stay in the vicinity of their own homes and "depend on their Guns for Subsistence" before it was time to rendezvous.[51]

On January 18, sixty-five Cherokees, along with a greater number of National Creeks, joined Jackson's men at Talladega for the push south to infiltrate the heart of Red Stick territory. After three days' travel, the expedition came within twelve miles of Emuckfau Creek and camped for the night at an abandoned Hillabee town on Enitachopco Creek. At daybreak on January 24, the Red Sticks attacked but were repulsed after heavy fighting. Jackson later reported, "The enemy was completely routed at every point, and the friendly indians joining the pursuit, they were chased about two miles with great slaughter."[52] The forward scouts soon afterward located, just as Jackson had anticipated, a large body of Red Sticks. They reported that "the enemy were fortified by a high log wall extending across the Tallapoosa River."[53] Because of the formidable barricade and the strength of the Red Stick force, Jackson concluded that Coffee and the Indian force should not attack at that time and so ordered a retreat to secure some provisions, bury the dead, and care for the wounded.[54]

The Red Sticks launched another assault at Emuckfau Creek. Jackson "ordered 200 of the friendly Indians to fall in upon the right flank of the enemy" to aid Coffee, who was only supported by about fifty-four men. Colonel William Carroll and this group, led by the Creek head warrior Jim Fife, struck "with a galling and destructive fire."[55] Jackson believed he had put the Red Sticks on the run. Yet again, the lack of sufficient provisions forced him to retreat toward Fort Strother.[56]

Soon reinforced, the enemy made another direct assault on the troops as they retreated across Enitachopco Creek and almost succeeded in cutting off Jackson's rear guard and the artillery. This group of new recruits panicked until some of Coffee's hardened veterans and artillerymen rallied and successfully repulsed the onslaught. One of Coffee's men, Richard Call, later recalled that when the situation looked its bleakest for the Americans,

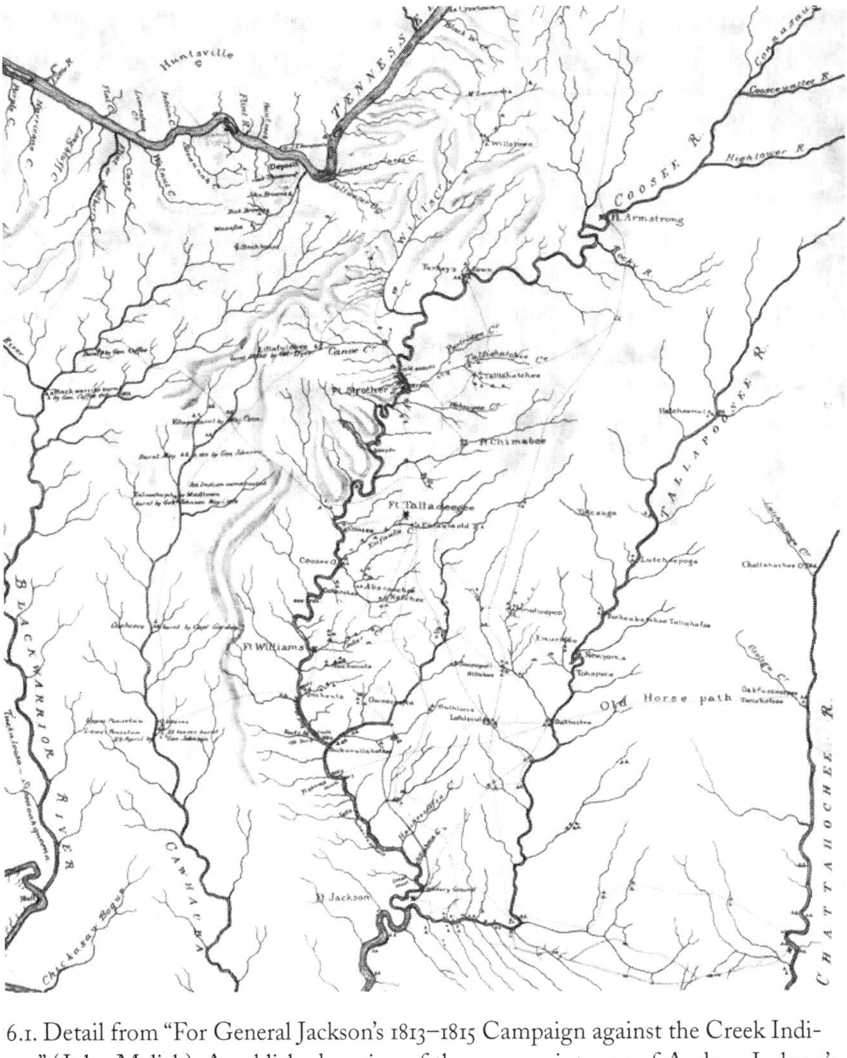

6.1. Detail from "For General Jackson's 1813–1815 Campaign against the Creek Indians" (John Melish). A published version of the manuscript map of Andrew Jackson's campaign. Record Group 77, CWMR, Misc. 11, 1813 and 1814, National Archives and Records Administration, Washington, D.C. Courtesy of the Alabama Department of Archives and History, Montgomery, Alabama.

Colonel Richard Brown and his "little band of mounted Cherokees" rode into the fray and drew the fire of the enemy, thus greatly contributing to a successful retreat.[57]

A few weeks later Jackson's intelligence indicated that the Red Sticks were massing in the river bend near Emuckfau, a tributary of the Tallapoosa.[58] Jackson deemed this an opportune time to kill "the hot bed of the war party" and feared that they might "endeavor to destroy some of the friendly Cherokees" if he did not move quickly.[59] He ordered the Cherokees under Colonel Brown to "scour the country" for any hostiles between the Coosa and Tallapoosa Rivers.[60] They were also to act in conjunction with Jackson's cavalry between the Black Warrior and Cahaba Rivers and then proceed up the Coosa to Fort Strother at Ten Islands. Their orders were to "kill and destroy all warriors . . . [and] burn all houses & villages & take all women & children prisoners" so as to eradicate any rear threat to Jackson's army.[61]

The Cherokees continued to operate within Jackson's military circle, providing valuable and varied services. Jackson heavily depended upon Cherokee mounted warriors as guides and translators. As the vast number of Jackson's men left for home or deserted, the Cherokees remained to protect Fort Strother until US reinforcements arrived.[62] Jackson furloughed the Cherokees to conserve provisions, but some remained on reconnaissance duty. The Cherokees "were permitted to Return to their Respective homes" for a short furlough to conserve precious provisions but were expected to return by February 20.[63] Most furloughed companies opted to stay in Wills Valley rather than return home. Morgan estimated that the Cherokees could field a force of about five hundred for the coming infiltration into Red Stick territory, though many were poorly armed.

On March 2, 1814, Cherokee adjutant John Ross received his marching orders from Morgan to rendezvous at Fort Armstrong and head for Fort Strother.[64] Colonel John Williams and the Thirty-Ninth US Regiment oversaw the transfer of provisions down the Coosa from Fort Armstrong to Fort Williams for the anticipated excursion into Red Stick territory.[65] This time Jackson was determined to field adequate troop numbers sufficiently provisioned.

The most significant action in the Creek War was the Battle of Horseshoe Bend, March 27, 1814. Jackson's invasion aimed at the heart of Red Stick power centered at the Red Stick encampment of Tohopeka.[66] This fortification encompassed approximately one hundred acres with dwellings and numerous beached canoes near the lower end of the horseshoe-shaped peninsula. At its neck, the Red Sticks had erected a log barrier that was "five to eight feet high of large pine logs fitted in with greater skill & strength."[67] This configuration allowed them to lay down a deadly crossfire through portholes if frontally attacked. The defenders used the felled brush and timber left from the barrier's construction to create redoubts behind the front line. The Red Sticks had also excavated some of the Tallapoosa's steeper banks to enlarge an area with an overhang as emergency shelters. A hill rose fairly steeply from the living area toward the neck of the horseshoe. Its elevation rose especially high on its right side. The prophets chose this hillock as the refuge's ceremonial area.

Jackson reached the Tallapoosa River and placed General Coffee's regiment, consisting of seven hundred mounted men along with five hundred Cherokees and one hundred National Creeks, around the entire peninsula to prevent any Red Sticks from escaping.[68] When his men were in place by mid-morning on March 27, Jackson began firing two pieces of artillery set on a rise about two hundred yards to the front and left of the barricade. Continuous cannonading against the massive log barrier bore no visible results. The effectiveness of the Red Stick frontal defenses made it suicidal to send men into a frontal assault.

Coffee later reported that his Indian soldiers "could no longer remain silent spectators. While some kept up a fire across the river . . . to prevent the enemy's approach to the bank, others plunged into the water and swam the river for canoes that lay at the other shore in considerable numbers, and brought them over, in which crafts a number of them embarked, and landed on the bend with the enemy."[69] The first of three daring Cherokees to swim the rain-swollen Tallapoosa was The Whale (Tuq-qua, Tucfo, or Tuck Wah), "a very large man" about thirty-seven years old, who served as a private under Captain Rain Crow. He, assisted by two other Cherokee warriors who also swam the river, returned with canoes, and began to ferry their comrades back across to the village.[70] They then attacked the village and set some structures afire, engaging the enemy's rear.[71]

This unplanned but successful rear assault meant that Red Sticks from the front line had to rush away, leaving the front more exposed to an attempt to breach the log defenses. Morgan rode to inform Colonel Lemuel Montgomery of the Thirty-Ninth of the events and upon returning found that approximately two hundred Cherokees were then engaging the enemy. Morgan, Walker, and thirty other Cherokees hurried across and, along with their fellow warriors, took possession of the high ground by fighting mostly in hand-to-hand combat. Morgan, who soon received a severe head wound over his right eye, later recalled that they only succeeded "by the dint of hard fighting."[72]

This unexpected attack by the Cherokees gave Jackson an opportunity to storm the barricade. With this simultaneous assault to the front and rear, the Red Sticks fought desperately but to no avail. According to one sol-

6.2. Major Ridge. From Thomas L. McKenney and James Hall's *History of the Indian Tribes of North America.*

dier, "the Tallapoosa might truly be called a River of blood for the water was so stained . . . it could not be used" because of the massive numbers of Red Sticks killed while attempting to escape by swimming the river or crossing on felled trees where "they would drop like turtles into the water" when shot.[73] Much close combat ensued. McKenney and Hall, while recounting the career of the then-famous Cherokee statesman Major Ridge, reported: "As he attempted to plunge his sword in one of these, the Creek closed with him, and a severe contest ensued. . . . Ridge, forgetting his own knife, seized one which his antagonist wore, and stabbed him; but the wound was not fatal, and the Creek still fought with an equal chance of success, when he was stabbed with a spear by one of Ridge's friends."[74]

One injured Red Stick warrior managed to reach the opposite side of the Tallapoosa, but a Cherokee quickly captured him and brought him before Coffee. He failed to cooperate even when "a tomahawk was raised in a threatening manner."[75] Elsewhere, Ensign Sam Houston, an adopted Cherokee serving in the Thirty-Ninth US Infantry, despite an arrow wound he had received earlier during the assault on the barrier, led a group of men to smoke out Red Sticks hidden among the brush redoubts. While systematically cleaning out these nests of the enemy, he suffered gunshot wounds to his right arm and shoulder.[76] All close fighting ceased with the coming darkness of night.

The next morning, troops made short work of sixteen Red Sticks who had entrenched themselves under the river embankment by caving in the dirt roofs of their hideout, which "completely buried them alive."[77] Jackson's men then proceeded to count 557 nose tips severed from the bodies of their enemies. They estimated that another 250 to 300 went to their watery graves when shot trying to cross the Tallapoosa. Some of Jackson's men then fashioned straps of human leather flayed from the corpses into bridle reins as trophies.[78] All in all, US forces slew approximately 800 Red Sticks and took about 500 women and children prisoners.[79]

Fifteen Cherokees lost their lives on the battlefield, while thirty-six received wounds, many severe, during the feverish hostilities that spanned the first few hours of the engagement. Three warriors died shortly afterward, directly related to their injuries.[80] The companies of Captains John Speers, John McLemore, James Foster, and John Brown received the most casualties, followed by those of Captains Rain Crow, John McIntosh, and, finally, Shoe Boots, who lost only two men and had no wounded.[81] Speers's and Brown's men lost the greatest number of horses, guns, hatchets, knives, and even clothing during the battle. Some horses expired during or shortly after the fighting due to battle wounds, while some died on the journey home, perhaps due to the lack of proper forage.

Though the numbers remain contested, the cumulative death toll of warriors during the Red Stick War might have reached 1,900 warriors, accounting for approximately 40 percent of the able-bodied male Creeks. Many Creek women and children prisoners would remain among their Cherokee captors. The Americans and their Indian allies had killed greater than three times their own losses and destroyed approximately forty-eight Red Stick towns, while another twelve would remain abandoned. The war's devastation left about 8,200 Creek refugees homeless and hungry.[82]

A few months later, Meigs, in reporting to the secretary of war, bragged about his Cherokee charges, noting "gentlemen of rank and character who were present at the decisive Battle at the Horseshoe," and concluded that the "daring intrepid & preserving bravery of the Cherokee warriors probably saved the loss of 1000 white men." He stressed that these warrior-soldiers had "distinguished themselves in every action in this barbarous war & according to their number [had] destroyed more of the enemy than any other part of the Army." Meigs concluded that many Cherokees had been wounded or fallen in battle, and "they deserve well of the United States."[83]

Yet while there were victory celebrations held throughout the Cherokee Nation, many towns and families mourned those who died in the war. The Cherokees would also continue to suffer from other hardships as a result of the war. The east wing of Jackson's army under General Cocke had devastated the Cherokee countryside, both in a sanctioned manner, such as through the impressments of supplies, and maliciously, as with the damages inflicted by the passage of troops through Cherokee territory. Issues such as war reparations and boundary settlements had to be resolved. In addition, as part of the military establishment at the termination of hostilities, Cherokee leadership did not expect the federal government to abandon disabled Cherokee veterans or widows and dependants of those warriors who died in service to the United States. The war resulted in a plethora of concerns that would require Cherokee leaders to continue to closely interact and negotiate with their neighbor and ally. The elder councilmen continued to trust and rely upon the community headmen and military leaders to protect the membership and interests of the Cherokee Nation. Though these Cherokees remained optimistic about their future relationship with the United States, their "band of brothers," they would soon begin a new battle to receive the respect they deserved as a proud people who firmly identified themselves as a distinct nation and not as a military appendage of the United States.

Notes

1. East Tennessee major James Baxter to Return Jonathan Meigs, March 20, 1814, and Charles Hicks to Meigs, March 21, 1814, Records of the Cherokee Indian Agency in Tennessee, 1801–1835 (hereafter cited as CIART), Record Group 75, microfilm M208, roll 6, National Archives and Records Administration (hereafter cited as NARA), Washington, D.C.; and diary entry, November 6, 1813, in Moravian Sprin*gplace Mission to the Cherokees* (hereafter cited as *Springplace Diaries*), ed. Rowena McClinton, 2 vols. (Lincoln: University of Nebraska Press, 2007), 1:546.

2. The Creek War of 1813–1814 was part of the larger War of 1812, which ended with the defeat of British forces at New Orleans in January 1815. See Henry S. Halbert and Timothy H. Ball, *Creek War of 1813 and 1814,* ed. Frank L. Owsley Jr., Southern Historical Publications, no. 15 (Montgomery, AL: White, Woodruff, & Fowler, 1895; reprint, Tuscaloosa: University of Alabama Press, 1969); Frank Lawrence Owsley Jr., *Struggle for the Gulf Borderlands: The Creek War and the Battle of New Orleans, 1812–1815* (Gainesville: University Presses of

Florida, 1981); Gregory Evans Dowd, *A Spirited Resistance: The North American Indian Struggle for Unity, 1745–1815*, Johns Hopkins University Studies in Historical and Political Science, 109th series, no. 4, 1991 (Baltimore: Johns Hopkins University Press, 1992), 185–90.

3. Diary entry, September 15, 1813, in *Springplace Diaries,* ed. McClinton, 2:558–59. Brigadier General James White to John Walker, September 26, 1813, and John Walker to Return J. Meigs, October 5, 1813, CIART, roll 6; Muster Rolls and Pay Rolls of Colonel Morgan's Regiment of Cherokee Indians, October 7, 1813, to April 11, 1814 (hereafter cited as Cherokee Muster Rolls), Record Group 94, Adjutant General's Office, NARA, Washington, DC (hereafter cited as RG 94, AGO).

4. Andrew Jackson to John Coffee, October 7, 1813, in *Correspondence of Andrew Jackson,* ed. John Spencer Bassett, 7 vols. Papers of the Department of Historical Resource, no. 371 (Washington, DC: Carnegie Institution of Washington, 1926), 1:328.

5. Cherokee Muster Rolls, RG 94, AGO. Meigs became acquainted with Morgan when he granted him a federal permit to reside in Cherokee territory for the purpose of leasing and working a saltpeter cave. Brown and Lowry were the headmen from the Cherokee communities of Brown's Town and Battle Creek in today's northeastern Alabama.

6. Meigs to Armstrong, October 30, 1813, Southeastern Native American Documents, GALILEO Digital Library of Georgia, doc. PA0032, from Penelope Johnson Allen Papers, Hoskins Special Collections Library, University of Tennessee, Knoxville, 1–2 (hereafter cited as GALILEO).

7. Meigs to Armstrong, October 30, 1813, and July 30, 1813, CIART, roll 6.

8. Meigs to the Cherokee troops, October 30, 1813, Cherokee Nation Papers, microfilm reel 49, Division of Manuscripts Collection, Item 24, Box 6, Folder 1, item 10, Western History Collections, University of Oklahoma, Norman, OK.

9. Mary Hardin McCown, ed., "'J. Hartsell Memora': Journal of a Tennessee Captain in the War of 1812," *East Tennessee Historical Society's Publication* 11 (1939): 102.

10. Tom Kanon, "Regimental Histories of Tennessee Units during the War of 1812," Tennessee State Library and Archives, Nashville, TN, (hereafter cited as TSLA), http://www.tennessee.gov/tsla/history/military/1812reg.htm (accessed February 10, 2007). The Moravians also recorded the presence of East Tennessee soldiers, who were building boats on the Conasauga River. Diary entry, March 20, 1814, *Springplace Diaries,* ed. McClinton, 2:12.

11. Cherokee Muster Rolls, RG 94, AGO. Cherokee troops guarded the fort from January 11 to February 10, 1814.

12. Narrative from Chulio, Creek interpreter, October 10, 1813, CIART, roll 6;

Gregory A. Waselkov and Brian M. Wood, "Creek War of 1813–1814: Effect on Creek Society and Settlement Patterns," *Journal of Alabama Archaeology* 32 (June 1986): 9.

13. Walker to Meigs, October 15, 1813, CIART, roll 6; diary entry, October 15, 1813, *Springplace Diaries,* ed. McClinton, 1:563. See also Colonel Morgan's Declaration, February 7, 1834, Gideon Morgan, no. 20844, Record Group 15, Records of the Veterans Administration, Old War Invalid Files (hereafter cited as OWIF). Defenders of the stockade had apparently panicked when some of Major John Coffee's cavalry had arrived shooting their guns into the air.

14. John Reid Memoir/Journal Entry, October 9, 1813, John Reid Memoir/Journal, MS AC 72–180, TSLA; Jackson to Path Killer and Hicks, October 23, 1813, in *The Papers of Andrew Jackson, 1770–1845: A Microfilm Supplement,* ed. Harold D. Moser et al., 39 reels (Wilmington, DE: Scholarly Resources, 1986), reel 3, folder 1, no. 4299.

15. Jackson to Path Killer, October 23, 1813, in *Papers of Andrew Jackson,* ed. Moser et al., reel 3, folder 1, no. 4299; John Reid to Maj. William B. Lewis, October 24, 1813, Tennessee Historical Society (hereafter cited as TSH), microfilm 678, reel 5, box 9, L48½, TSLA; Jackson to Coffee, October 9, 1813, in *Correspondence of Andrew Jackson,* ed. Bassett, 1:329.

16. Jackson to Coffee, October 9, 1813, *Correspondence of Andrew Jackson,* ed. Bassett, 1:330.

17. David Crockett, *Autobiography of David Crockett* (originally printed as *A Narrative of the Life of David Crockett, of the State of Tennessee,* 1834; reprint, New York: Charles Scribner's Sons, 1923), 54; Stanley J. Folmsbee and Anna Grace Catron, "Early Career of David Crockett," in *Houston and Crockett: Heroes of Tennessee and Texas: An Anthology,* ed. Herbert L. Harper (Nashville: Tennessee Historical Commission, 1986), 138–40.

18. John Reid and John Henry Eaton, *The Life of Andrew Jackson: Major General in the United States Comprising a History of the War in the South, from the Commencement of the Creek Campaign to the Termination of Hostilities before New Orleans,* ed. Frank Lawrence Owsley Jr., Southern Historical Publication 19 (Philadelphia: M. Carey & Son, 1817; reprint, Tuscaloosa: University of Alabama Press, 1974), 37.

19. Coffee to His Wife, October 24, 1813, in "Letters of General John Coffee to His Wife, 1813–1815," ed. John H. DeWitt with introduction and notes, *Tennessee Historical Magazine* 2 (December 1916): 275; Arthur S. Colyar, *Life and Times of Andrew Jackson: Soldier—Statesman—President,* vol. 1 (Nashville, TN: Press of Marshall & Bruce, 1904), 1; Coffee to Jackson, October 22, 1813, in *Correspondence of Andrew Jackson,* ed. Bassett, 1:334–35; Walker to Meigs, November 5, 1813, CIART, roll 6; Richard Breckenbridge, a traveler from Mississippi in 1816, in *History of Walker County: Its Towns and Its Peoples,* by John Martin

Dombhart (Thornton, AR: Cayce Publishing, 1937), 14; Reid and Eaton, *Life of Andrew Jackson,* 48.

20. George Mayfield to Jackson, November 2, 1813, "Forts," in Public Information Subject Files—Alabamians at War, War of 1812 and First Creek War, SG0013378, Alabama Department of Archives and History (hereafter cited as ADAH), Montgomery; John Lowry from Jackson, November 7, 1813, *Correspondence of Andrew Jackson,* ed. Bassett, 1:342; Colyar, *Life and Times of Jackson,* 5; James Mooney, *Myths of the Cherokees,* 19th Annual Report, Bureau of American Ethnology, Smithsonian Institute (Washington, D.C., Government Printing Office, 1900), 90.

21. Jackson to Tennessee governor Willie Blount, November 4, 1813, *Correspondence of Andrew Jackson,* ed. Bassett, 1:341.

22. John Reid Memoir/Journal Entry, November 1, 1813, and November 7, 1813, TSLA; Colyar, *Life and Times of Jackson,* 11.

23. John Reid Memoir/Journal Entry, November 7, 1813, TSLA; John Lowry from Jackson, November 7, 1813, in *Correspondence of Andrew Jackson,* ed. Bassett, 1:342; Mooney, *Myths of the Cherokees,* 91; Crockett, *Autobiography of David Crockett,* 61.

24. Walker to Meigs, November 5, 1813, CIART, roll 6; Reid and Eaton, *Life of Andrew Jackson,* 50–51. It was after this engagement that Jackson claimed the Creek infant Lyncoya, whose mother was killed during the battle. Jackson sent another Creek boy to Rachel's nephew. Another white family also stole a Creek child, who had received wounds in the encounter, but he later ran away. Jackson to Col. W. Moore, November 15, 1833, in *Correspondence of Andrew Jackson,* ed. Bassett, 5:225; Jackson to wife, Rachel, March 12, 1814, in *Correspondence of Andrew Jackson,* ed. Bassett, 1:478; and Herbert J. Doherty Jr., *Richard Keith Call: Southern Unionist* (Gainesville: University of Florida Press, 1961), 6.

25. Reid and Eaton, *Life of Andrew Jackson,* 53–55; Cherokee Muster Rolls, RG 94, AGO; George Fields, no. 25091, OWIF. For further accounts on the Battles of Tallushatchee and Talladega, see Ephraim Foster to his father, R. C. Foster, January 29, 1814, Ephraim Hubbard Foster Papers, MS AC. no. 79-26, V-L-5, box 11-4, TSLA; and Benson John Lossing, "War with Creek Indians," in Scenes in the War of 1812 series, *Harpers' New Monthly Magazine* 28, no. 167 (April 1864): 605–7.

26. McCown, "'Hartsell Memora,'" 104, 107. This was at the future site of Fort Williams, built in March 1814.

27. Morgan to Meigs, November 23, 1813, CIART, roll 6; Gideon Morgan Papers, MS AC 78–31, TSLA; Reid and Eaton, *Life of Andrew Jackson,* 71; Owsley, *Struggle for the Gulf Borderlands,* 66–67; Cherokee Muster Rolls, RG 94, AGO; and Brig. Gen. James White to Maj. Gen. John Cocke, November 24, 1813, reprinted in the *Weekly Register,* December 25, 1813, 283. See also John and Anna

Gambold to Meigs, April 21, 1814, CIART, roll 6; and Lossing, "War with Creek Indians," 608–9, for more information on prisoners.

28. Morgan to Meigs, November 23, 1813, Gideon Morgan Papers, MS AC no. 78–31, TSLA.

29. Ibid. McNair's company sometimes acted along with Captain William Russell's scouts/spies from October 4, 1813, to April 4, 1814. See "William Russell," in "Soldiers," Public Information Subject Files—Alabamians at War, War of 1812 and First Creek War, SG0013378, folder 19, ADAH. According to "Old Times," January 27, 1877, in *Cherokee Advocate,* vol. 1, no. 1, Book One, May 1, 1845–June 27, 1877, from microfilm copies in Oklahoma Historical Society's Collection, ed. Dorothy Tincup Maulden (Tulsa: Oklahoma Yesterday Publications, 1991), 153, McNair was a Cherokee countryman, originally a carpenter from Virginia, who married Joseph Vann's older sister. See also the character reference in Remarks on the Testimony Taken of Disputed Country to John Coffee, December 30, 1829, Cherokee Collection, Tennessee Historical Society, mf #815, reel 4, box 3, folder 6, TSLA. Other companies may have participated, but the evidence cannot confirm this. Cherokee Muster Rolls, RG 94, AGO.

30. Jackson, quoted in *Carthage Gazette,* December 18, 1813; Samuel Baines to wife, Christiana, November 25, 1813, SPR 542, ADAH.

31. Morgan to Meigs, November 23, 1813, Morgan Papers, MS AC no. 78-31, TSLA; Gary E. Moulton, *John Ross: Cherokee Chief* (Athens: University of Georgia Press, 1978), 11.

32. McCown, "'Hartsell Memora,'" 110.

33. Maj. Gen. David Adams to Georgia Gov. Peter Early, December 24, 1813, in Georgia Military Affairs, January 4, 1814–October 9, 1819, 4 vols. (unpublished: Georgia Department of Archives and History, Morrow, GA), 4:317, 320. For a discussion of the founding of Tohopeka by Abeika Creeks from six nearby towns, see Waselkov and Wood, "Creek War of 1813–1814," 9. For further discussion of Georgia troop movements in the Red Stick War, see Susan K. Barnard and Grace M. Schwartman, "Tecumseh and the Creek Indian War of 1813–1814 in North Georgia," *Georgia Historical Quarterly* 82 (Fall 1998): 489–506; Hugh M. Thomason, "Governor Peter Early and the Creek Indian Frontier, 1813–1815," *Georgia Historical Quarterly* 45 (September 1961): 225–32.

34. John Sugden, "Southern Indians in the War of 1812: The Closing Phase," *Florida Historical Quarterly* (January 1982): 279; Benjamin W. Griffith Jr., *McIntosh and Weatherford: Creek Indian Leaders* (Tuscaloosa: University of Alabama Press, 1988), 133–38. See also Lossing, "War with Creek Indians," 609–11; and Owsley, *Struggle for the Gulf Borderlands,* 54–57.

35. Bill of exchange relating to supplies to Cherokee warriors from Meigs to Armstrong, December 1813, CIART, roll 6; Receipt of Timothy Meigs for

goods given the Cherokees, March 31, 1814, GALILEO, Doc. PA0216, Penelope Johnson Allen Papers, Mss. 2033, box 1, folder 75, doc. PA0216, Hoskins Special Collections Library, University of Tennessee, Knoxville, TN; Jackson to Path Killer and Hicks, October 23, 1813, in *Papers of Andrew Jackson,* ed. Moser, reel 3, folder 1, no. 4299.

36. John Lowry to Meigs, October 27, 1813, and Big Halfbreed, Ri[d]ge, Birdseye, Oald [*sic*] Wakeygiskee to Meigs, January 16, 1814, CIART, roll 6; General Order from Jackson to Adjutant Gen. Robert Searcey, January 14, 1814, Jackson Papers, series 3, vols. A–E, reel 61, Library of Congress (hereafter cited as LOC); Big Halfbreed, Ri[d]ge, Birdseye, Oald [*sic*] Wakeygiskee to Meigs, January 16, 1814, CIART, roll 6.

37. Petition of Sundry Indians [including Willioe, John Acorn, Thomas Maw, Corn Tassle, and John Nettle] at Tuskegee to Meigs, February 15, 1814, CIART, roll 6.

38. Richard Brown to Meigs, February 18, 1814; Riley to Meigs, February 20, 1814; Daniel Ross to Meigs, March 3, 1814; Duck and Whooping Boy to Meigs, March 4, 1814, all in CIART, roll 6; Cocke to Jackson, November 27, 1813, in *Correspondence of Andrew Jackson,* ed. Bassett, 1:361. See also Cocke to Jackson, December 3, 1813, in *Correspondence of Andrew Jackson,* ed. Bassett, 1:368; and Jackson to Cocke, December 15, 1813, in *Correspondence of Andrew Jackson,* ed. Bassett, 1:395.

39. Morgan to Meigs, February 11, 1814, GALILEO, Doc. MP017, Morgan Papers, box 10, folder VA, doc. t1017, TSLA, 1-21-2; Jackson to Pinckney, March 2, 1814, Jackson Papers, series 3, vols. A–E, reel 61, LOC.

40. Jackson to Morgan, February 21, 1814, Jackson Papers, series 3, vols. A–E, reel 61, LOC.

41. Path Killer to John Strother, December 28, 1813, CIART, roll 6.

42. Jackson to Col. John Lowry, January 8, 1814, Jackson Papers, series 3, vols. A–E, reel 61, LOC.

43. Kanon, "Regimental Histories, http://www.tennessee.gov/tsla/history/military/1812reg.htm (accessed February 26, 2011). See also Colyar, *Life and Times of Jackson,* 3; Cherokee Muster Rolls, RG 94, AGO.

44. E. Shackelford to F. Shackelford, November 26, 1813, Society for Georgia Archaeology, MSS 4911, Macon, GA.

45. Cherokee Muster Rolls, RG 94, AGO.

46. Because of a delay in receiving the message, the Valley Town/Mountain Warriors did not arrive at the designated date. Yonah Equah or Big Bear to Meigs, March 5, 1814, CIART, roll 6. For a familiar account of the battle, see Lossing, "War with Creek Indians," 612–13. See also, Jackson to wife, Rachel, January 28, 1813, in *Correspondence of Andrew Jackson,* ed. Bassett, 1:444–47.

47. John Lowry to Meigs, January 5, 1814, CIART, roll 6.

48. Meigs to Jackson, February 11, 1814, in *Papers of Andrew Jackson,* ed. Moser, reel 8.

49. Morgan to Meigs, February 4, 1814, GALILEO, Doc. MP018, Morgan Papers, box 10, folder n/a, doc. t1018, TSLA, 1; Morgan to Jackson, February 5, 1814, in *Papers of Andrew Jackson,* ed. Moser, reel 8.

50. Jackson to Carroll, 28 January 1814, in *Correspondence of Andrew Jackson,* ed. Bassett, 1:472.

51. Morgan to Jackson, February 9, 1814, in *Papers of Andrew Jackson,* ed. Moser, reel 8.

52. Jackson to Pinckney, January 29, 1814, in *Correspondence of Andrew Jackson,* ed. Bassett, 1:448.

53. Entry from Journal of Governor Richard K. Call, "Lake Jackson, August 5, 1861," Fla 921 Call, DBCN ACI-9781, M82-4, 82, State Library of Florida, Tallahassee (hereafter cited as Call Papers).

54. Jackson noted that the Indians who joined him at Talladega had not drawn any rations and were really in need. Jackson to Pinckney, January 29, 1814, in *Correspondence of Andrew Jackson,* ed. Bassett, 1:450–51.

55. Jackson to Pinckney, January 29, 1814, in *Correspondence of Andrew Jackson,* ed. Bassett, 1:450.

56. Thurman Wilkins, *Cherokee Tragedy: The Ridge Family and the Decimation of a People,* Civilization of the American Indian, no. 169, 2nd ed., rev. (1970; repr., Norman: University of Oklahoma Press, 1986), 72–73.

57. Entry from Journal of Governor Richard K. Call, Call Papers, 84–85.

58. Later they would identify this collection point as the Red Stick stronghold refuge of Tohopeka at Horseshoe Bend on the Tallapoosa River.

59. Jackson to Pinckney, February 11, 1814, Jackson Papers, series 3, vols. A–E, reel 61, LOC.

60. Jackson to Maj. William McIntosh, February 17, 1814, and Jackson to Col. Robert Dyer, February 23, 1814, Jackson Papers, series 3, vols. A–E, reel 61, LOC.

61. Jackson to Col. John Brown, February 17, 1814, and Jackson to Col. Richard Brown, February 18, 1814, Jackson Papers, series 3, vols. A–E, reel 61, LOC.

62. Jackson to Capt. Eli Hammond, February 15, 1814, Jackson Papers, series 3, Letters and Orders, vol. F, LOC, 5; Jackson to Col. William Snodgrass, February 2, 1814, Jackson Papers, series 3, vols. A–E, reel 61, LOC.

63. Morgan to Meigs, February 4, 1814, GALILEO, Doc. MP018, Morgan Papers, box 10, folder n/a, doc. t1018, TSLA, 2.

64. John Ross to Meigs, March 2, 1814, CIART, roll 6; Moulton, *John Ross,* 11.

65. Leota Driver Maiden, "Colonel John Williams," *East Tennessee Historical Society Publications* 30 (1958): 23.

66. Some of the most familiar literature regarding this battle are James W. Holland, "Andrew Jackson and the Creek War: Victory at the Horseshoe," *Alabama Review* 21 (October 1968): 243–75; W. H. Brantley Jr., *Battle of Horseshoe Bend in Tallapoosa County, Alabama, March 27, 1814* (Np: Horseshoe Bend Battle Park Association, 1955); Thomas Kanon, "'A Slow, Laborious Slaughter': The Battle of Horseshoe Bend," *Tennessee Historical Quarterly* 58 (Spring 1999): 2–15; Lossing, "War with Creek Indians," 614–15; Robert V. Remini, *Andrew Jackson and the Course of American Empire, 1767–1821* (New York: Harper & Row, 1977), 207–16. For a recent study offering a detailed examination of the battle, see Mike Bunn and Clay Williams, *Battle For the Southern Frontier: The Creek War and the War of 1812* (Charleston: History Press, 2008). See also Charles H. Fairbanks, "Excavations at Horseshoe Bend, Alabama," *Florida Anthropologist* 15 (June 1962): 48–49. Numerous articles and books cover this battle, which propelled Andrew Jackson to the presidency. For discussion focusing on Jackson and the action of his troops, see Finley McIlwaine, "The Horseshoe," *Tennessee Valley Historical Review* 2 (Fall 1973): 2–11; C. Jack Coley, "Battle of Horseshoe Bend," *Alabama Historical Quarterly* 14 (January 1952): 129–34; Marcus J. Wright, "Battle of Tohopeka, or Horse-Shoe: General Andrew Jackson's Original Report," *Magazine of American History* 19 (1888): 45–49; Holland, "Andrew Jackson and the Creek War," 243–75; Letter from Lt. Alexander McCulloch to his wife, Frances, April 1, 1813 [1814], Center for American History, University of Texas, Austin.

67. Reid to his wife, Betsy, April 1, 1814, in John Reid Papers, 1802–1842, MSS 37507, Library of Congress, Washington, DC (microfilm) 425. See also Roy S. Dickens Jr., *Archaeological Investigations at Horseshoe Bend National Military Park, Alabama,* Special Publications No. 3, Alabama Archaeological Society (Tuscaloosa: University of Alabama, 1979), 48; Gregory A. Waselkov, "A Reinterpretation of the Creek Indian Barricade at Horseshoe Bend," *Journal of Alabama Archaeology* 32 (1986): 94–107; and George C. Mackenzie, *The Indian Breastwork in the Battle of Horseshoe Bend: Its Size, Location, and Construction* (Washington, DC: US Department of Interior, Office of Archaeology and Historic Preservation, 1969).

68. Report from Coffee to Jackson, April 1, 1814, reprinted in *Niles Weekly Register,* April 30, 1814, 148, and *Carthage Gazette,* April 23, 1814; DeWitt, "Letters of John Coffee," 283; Cherokee Muster Rolls, RG 94, AGO. Muster records confirm that 632 Cherokee warriors, divided into seven companies, were enlisted at this time.

69. Report from Coffee to Jackson, April 1, 1814, reprinted in *Niles Weekly Register,* April 30, 1814, 148.

70. "Bounty Application for Whale," Horseshoe Bend National Military Park files, Bounty Land Files, War of 1812, #1298, NARA, Washington, DC; "Long

Ago," *Cherokee Advocate,* February 28, 1877, 163; Calvin Jones, "Account of the Cherokee Schools, communicated by Gen. Calvin Jones, of Raleigh to the editor of *the Register," American Monthly Magazine* (December 1813): 117–24. Reproduced in Southeastern Native American Documents, 1730–1842, GALILEO Digital Library of Georgia Database.

71. Cherokee Nation Papers, box 177, folder 7729, 1:218; William G. McLoughlin, *Cherokee Renascence in the New Republic* (Princeton: Princeton University Press, 1986), 192–93.

72. Report from Colonel Gideon Morgan to Blount, April 1, 1814, reprinted in *Niles Weekly Register,* April 30, 1814, 149, and *Clarion,* April 12, 1814; Confederate Soldier, "Our Correspondence," Interview with Captain James Campbell, September 10, 1861, *Richmond (VA) Daily Dispatch,* September 16, 1861.

73. McCulloch to Francis, April 1, 1813, Center for American History, University of Texas, Austin; Confederate Soldier, "Our Correspondence," September 10, 1861, *Daily Dispatch,* September 16, 1861.

74. Thomas L. McKenney and James Hall, *The Indian Tribes of North America, with Biographical Sketches and Anecdotes of the Principal Chiefs,* 2 vols. (1836–1844; Repr., Kent, OH: Vilair, Ltd., 1978 Cherokee Nation Papers, box 177, folder 7729, mf. reel 50, 219.

75. Confederate Soldier, "Our Correspondence," September 10, 1861, *Daily Dispatch,* September 16, 1861.

76. Marquis James, *Raven: A Biography of Sam Houston* (New York: Blue Ribbon Books, 1929; repr., Austin: University of Texas Press, 1994), 20, 34, 150; Clifford Hopewell, *Sam Houston: Man of Destiny* (Austin, TX: Eakin Press, 1987), 14, 27, 111; Kanon, "'A Slow, Laborious Slaughter,'" 10; Sam Houston, *Autobiography of Sam Houston: Compiled from His Writings and Letters,* ed. Donald Day and Harry Herbert Ullom (Norman: University of Oklahoma Press, 1954); James Parton, *Life of Andrew Jackson,* 3 vols. (Boston: Ticknor and Fields, 1866; repr., New York: Johnson Reprint, 1967), 1:519.

77. Henry S. Halbert, ed., Draper Manuscripts, Tecumseh Papers, Series YY, vol. 10, reel 119, State Historical Society of Wisconsin, Madison; John Harris, *A Review of the Battle of the Horse Shoe, and of the Facts Relating to the Killing of Sixteen Indians on the Morning after the Battle by the Orders of Gen. Andrew Jackson* (n.p.: 1928), LOC, Washington, DC; and Braund, "Warriors and Society," 4–5, 28–30.

78. Kanon, "'A Slow, Laborious Slaughter,'" 14, fn. 23; Henry S. Halbert, "Horse Shoe Incidents," Draper Manuscripts, Tecumseh Papers, Series YY, vol. 10, reel 119; Halbert and Ball, *Creek War,* 276–77.

79. Jackson to wife, Rachel, April 1, 1814, in *Correspondence of Andrew Jackson,* ed. Bassett, 1:493; Halbert and Ball, *Creek War,* 276–77. For a more extended ac-

count, see Coley, " Battle of Horseshoe Bend," 129–34; Brantley, *Battle of Horseshoe Bend in Tallapoosa County;* and Holland, "Andrew Jackson and the Creek War," 283.

80. Jackson to Blount, March 31, 1814, in *Correspondence of Andrew Jackson,* ed. Bassett, 1:492; John Ross, "Report of the killed and wounded," Ayer MSS 781, Newberry Library, Chicago, IL; "Casualty Report," in *Papers of Chief John Ross,* ed. Gary E. Moulton, 2 vols. (Norman: University of Oklahoma Press, 1985), 1:20–21; Penelope Johnson Allen, "The Creek War," MSS Chattanooga Public Library (1935), TSLA, 138.

81. Muster Rolls and Pay Rolls of Colonel Morgan's Regiment of Cherokee Indians, October 7, 1813, to April 11, 1814, Cherokee Muster Rolls, RG 94, AGO.

82. Frank H. Akers Jr., "The Unexpected Challenge: The Creek War of 1813–1814" (PhD diss., Duke University, 1975), 241. Michael Green, in *Politics of Indian Removal: Creek Removal and Society in Crisis* (Lincoln: University of Nebraska Press, 1982), 42, estimated that approximately 15 percent of the total Creek population, or about three thousand warriors, lost their lives during the war. Affidavit of Switzler Lowrey, January 10, 1878, Charles Reece, no. 13828, RG 15, OWIF. The practice of taking in captives was not unusual among whites and native peoples along the frontier borders. For examples, see Christina Nicole Snyder, *Slavery in Indian Country: The Changing Face of Captivity in Early America* (Cambridge: Harvard University Press, 2010); Waselkov and Wood, "Creek War of 1813–1814," 10; Owsley, *Struggle for the Gulf Borderlands,* 71.

83. Meigs to Secretary of War, June 4, 1814, CIART, roll 6.

7
Horseshoe Bend

A Living Memorial

Ove Jensen

Horseshoe Bend National Military Park is one of 392 units in the National Park System and one of only two dozen battlefield or military parks. It is the only national military park in Alabama. The 2,040-acre park receives some fifty to sixty thousand visitors annually. Most people come to enjoy the serene landscape, view wildlife, and have a quiet experience in a natural environment. However, many come specifically to visit the site of the battle in order to learn more about the history of the Creek Indians and the war that ended on the banks of the Tallapoosa River. Historic sites are essential to our understanding of history and help "fix the subject" or make the subject real in the mind of the visitor. As a former Horseshoe Bend ranger observed, visiting a site "breathes life into the dry leaves of the past." In a real sense, the *place* provides a tangible, living, and lingering connection to the past. In the case of Horseshoe Bend, it also makes it possible for modern people to comprehend the complexities of the nineteenth-century battle and the difficulties and opportunities presented by the terrain.

From a Creek perspective, aside from any spiritual reasons for selecting the location, the topography must have seemed a particularly good place to make a stand. Based on prior experience, with the opposing forces roughly equal in strength, the area seemed to offer obvious advantages and provide an easily defended piece of ground. Indeed, there seems to have been a pattern. For example, at Holy Ground, the basic layout was similar, with a rudimentary barrier providing frontal protection to forces whose rear was protected by a river. Prior to the battle, the Tallapoosa River provided a means of communication and travel, and if the initial barriers were breached, the river could provide a means of escape. Compared to US forces, Red Sticks moved faster and used obstacles to their advantage. Their goal was not necessarily the destruction of enemy forces, but the protection of their ground;

and when that proved impossible, they did not hesitate to use their surroundings to their advantage and retreat into canebreaks and swamps and over rivers, which, generally speaking, Americans could not cross as fast or effectively. In earlier battles of the Creek War, US forces and Red Sticks were on relatively equal standing. When surrounded, the Red Sticks would choose a point of the line, break through, and retreat. Undoubtedly, they expected to be able to do that at Horseshoe Bend; however, by March of 1814, General Andrew Jackson's numbers were vastly superior and the advantage gained by geography was lost as his total force swelled to some five thousand. Even though he did not deploy his entire force at Horseshoe Bend, he still had sufficient troops to effectively surround them and prevent retreat. One factor that is difficult for modern people to comprehend is the spiritual or supernatural force that the site offered in the Red Stick worldview. An early account of the battle described the bend as "a consecrated spot, where they considered themselves protected by friendly spirits."[1] But clearly, real as well as spiritual defenses were important to the Red Stick defenders of the barricade or fortification, known in the Creek language as Tohopeka.

Jackson gained considerable experience from his earlier engagements at Tallushatchee, Talladega, Emuckfau Creek, and Enitachopco Creek. By the time he set his sights on the Horseshoe, he possessed a larger and better-organized army. Prior to the battle, the bulk of Jackson's forces were garrisoned at Fort Williams on the Coosa River, near modern Sylacauga. The army set off in late March for Horseshoe Bend, which Jackson knew from prior intelligence reports was heavily fortified and manned by a massed force of Okfuskee warriors. His army cut a fifty-two-mile path through the woods, and by the evening of March 26, they were camped five or six miles from Tohopeka, as the Creeks called the fortified site. Jackson's exact route from Fort Williams to Emuckfau Creek is not known, nor is the exact location of his campsite, but "best guess" reasoning places the camp near modern New Site, Alabama.[2]

Jackson's experience in January, when he engaged the Creeks at the Battles of Emuckfau and Enitachopco, seems to have guided his thinking as he planned his campaign. At Emuckfau, on January 22, Red Stick forces launched a surprise attack on his camp. Thus, Jackson put some distance between his camp and that of his enemy. The Battles of Emuckfau and Enitachopco are frequently overlooked but were crucial to the ultimate success at Horseshoe Bend. Although neither were clear victories for either side—one could argue they were both draws—Jackson was forced to relinquish ground and retreat, but he did so as a cohesive force. Even so, in military circles, to relinquish ground does not present a positive picture. At Enitachopco Creek, a portion of his army broke, which Jackson viewed as weakness. Having been forced into retreat and seeing his lines broken, Jackson railed at insubordination, cowardice, the disintegration of his rear guard, and the limitation of his amateur force. After receiving reinforcement in late winter, including the Thirty-Ninth Regiment, a regular US infantry unit, he was presented with a wider range of options and could deploy strength in ways not possible before. In addition, the greater professionalism of the regulars imposed discipline on his army. Thus, his Red Stick enemies, who had proved it was possible to break his line, create disorder in the US ranks, and generally do well against them, framed their actions on these past perceptions. By the time Jackson came to them on March 27, he had a vastly more disciplined and stronger army.[3]

From their camp north of Emuckfau Creek, the Americans set out about 6:30 a.m. and reached Horseshoe Bend by 10:00 a.m. on the morning of the twenty-seventh.[4] Accounts vary as to Jackson's actual numbers, ranging from 3,000 to 3,300, but his force included 600 regulars from the Thirty-Ninth US Infantry, 500 Cherokee auxiliaries, 100 allied Creek auxiliaries, and approximately 2,100 Tennessee militia organized into three brigades. When Jackson broke camp, he divided his force into two contingents. While dividing a force in the face of an enemy is contrary to the traditional tenets of war, Jackson never intended that his force should stay divided or fight separately. Rather he had devised a precise strategy based on intelligence gathered by John Coffee in January, who saw the barricade while pursuing a group of Red Sticks from Emuckfau Creek. His aim was to "exterminate" them—eliminate them as a threat. He knew that the barricade they constructed would be a formidable barrier.[5] As he set out on March 27, he divided his force in order to contain the enemy. His objective was to encircle the Red Stick force gathered to meet him. The main force of about 2,000 men, with artillery, proceeded with Jackson directly to the barricade at Tohopeka. A mobile force of 700 Tennessee riflemen and 600 allied Creek warriors under John Coffee proceeded to cross the Tallapoosa River and take up positions at the Red Stick rear. Initially, the riflemen faced away from the action to protect the field in the event that Red Stick reinforcements arrived, while the Cherokee and Creek allies lined the riverbank directly opposite Tohopeka village. Jackson had two field guns with him: a six-pounder and a three-pounder. Neither gun was capable of knocking down the heavily fortified barricade, but Jackson intended to use his cannon to hammer away at a weak point and eventually soften it or create a gap. Jackson himself was impressed with the site chosen by the Red Sticks. In a letter, he astutely summed up the location: "This bend, which resembles in its curvature that of a horseshoe includes I conjecture, eighty or a hundred acres. The river immediately around it, is deep, and somewhat upwards of 100 yards wide. As a situation for defense it was selected with judgment, and improved with great industry and art."[6]

The cannon were placed on a high point of land—today known as Gun Hill—roughly eighty yards from the Red Stick barricade. The remainder of Jackson's forces—the Thirty-Ninth and most of the militia—was stationed three to four hundred yards away from the barricade. Jackson, intent on precision bombing of the barricade, placed his guns very close, putting his artillery crews well in range of the Red Stick muskets. To distract the Red Sticks from firing against the cannon crews, Jackson deployed a skirmishing force of riflemen to maintain a harassing fire upon the barricade. During this early phase of the battle, the artillerymen faced the greatest danger. With one dead and ten wounded, one in three US casualties came during this initial artillery assault against the Red Stick barricade. Although there is evidence that some of the cannon shot penetrated the barricade, thus killing or injuring Red Sticks, overall, the bombardment was ineffective. After two hours of fire, the artillery had failed at knocking down a section of the wall.[7]

Everyone who saw the barricade was impressed. Unfortunately, aside from comments about its "ingenuous" construction and general sketches on maps, no comprehensive description exists. We do know the basics: the structure was four hundred yards long and stretched from one end of the peninsula to the other. It was from five to eight feet high and contained two rows of firing ports cut through the horizontal log wall. Generally, it was shaped in a shallow "V" with the point heading toward the bend; thus, as Jackson noted, it could not be breached without exposing men to fire from two angles. The huge pine logs—archaeological excavations have revealed they were forty feet long at the base—were laid horizontally and stacked atop each other. Four to five large trees would have been required to achieve the minimum height of five feet, since the trees were a foot and a half in diameter.[8] Work on the barricade was generally believed to have begun in December 1813, and when Coffee saw it on January 22, it was largely in place, although no doubt lacking in refinements. The construction of such a formidable barrier was an impressive task for men using hand tools and, mostly likely, no draft animals. Trees are thought to have been harvested from the peninsula or nearby and hauled by hand to the site, using wedges and ropes. The manner in which the construction project was directed and under whose direction it was constructed remain a mystery. Today, the area encompassing the barricade is an open grassy field surrounded by a mixed pine and hardwood forest. A straight line of white posts marks the approximate location of the Red Sticks' log wall. Supporting this main continuous fortification, the Red Sticks constructed a series of smaller "fall back" positions from logs piled up with hollowed areas under them. These secondary positions were scat-

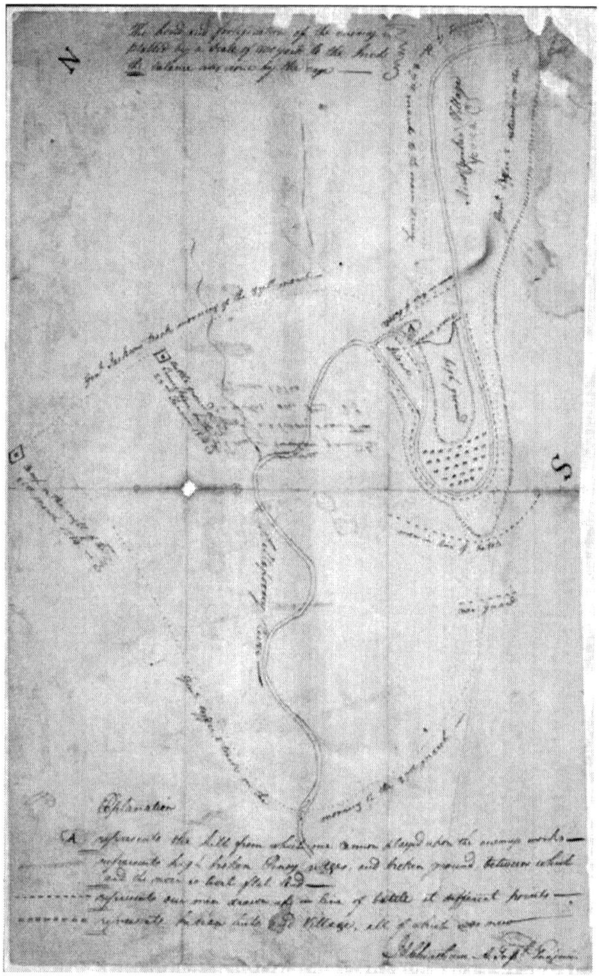

7.1. John Cheatham's battle map of Horseshoe Bend, March 27, 1814. President William H. Harrison Papers, Record Group 77, CWMF, Misc. 11-2, National Archives and Records Administration, Washington, D.C.

tered across what became known as the "high ground" or "rough ground" in contemporary accounts of the battle. This area is the center portion of the one-hundred-acre bend and today still conveys a close approximation of the rough, tangled ground fought over in 1814.

By 10:30 a.m., Jackson's forces had come together. As the bombardment of the barricade began, the carefully choreographed encirclement took on a new dimension as three Cherokee warriors, eager to engage in the battle, abandoned their positions on the perimeter and swam the Tallapoosa River. Once there, they encountered some slight resistance and one, The Whale, was wounded. The remaining two procured canoes and crossed back to the far side of the river. With that, the bulk of the Cherokee and allied Creek warriors and a few of the Tennessee militia began the process of crossing the river toward the rear of the Red Stick positions. No record reveals who gave the order to cross the river or even if there was an order to cross. We assume that this was an act of battlefield initiative on the part of the young Cherokee warriors, and it changed the course of the battle. For once across the river, the Cherokees and allied Creeks set fire to the area we know as the village—where Creek habitations had been constructed. Most of the Red Stick warriors were at the barricade, and the Cherokees and allied Creeks encountered virtually no resistance until Red Stick warriors realized a rear action was under way, and some began to fall back to protect the village.[9] With this, the Red Stick Creeks lost control of their destiny as the obvious advantage of the barricade was negated and opportunities for escape by canoe dwindled. The battle became a desperate fight for survival.

When Jackson saw obvious signs of combat deeper in the bend, along with the smoke from burning huts, he realized that an attack on the Red Stick rear was under way. He promptly halted the cannonade and launched a bayonet assault of the barricade by his regular troops. By this time, approximately 12:30 p.m., many Red Stick defenders had dropped back to defend the village, now under attack by what appeared to be the bulk of the Cherokees.

The number of Red Sticks at Horseshoe Bend is a matter of some speculation and estimation. One captive Cherokee woman estimated there were one thousand Red Sticks warriors gathered there. These were Abeika Creeks, from the nearby towns of Okfuskee, Okchai, Nuyaka, Hillabee, Fish Ponds, and Eufaula.[10] Even though they were attacked from the rear by a force nearly as large as their own, the action failed, as Jackson observed, to "dislodge" the defenders. According to Jackson, when he ordered the fortification to be taken "by storm," his men "hailed it with acclamation." Jackson's men gained the advantage and took control of the barricade rather quickly; however, it was not without cost. Indeed, it was the bloodiest, most intense fighting of the day.[11]

Once the barricade was breached, the Red Sticks relinquished their forward positions and fell back to secondary defensive positions. These were radically different from the massive barricade, being widely spaced and more rudimentary in nature. According to Jackson, the battle "continued with some severity for five hours," or until dark. During this time, the Ameri-

7.2. Selocta, the son of Chinnabee, a Natchee (Natchez) Creek chief. He served as a guide for Andrew Jackson and fought with the allied Creeks against the Red Sticks at Horseshoe Bend. From Thomas L. McKenney and James Hall's *History of the Indian Tribes of North America.*

cans and Cherokees and allied Creeks carefully scoured the peninsula, killing Red Sticks they encountered. Those who reached the river found escape impossible. Coffee's mounted riflemen moved in, taking up positions along the riverbank. Forty Tennessee riflemen under Lieutenant Jesse Bean positioned themselves on an island that today bears his name, thereby preventing Red Sticks from escaping in that vicinity.[12]

Andrew Jackson's plan to encircle and destroy his enemy had worked beautifully. On the other hand, the Red Stick plan, which no doubt was designed to hold up against US guns and militia, failed. Perhaps the biggest failure was the absence of a rear guard to protect the canoes they had assembled to aid a retreat if necessary, for with the loss of mobility, the badly outnumbered and more poorly equipped Red Sticks, even though they fought valiantly and desperately, were caught in an untenable position.

Jackson's losses were 49 killed, with 154 wounded. The day after the battle, Jackson detailed officers to count enemy dead, which they listed at 557 on the battlefield. Estimates by the Americans placed those shot dead in the river by the mounted riflemen at 250 to 300. Total loss to the Red Stick force may have exceeded 800. Given the lack of a positive count of those killed while in the river, it is impossible to devise an accurate count of Red Stick losses. On one point most observers agreed: very few had escaped the battlefield with their lives. Jackson himself wrote, "It is believed that not more than 20 have escaped."[13] Virtually no Red Sticks surrendered, but women and children from the village were captured. Jackson first noted that the number of captives was 250, but later increased the number to 350. In any case, these became the property of Cherokees and allied Creeks, who treated them as slaves.

One of the few to escape was perhaps one of the most famous of all Creeks: Menawa of Okfuskee. Wounded seven times, including a shot through the mouth, he lay unconscious on the field as the battle raged around him. Regaining consciousness after night fell, he managed to make his way to the river and launch a canoe into the water. The river carried him downstream to Elkahatchee Creek, where most of the elderly and women had been secreted prior to the battle. The few Red Stick survivors of the battle appear to have escaped after dark, and most of them were severely wounded.[14]

The day after the battle, US forces buried their own dead by sinking them in the Tallapoosa River in order to prevent desecration of their bodies by Red Sticks. Only one man, Major Lemuel Montgomery, who was killed leading the assault on the barricade, was buried on the battlefield. The dead Red Sticks were left on the battlefield. Years later, white settlers who visited the site would report that their bleached bones were scattered about the field.

The Battle of Horseshoe Bend essentially ended the Creek War. It was a watershed event in Creek Indian history, as well as US history. The participants of the battle on both sides read like a roll call in southern history. In addition to Andrew Jackson, Sam Houston, and John Coffee, many of the most important Cherokee men of the age fought at the Horseshoe: John Ross, The Ridge, Sequoyah, Junaluska. The heavy losses suffered by the Red Stick Creeks obliterated a generation of leaders, but one who survived, Menawa, came to be among the most respected and revered of all

7.3. Menawa, the military leader of Red Stick forces at Horseshoe Bend. This Okfuskee warrior, although gravely wounded, survived the battle. From Thomas L. McKenney and James Hall's *History of the Indian Tribes of North America.*

Creek warriors. On the other hand, William McIntosh of Coweta, who led the allied Creeks in Jackson's force, became the most reviled for his actions in signing the Treaty of Indian Springs in 1825, which turned over all Creek lands in Georgia to the United States by that fraudulent treaty.

Visitors to the battle site today will encounter a carefully maintained park of 2,040 acres. The visitors' center includes museum exhibits about Creek

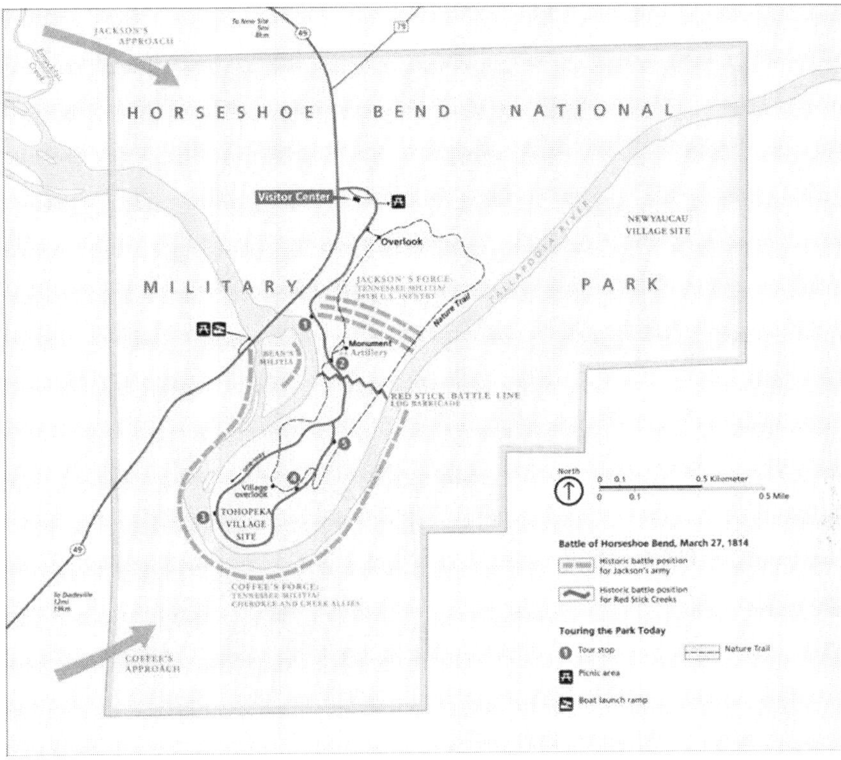

7.4. Horseshoe Bend National Military Park. Courtesy of the National Park Service.

culture and the war and a theater that shows a documentary film about the battle. The first stop on the driving tour of the area is the Overlook, which provides the best view of the battlefield. Today, visitors see an open pasture leading down to the barricade site—a very different vista than that encountered by Andrew Jackson. Absent tree stumps and the massive Red Stick barricade, people can nonetheless view the slope upon which Jackson's forces arrayed before battle, the small hill upon which he placed his artillery, and the sight of the barricade, which is marked by posts.

Other stops provide a close-up view of the barricade area and provide access to the 1918 congressional monument commemorating the battle site. As visitors proceed along the tour road, they can view the site where Cherokee and allied Creek warriors crossed the river to attack the village. Although not open to foot traffic, the fifteen-acre island in the Tallapoosa River where Tennessee militiamen under Lieutenant Bean were situated during the battle is visible as well. Bean's riflemen stationed on the small island prevented Red Stick warriors from taking refuge on that spot of land or escaping downstream. The modern calm and beauty of the site can never adequately convey the roar and carnage of the great battle that took place there; however, a visit to the site does allow a brief connection with our past. It points to the shared history between two nations that are now one. From a brief visit, modern people may gain insight into the mindset and lives of people who lived and fought here two centuries ago. Young visitors, while not fully comprehending the meaning of armed conflict, are capable of understanding disagreements and differences. They comprehend the fact that two groups can be at odds, and they appreciate the diversity and dignity of the people whose lives were forever changed by the Battle of Horseshoe Bend.

The past is often described as another world because it is removed from us in time; yet we are drawn to historic places, and these special places allow us to maintain our connections to distant events. The bicentennial of the Creek War and the Battle of Horseshoe Bend presents a unique opportunity to reexamine and commemorate those distant events that still affect our lives to this day. Though the timeline separating us from the actual events of two hundred years ago grows longer, Horseshoe Bend National Military Park remains our touchstone to the past. It connects us and future generations to our shared past. It remains a living memorial.

Notes

1. Thomas L. McKenney and James Hall, *The Indian Tribes of North America with Biographical Sketches and Anecdotes of the Principal Chiefs,* 3 vols. Ed. by Frederick Webb Hodge. (Philadelphia: Rice & Hart, 1855; repr., Edinburgh: John Grant, 1934), 2:184.

2. The standard account of the battle is James W. Holland, "Andrew Jackson and the Creek War: Victory at Horseshoe Bend," *Alabama Review* 21 (1968): 243–75. See also the more recent work: Tom Kanon, "'A Slow, Laborious Slaughter': The Battle of Horseshoe Bend," *Tennessee Historical Quarterly* 58 (1999): 3–15.

3. See chapter by Tom Kanon, "Before Horseshoe: Andrew Jackson's Campaigns in the Creek War prior to Horseshoe Bend," this volume.

4. Andrew Jackson to Thomas Pinckney, March 28, 1814, in *The Papers of Andrew Jackson,* vol. 3, *1814–1815,* ed. Harold D. Moser, David R. Hoth, Sharon Macpherson, and John H. Reinbold (Knoxville: University of Tennessee Press, 1991), 3:52.

5. Andrew Jackson to Rachel Jackson, January 28, 1814, in *Papers of Andrew Jackson,* ed. Moser et al., 3:18. Holland, "Andrew Jackson," 21–23.

6. Andrew Jackson to Governor Willie Blount, April 5, 1814, *Nashville Whig,* May 25, 1814.

7. Ibid.; Andrew Jackson to Thomas Pinckney, March 28, 1814, in *Papers of Andrew Jackson,* ed. Moser et al., 3:52.

8. Roy S. Dickens Jr., *Archaeological Investigations at Horseshoe Bend National*

Military Park, Alabama, Special Publications No. 3, Alabama Archaeological Society (Tuscaloosa: University of Alabama, 1979), 79–81.

9. For Cherokee participation in the battle, see Susan M. Abram, "Cherokees in the Creek War: A Band of Brothers," in this volume.

10. Andrew Jackson to Thomas Pinckney, March 28, 1814, in *Papers of Andrew Jackson,* ed. Moser et al., 3:52. Scholars recognize three main divisions among the Upper Creeks: the Tallapoosa, Abeika, and Alabama. Although a number of scholars separate the Okfuskee towns as a separate division, throughout the eighteenth century they were included by earlier British observers—and the Creeks—as a significant element of the Abeika towns.

11. Andrew Jackson to Thomas Pinckney, March 28, 1814, in *Papers of Andrew Jackson,* ed. Moser et al., 3:52.

12. Ibid., 3:53.

13. Ibid., 3:52.

14. McKenney and Hall, *The Indian Tribes of North America,* 1:106–107.

8
Fort Jackson and the Aftermath

Gregory A. Waselkov

The battle at the Horseshoe on March 27, 1814, is almost invariably described as the end of the Creek War, the final climactic act of an exceptionally violent though—at barely seven months—brief conflict between the United States and a large segment of the Creek Nation. In its immediate aftermath, however, the decisive impact of that bloody day was not at all certain to US commanders of forces converging from the north, east, and south on the Hickory Ground at the confluence of the Coosa and Tallapoosa Rivers. For some Red Stick Creeks the fight did not end then, or for many years to come. The prophets' teachings that had inspired a movement to reclaim lands for Indians alone, for Indian ways free from interference by whites, were not easily forgotten even in the face of massive battlefield losses and the famine suffered by surviving warriors and their families. Flight south to Spanish Florida and their kin, the Seminoles, sustained those determined to continue the fight, which, in fact, some did for another four decades. However, the utter devastation of their country and the destruction of every one of the sixty towns in the Upper Creek country did persuade many of the estimated eight thousand homeless Red Sticks to accept defeat and seek food and aid from their enemies.

After Horseshoe Bend, rumors reached US commanders of Red Stick intentions to make another stand at the Hickory Ground, a major town on the lower Coosa River that had served over the previous half century as a meeting place for the leadership of the Creek Nation on occasions of crisis. Other more accurate reports told of one last remaining Red Stick stronghold, the Cluwallee Camps near the old town of Hoithlewaulee on the lower Tallapoosa River.[1]

On April 7, with his militia's three-month enlistment drawing to a close and only eight days' rations on hand, General Andrew Jackson set his three-thousand-strong army of Tennesseans, Cherokees, and Thirty-Ninth US Infantry regulars down the Tallapoosa valley toward those objectives, marching as rapidly as they could in heavy rains. Near the falls of the Tallapoosa, he made contact with Colonel Homer Milton, commanding elements of the Third US Infantry and General Joseph Graham's Carolina Brigade. Graham's army of North Carolina and South Carolina militia units relieved Georgia militia that had twice attacked the Red Sticks from the east. The Carolina Brigade crossed the Chattahoochee River and swept the south bank of the Tallapoosa, while Jackson's army proceeded along the north bank. They located and burned many deserted towns, including the Cluwallee Camps. Upon reaching the forks of the Alabama River on April 17, Jackson discovered the Hickory Ground and the nearby town of Tuskegee (Taskigi) in ashes, destroyed by Milton's advance troops, and the remaining Red Sticks dispersed.[2]

General Jackson determined to fortify the site of Tuskegee in order to dominate the Red Stick heartland and defend his conquests from anticipated British military incursions. US political and military leaders had always (wrongly) attributed Red Stick militancy to meddling by British agents thought to be circulating among the Creeks. But now there were increasing signs of British naval activity in the Gulf of Mexico, and an attack on Mobile seemed likely. General Graham's Carolinians were tasked with construction of a large earthen structure, Fort Jackson, on a high bluff overlooking the Coosa River. The US engineers chose a strategic spot on an isthmus between the Coosa and Tallapoosa Rivers, where French colonizers had maintained Fort Toulouse among the Creeks during the early eighteenth century. Fort Jackson, with its impressive dry moat, drawbridge, and artillery-mounted bastions, was designed to withstand British attack as well as serve as a central supply base for operations against the remaining Red Sticks. Thousands of US troops were billeted on the Tallapoosa side of the isthmus at Camp Jackson, an equally imposing tent city with hospital, guardhouse, ovens, and other structures.[3]

Within hours of Jackson's arrival at the Forks on April 17, hundreds of starving Creek men, women, and children began to gather around the Americans' camp, as did others at all the US forts established along the lines of march into Upper Creek country. Among them were Polly Jones and her three young children (Seaborn, Samuel, and little Jeffersonia Hawkins Jones), *métis* Creeks taken at Fort Mims on August 30, 1813, held at Wewocau during the war, and left at the Hickory Ground as their liberators approached. The following day, William Weatherford rode into the midst of the US Army and walked boldly up to Jackson's marquis to surrender.[4]

Weatherford was undoubtedly the Red Stick leader best known to the US public. Early in the war he had been widely vilified for his role in planning and executing the stunningly successful Red Stick attack on Fort Mims, a palisaded plantation home sheltering hundreds of civilians under the protection of about forty-five local militia and one hundred Mississippi Territorial Volunteers. In addition to numerous white settlers and enslaved blacks, many of the families taking refuge in Fort Mims were métis Creeks, mixed-race members of the Creek Nation who had rejected the Red Stick religion's militant anti-Americanism and sided with their neighbors and friends living in the Tensaw district immediately north of Mobile. William Weatherford had deep kin and commercial ties to Tensaw métis, but his growing alienation from them reflected a widening social rift that culminated in a civil war among the Creeks during the summer of 1813. His hesitation vanished when US militia crossed into the Creek Nation and joined with Tensaw métis to attack a Red Stick packhorse train at the Wolf Trail crossing on Burnt Corn Creek in July 1813. Weatherford and other Alabama and Koasati members of the Red Stick movement thereafter resolved to destroy the Tensaw métis and their US allies taking shelter within Fort Mims. At the end of the long battle, as the American and métis defense collapsed, numerous civilians were mutilated and killed by Red Stick warriors. Weatherford evidently tried ineffectually to halt the massacre. Although he was only in the second rank of the Red Stick war party, US officials attributed leadership of the attacking force at Fort Mims principally to him, probably because he was highly acculturated to US society, and a US defeat of this shocking scale seemed somehow easier to accept if masterminded by a light-skinned, English-speaking Indian with a pronounceable name.[5]

When William Weatherford strode into Jackson's presence, many in the US Army expected (and some no doubt hoped) that the man widely held responsible for the massacre at Fort Mims would be summarily executed. No one doubted Andrew Jackson's capacity for swift, brutal, frontier justice. He had not stayed his troops at Horseshoe Bend from methodically annihilating the remnants of that Red Stick army long after the barricade had fallen, and he did not hesitate to hang Josiah Francis, the Alabama prophet, and other prominent British and Red Stick opponents who fell into his hands later in the conflict. What caused Jackson to pardon this particular Red Stick? Weatherford was, by all accounts, fearless, and, although there were no other witnesses to the meeting, second-hand reports agree that he gave a brief but eloquent speech accepting responsibility for the damage he inflicted on his military adversaries while regretting his inability to avert the deaths of civilians at Fort Mims. Whatever his reasons, Jackson evidently admired Weatherford's courage and forthright nature, and Weatherford, in turn, worked strenuously to reconcile defeated Red Sticks to US subjugation.[6]

After gaining an assurance of safe conduct for his own extended family, who had hidden from the conquerors on an island in the upper Alabama River, Weatherford agreed to work with the Americans for the surrender of other scattered bands. In late May he and 70 other former Red Stick warriors joined Colonel John Pearson's command of 300 Carolinians on a sweep through the central Alabama River valley south of the Cahaba. This mixed force persuaded nearly 300 Creeks to surrender, including the Coosada King and 75 of his followers, mostly women and children, part of the Koasati ethnic group to which Weatherford belonged. They pursued but could not catch one forlorn Creek family, which abandoned their dugout canoe containing the half-consumed legs and thigh of a colt. Pearson's detachment also brought in 35 African women and children taken during the fighting at Fort Mims and elsewhere to the south. The return of his force to Fort Jackson on June 5 brought the total number of surrendered Red Sticks there to 1,321, and all depended upon rations from the US military.[7]

The dispersal of surviving Red Sticks as the US troops advanced on the Hickory Ground was partly a tactical response to the overwhelming force bearing down upon them and partly due to the necessity to search widely for the meager foods available at that time of year in the forests of central Alabama. Unrelenting US campaigns through the fall, winter, and spring had destroyed town after town, along with their granaries and other stored food supplies, and pushed survivors further into the heart of the Upper Creek country, into a few increasingly overcrowded towns along the lower Coosa and Tallapoosa Rivers. Compounding the hunger caused by this refugee influx was the Red Stick prophets' injunction to turn away from US-style plantation agriculture, which had become highly symbolic, contested ground. For Creek traditionalists, US insistence that Creek men set aside the hunting way of life and take up the plow, to work in fields that had been the realm of women, tainted the whole endeavor. Many Red Stick families gave up on farming altogether, and for a while the untended land returned a bounty. The panic that followed the fall of Fort Mims emptied the Creek frontier and, for a time, the abandoned fields of the defeated Americans and Creek métis in the Tensaw and Tombigbee districts did furnish ample corn and sweet potatoes for Red Stick warriors and families assembled at the Holy Ground and the Cluwallee Camps and other warring towns. But those towns had been destroyed, and their former inhabitants now needed seeds to replant and rations to sustain them until the summer harvest.

The task of provisioning the US troops and their new charges became a major challenge. Boatloads of provisions were dispatched up the Alabama River from Mobile and down the Coosa River from Tennessee, and the state of Georgia sent food across the Chattahoochee River along the Federal Road. General Graham found these lifelines brittle, and he fretted constantly about food shortages. Benjamin Hawkins, principal US agent to the Creek Indians, appointed Major James Warren, Graham's topographical engineer, to be assistant Indian agent at Fort Jackson and see that the surrendered Red Sticks were fed, clothed, and treated well. Warren embraced his new role enthusiastically, earning Graham's exasperation at his "prepossession in favor of the red people, having now become bone of their bone & flesh of their flesh." Hawkins ordered the quartermaster to issue two gallons of corn to each Indian family for planting. Graham felt he could ill afford such a generous provision without placing his army at risk and ordered Warren to reduce the amount to two quarts per family.[8]

Surrender to the Americans did not necessarily ensure good treatment by the militia or by other Creeks. Hopoithle Mico, the Tallassee King, suffered some unspecified abuse on May 30 while under guard at Fort Jackson. Sergeant John Gray, officer of the guard, who claimed that he did "not know who it was that done it," merely received a reprimand from General Graham. The reputedly ninety-five-year-old Tallassee King died on June 12 and was buried on the Coosa River bluff north of the fort. Old animosities from the Creek civil war festered long after the Red Sticks' surrender. Graham returned to camp one evening to find six hundred Alabamas clustered around his tent, seeking protection from some Cussitas and Tuckabatchees who had allied with the Americans during the war and now wanted to plunder the few possessions of their former enemies.[9]

While General Graham oversaw construction of Fort Jackson and dealt with the refugee crisis, General Jackson remained preoccupied with the several thousand unrepentant Red Sticks who continued to evade US forces. Peter McQueen, a Scots-Creek métis and head warrior (*tastanagi*) of Tallassee, and his followers were south of the Tallapoosa River in the vicinity of Line Creek; and the prophet Josiah Francis led a band of Alabamas in the Catoma Creek area not far south of the new US stronghold. These and other isolated Red Stick forces drifted south over the coming months toward a haven in Spanish West Florida, where they could hope for resupply of ammunition and food and a respite from harassment by the Americans. At first, US forces respected Spanish neutrality and the international border on the thirty-first parallel just north of Pensacola. In addition to Colonel Pearson's foray to the central Alabama River valley in late May and June, the Thirty-Ninth US Infantry and Colonel George Nixon's Mississippi Territorial Volunteers searched the Escambia River valley for Red Sticks in July. At about that time, however, Colonel Joseph Carson's Mississippi territorial dragoons, accompanied by William Weatherford, crossed the boundary and attacked a Red Stick settlement called Coneta near Pensacola. According to

British reports, the Americans "killed all the Indians they could lay hands on" and took "what Women and Children could be found." By late summer an estimated seventeen hundred Red Stick Creeks had reached Spanish West Florida, where they established new towns, found common cause with the Seminoles, and showed every intention of continuing their struggle against the Americans.[10]

During the first nine days in August, Jackson, Hawkins, and Thomas Pinckney, representing the US government, met with assembled Creek leaders, nearly all of whom had sided with the Americans in the war against the Red Sticks, to negotiate a peace treaty. In fact, the treaty's terms were dictated by Jackson, who was determined to sever the Creek Nation from Spanish and British support to the south and to seize the majority of Creek lands as war reparations, for eventual sale to US settlers. Ignoring objections from all sides, including his fellow commissioners, Jackson imposed punitive terms on the assembly. The Treaty of Fort Jackson claimed 21,086,793 acres from the Creek Nation, including most of the best hunting territories of the Lower and Upper Creeks, the largest seizure of Indian lands to that point in US history. In return the Creeks were promised autonomy within their remaining lands, as well as food and clothing during the coming winter. A number of prominent Creeks who had sided with the Americans, mostly métis and a few white men adopted by the Creek Nation, were permitted to retain tracts outside the treaty reservation. (One of these tracts formed the nucleus of the community that has since become the Poarch Band of Creek Indians, near Atmore, Alabama.)[11]

In mid-September about 200 Red Sticks led by McQueen and Francis, along with a number of Seminoles, joined a British naval expedition intent on capturing Fort Bowyer, a small US battery at the mouth of Mobile Bay. This first British military attack of the war on the US Gulf Coast failed when one of their vessels, the frigate HMS *Hermes,* was disabled by US artillery fire and had to be destroyed. Despite this failure, the British attempt on Fort Bowyer convinced Jackson that Mobile (not New Orleans) was their principal objective, and he recognized the continuing threat posed by unsubdued Red Sticks on the southern frontier. At this crucial moment, with a British expeditionary force offshore, 356 militiamen from Colonel Philip Pipkin's First Tennessee Regiment deserted from Forts Jackson, Williams, and Strother (the latter two higher up the Coosa River), believing they had fulfilled their obligation to serve just three months of military service. Most were soon recaptured or voluntarily returned to duty, and Jackson pardoned all but six identified as ringleaders, who were executed for mutiny. This unfortunate incident, and an earlier execution of a militia private at Jackson's command, became the subject of broadsides proclaiming the Gen-

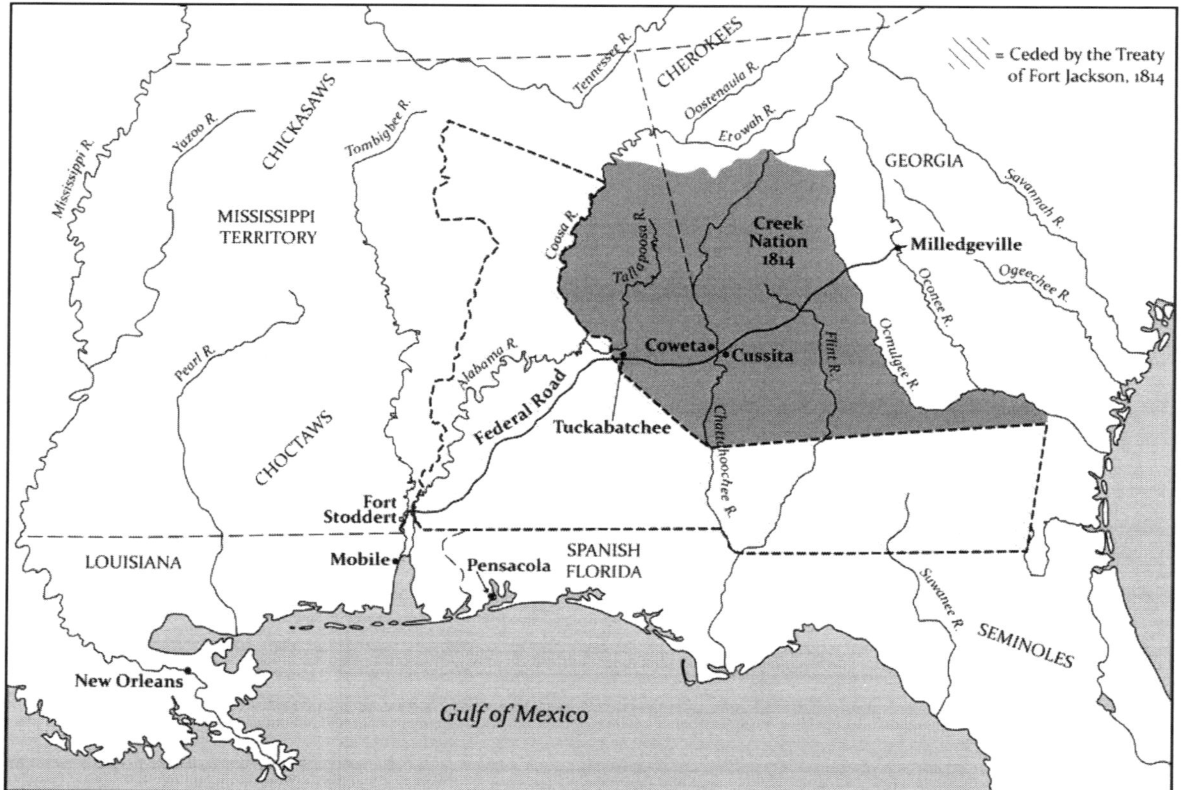

8.1. The Creek Nation following the Treaty of Fort Jackson. Map by Sarah Mattics, Center for Archaeological Studies, University of South Alabama.

eral's "Bloody Deeds," circulated by Thomas Hart Benton and other political opponents during Jackson's presidential campaigns many years later.[12]

According to testimony at the court martial, the discontents had "frequently collected in front of Lieutenant James McCauley's tent to make use of the *black drink* before their departure from Fort Jackson," and the men had often been heard "uttering mutinous language" while "using the *black drink*." McCauley ordered his men to discontinue use of the drink and berated them for behaving "like a parcel of savages." A caffeinated tea brewed from the leaves of yaupon holly (*Ilex vomitoria*), the black drink was consumed in quantity by Creek men in purification rituals, to strengthen social ties, and as a "war physic" before going into battle. McCauley's men had not merely adopted a Creek tea, but had accepted the drink's social associations and symbolically transgressed US cultural boundaries. Correspondence of officers stationed at Fort Jackson before and after the mutiny confirms that militiamen honestly believed they were being wrongfully detained in service beyond their enlistments. They also suffered from lack of provisions, spoiled flour, and widespread sickness (described as chronic rheumatism, general debility, and emaciation of the system). Indeed, living conditions of militia troops differed little from those of the Red Stick refugees in their charge, with similar levels of illness and mortality in the two camps around Fort Jackson, a situation in which militiamen may have felt they had more in common with the Creeks than with their own officers.[13]

By the time the Treaty of Fort Jackson was signed on August 9, eighty-two hundred Indians were drawing rations at a half dozen American forts. When provisions were ample, each one was issued three-quarters of a pound of flour and one-quarter of a pound of beef or pork daily; more commonly, they received a smaller ration of flour and were expected to eke out an existence by gathering edible plants and hunting for game in the forest. Standard fare for the soldiers consisted of about a pound of flour, some salt pork, and a gill (four ounces) of whiskey. In April General Graham had to prohibit his officers and men from purchasing game from Creek hunters he had hired to supply meat for the sick. The Creeks much preferred corn to wheat flour and occasionally were issued two-thirds of a quart of corn in place of flour rations. But corn, like everything else, was difficult to obtain, and what quantity was available was preferentially allocated as forage for draft animals and the officers' and dragoons' mounts. Even so, horses were seldom fed their full forage allowance of twelve quarts a day, and most of the South Carolina cavalry was dismissed for lack of forage.[14]

Fort Bowyer's defense against a British and Indian force organized in Spanish West Florida led Jackson to push forward with plans he had been crafting since August for a preemptive attack on Pensacola. At the newly established post in the Tensaw, Fort Montgomery, just a mile from the charred remnants of Fort Mims, he gathered elements of the Third, Thirty-Ninth, and Forty-Fourth US Infantry regiments, as well as Tennessee and Mississippi territorial troops and 750 Chickasaw and Choctaw warriors. Hundreds more Creeks led by William McIntosh would coordinate their own march down the Chattahoochee River. In late October, Jackson's army of 4,000 advanced against Pensacola and took the old Spanish colonial town on November 7. British and Red Stick combatants and civilians withdrew eastward to Fort Apalachicola, commonly called Prospect Bluff, where Major Edward Nicolls of the Royal Marines had established a base that attracted not only Red Sticks and Seminoles, but also runaway slaves who would fight to maintain their freedom. When Jackson withdrew most of his regulars to prepare the defenses of Mobile and New Orleans, he dispatched an expedition to the Escambia valley under the command of Major Uriah Blue with a large force of William Colbert's Chickasaws. Throughout December, Blue searched the endless scrub and longleaf pine forests as far east as the Choctawhatchee River without making significant contact with Red Stick Creeks. McIntosh's Creeks and Georgia militia likewise made little progress in their march toward Prospect Bluff.[15]

On January 8, Josiah Francis and other Red Stick and Seminole guests of the British watched Lieutenant General Sir Edward Pakenham's attack on Jackson's army outside of New Orleans fail disastrously. But even that debacle and the withdrawal of the British invasion force from the Gulf of Mexico did not weaken the British–Red Stick alliance forged on the ground by Nicolls, Francis, and McQueen. Early in 1815 Nicolls and the hundred Royal Marines in his command remained at Prospect Bluff, where some three thousand Indians and hundreds more free blacks had gathered for mutual defense.[16]

However, British resolve finally withered at higher levels once the implications of the Treaty of Ghent became clear to all parties. By the terms of Article Nine the United States agreed to restore all rights and lands to British-allied Indians with whom the United States was still at war at the time of the treaty signing. In fact, the United States uniformly failed to carry out the provisions of Article Nine along the entire western frontier. In any case, in the South the Treaty of Fort Jackson seemed to exempt the Red Sticks, despite the obvious fact that hostilities continued still between them and the United States. Finally, in June 1815, Nicolls was forced to evacuate his marines, along with Josiah Francis and his son, whom he took to London, where they found no support for renewed military action to support the Red Stick cause. (In 1817 Francis returned to Florida, where he was captured and hanged a year later by Americans during General Jackson's second invasion of Spanish Florida.)[17]

With the withdrawal of British and Red Stick forces, Prospect Bluff was left to the armed runaway slaves and became known as Negro Fort. One of the three black leaders of this very sizeable maroon community was Cyrus, probably the former slave of Sam Moniac, who, in August 1813, had taken an axe to the palisade at Fort Mims to assist the Red Stick assault at the beginning of the Creek War. The presence of black Red Sticks at Negro Fort, and the racial divide that occurred when most Indian and white-Indian métis Red Sticks left Prospect Bluff in June 1815, reflected a growing racialist sentiment shared by many Creeks and Seminoles by this time.[18]

Red Stick resistance to the Americans continued unabated in successive years. Late in 1817, a war party led by Neamathla ambushed a US military keelboat on the Flint River, killing thirty-four soldiers and their wives and children. This horrifying event, which had been provoked by repeated incursions of US troops on the Spanish/Red Stick side of the international boundary, triggered the First Seminole War. From this point forward, Red Stick Creeks and Seminoles in Florida would become one and the same to nearly all Americans opposing them.[19]

One conclusion is certain. Horseshoe Bend was a milestone in many ways. It virtually ended the war in the Creek Nation. But that battle did not bring an end to the Red Stick War, which simply shifted further south with considerable continuity in the individuals involved on both sides. One could argue that it did not conclude until 1858, when the United States unilaterally declared an end to the Third Seminole War.

Notes

1. George Stiggins, "A Historical narration of the Genealogy traditions and downfall of the Ispocaga or Creek tribe of Indians, written by one of the tribe," 47, 74–75, 77–78, in vol. 1, ser. 5, Georgia, Alabama, and South Carolina Papers, Lyman Draper Manuscript Collection, Wisconsin Historical Society; *American State Papers, Military Affairs,* ed. by Asbury Dickins and John W. Forney, vol. 3, *1823–1828* (Washington, DC: Gales & Seaton, 1860): 788–90 (hereafter cited as *ASPMA*); Frank L. Owsley Jr., *Struggle for the Gulf Borderlands: The Creek War and the Battle of New Orleans, 1812–1815* (Gainesville: University Presses of Florida, 1981), 82.

2. John Spencer Bassett, ed., *Correspondence of Andrew Jackson,* 7 vols. (Washington, DC: Carnegie Institution of Washington, 1926–1935), 1:500–503; Owsley, *Struggle for the Gulf Borderlands,* 82–83.

3. Gregory A. Waselkov, Brian M. Wood, and Joseph M. Herbert, *Coloni-*

zation and Conquest: The 1980 Archaeological Excavations at Fort Toulouse and Fort Jackson, Alabama, Auburn University Archaeological Monograph 4 (Montgomery, AL: Auburn University at Montgomery, 1982), 235–47.

4. *ASPMA,* 3:790; Bassett, *Correspondence of Andrew Jackson,* 1:503, 507.

5. Gregory A. Waselkov, *A Conquering Spirit: Fort Mims and the Redstick War of 1813–1814* (Tuscaloosa: University of Alabama Press, 2006). I borrow the term "métis," and the related "métissage," from modern critical theory to refer to people of mixed race who creatively develop an ethnicity distinct from their parent cultures. The Creeks of the Tensaw descended (mostly) from European men who married Creek women. For a variety of reasons, these particular multiracial families moved to the southern edge of the Creek Nation, at the limits of traditional Creek social control, where they experimented with novel forms of economic and political expression. Describing the Tensaw Creeks as métis highlights their creative ethnic reformulation as a specific example of a social process recognized in many other modern and historical contexts.

6. Waselkov, *A Conquering Spirit,*, 173–74, 326n.25.

7. Ibid., 174; Waselkov, Wood, and Herbert, *Colonization and Conquest,* 208; C. L. Grant, *Letters, Journals, and Writings of Benjamin Hawkins,* 2 vols. (Savannah, GA: Beehive Press, 1980), 2:680–81, 688; General Joseph Graham to General Andrew Jackson, near Fort Jackson, June 7, 1814, Joseph Graham Papers, 1780–1836, North Carolina State Archives, Raleigh, NC (hereafter cited as Graham Papers); "Report of Col Pearsons Expedition Against the Hostile Creeks on the Alabama, Camp Ho-to-wa Ninety four miles from Fort Jackson, East bank of the Allabama [*sic*] and half a days journey below the mouth of Ka-ha-ba, June 1st 1814," enclosure in letter, General Thomas Pinckney to Secretary of War, June 28, 1814, Letters Received by the Secretary of War, Registered Series (1801–1870), Record Group 107, Records of the Office of the Secretary of War, National Archives and Records Administration, Washington, DC (M221, 317 rolls), roll 65, P27.

8. Waselkov, Wood, and Herbert, *Colonization and Conquest,* 209–10; Graham to Benjamin Hawkins, and Graham to Pinckney, May 24, 1814, Graham Papers.

9. Waselkov, Wood, and Herbert, *Colonization and Conquest,* 209–10; Graham Orderly Books, May 30, 1814, and Graham to Pinckney, June 14, 1814, Graham Papers.

10. Sean Michael O'Brien, *In Bitterness and Tears: Andrew Jackson's Destruction of the Creeks and Seminoles* (Westport, CT: Praeger, 2003), 155, 159, 167; Waselkov, *A Conquering Spirit,* 175, 327n.29.

11. Charles J. Kappler, comp. and ed. *Indian Affairs: Laws and Treaties,* 7 vols. (Washington, DC: Government Printing Office, 1904), 2:107–10; Waselkov, Wood, and Herbert, *Colonization and Conquest,* 211; Owsley, *Struggle for the Gulf*

Borderlands, 86–94; Waselkov, *A Conquering Spirit,* 205–6; Judith Royster, "Indian Land Claims," in *Handbook of North American Indians,* vol. 2: *Indians in Contemporary Society,* ed. by Garrick A. Bailey, 28–37 (Washington, DC: Smithsonian Institution, 2008), 32; J. Anthony Paredes, "Creek in the East since Removal," in *Handbook of North American Indians,* vol. 14: *Southeast,* ed. by Raymond D. Fogelson, 404 (Washington, DC: Smithsonian Institution, 2004).

12. Owsley, *Struggle for the Gulf Borderlands,* 109–12; O'Brien, *In Bitterness and Tears,* 172–74; *ASPMA,* 3:693–793 [No. 371], also published as Report of the Committee on Military Affairs, *The Proceedings of a Court Martial Ordered for the Trial of Certain Tennessee Militiamen,* Report No. 140, House of Representatives, 20th Congress, 1st Session (Washington, DC: Gales & Seaton, 1828); Waselkov, Wood, and Herbert, *Colonization and Conquest,* 210–12, 223.

13. *ASPMA,* 3:705–7; Waselkov, Wood, and Herbert, *Colonization and Conquest,* 225–26; Charles H. Fairbanks, "The Function of Black Drink among the Creeks," in *Black Drink: A Native American Tea,* ed. by Charles M. Hudson (Athens: University of Georgia Press, 1979), 124–27.

14. Waselkov, Wood, and Herbert, *Colonization and Conquest,* 229–33.

15. O'Brien, *In Bitterness and Tears,* 175–83; Owsley, *Struggle for the Gulf Borderlands,* 112–19, 125–26, 135; Grant, *Letters, Journals, and Writings of Benjamin Hawkins,* 2:708–17; Brian R. Rucker, "In the Shadow of Jackson: Uriah Blue's Expedition into West Florida," *Florida Historical Quarterly* 73 (January 1995): 325–38.

16. Grant, *Letters, Journals, and Writings of Benjamin Hawkins,* 2:717–18; O'Brien, *In Bitterness and Tears,* 183–84; Owsley, *Struggle for the Gulf Borderlands,* 175; Claudio Saunt, *A New Order of Things: Poverty, Power, and Transformation of the Creek Indians, 1733–1816* (New York: Cambridge University Press, 1999), 279–80.

17. Owsley, *Struggle for the Gulf Borderlands,* 179–83; and Frank L. Owsley Jr., "Prophet of War: Josiah Francis and the Creek War," *American Indian Quarterly* 9 (Summer 1985): 273–93.

18. Joel W. Martin, *Sacred Revolt: The Muskogees' Struggle for a New World* (Boston, MA: Beacon Press, 1991), 222–23, 223n.41; Saunt, *A New Order of Things,* 283–84; O'Brien, *In Bitterness and Tears,* 192; Waselkov, *A Conquering Spirit,* 234.

19. O'Brien, *In Bitterness and Tears,* 198.

9
"We Bleed Our Enemies in Such Cases to Give Them Their Senses"

Americans' Unrelenting Wars on the Indians of the Trans-Appalachian West, 1810–1814

John E. Grenier

This chapter addresses the unrelenting wars that Americans waged in the early 1810s against the Indians of the trans-Appalachian West. Two major Indian conflicts—the Northwest Indian War of 1810–1813 and the Red Stick War of 1813–1814—wracked the trans-Appalachian frontier preceding and concurrent with the War of 1812. At the conclusion of these wars, US frontiersmen had crushed Indian hopes of blocking the expansion of the early republic as far west as the Mississippi River. Major General Andrew Jackson's rejoinder to the Creek headmen, those who had fought alongside him as allies and traveled to the treaty talks at Fort Jackson to salvage a semblance of independence for their people, was hardly hyperbole. He told them, "We [Americans] bleed our enemies in such cases to give them their senses."[1] Between 1810 and 1814, US arms literally and figuratively bled white the Indian peoples of the old Northwest and old Southwest.

This chapter explains the nature of Americans' wars on the early nineteenth-century frontier. The goal is to provide a context from which readers of this book can better understand Americans' actions—both their military operations and their resort to extreme and indiscriminate violence—that shaped the Creek War. The focus is on three key points regarding the Northwest Indian War and the Red Stick War: the wars' character, their purpose, and their legacy.

First, the character of US wars against the Indians remained consistent in both words and deed. I have described Americans' "first way of war" in my book of that title, and I have argued that from the early seventeenth century onward, Americans on the frontier—whether in New England, the Tidewater of Virginia, the Appalachian Piedmont, or the frontiers of the 1790s—generally waged war in an unlimited and unrelenting manner. Americans made little distinction between combatants and noncombatants, and the goal of their wars against Indians usually remained the total conquest and subjugation of their enemies.[2] The same pattern held true for both the Red Stick War and the Northwest Indian War. Americans stood unified and determined to crush the Indians at any cost, and by any means. As Jackson prepared for war in July 1813, he clearly laid out the fundamental US strategic objectives for the Red Stick War: "Drive the Indians and their allies into the ocean [the Gulf of Mexico]."[3] Americans conceived both these wars as no-holds-barred, unlimited conflicts to destroy their Indian enemies and seize their lands.

Second, the purpose of these wars was imperial conquest. Particularly among westerners—the Kentucky, Indiana, and Illinois militiamen who fought in the North and the Tennessee, Georgia, and Mississippi volunteers who campaigned against the Red Sticks—the fighting on the frontier had little to do with the United States' place in the Napoleonic Wars that then raged in Europe. The Indian wars became opportunities to gain Indian lands, not a national statement about impressment, interference with US trade on the high seas, or the economic woes that resulted from Thomas Jefferson and James Madison's failed embargoes. Of course, frontier Americans held deep antipathy for the British. A war with the Creeks also served the added benefit of driving British and Spanish influence from the Gulf borderlands, while a war against the Indians in the North offered the chance to eliminate what frontiersmen believed to be British manipulation of the Indians that hindered settlement of the Northwest Territory. Tennessee's governor Willie Blount observed that southern frontiersmen had an "ardent desire for the general improvement of the face of the country inhabited by the hostile Creeks, and that they [felt] too little inclination, after knowing the present and past conduct of these people, to permit their longer residence thereon." Tennesseans, Blount continued, expected to "soon become the cultivators of the rich soil, which they may, in that time, soon become possessed of by their valor."[4] Both the Northwest Indian War and the Red Stick War thus stand as manifestations of early nineteenth-century Americans' insatiable land hunger and their collective desire to establish dominion over the peoples and lands between the Appalachian Mountains and the Mississippi River.[5]

Last, the wars' character and purpose combined to shape their legacy. The wars fueled the dark legacy of segregation in US culture. At this time, segregation did not mean the practice of separating peoples of different races as a form of discrimination, but instead it meant totally removing them from the cultural and social landscape. As late as the middle decades of the eighteenth century, Americans tolerated some Indians among them, provided those Indians remained tractable and subservient to Americans' wishes.[6] By the end of the Indian wars of the early 1810s, however, few frontier Americans accepted Indians in their midst, even those Indians who prostrated themselves and acquiesced to being neither heard nor seen. Indeed, the Red Stick War, which began as a civil war among the Creek people and ended with some Creeks seeking US assistance against the Red Stick faction, served only to turn public opinion against the entire Creek Nation. By the war's end, newspapers and politicians' screeds had convinced the citizens of Mississippi that the Creeks, not just the Red Sticks, had visited upon them a war "unrestrained by any principles, which govern warfare among civilized nations."[7] Many Mississippians therefore expressed incredulity when they learned that the federal government had considered carving out a few dozen acres from the approximately 21,000,000-acre Creek cession for a Creek reservation on their Tuckabatchee town site. It did not matter that the leadership at Tuckabatchee had been the chief target of the Red Sticks at the beginning of the war. Henceforth, Americans no longer considered Indians as potential neighbors, but instead peoples whom they should segregate and, in the end, expel to the vast "American desert" west of the Mississippi River. The legacy of the Red Stick War and the Northwest Indian War proved a US antipathy for Indians that shaped white-Indian relations well into the twentieth century.

The means by which Americans executed the Northwest Indian War and the Red Stick War point to the wars' character, purpose, and legacy. Americans proved unrelenting in waging those wars. Although US military operations proved ad hoc, disorganized, and poorly coordinated, their grand strategic design remained consistent. Americans determined to extirpate their Indian enemies, expropriate their lands, and segregate from white US society those few Indians who survived.

There remains little debate that frontiersmen's actions precipitated these wars. Although by the early 1810s some Indians in the old Northwest had seen enough of settler encroachments on their lands to follow the calls of Tecumseh and his brother Tenskwatawa—also known as the Shawnee Prophet—to resist, just as many, if not more, Indians remained committed to peace with the Americans. Since the conclusion of the Ohio Indian War of the early 1790s, Indians who once led the opposition to the Americans, leaders like Little Turtle and Blue Jacket, had become agency chiefs. At the 1809 Treaty of Fort Wayne, for instance, Indiana territorial governor William Henry Harrison had convinced several destitute Delaware, Miami, and Potawatomi chiefs to abandon their claims to most of southern Indiana for an annuity of just over $5,200.[8] Tecumseh and his followers scorned the agency chiefs as weak and old men. The core of Tecumseh's compelling rhetoric of resistance centered in his call for Indian co-ownership of all the lands of the West, which left little to no room for US expansion.

Harrison's face-to-face meetings with Tecumseh convinced the former that only war could solve the Indian problem on the Northwest frontier. First, in 1810 at Vincennes, Tecumseh vociferously protested the previous year's Treaty of Fort Wayne. Then, in 1811, Tecumseh brought canoes loaded with militant Kickapoos, Wyandots, Peorias, Ojibwes, Potawatomis, Winnebagos, Shawnees, and other western Indians for the second round of diplomacy at Vincennes. This, coupled with a settler petition to President James Madison that read, "The safety of the persons and property of this frontier can never be effectually secured, but by the breaking up of the combination formed by the Shawnee Prophet on the Wabash," made Harrison believe his options for negotiation had dwindled.[9] After weeks of talks that settled none of the issues dividing the Americans and Indians, Tecumseh left Vincennes for a preplanned trip to the South to bring the Creeks, Choctaws, and Chickasaws into his burgeoning Indian confederacy. Harrison thereupon chose to start a war with the Northwest Indians.

Harrison hoped that if he destroyed Prophet's Town, at the confluence of the Tippecanoe and Wabash Rivers, he might discredit Tecumseh's faction among Indians. He marshaled a mixed force of Indiana and Kentucky frontiersmen and US regulars and advanced up the Wabash Valley. Harrison stopped at present-day Terre Haute, Indiana, and constructed Fort Harrison on contested lands. The fort showed any Indians who might have misunderstood that the Americans had claimed the Wabash Valley as US land. The time for negotiations and a peaceful resolution to the land dispute had passed.

The Indians in Prophet's Town, meanwhile, waited for the right moment. Tecumseh, then in the South, had warned his brother not to let the Americans draw him into a fight. The Prophet, however, believed that he had no other option but to lead his followers into battle in the early morning hours of November 7, 1811. He had convinced his warriors that he had imbued them with special powers that protected them from Americans' bullets. Whether from belief in those powers or from knowledge that they faced a desperate situation, the warriors "manifested a ferocity, uncommon even with them," Harrison later reported. At the cost of nearly two hundred casualties, Harrison drove the Indians from Prophet's Town. He burned the town, destroyed the Indians' granary, and allowed his troops to pillage what they could. In his post-battle report, Harrison claimed a major victory for the forces of US expansionism.[10]

While Harrison much later leveraged his role at Tippecanoe into the presidency of the United States, in the immediate term, the Battle of Tippecanoe drove hundreds of Indian warriors and their families to British-held Fort Malden in today's Ontario. Because of Americans' aggressive actions, the great fear of the frontier settlers loomed on the immediate horizon: well-armed and angry Indians now stood poised to unleash hell on the frontier. From the Indian agency at Fort Wayne in the Indiana Territory in March 1812, Captain James Rhea ominously predicted that Americans faced "an Indian war this spring, whether we have a British war or not."[11]

Rhea proved prescient. Indian war parties swept across the Northwest frontier in the summer of 1812. The US forts at Michilimackinac, Detroit, and Dearborn (present-day Chicago) capitulated to Indian besiegers. After the initial Indian onslaught, only Fort Wayne and Fort Harrison stood. Outside both the fort's walls and on distant farms, Indians massacred their captives. They killed the fifty-two Americans who had surrendered at Fort Dearborn, and they slaughtered men, women, and children at Pigeon Roost, north of Louisville, and on the O'Neal farm outside Peoria. Thousands of US settlers fled the frontier. In the end, the chaos on the frontier only hardened the attitudes of Indian haters and supplied them with further self-righteous justification for the bloodshed that followed.

US frontiersmen answered the Indian massacres with a series of punitive raids. The immediate goal focused on punishing Indians. Harrison arrived at Fort Wayne in September 1812 with two thousand Northwest militiamen, intent on "avenging his country and saving the frontier."[12] He turned the militia loose on Indians' fields to destroy the Indians' means of sustenance and drive them to starvation in the winter. Governor Samuel Hopkins of Kentucky mustered two thousand mounted volunteers to destroy the Indian towns and crops near Peoria. Hopkins's campaign proved a bust, but in October, Illinois governor Ninian Edwards and Colonel William Russell led a mixed force of militia and US Rangers against Pimartam's Town near Lake Peoria. They killed twenty Indians and, as was their practice, burned Indian food supplies. In November, Hopkins reconstituted his force and drove northward; he destroyed dozens of deserted Indian towns and fields—most Indians wisely had fled in the face of the US columns. While he undoubtedly preferred to have killed more Indians, Hopkins at least could find solace in that he had driven the Indians from the frontier. Indeed, there proved no rest for the Indians. Lieutenant Colonel John Campbell unleashed six hundred mounted rangers in a winter campaign in December against the Shawnees' towns in the Mississinewa River Valley. US rangers took to the Indiana and Illinois frontier to intercept any Indian raiders who ventured forth in the winter. Very few Indians dared leave the safety of their winter camps.

While renewed Indian attacks in the spring of 1813 temporarily stalled the pace of US offensive actions, by early summer hundreds of US forces again flooded the frontier to ethnically cleanse it. The target of these operations remained noncombatants, fields, and Indian shelters. In June and July, Indiana's rangers marched five hundred miles against the Indian village of Villonia, from which the springtime raids had originated. They put Villonia to the torch and turned the surrounding area into a wasteland. Although they returned home without having killed any Indians, Americans judged the campaign a success because they had made Villonia uninhabitable for Indians. In September, over thirteen hundred Missouri territorial militiamen similarly occupied the area around Peoria, which henceforth became a US "possession."

With the Indiana and Illinois frontiers relatively secure in 1813, US forces in the West directed their energies on the British-held base of support for the Indians in Ontario. Kentuckians had grown particularly enraged when they learned that British officers had stood by and watched their Indian allies scalp, immolate, and kill wounded prisoners in the River Raisin Massacre that followed the surrender of Fort Detroit. Kentucky militiamen, mounted on the prime horses of the Bluegrass State, therefore aggressively led the van of William Henry Harrison's pursuit of British major general Henry Proctor and Tecumseh's forces, resulting in the US victory at the Battle of Moraviantown in October 1813. Beyond cementing Harrison's place as a US hero, which he had first garnered at Tippecanoe, Moraviantown stood as the denouement of the Northwest Indian War. Indeed, few battles in US history proved more decisive. It stood as the final act of the US campaign to drive all Indians from the old Northwest. Thus, while the regular US Army found itself mired in the better-known struggle outside Niagara and in the Chesapeake, US frontiersmen of Kentucky, Ohio, Indiana, and Illinois had used the Northwest Indian War to conquer the old Northwest.

In the South, meanwhile, the War of 1812 stood as essentially an Indian war, the Red Stick War, until the Battle of New Orleans in January 1815. Like the settlers of Indiana and Illinois, many Georgians, Tennesseans, and Mississippians feared and loathed their Creek neighbors. The frontiersmen of the North and South had formed to march in lockstep against all Indians, regardless of their friendship or hostility. While both the Choctaws and the Chickasaws had prostrated themselves to the Americans and sold their lands at bargain-basement rates, the Creeks proved more troublesome. Many Creeks had adopted US ways—large numbers of Creek mestizos thoroughly had embraced US cultural and social mores. Many other Creeks wanted an end to US encroachments on their lands. A sizable faction found the actions of the Creek National Council, which sought accommodation rather than confrontation, particularly unpalatable. They ultimately raised the "red stick" of war and sought to destroy their leading chiefs. Even the pleading of Indian agent Benjamin Hawkins, who had lived among the Creeks for nearly twenty years and who feared the devastation that war promised, was not enough to calm tensions—indeed, his actions helped further fuel the Red Sticks' anger. Naturally, the frontiersmen of the South focused on the Red Sticks rather than the assimilationist Creeks. Although the Creek National Council members actively sought US assistance to defeat their Red Stick enemies—and fought against them in the war—US frontiersmen hungry for Creek lands took the actions of the Red Stick faction as expressions of the entire Creek Nation's will.

Civil war tore asunder the Creek Confederacy in 1813. Americans from the settlements along the Tombigbee River took the opportunity to insert themselves into a Creek internal affair at Burnt Corn Creek. The skirmish there among assimilationist Creeks, Red Sticks, and Americans sounded alarm bells across the American settlements in what is now Alabama and Mississippi. Settlers rushed to the putative safety of Fort Mims; Red Sticks massacred them there on August 30, 1813. Only 250 of the nearly 400 American, Creek, and mestizo men, women, and children, as well as African American slaves, who had sought refuge there escaped with their lives.[13] Like the massacres in the north at Fort Dearborn, Pigeon Roost, and River Raisin, the killings at Fort Mims enraged US sensibilities. After the Fort Mims Massacre, frontiersmen determined to extirpate the Creek Nation. Tennessee called up its militia, and Jackson prepared to lead a war of punishment, conquest, and finality into the Creek country.

Although dozens of Creek towns continued to profess their fidelity to the Americans, pointed out their allegiance in the effort to suppress the Red Sticks, and suffered terribly under Red Stick sieges, the Americans heard nothing of it. Americans refused to differentiate among the Creeks, primarily because Indians sat on the land that they wanted. Willie Blount went as far as to dismiss reports of a Creek civil war as "altogether fudge—a mere tub for the whale,"[14] as little more than a distraction from conquest of the old Southwest. Four US armies, in the largest operation in the Southeast since the US campaign to destroy the Cherokee Nation in 1776 and another US war on the frontier lost in the larger context of an anti-British war, prepared to descend on the Creek Nation. The strategic objective was to drive the Creeks from the Southeast; the operational and tactical goals became to kill as many Red Sticks as possible and, short of that, destroy their dwellings and food caches and push them toward starvation.

The combined forces of two Tennessee militia armies divided between Jackson and John Cocke, Georgia militia commanded by General John Floyd, and Brigadier General Ferdinand Claiborne's Mississippi militia and US Army regulars were to form columns to cut huge swaths of destruction toward a rendezvous at the center of the Creek homelands, at Tuckabatchee. Ironically, Tuckabatchee, since the mid-1790s, had held symbolic meaning as a place of Creek amicability and progress for both the Creeks and the Americans. It was there that the Creek National Council as recently as 1811 had refused to heed Tecumseh's pleas to join in a unified confederacy with the Indians of the North. It was from Tuckabatchee that Red Sticks had driven the National Council at the start of the Creeks' civil war. In 1813, however, Americans saw it as the heart of Red Stick recalcitrance and determined that they must conquer it to rip that heart out of the Creek body politic.

Among the four armies that descended on the Red Sticks, Jackson's proved the most destructive. Some historians have criticized Jackson and observed that he lacked tactical finesse, both as a soldier and a politician. Finesse, however, played no part in Jackson's or frontier Americans' grand design for the Creeks. The goal was to extirpate, expropriate, and segregate. Thus, his campaign against Tallushatchee (186 Red Sticks killed and 84 made prisoner) and Talladega (another 290 Red Sticks killed) significantly weakened the Red Sticks.

Jackson became the most famous of the Creek fighters, but he was far from unique in his brutality and effectiveness. General Floyd, with the support of pro-American Creek William McIntosh, killed two hundred Red Sticks at Autossee in November; and General Claiborne's army, before its march stalled because of lack of supplies, cleared the lower Alabama River region of Red Sticks. In a particularly tragic act even for this dreadful war, James White, under Cocke's command, massacred sixty-four peaceful Creeks at Hillabee. The Hillabees earlier had sent representatives to negotiate with Jackson and therefore assumed that they were safe from attack when White's troops assaulted the village in the predawn hours of November 18, 1813. Jackson sent a message to tell Cocke of the Hillabees' capitulation, but it arrived too late to stop the orgy of destruction.

On the heels of the 1813 campaign's successes, Jackson placed his army in winter quarters. He was unable to continue his offensive operations; many of the militia chaffed under his authoritarian command and nearly mutinied when supplies grew dangerously short, which compelled him to retreat northward to Fort Strother on the Coosa River and regroup. He quickly assembled a powerful fighting force of nearly four thousand Tennessee militiamen, a mounted brigade of riflemen under John Coffee, the US Thirty-Ninth Infantry Regiment, and pro-assimilationist Creeks and Cherokee allies.

Jackson proved determined to finish the extirpation of the Red Sticks in 1814. In January, he conducted a reconnaissance in force of the Creek positions to the south of him. He wanted to confirm rumors that the Red Sticks had fortified the Horseshoe Bend of the Tallapoosa River near Tohopeka.

The reconnaissance to the south proved bloody going for Jackson and the US Army. On January 21, his scouts reported that the Red Sticks camped on Emuckfau Creek had discovered the army and had prepared a preemptive attack. The Indians surrounded Jackson's troops and attacked his front and rear in the next morning's predawn hours. The US lines held, but after he sent Coffee's mounted troops to reconnoiter further southward, Jackson, now deep in Indian country, decided to retreat to Fort Strother and reinforce his detachment with the rest of his force. On the morning of January 24, the Indians attacked and routed Jackson's rear guard of militia as it crossed Enitachopco Creek. Jackson's lead elements quickly turned about and, only after hand-to-hand fighting that prevented the Red Sticks from taking Jackson's only cannon, managed to fend off the Creek attack. Although the Americans claimed to have killed nearly 190 Red Sticks in the two engagements, the nearly 100 American casualties had shaken the militia. Jackson wisely chose to continue the retreat to Fort Strother.

In the end, US numbers simply overwhelmed the Red Sticks. On March 27, 1814, Jackson's army, with the support of Cherokees and allied Creeks under William McIntosh, attacked the Red Sticks on the peninsula at Horseshoe Bend. Jackson had "determined to exterminate them."[15] After a two-hour artillery barrage that failed to breach the formidable barrier that the Red Sticks had erected across the peninsula, Jackson ordered the Thirty-Ninth Regiment to prepare to assault the barricade with fixed bayonets. Coffee's mounted troopers, meanwhile, had cut off the Indians' retreat across the river, while a handful of Cherokee Indians swam the Tallapoosa, stole the Red Sticks' canoes, and set the village on fire by shooting flaming arrows into it. That was the decisive point in the battle—the Red Sticks realized that Jackson had cut off their retreat and they began to disengage from the barricade. The Thirty-Ninth's head-on assault into the teeth of Indian musket fire and arrows broke the weakened Red Stick line. The Red Sticks thereupon found themselves trapped within an increasingly constricting cordon raked by the Americans' heavy firepower. Coffee's mounted troops, armed with accurate rifles, shot the Red Sticks that tried to flee across the river, while Jackson's Indian allies attacked on the rear of the peninsula. All told, the Americans and their Indian allies needed five hours to root out and eliminate all the pockets of Red Stick resistance. At the end of the day, Jackson was well pleased with the outcome. His troops and Indian allies had killed over 800 Red Stick warriors and taken captive around 300 women and children, at a cost of less than 50 killed and 160 wounded. It was hardly an understatement when Jackson wrote in his initial post–Horseshoe Bend assessment that the Creek Nation was "forever broken."[16]

The crushing defeat that the Red Sticks suffered at Horseshoe Bend brings us to where we began. At the Treaty of Fort Jackson, when Jackson told the Creeks that he had bled them essentially for their own good, he reminded them that the "principles of national justice and honorable war" justified that Americans take "retribution."[17] Thus, he cast all Creeks as US enemies. He ignored that the war had begun as an internal Creek war and that the Creeks who signed the treaty represented the Creek National Council, which had called for US assistance against the Red Sticks in the first place. Jackson treated as vanquished foes even those Creeks who joined him to fight the Red Sticks.

For the United States, retribution, of course, meant dominion. No better tools existed to complete the work started on the battlefield than segregation, quickly followed by dispossession. The Red Stick War and the Northwest Indian War thoroughly had crushed Indian power in the trans-Appalachian West. By the start of the Black Hawk War and the era of removal of the Five Civilized Tribes twenty years later, Indians proved powerless in the face of the Americans. The pattern repeated itself in the trans-Mississippi West. Many of the heroes of the Creek War—Sam Houston and Davy Crockett became the most famous—began in the 1820s the two-generation-long process of cleansing Indians from what became the Lone Star State.[18] In the final analysis, then, the Northwest Indian War and the Red Stick War stand as the climatic events in the US conquest of the old Southwest and the old Northwest and, just as important, point to the means that Americans employed time after time in their conquest of the North American frontiers.

Notes

1. Andrew Jackson to Big Warrior, August 7, 1814, *The Papers of Andrew Jackson,* ed. Sam B. Smith and Harriet Chapelle Owsley, 5 vols. (Knoxville: University of Tennessee Press, 1980), 3, 110.

2. John Grenier, *The First Way of War: American War Making on the Frontier, 1607–1814* (New York: Cambridge University Press, 2005), 10.

3. Andrew Jackson to Willie Blount, July 13, 1813, in *American State Papers, Class II, Indian Affairs,* US Congress, ed. Walter Lowrie, 2 vols. (Washington, DC: Gales and Seaton, 1832–1834), 1:850 (hereafter cited as *ASPIA*).

4. Willie Blount to Thomas Flournoy, October 15, 1813, in *ASPIA,* 1:856.

5. Fred Anderson and Andrew Cayton observe, "American historians have generally approached the imperial dimension of the nation's history obliquely, treating occurrences of jingoism like the war fevers of 1812, 1846, and 1898 as unfortunate exceptions to the antimilitarist rule of republicanism." See Fred Anderson and Andrew Cayton, *The Dominion of War: Empire and Liberty in North*

America, 1500–2000 (New York: Viking, 2005), xi. Like them, I contend that the Indian wars were not an "unfortunate exception," but instead a fundamental piece of the story of the US conquest, not settlement, of the nineteenth-century frontier.

6. For the emergence of racism directed at Indians in the middle and late eighteenth century, see Peter Silver, *Our Savage Neighbors: How Indian War Transformed Early America* (New York: W. W. Norton & Company, 2008); and Patrick Griffin, *American Leviathan: Empire, Nation, and Revolutionary Frontier* (New York: Hill & Wang, 2007).

7. Memorial to Congress by the Territorial Legislature, December 23, 1814, in *The Territorial Papers of the United States*, comp. and ed. Clarence Edwin Carter, 12 vols. (Washington, DC: Government Printing Office, 1934–1945), 6:481.

8. For the terms of the treaty, see http://digital.library.okstate.edu/kappler/Vol2/treaties/del0101.htm (accessed November 7, 2011). In subsequent amendments to the treaty, Harrison doled out additional annuities. The Miamis could consider themselves lucky, compared to other Indians; they received a $200 annuity, plus $500 worth of domestic animals. See http://digital.library.okstate.edu/kappler/Vol2/treaties/mia0103.htm (accessed November 7, 2011).

9. Memorials from the Inhabitants of the Indiana and Illinois Territories, Addressed to the President of the United States, July 1811, in *ASPIA*, 1:802.

10. Harrison to William Eustis [secretary of war], November 18, 1811, in *ASPIA*, 1:780.

11. Extract of a letter from J[ames] Rhea, March 14, 1812, in *ASPIA*, 1:806.

12. Harrison to [Kentucky] Governor Isaac Shelby, September 5, 1812, in *Official Letters of the Military and Naval Officers of the United States during the War with Great Britain in the Years 1812, 13, 14, & 15. With Some Additional Letters and Documents Elucidating the History of that Period*, comp. John Brannan (Washington, DC: Way & Gideon, for the editors, 1823), 56.

13. Gregory A. Waselkov, *A Conquering Spirit: Fort Mims and the Redstick War of 1813–1814* (Tuscaloosa: University of Alabama Press, 2006), 149–52.

14. Willie Blount to Thomas Flournoy, October 15, 1813, in *ASPIA*, 1:855. William Pulleyn's *Etymological Companion* of 1853 described how "the Greenland vessels, and indeed the South Sea vessels, are sometimes (especially after stormy weather) so surrounded with whales, that the situation of the crew becomes dangerous. When this is the case, it is usual to throw out a tub in order to divert their attention; when the marine monsters amuse themselves in tossing this singular sort of a plaything into the air, to and fro, as children do a shuttlecock. Their attention being drawn, every sail is hoisted, and the vessel pursues its course to its destination. Hence came the saying, 'Throwing a Tub to the Whale!'" See http://www.worldwidewords.org/qa/qa-thr3.htm (accessed November 7, 2011).

15. Jackson to Pinckney, March 28, 1814, in *ASPIA,* 1:319–20.
16. Ibid.
17. Articles of Agreement and Capitulation, in *APSIA,* 1:826.
18. Gary Clayton Anderson, *The Conquest of Texas: Ethnic Cleansing in the Promised Land, 1820–1875* (Norman: University of Oklahoma Press, 2005).

10

"Where All Behave Well"

Fort Bowyer and the War on the Gulf, 1814–1815

David S. Heidler and Jeanne T. Heidler

In the predawn twilight of February 8, 1815, Lieutenant Colonel William Lawrence awoke to a troubling tableau. He stared intently into the fading darkness from the ramparts of Fort Bowyer out at the gray waters of the Gulf of Mexico. There was movement to the west and the south, and the rising sun soon revealed an alarming amount of sail bearing down on Lawrence's position at Mobile Point. Indeed, the growing light made clear a developing situation that was more than alarming. The ships were veritable clouds of canvass, their massive hulls and numerous gun ports showing at least five of them to be third-raters, two-decker ships of the line, each with more than seventy guns. They were in the company of eight frigates, all soon to anchor just across the entrance of Mobile Bay off Dauphin Island. The glittering Gulf was peppered with scores of smaller craft as well. Lawrence stopped counting when he at last comprehended the mysterious, faint sounds of cadenced splashing that had been chilling enough in the darkness. Now in the light, their import was terrifying. The ships had disgorged thousands of British regular soldiers; barges had been landing them to the east of Fort Bowyer, both on the northern shore of Mobile Point at Navy Cove and on the Gulf side. Thousands. Lawrence had 320 effectives and a gaggle of women and children. It was one month to the day after Andrew Jackson's great victory at New Orleans. Now the people Jackson had defeated were at the mouth of Mobile Bay. William Lawrence and Fort Bowyer were in a great deal of trouble.[1]

It was little consolation that Lawrence's command was in itself relatively unimportant to the British. From the start of British strategic planning for the Gulf campaigns, the objective had always been and remained New Orleans, and establishing control of the Mississippi River Valley. As early as 1812, these plans had been ruminated over by British authorities in the West

Indies, Bahamian governor Charles Cameron most prominent among them.[2] The Gulf Coast was a promising entryway, in part because of Indians antagonized by attempted US encroachments into Spanish Florida, especially during the recent Patriot War in East Florida.[3] The likelihood that Britain could exploit Indian anger was combined with Spain's diminishing sway over the Floridas. In fact, Spanish authorities in West Florida looked on Indians as a way to protect their fragile hold on the province in the face of US expansion.

The Spanish provincial government in Pensacola, after all, had hard evidence of those intentions in the spring of 1813 when General James Wilkinson sallied forth from New Orleans to occupy and claim Mobile. Wilkinson operated under the authority of congressional legislation and presidential approval. Both were grounded in a persistent US claim concerning the Louisiana Purchase, which held that the lands east of New Orleans to the Perdido River were part of Louisiana, not West Florida. Spain had always disputed the claim, but the tiny Spanish garrison at Mobile's Fort Carlota was hardly in a position to make an issue of it with Wilkinson.[4]

The US seizure of Mobile was more than an expression of territorial legalisms, however. It was a sign that everyone realized Mobile's crucial importance in the defense of Louisiana. British strategic plans from the start had always included taking Mobile as the initial stage of a Gulf offensive, a sensible way to approach its problem of taking the Crescent City. Possessing Mobile would allow easy and unchallenged access to interior lines of approach to Baton Rouge, making for a northern assault on New Orleans. Lines of communication and supply through Mobile would have prevented the isolation of an overland march from its greatest protection, the Royal Navy, which would have undisputed control of the Gulf.[5]

Yet the British did not implement these plans from late 1812 thru 1813. The reasons for their inaction are clear: the European contest with Napoleon was in its endgame and always had been more important than the distracting US war, and the stretching of British resources to address that reality had compelled a reliance on Canadian forces that were primarily defensive. The focus on the northern border meant the opportunities afforded by the southern frontier went unexploited by the British for all of eighteen months, and that delay was to prove extremely consequential when Britain did turn its attention to the Gulf.

For one thing, a great deal happened in the Southeast during that time. In addition to Wilkinson's seizing Mobile—an obvious setback to British plans in itself—the civil war within the Creek Nation broke out and ultimately brought on US intervention after nativist Red Sticks clashed with American militia at Burnt Corn Creek and then staged the attack on Fort Mims. The

Creek War brought into play militias from Georgia, the Mississippi Territory, and, most notably, Tennessee, this last led in part by Andrew Jackson.

Jackson's campaign against the Red Sticks not only crushed their resistance at Horseshoe Bend in March 1814, it achieved three other important objectives: (1) it essentially broke the back of the very Indian hostility the British would rely on after they began to focus on the Gulf a few months later, (2) it placed a sizable American force in the field in the very region the British would be vying for in 1814, and (3) it laid bare Spanish complicity in abetting Indian hostility during the Creek civil war and the Creek War. Each of these consequences had a bearing on what would happen from mid-1814 through the following winter.

Just a handful of weeks after the Battle of Horseshoe Bend, the British finally appeared in the Gulf to begin the long-laid plans for a southern campaign. Napoleon's defeat and the apparent end of the European war would soon free up thousands of seasoned British soldiers to come to the United States and mount offensive operations. Increased raids in Chesapeake Bay and a late summer invasion on Lake Champlain resulted. Another was the dispatch of Captain Hugh Pigot, commanding HMS *Orpheus,* to establish contact with Seminoles and Creeks at the Apalachicola in May 1814. Soon Captain George Woodbine of the Royal Marines was sent with supplies and arms to equip and train these Indians. He established his headquarters about a half-mile from the store operated by William Hambly and Edmund Doyle, employees of John Forbes and Company, a British trading concern headquartered at Spanish Pensacola. Early on, Hambly and Doyle were compliant, if wary, as they helped Woodbine obtain supplies and served as interpreters. Yet the Royal Marine soon began requisitioning materials and commandeering cattle with a cavalier disregard for the injury it did to the Forbes inventories. Woodbine's curt explanations that he needed to feed his growing army of Seminoles offered little comfort to the victimized agents, and they became less cooperative.[6]

Jackson sealed his victory over the Creek Indians with the Treaty of Fort Jackson in August 1814. The Creek territorial cession under the treaty's terms was shockingly vast (more than 21 million acres), but it also spanned what Jackson boasted was "the cream of the Creek country."[7] That much at least was true, but left unspoken was the fact that this punitive peace injured the United States' Creek allies as much as the Red Stick Creeks. The potential for ominous consequences stemming from that reality gave the British heart because an increasing number of disgruntled Indians were more likely to become British allies. Many Red Stick leaders—Peter McQueen, Josiah Francis, and Homathle Mico among them—had already fled with their people to West Florida, where they clustered in encampments outside Pensacola. Rumors also told of how the Treaty of Fort Jackson had provoked angry Creek attacks all across the Georgia frontier. Seeking to exploit the Red Stick exodus and their hostility to Americans, Woodbine planned to organize these refugees.[8]

The British design to rely on Indian anger toward the United States would permit a British campaign by surrogacy, reducing the need for large amounts of British manpower and allowing the northern campaigns to proceed against US forces presumably diminished by the need to protect the southern frontier. Yet this plan ignored several unsettling realities about their Indian allies. Most importantly, the idea that they needed only organization and supplies to pose a serious military menace was wishful thinking at best. In fact, the Indians—especially the Red Stick Creeks—though furious, were starving and demoralized, and to imagine them rebounding to carry the burdens of a coherent campaign was simply unrealistic. Nonetheless, this thinking continued to dominate British actions even after additional British ships arrived in Florida and operations at Prospect Bluff on the Apalachicola came under the command of Royal Marine lieutenant colonel Edward Nicolls. When Nicolls arrived at the bluff in August 1814, Woodbine had gone to Pensacola to reassure nervous Spaniards there and to begin training the Red Sticks outside of town. Nicolls continued the training at Prospect Bluff, and glowing, or at least vaguely misleading, reports about Indian strength, fealty, and potential contributions were regularly fed to Admiral Alexander Cochrane, who swallowed them whole.[9]

The other part of the equation for the British was the attitude of their reluctant hosts, the Spaniards, who nominally owned Florida. By any measure, the British botched this part of their operation. Governor Mateo González Manrique in Pensacola found himself that summer between the rock of Andrew Jackson's displeasure and the hard place of British plans. As disillusioned Red Sticks moved into West Florida, Jackson demanded that González turn them over to the United States. The governor refused, and he likewise refused to join the British plans to assail Mobile. There was little he could do, however, about the British presence in West Florida, including their increasingly overbearing attitude in his own provincial capital.[10]

Aboard the British ships *Hermes* and *Caron,* Nicolls took those Indian allies who were fit for campaigning to Pensacola at the end of August, where a reluctant González allowed the British soldiers to strengthen the town's defenses and to occupy Fort San Miguel. Nicolls's recruitment, arming, and drilling of Pensacola's slaves began to alarm the townspeople and cooled González toward his increasingly officious guests. Nicolls was proving obnoxious with everyone and continued the alienation of Hambly and Doyle at Prospect Bluff begun by Woodbine. In Pensacola, he was equally insufferable with Forbes's directors, the Innerarity brothers. The British continued to be light-fingered with Forbes property, especially slaves commandeered for soldiering and manual labor. With such behavior Woodbine and Nicolls recklessly gained the enmity of powerful and connected men.[11]

Fort Bowyer, the British objective at Mobile Point, had always been a makeshift affair, an ad hoc bastion in every sense of the word. Immediately after Wilkinson took Mobile in the spring of 1813, the need to protect the isolated little village of 500 souls from an assault by water required a citadel at the mouth of the bay. Under the direction of Colonel John Bowyer, the fort's first commander, a log enclosure was planted on the sands of Mobile Point and outfitted with enough cannon (including nine heavy pieces captured from the Spaniards in Mobile) to pass for a reasonably formidable coastal defense. Yet its strength was decidedly one-faceted and one-dimensional: it lacked casemates to protect both people and powder and boasted ramparts and heavy artillery only on its coastal face; its eastern side was lightly armed and consisted of embrasures, making Fort Bowyer indefensible from a strong land assault. Further, the fort's location thirty miles from Mobile by water and sixty-five miles by land made it difficult for troops from Mobile to reinforce it with any speed. Its vulnerability was so obvious that Wilkinson's successor, General Thomas Flournoy, ordered it abandoned. Then Flournoy's successor, Andrew Jackson, who was appointed major general in the regular army in the wake of Horseshoe Bend, sent forces back into it, this time under Major William Lawrence, who nervously took up the post with some 150 men in August 1814. Lawrence, a Marylander with more than a decade of service in the army, had no illusions about Fort Bowyer and its fatal weakness.[12]

Neither did Edward Nicolls, though he did reveal some misgivings about his ability to exploit the fort's vulnerability. A hint that the British had begun to doubt the effectiveness of the Indian allies is provided by the effort to recruit Jean Lafitte and his Baratarian pirates. Captain Nicholas Lockyer, commanding HMS *Sophia,* carried an invitation to Lafitte with the attractive offer to help seize New Orleans and partake of the ensuing swag, but he politely refused. The British also tried to stir up French and Spanish Louisianans with a bombastic proclamation that described their impending invasion as a campaign to liberate Louisiana from US tyranny. As it happened, Lafitte would cast his lot with the Americans. When Andrew Jackson later placed New Orleans under martial law, he might have been perceived as proving the British point about despotism, but Old Hickory's iron grip on any disgruntled Creoles made the British proclamation irrelevant.[13]

The British marine and naval forces at Pensacola intended to use the town as a base to launch an attack on Fort Bowyer. With unimpeded access to Mobile Bay, securing Mobile would be an easy prelude to a larger British overland march on New Orleans. In early September 1814, Nicolls set about launching the first phase of this operation, but he began with a major mistake. He took González into his confidence by apparently trying to enlist the governor's aid. Rather than throw in with the British, González instead told his priest about the British plans. Father James Coleman might have heard this information in the confessional (how and where González related it to him was never clear), but Father Coleman wasted no time in telling it to John Innerarity. Already at odds with thieving redcoats in West Florida, Innerarity hoped that the Americans would be able to protect the Forbes and Company store at Bon Secour near Mobile Point. Accordingly, he immediately sent a messenger flying to Fort Bowyer. Nicolls learned of the messenger, but his attempt to have him captured failed. Even before the British started their operation, the US targets of it knew many of its particulars.[14]

Andrew Jackson had already moved down from Fort Jackson to Mobile. He rightly suspected that the British in Pensacola would attack Fort Bowyer sooner or later, and his response was to reinforce it. Yet at the same time Jackson believed it more likely that the British were simply helping the Spaniards prepare Pensacola's defenses against a US attack.[15] Out on Mobile Point, William Lawrence and his lonely, exposed garrison did not have the luxury of being wrong about British intentions, and even before Innerarity's messenger brought his news, Lawrence put his men to work strengthening the fort in early September. On September 12, when the garrison at Fort Bowyer spotted the British in the Gulf of Mexico, everyone knew what was about to happen.

Nobody, however, could have predicted how it would end so badly for the British. In fact, their expedition, though small, seemed entirely adequate. They had two sloops of war and two brigs, with HMS *Hermes* in the lead carrying 130 Royal Marines and 600 Indians to mount the land assault. They were all dropped off about nine miles southeast of the fort, and it was so far so good for Nicolls, although he was ill and had to stay aboard the *Hermes*.[16]

That hardly seemed to matter, though. This first British campaign in the Gulf was rising on an irresistible British momentum from all other fronts in the North, including the burning of Washington in August and apparently inevitable British victories on Lake Champlain and at Baltimore. Yet that inevitability, we now know, was hardly that at all. The momentum had crested by the fall of 1814, a victim of British impetuosity, arrogance, and overreach. The Champlain offensive stalled at Plattsburgh, and Baltimore's Fort McHenry proved impossible to reduce. The much smaller-scale disaster at the mouth of Mobile Bay was no less consequential.

William Lawrence had twenty artillery pieces, with the eight largest

10.1. Oil portrait of General Andrew Jackson, ca. 1814, by Samuel Lovett Waldo. Courtesy of the Historic New Orleans Collection, New Orleans, Louisiana.

mounted to overlook the water approaches to the bay. To fire the other guns facing the land approach, the men were exposed above their knees to enemy fire. By the evening of September 12, Lawrence had reports of the British landing that counted some 600 Creeks and Seminoles and 130 Royal Marines southeast of Bowyer. The following day, this landing force had moved to within three-quarters of a mile of the fort. Using the dunes for cover, it also staked out positions to the northwest, placing those forces even closer in. At half past noon, they unlimbered a couple of artillery pieces and fired off three shells, which exploded before reaching the fort, and a cannon ball that more menacingly shattered a part of Bowyer's rampart. American bullets scattered the British marines who had started to dig entrenchments, and American grapeshot harassed the small British boats trying to take soundings in the channel just off the fort's coastal face. Surprisingly, this peppery response gave the British pause, and Fort Bowyer's weaknesses on the land side remained unexploited for the next thirty-six hours.[17]

Finally, in the early afternoon of September 15, the British ships weighed anchor and moved out into the Gulf. They began a series of maneuvers to form a line of battle, but the wind was uncooperative, and for two hours they labored to bear down upon the fort. Lawrence and his men watched this development with justifiable concern, and he called his officers into a council of war. They resolved not even to offer to surrender unless Bowyer's walls were obliterated, exposing the garrison to overwhelming fire from the water and an irresistible assault by land. Even at that they pledged to each other that the fight would continue to the last man unless the British were willing to extend the full honors of war.[18]

It took a good part of the afternoon, but by 4:00 p.m. the *Hermes* was pulling within range. The fort's largest guns opened up, but the Americans firing them could not find their target, very likely because they were untrained at artillery, an incredible lapse in a coastal fortification. The *Hermes,* though, fared no better when it returned fire with its forward gun, and as the other three ships paraded before the fort, their relatively ineffective broadsides proved that Fort Bowyer was to be a tough nut to crack, at least from the Gulf. The ships anchored out from the fort to attempt a continuous pounding of the ramparts.[19]

The noise from all this cannonading was spectacular, but the effects were mostly unnerving rather than decisive; and as the battle raged toward and from the water, Captain Robert Henry, in command of the land operation, decided it was time to force the issue. Yet when he tried to move his two artillery pieces closer to the fort, he lobbed only a few shots before discovering that Bowyer's eastern guns were hardly paper tigers. In the meantime, a lucky shot by Lawrence's amateur gunners on the other side of the fort had sheared the flag halyard on the *Hermes,* causing the Americans to think that the British were striking colors to give up the fight. Lawrence ordered his men to cease firing while he assessed this development, but in the eerie quiet after the fusillades, the US garrison uneasily reloaded every gun facing the water. The British answered the American silence with a raking broadside that removed all doubt about their intentions, and at the order to return fire, every piece of Bowyer's coastal ordnance discharged more or less simultaneously to send a wall of metal hurtling toward the four British ships.

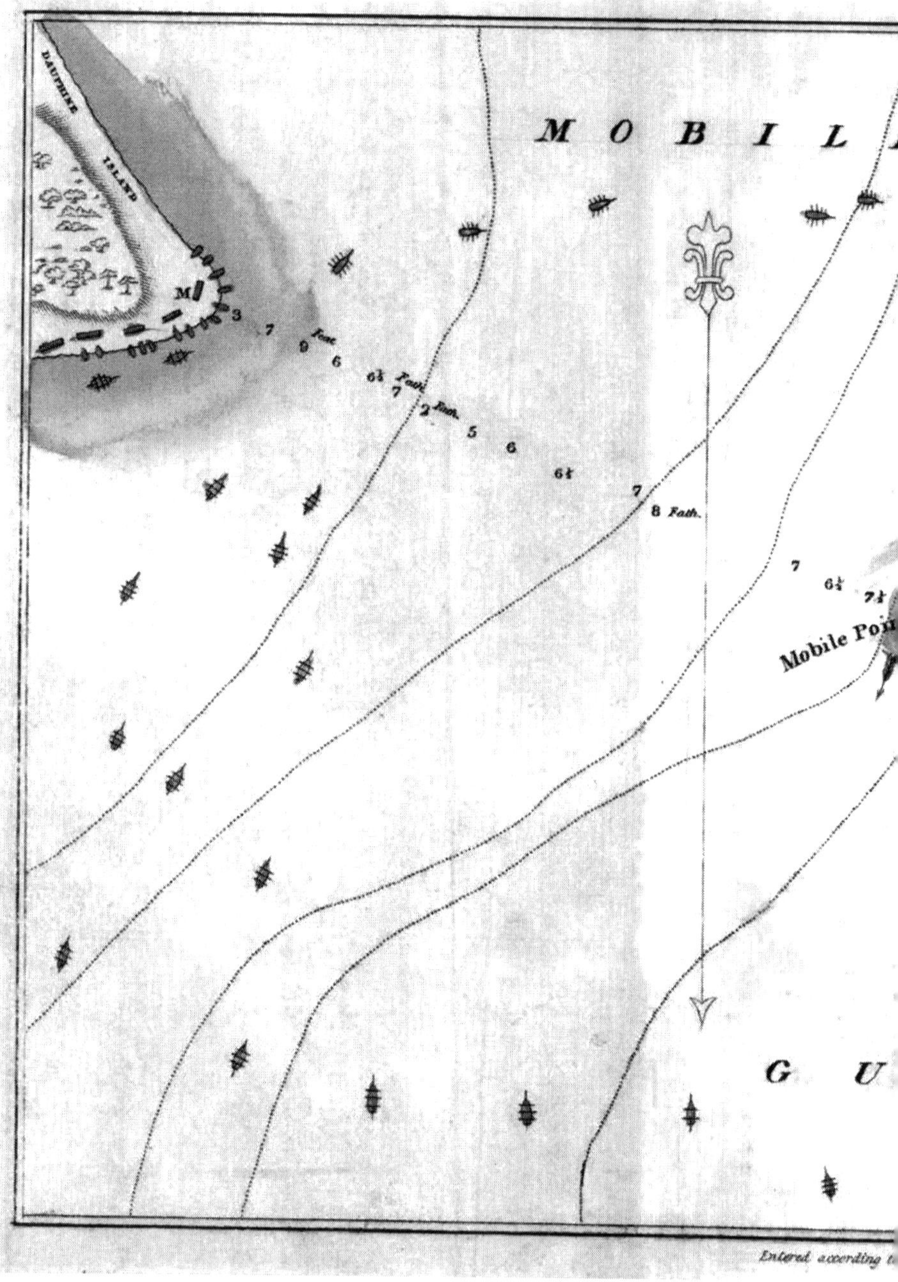

10.2. Map of Mobile Point and part of the bay and Dauphin Island, showing the position of the British land and naval forces investing Fort Bowyer, the batteries erected, and the trenches opened when the summons was made to the garrison. From Major

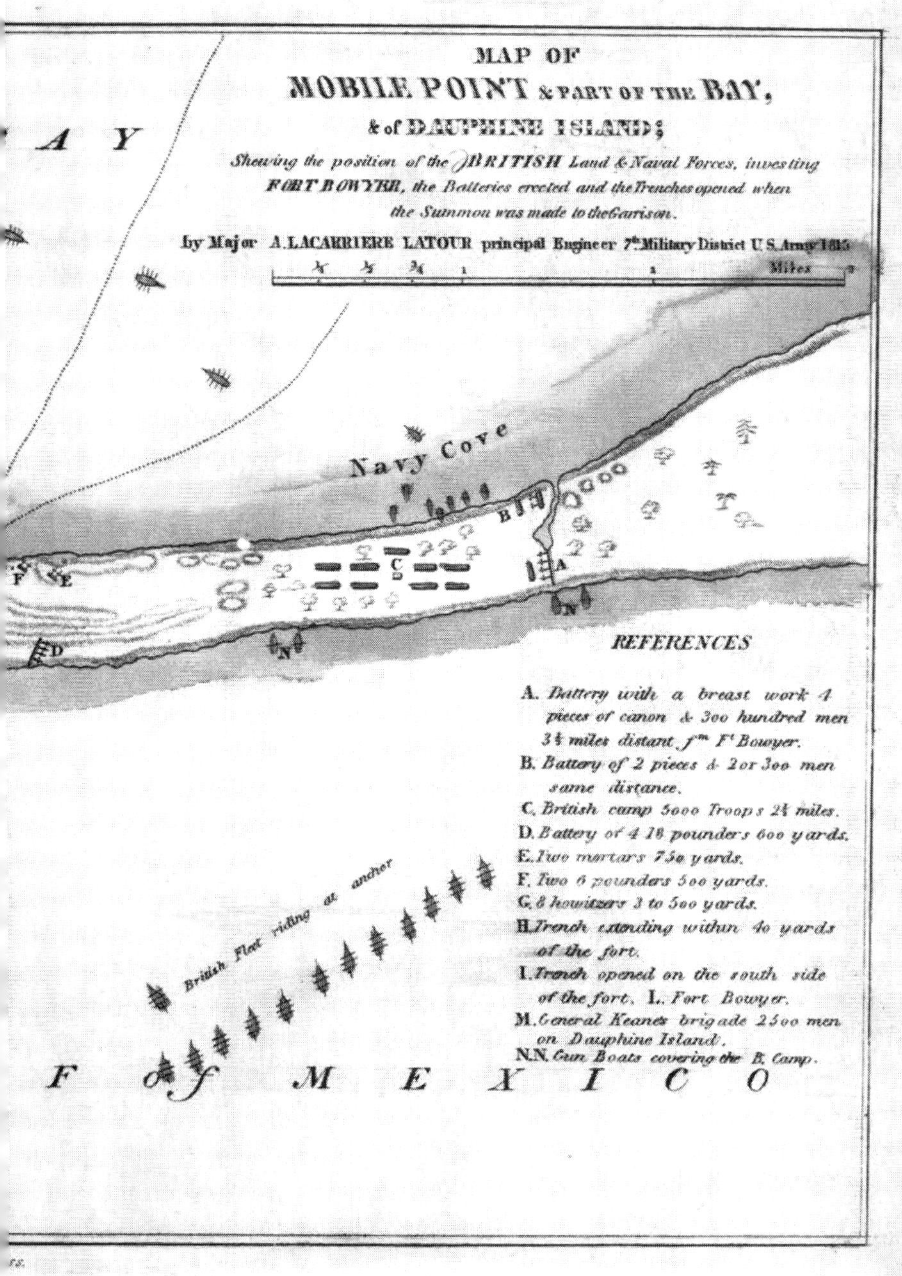

Arsène Lacarrière Latour, *Historical Memoir of the War in West Florida and Louisiana in 1814–15, with an Atlas* (n.p., 1816), 238. Courtesy of the Alabama Department of Archives and History, Montgomery, Alabama.

Out on the water, it was more than impressive; it was spectacularly terrifying, and the British that afternoon never really recovered from it. As the battle resumed, another lucky American shot disabled the *Hermes.* Winds and currents drifted the ship well into range of Bowyer's deadly guns. The Americans raked the helpless ship, sending huge fragments of razor-sharp wood flying through the air, enormous splinters as lethal as any shot or shell. One put out Edward Nicolls's right eye, the worst of several wounds he suffered during this ordeal. The *Hermes* finally ran aground, and her crew eagerly scampered overboard, but not before setting her on fire to prevent her from falling into US hands. The flames ultimately reached the ship's powder, causing a deafening explosion that was heard in Mobile. By then, the rest of the British force on both sea and land had already left.[20]

William Lawrence and his brave band were lionized as heroes, not the least by Andrew Jackson, who boasted that Lawrence and his men had given the British "a severe mauling."[21] Lawrence's understated after-action report was a model of modesty: "Where all behave well, it [is] unnecessary to discriminate[;] suffice it to say every Officer and Man did his *duty.*"[22] A grateful nation soon made this new champion a lieutenant colonel. The small number of defenders at Fort Bowyer had held their position while losing only 4 killed and 5 wounded. The British, who had entered the battle with a ten to one advantage in manpower and a five to one advantage in artillery, had indeed been mauled. They lost 162 killed and 70 wounded.[23]

Aside from gaining Lawrence and his command plaudits, the action at Bowyer had serious repercussions for British plans in the Gulf. The Indians who participated in the attack left it considerably sadder but much wiser about the British ability to help them exact vengeance on the United States. The acquiescent Spaniards in Pensacola, already unhappy about Britain's high-handed ways, grew positively chilly, refused to strengthen the town, and became increasingly reluctant to do anything that the Americans might see as provocative. The Innerarity brothers gave up any pretense of neutrality, partly because when the British retreated from Mobile Point they had encouraged their Indian allies to loot the store at Bon Secour of livestock, trade goods, and ten slaves, but also because it appeared that the British were not willing to expend the necessary resources to mount a successful campaign in the Gulf.[24]

Now that the British had revealed their intentions, Old Hickory began assembling enough men and equipment to invade Florida. He had been considering a campaign against Pensacola at least since July, but now there was a concern that the British not only would use their position at Prospect Bluff to harry the Georgia frontier, but also would use it as a central place from which they could link up with British raids to be conducted on Georgia's sea islands and the Atlantic coast. Both Jackson and Creek Indian agent Benjamin Hawkins believed that the British were using their presence at Prospect Bluff and Pensacola to encourage Creek and Seminole raids into Georgia, and rumors told of British efforts to recruit Creeks within the borders of the United States to their cause. Jackson hoped that taking Pensacola would force the British out of Florida.[25]

As Jackson and his army of about three thousand men approached Pensacola, Nicolls tried to shore up the town's defenses, but the locals, especially Governor González, balked. Nicolls continued to conscript the town's slaves for soldiering and to requisition supplies, but his situation had obviously become quite awkward and was verging on being untenable. Scouts reported on November 2 that Jackson was approaching Pensacola, and Nicolls coerced cooperation from González by threatening to sail away with his marines and Indians. But the governor only reluctantly gave in to Nicolls, and soon the Royal Marine completely wore out his welcome. He barked orders at everyone, including Spanish soldiers, and the town's inhabitants concluded that Pensacola would be better off under US control. As Jackson neared the town on November 6, Nicolls angrily repeated to González his threat to leave Pensacola defenseless, promising to destroy Fort Barrancas and the bastion on Santa Rosa Island as he left the town to the Americans.[26]

It was no use, though, and Nicolls began sending his Indian allies and Spanish slaves toward the Apalachicola. The next morning (November 7) the Americans arrived as British ships in Pensacola Bay lobbed a few shells into town but mostly leveled their guns at the forts before making sail for the Apalachicola River. Jackson had captured a defenseless village, and he quickly restored it to Spanish authorities because he was now quite concerned that Mobile was in peril more than ever.[27]

Indeed, Nicolls at Prospect Bluff seemed to threaten Mobile until the end of the war, but only after leaving Pensacola did Andrew Jackson gradually realize that British plans for New Orleans had actually changed. Instead of an initial assault on Mobile, followed by an overland march to Baton Rouge, the Royal Navy and British army intended to attack the Crescent City directly. In December, Jackson all but stripped Mobile of its defenses and raced to New Orleans, frantic that he might be too late. Left in command at Mobile, General James Winchester coped with an impossible situation. He had at best a paper army whose actual numbers were nowhere near the figures on muster rolls. The scant forces he did have were always hungry, victims of the inadequate and ineffective commissary contract system. Nervous about his weakness and the continued presence of Nicolls on the Apalachicola, he agreed to Jackson's plan to send a force under Major Uriah Blue to attack Prospect Bluff, though that expedition never reached the bluff and left Blue's men exhausted and famished, making them little good for anything else. Out on Mobile Point, the hero Lawrence had seen his command double in number, but more important, his repeated warnings about Fort Bowyer's indefensible eastern approach brought no corrections.[28]

The British abandonment of Plan A for New Orleans stemmed from several considerations. The setbacks in the North put considerable pressure on forces in North America to give British commissioners at the peace negotiations in Ghent something with which to wring concessions from the United States. Time was of the essence, and it must have appeared that an overland campaign would waste it. As we know, the decision to move on New Orleans by way of Lake Pontchartrain and from the South did not pan out. Bad weather and delays plagued the British, but incoherent leadership (General Edward Pakenham did not arrive until Christmas and thought it too late to change the army's disposition, despite his extreme dissatisfaction with it) together with Jackson's preparations caused the British disaster of January 8.

Yet the British defeat at New Orleans did not really change things from the US perspective. Jackson was slow to comprehend that his victory had all but quashed British plans for a direct assault on New Orleans—Cochrane's failure to reduce Fort St. Philip in the aftermath of New Orleans completed the abandonment. Nevertheless, Jackson remained worried that the British were merely taking a breather, and he accordingly and controversially continued martial law in New Orleans.[29] He meanwhile peppered poor Winchester with demands for reinforcements Mobile could not spare and exhorted him at the same time to remain vigilant.[30]

The advice was reflexive but apt, for the British had, in fact, quit Louisiana to revert to Plan A, meaning the overland march to Baton Rouge from Mobile. Andrew Jackson never understood this and, consequently, did nothing to stop it. In fact, he did not even realize that the British were heading to Mobile until after Fort Bowyer had fallen.[31] In the aftermath, Jackson's chief engineer would attribute the British return to Fort Bowyer as merely a gesture to salve British pride wounded at New Orleans with a meaningless victory, but the claim was preposterous.[32] Cochrane and the general staff who had survived New Orleans were thoroughgoing professionals, the men they commanded both afloat and on foot were battle-hardened veterans of Napoleonic campaigns, and the task before them had to do with military objectives, not British military vindication. When the enormous British force appeared off Mobile Point on February 8, 1815, and began landing men on Fort Bowyer's eastern face, its Achilles' heel, they were commencing the first stage of their renewed effort to take New Orleans.

Admiral Cochrane stood off, out of Fort Bowyer's range. The admiral had seen enough of efforts to reduce US forts with naval bombardments—Fort McHenry and, most recently, Fort St. Philip were cautionary tales, and the fate of the *Hermes* the previous September counseled prudence about capering before the fort's lethal artillery. Instead, the large British vessels remained near Dauphin Island while barges landed five thousand regulars, now under the command of General John Lambert since Pakenham's death at New Orleans, behind the safety of the large dunes east of the fort.[33]

British engineers east of Fort Bowyer were soon carving trenches in a classic but rapid siege advance, forgiving sand making quick work of it. Belatedly, as British plans had become relatively clear, Winchester had tried to do something about Fort Bowyer's fatal weakness, but the best he could muster were Uriah Blue's spent men. Contrary winds and an incoming tide made them late, too late, in fact, because the British were patrolling the waters with gunboats captured from Americans at New Orleans, but that was just as well. It is difficult to see how Blue, outnumbered and weary, could have been anything more than a minor irritation to the British soldiers quickly trenching their way toward Fort Bowyer.[34]

By the following morning, February 9, the British had placed 750 riflemen in a protected trench to shield the sappers as they dug ever closer to the fort. Lawrence watched helplessly, now deprived even of the satisfaction of taking potshots at the men placing batteries on dunes high enough that they actually allowed for declining fire into the fort. That work was completed by the morning of February 11, and the British messenger under a flag of truce (the flamboyant Harry Smith, as it happened, destined for a distinguished and colorful career) offered Lawrence terms of surrender or, barring that, the chance to evacuate the twenty women and sixteen children from the fort. Staring up at the muzzles of British batteries from a wooden fort with an exposed magazine and no casemates, Lawrence, who was among the ten wounded, knew his time was up.[35]

The best he could do was cavil at the thirty-minute deadline Smith proposed. Lawrence was able to negotiate for a bit more time but nothing else. His garrison stacked its arms and surrendered at noon on February 12. During the three-day siege both sides had suffered a combined casualty total of fourteen killed and twenty-eight wounded. Lawrence and his men were taken aboard the British fleet as prisoners, as both the Royal Navy and British army began laying plans to take Mobile, an easy objective now that they had control of the bay.[36]

We all know, of course, that Mobile was spared because close on the heels of Fort Bowyer's fall came news that the Treaty of Ghent had ended the war. Just that quickly the thoroughgoing professionals in Mobile Bay contacted Jackson to arrange the release of their prisoners.[37]

Lieutenant Colonel William Lawrence, the hero of September, unfairly became the goat of February. Andrew Jackson heaped harsh criticism on him for surrendering his command without firing a shot, which was not altogether true, and implied Lawrence had fallen prey to a want of nerve if not contemptible cowardice, which was patently unfair. Ignorant of rudimentary engineering tenets concerning fortifications and coastal defense, Jackson defined strengthening Fort Bowyer as putting more men into it, an inadequate bastion exposed to and indefensible against the most marginally determined attack. Apparently misled by Lawrence's success against the September assault, Jackson put these men in a hopeless situation and burdened them with an impossible task. Lawrence knew that he had been fortunate in September, the beneficiary of British shortages in men, ships, and field artillery, and he persistently warned that next time he and Fort Bowyer were not likely to be so lucky.[38]

He was right, and the Court of Inquiry that he requested to investigate his conduct completely vindicated his actions on February 11 and 12 as justifiable and prudent.[39] The news of the peace, moreover, proved a remarkable instance of good fortune for the United States, in general, and Old Hickory, in particular. Had the British gained the US interior by way of Mobile, there was nothing to stop them from reaching Baton Rouge and from there overwhelming even the most stalwart defense of New Orleans. Andrew Jackson then would himself have experienced the fate of William Lawrence, to discover what it feels like to go from hero to goat in the space of weeks. In that regard, rather than victory at New Orleans saving the country, negotiations at Ghent saved victory at New Orleans. Such are the unexpected ironies of war.

Notes

1. Robert Ricketts, "The Men and the Ships of the British Attack on Fort Bowyer—February 1815," *Gulf Coast Historical Review* 5 (1990): 14–15; Arsène Lacarrière Latour, *Historical Memoir of the War in West Florida and Louisiana in 1814–15, with an Atlas*, edited by Gene A. Smith (Gainesville: University Press of Florida, 1999), 141; William S. Coker, "The Last Battle of the War of 1812: New Orleans. No, Fort Bowyer!" *Alabama Historical Quarterly* 43 (1981): 55.

2. John K. Mahon, "British Strategy and Southern Indians: War of 1812," *Florida Historical Quarterly* 44 (1966): 285; Frank L. Owsley Jr., "British and Indian Activities in Spanish West Florida during the War of 1812," *Florida Historical Quarterly* 46 (1967): 114.

3. For an excellent analysis of the Patriot War see James G. Cusick, *The Other War of 1812: The Patriot War and the American Invasion of Spanish East Florida* (Gainesville: University Press of Florida, 2003).

4. Harvey H. Jackson III, *Rivers of History: Life on the Coosa, Tallapoosa,*

Cahaba, and Alabama (Tuscaloosa: University of Alabama Press, 1995), 33–34; Coker, "The Last Battle," 45

5. Frank L. Owsley Jr., *Struggle for the Gulf Borderlands: The Creek War and the Battle of New Orleans* (Gainesville: University Presses of Florida, 1981), 101–2.

6. *Niles Weekly Register,* August 6, 1814; William S. Coker and Thomas D. Watson, *Indian Traders of the Southeastern Spanish Borderlands: Panton, Leslie & Company, and John Forbes & Company, 1783–1847* (Gainesville: University Presses of Florida, 1986), 281; Frank L. Owsley Jr., "Jackson's Capture of Pensacola," *Alabama Review* 19 (1966): 176; Arthur H. Hall, "The Red Stick War: Creek Indian Affairs during the War of 1812," *Chronicles of Oklahoma* 12 (1934): 288; Thomas C. Kennedy, "Sibling Stewards of a Commercial Empire: The Innerarity Brothers in the Floridas," *Florida Historical Quarterly* 67 (1989): 275; James W. Covington, "Migration into Florida of the Seminoles, 1700–1820," *Florida Historical Quarterly* 46 (1968): 355.

7. Jackson to Overton, August 10, 1814, Andrew Jackson Papers, Library of Congress, Washington, DC.

8. Hawkins to Early, November 3, 1814, "Unpublished Letters of Timothy Barnard," edited by Louise Frederick Hays, Georgia Department of Archives and History, Atlanta, GA; Mahon, "British Strategy," 287; J. Leitch Wright Jr., *Creeks and Seminoles: The Destruction and Regeneration of the Muscogulge People* (Lincoln: University of Nebraska Press, 1986), 186.

9. John Sugden, "The Southern Indians in the War of 1812: The Closing Phase," *Florida Historical Quarterly* 60 (1982): 283–87; Hawkins to Armstrong, July 13, 1814, in *American State Papers, Class II, Indian Affairs,* 2 vols., ed. Walter Lowrie (Washington, DC: Gales and Seaton, 1832–1834), 1:860; Wilburt S. Brown, *The Amphibious Campaign for West Florida and Louisiana, 1814–1815* (Tuscaloosa: University of Alabama Press, 1969), 27; Owsley, *Struggle for the Gulf Borderlands,* 105.

10. Jackson to González Manrique, July 12, 1814, Jackson to Armstrong, July 14, 1814, Gonzalez Manrique to Jackson, July 26, 1814, in *The Papers of Andrew Jackson,* by Andrew Jackson, 7 vols., edited by Harold D. Moser et al. (Knoxville: University of Tennessee Press, 1980–2007), 3:85–87, 95; Report of John Gordon, July 20, 1814, in *Correspondence of Andrew Jackson,* 7 vols., ed. John Spencer Bassett (Washington, DC: Carnegie Institute, 1926–1935), 2:17; David S. Heidler and Jeanne T. Heidler, *Old Hickory's War: Andrew Jackson and the Quest for Empire* (Baton Rouge: Louisiana State University Press, 2003), 44.

11. Owsley, *Struggle for the Gulf Borderlands,* 105; Sugden, "Southern Indians," 287; Mark F. Boyd, "Events at Prospect Bluff on the Apalachicola River, 1808–1818: An Introduction to Twelve Letters of Edmund Doyle, Trader," *Florida Historical Quarterly* 16 (1937): 70; Owsley, "Jackson's Capture of Pensacola," 177.

12. Coker, "The Last Battle," 45–46; Gene A. Smith, "'Our Flag was Display'd

within Their Works': The Treaty of Ghent and the Conquest of Mobile," *Alabama Review* 52 (1999): 16–17; Joseph E. Brent, "A Visit to Fort Morgan: Mobile's Guardian on the Gulf," *Gulf Coast Historical Review* 3 (1987): 97; Latour, *Historical Memoir,* 34; Walter T. Durham, *James Winchester, Tennessee Pioneer* (Gallatin, TN: Sumner County Library Board, 1979), 157–58; Armstrong to Jackson, May 28, 1814, Jackson Papers, Library of Congress.

13. Latour, *Historical Memoir,* 25–27; Nicolls to Lafitte, August 31, 1814, Jean Lafitte Papers, Rare Book, Manuscript, and Special Collections Library, Duke University; Mahon, "British Strategy," 293.

14. Kennedy, "Sibling Stewards," 277; Coker, "The Last Battle," 49–50.

15. Jackson to Lawrence, September 12, 1814, Military Manuscript Collection, 1783–1888, Maryland Historical Society, Baltimore, MD.

16. Latour, *Historical Memoir,* 35; Coker, "The Last Battle," 51.

17. Latour, *Historical Memoir,* 35–36.

18. Ibid., 36–37.

19. Latour, *Historical Memoir,* 37; *Niles Weekly Register,* October 22, 1814.

20. *Niles Weekly Register,* October 15, 1814; Coker, "The Last Battle," 51, 53; Sugden, "Southern Indians," 291; Mahon, "British Strategy," 295; Latour, *Historical Memoir,* 37–38.

21. Jackson to Reid, September 18, 1814, Andrew Jackson Letters, Rare Book, Manuscript, and Special Collections Library, Duke University (hereafter cited as Jackson Letters).

22. Lawrence to Jackson, September 15, 1814, in *Papers,* by Jackson, 3:138.

23. Sugden, "Southern Indians," 292; Latour, *Historical Memoir,* 39.

24. Kennedy, "Sibling Stewards," 278; Coker, "The Last Battle," 53; Coker and Watson, *Indian Traders,* 285.

25. Jackson to Armstrong, July 30, 1814, in *Papers,* by Jackson, 3:97; Jackson to Reid, September 18, 1814, Jackson Letters; Hawkins to Early, October 26, 1814, Hawkins to commanders of Forts Lawrence, Perry, and Mitchell, November 3, 1814, in *Letters, Journals, and Writings of Benjamin Hawkins,* by Benjamin Hawkins, 2 vols., ed. C. L. Grant (Savannah: Beehive Press, 1980), 2:698–99; Coker and Watson, *Indian Traders,* 292; Bowen to Warren, October 8, 1814, Alabamians at War, War of 1812, and 1st Creek War, Alabama Department of Archives and History, Montgomery; Cook to Early, November 7, 1814, Creek Letters, talks, and treaties, 1705–1839, Georgia Department of Archives and History, Morrow; Barnard to Hawkins, November 3, 1814, Telamon Cuyler Collection, University of Georgia Libraries, Special Collections, Manuscript Department, Athens.

26. Sugden, "Southern Indians," 293–95; Owsley, "Jackson's Capture of Pensacola," 177; Ruth Anna Fisher, "The Surrender of Pensacola as Told by the British," *American Historical Review* 54 (1949): 327; Innerarity to Innerarity, Novem-

ber 10, 1814, in Marie Greenslade, ed., "Letters of John Innerarity: The Seizure of Pensacola by Andrew Jackson, November 7, 1814," *Florida Historical Quarterly* 9 (1931): 128; Mahon, "British Strategy," 296; Heidler and Heidler, *Old Hickory's War,* 44.

27. Fisher, "Surrender of Pensacola," 327–28; Owsley, "Jackson's Capture of Pensacola," 175, 184; Innerarity to Innerarity, November 10, 1814, in "Seizure of Pensacola," by Fisher, 129. Unbeknownst to Jackson, acting Secretary of War James Monroe had sent him instructions on October 21 not to move against Spanish territory. By the time Jackson learned of these instructions, he had already taken and returned Pensacola. See Monroe to Jackson, October 21, 1814, in *Papers,* by Jackson, 3:171; Heidler and Heidler, *Old Hickory's War,* 46.

28. Durham, *James Winchester,* 156–58; Brian R. Rucker, "In the Shadow of Jackson: Uriah Blue's Expedition into West Florida," *Florida Historical Quarterly* 73 (January 1995): 325–38; Sugden, "Southern Indians," 297; *Augusta Chronicle,* January 13, 1815.

29. For Jackson's use of martial law in New Orleans see Matthew Warshauer, *Andrew Jackson and the Politics of Martial Law: Nationalism, Civil Liberties, and Partisanship* (Knoxville: University of Tennessee Press, 2006).

30. Jackson to Winchester, December 16, 1814, January 10, 1815, and January 31, 1815, in *Papers,* by Jackson, 3:208, 231n1, 242, 262.

31. Jackson to Hays, February 17, 1815, Jackson Letters.

32. Latour, *Historical Memoir,* 140.

33. Ricketts, "The Men and the Ships," 8; George Robert Gleig, *A Narrative of the Campaigns of the British Army, At Washington and New Orleans, Under Generals Ross, Pakenham, & Lambert, in the Years 1814 and 1815; with Some Account of the Countries Visited. By an Officer Who served in the Expedition* (Philadelphia: M. Carey, 1821), 355–57; Latour, *Historical Memoir,* 140–41.

34. Coker, "The Last Battle," 57–58; Latour, *Historical Memoir,* 141; Durham, *James Winchester,* 171.

35. Latour, *Historical Memoir,* 35, 142–43; Coker, "The Last Battle," 57–59.

36. Coker, "The Last Battle," 44, 59; Latour, *Historical Memoir,* 143; Owsley, "British and Indian Activities," 121.

37. Durham, *James Winchester,* 172; Hawkins to Early, February 26, 1815, in *Letters,* by Hawkins, 2:720; Latour, *Historical Memoir,* 261–62.

38. Latour, *Historical Memoir,* 272; Coker, "The Last Battle," 59–60.

39. Latour, *Historical Memoir,* 265; Coker, "The Last Battle," 60–62; *Niles Weekly Register,* May 20, 1815.

11

Archaeology, Geography, and the Creek War in Alabama

Craig T. Sheldon Jr.

This chapter is a brief survey of geographical and archaeological information relating to the Creek War during the period between the Battle of Burnt Corn (July 27, 1813) and the Treaty of Fort Jackson (August 9, 1814). My particular focus is on the Upper Creeks and their role in the conflict due to the simple fact that their territory was overwhelmingly the scene of most action during the war.[1]

Based on historic accounts, we can identify hundreds of Creek War–era archaeological sites built by both Creeks and Americans, including towns, camps for hunting, war and refugee areas, homesteads, mills, battle sites, and forts. The physical locations of most are not known. Presently, over two hundred sites with diagnostic Creek artifacts are recorded, but how many of these were occupied during the war is also unknown. Systematical investigations of historic Indian sites in the Southeast are comparatively new. Most early archaeological research concentrated on prehistoric sites "uncontaminated" by European contact. In 1948, during a search for the Hernando de Soto–period site of Coosa, David DeJarnette excavated 1TA1, which proved to be a mid-eighteenth-century Creek site. Since then, surveys and excavations in Alabama and Georgia have produced an increasing body of data on historic Creek Indian settlement patterns, architecture, mortuary customs, diet, culture change, and material culture, mostly related to the seventeenth and eighteenth century. During the 1960s and 1970s, preconstruction and post-construction surveys and salvage excavation projects were conducted in the reservoir areas of Logan Martin, H. Neely Henry, and Weiss Dams on the upper Coosa River and R. L. Harris Dam on the Tallapoosa River. Similar investigations in the reservoir areas of the West Point, Walter F. George, George W. Andrews, and Jim Woodruff Dams on the Chattahoochee River provided information on the distribution of Lower Creek sites.

Surveys and excavations in the areas flooded by Claiborne, Millers Ferry, and Jones Bluff Dams on the Alabama River revealed an overall lack of historic Indian sites, except in the vicinity of Montgomery. A similar dearth of historic-period aboriginal sites was found in surveys along the Tombigbee, Black Warrior, and Conecuh Rivers.[2]

Archaeological excavations have occurred at over fifteen historic late eighteenth- and early nineteenth-century Creek sites in Alabama. On the upper Coosa, in the vicinity of Gadsden, a number of sites were excavated, but they dated to the seventeenth century. Moving south along the Coosa River, major archaeological excavations have been conducted at the early eighteenth-century Creek sites at Woods Island (1SC40) and Coosa (1TA1) and at the Creek War sites of Talladega (1TA308) and Tallushatchee (1CA162). Near the junction of the Coosa and Tallapoosa Rivers, there have been large-scale investigations at Ocheaupofau or Hickory Ground (1EE89) and amateur collections made at Tuskegee (1EE1). Along the Tallapoosa River, there have been excavations at Nuyaka (1TP25), Horseshoe Bend battlefield (1TP 23), Tohopeka (1TP24), Tuckabatchee (1EE 52), Hoithlewaulee (1EE328), Fusihatchee (1EE191), and Coolome (1MT3). Most of the occupations found at these sites date from the eighteenth century; very few of the artifacts and features could be specifically attributed to the early nineteenth-century Creeks. Vernon Knight's excavations at Tuckabatchee, which was occupied until 1836, yielded one of the better-defined nineteenth-century archaeological assemblages. Some of the artifacts and features reported by Gregory Waselkov and John Cottier probably relate to one of the war camps at the refugee settlement of Hoithlewaulee (1EE328).[3]

A number of contemporaneous US sites, mostly military, have also been archaeologically investigated in Alabama. These include Forts Strother, Williams, and Jackson on the Coosa River, Fort Decatur on the Tallapoosa River, Fort Mitchell on the Chattahoochee River, and Forts Montgomery and Mims on the lower Alabama.[4]

Before examining the actual and possible physical signs of the Creek War of 1813 and 1814 in central Alabama that might be detected through combined historic archaeological and ethnohistorical approaches, it is important to remember the limitations of archaeology. Over 190 years of agricultural activity in central Alabama have destroyed many architectural and other archaeological features and have mixed artifacts from the war period with those of earlier deposits. Fort Mims, Horseshoe Bend, Autossee, Tuskegee, Fusihatchee, and many other Creek sites have been damaged by artifact looting and selective surface collecting. Many of the iconic insignia of the Red Stick faction, such as animal skins, war paint, and the red-painted *atássa,* or "war clubs," decayed in the humid southeastern climate.

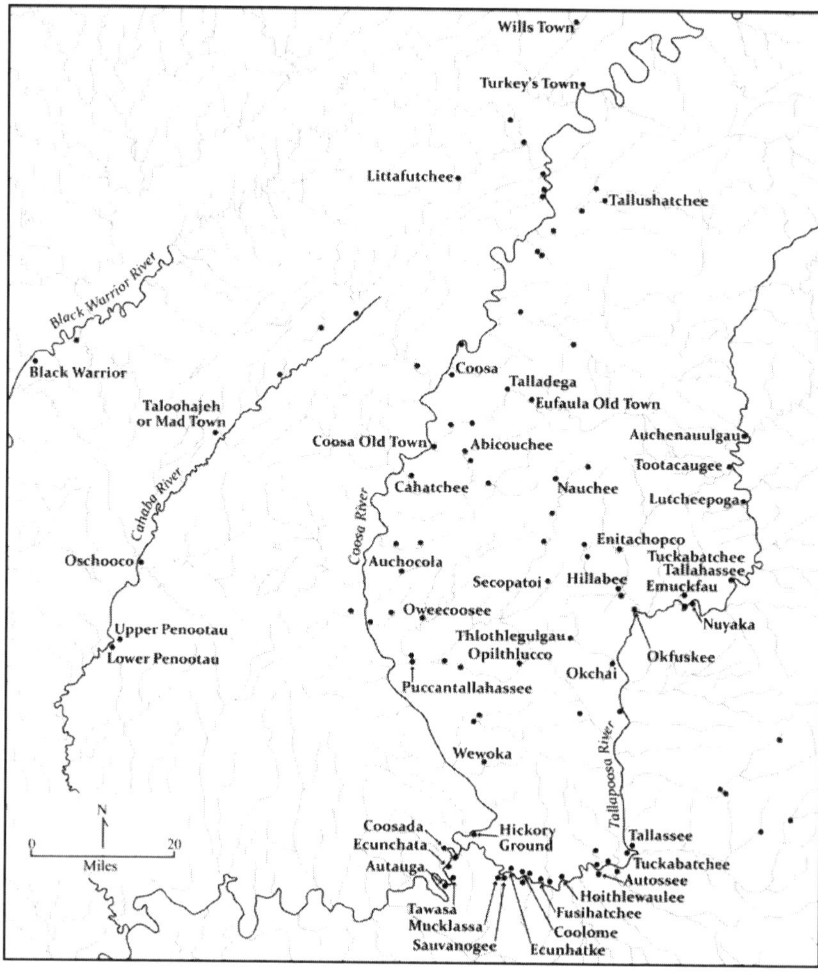

11.1. The Upper Creek country on the eve of the Creek War, adapted from "General Jackson's Campaign against the Creek Indians, 1813 & 1814," Record Group 77, CWMF, Misc. 11, 1813 and 1814, National Archives and Records Administration, Washington, D.C. Map by Sarah Mattics, Center for Archaeological Studies, University of South Alabama.

The war itself was brief, too short a time for many actions and events of conflict to have left visible marks in the archaeological record. Souvenir hunting, looting of bodies and houses, and collecting of guns and other weapons would have left little other than lead or iron balls as markers of battlefields.

Determination of the precise period when a Creek town or camp was abandoned or attacked may be very difficult. Even the practice of deliberate burning of Indian houses and cornfields, so commonly mentioned in US military reports, is not easily identified at Indian archaeological sites. Creek houses, with their wooden superstructures and internal hearths, frequently burned due to accidents. Only in the cases where burning is specifically reported, such as Fort Mims, Eccanachaca, the settlements on the Black Warrior River destroyed by General John Coffee in October 1813, or the short-term refugee camps on the Cahaba River, can we identify deliberate destruction.[5]

Archaeology can resolve some poorly documented issues of the Creek War. Foremost of these are the actual effects of supposed incitements by Tecumseh and local prophets for the Creeks to abandon items and customs of US and European origins and to return to traditional ways. Aside from a questionable interpretation by Benjamin Hawkins, there are no reliable accounts of Tecumseh's speech to the Creeks, but Albert Pickett and other scholars continued to refer to a prohibition on trade items in Red Stick culture. Accounts of the subsequent war, however, include many references to the Red Sticks' continued use of iron axes, knives, and guns and the need for ammunition, suggesting that religiosity was tempered by military practicality. Changes in architecture, settlement pattern, and non-military culture are much less historically documented. Excavations of artifact assemblages from Red Stick sites would resolve many of these questions.[6]

Geography and Upper Creek Settlement Patterns

Settlement patterns describe the distribution of human settlements and other activities in relation to natural landscapes and resources. Distribution data from historical, geographical, and archaeological surveys are used to create descriptive and explanatory models of how indigenous populations occupied and used their landscape. Settlement patterns are never static: they make frequent dynamic adjustments to changes in environment, technology, society, and external cultures.[7]

Moreover, while the mountains, valleys, and plains of Alabama have changed little since the Creek War, other geographic characteristics have altered, some almost beyond recognition. Most of the major rivers have been dammed or rechanneled. Nearly two centuries of agriculture, lumbering, and urban sprawl have caused extensive deforestation, soil erosion, and dramatic shifts in plant and animal populations. To understand the early nineteenth-century landscape, it is necessary to reconstruct it using historic accounts and ecological and archaeological data. Late eighteenth-century descriptions of terrain, streams, forests, and indigenous settlements together with modern analysis of pollen and botanical remains from archaeological sites, remnant stands of original plant communities, and witness trees in land survey records of the 1820s and 1830s have been used in hypothetical reconstructions of forest composition. The environment was not static; the relationship between it and the resident Creek communities was dynamic, with both constantly re-adapting to each other.[8]

The Creek War involved persons and supplies from eight modern southeastern states, but the actual arena of war was largely confined to Alabama. The war was not raged over the flat, clean maps found in documents and modern literature, but rather over fifty thousand square miles of the most geographically and ecologically diverse regions of eastern America. North to south, the Tennessee Valley; Cumberland Plateau, Ridge, and Valley; Piedmont; and Coastal Plain presented opportunities and challenges to the native Creeks and the US invaders. Crosscutting these physiographic zones were the rivers. The Tennessee, Alabama, and Tombigbee Rivers were largely navigable while much of the Coosa and Tallapoosa Rivers contained some of the worse rapids in the eastern United States. Except for the Federal Road running from the vicinity of Mobile to Columbus, Georgia, there were almost no improved roads—only horse paths used by the Creeks and US traders.[9]

The iconic views of US soldiers fighting savages in a trackless wilderness are not entirely correct. True, there were vast evergreen and hardwood forests in the Alabama hinterlands, and some battles, such as at Burnt Corn or Calebee Creek, were fought in such isolated areas. However, most of the Upper Creeks lived in settled agricultural landscapes of towns (or as the Creeks termed them, talwas), hamlets, single houses (or *talofas*), paths, fields, livestock, and rich bottomlands along the major rivers and their tributaries. While they could be identified with specific geographical locations at one time or another, talwas were actually large social units of persons related by matrilineal and affinal kinship. The center of each town was a nucleated settlement of a rotunda or council house, square ground, ball yard, and trader's compound, surrounded by clusters of domestic structures. As discussed elsewhere, in the late eighteenth and early nineteenth centuries, a trend toward a more dispersed settlement pattern began with individual families moving away from the centers, but most Creeks remained loyal to their talwas despite geographical separation.[10]

Historic descriptions by eighteenth- and nineteenth-century visitors and archaeological excavations give us glimpses into Creek settlements and landscapes. Much of the primeval floodplain forest had been cut for fields and houses, creating a mosaic landscape of large trees, canebrakes, cypress and gum swamps, active and abandoned fields, fences, paths, and individual homesteads. Within each talwa, which could vary in size and population, scattered houses and hamlets were situated on levees, higher terraces, and other elevated areas. Occasionally, wooden fences enclosed agricultural fields, some active, some overgrown, which lay on both sides of the rivers.

Horse paths connected the scattered houses, hamlets, and talwas. Numerous canebrakes, swamps, gravel bars, and abandoned fields served as sources of food for livestock, livestock grazing, and building and other raw materials.[11]

Due to the Creek policy of allowing Indian refugees to settle nearby, aboriginal populations in the river valleys of eastern Alabama grew in the late eighteenth and early nineteenth centuries to be some of the densest and most ethnically diverse in eastern North America. The region's rich soils, abundant natural resources, and ecological diversity allowed it to absorb large numbers of emigrants without straining local capacity. The resultant Creek society was a complex mixture of social, political, and ethnic groups.

Although Creek settlements were largely confined to stream valleys, topography in adjacent uplands had its effects upon local settlement patterns. In the north, the eastern Cumberland Plateau region extended from the northeast corner of Alabama southward to near Birmingham. A series of northeast-southwest-trending mountains and ridges and narrow valleys lay between Andrew Jackson's base of operations at Fort Strother on the Coosa River and his principal supply depots in the Tennessee Valley. Sand Mountain, a five-hundred-foot-high flat-topped mountain with no roads, was the greatest obstacle. To the northeast, Lookout Mountain and lesser mountains, with differences in local relief of two hundred to eight hundred feet, paralleled the Coosa River and were additional impediments to the movements of troops and supplies. There were no major Creek towns in this part of the Cumberland Plateau, but there are certainly archaeological sites of US military camps, roads, and supply depots.[12]

Along the Coosa River in the Ridge and Valley Province of Cherokee, Etowah, and Calhoun Counties, northeast- to southwest–trending narrow ridges and hills lay on both sides of the river. The lower topographic relief presented some hindrances to troop movements, but nowhere near as much as in the eastern Cumberland Plateau. Some transportation in flatboats was possible on the Coosa River in Etowah and Cherokee Counties. A drop of only forty-nine feet in the river's elevation in the 133 miles between Rome, Georgia, and Greenport in St. Clair County (the location of Fort Strother, established by General Jackson in 1813) allowed for some regular boat traffic. Due in part to the proximity to the Cherokees in Georgia, Creek settlement in this region was sparse in the nineteenth century, with the northernmost Creek town being Tallushatchee, near Jacksonville, in Calhoun County.[13]

In the southern Ridge and Valley Province in St. Clair, Shelby, and Talladega Counties and the northern Piedmont Province in Coosa and Elmore Counties, local topographic relief was more subdued but still sufficient to slow movements of US forces. Between Greenport and Wetumpka at the fall line in Elmore County, the Coosa River descended 339 feet in 142 miles, producing some of the most severe rapids in the eastern United States, passable by flatboats and other craft only during periods of high water. The river was deeply entrenched in a narrow, rocky gorge subject to high floods and with limited land for agriculture on either side. Only at certain points in this region, such as the town of Coosa near Childersburg and Woods Island, was the terrain favorable for settlement adjacent to the river. By the late eighteenth century, these riverine locations were abandoned. Talladega, Abicouchee, Nauchee, Opilthlucco, Weoka, and most other talwas of the Abeikas lay some distance to the east of the river along fertile but less entrenched tributaries like Nauchee, Talladega, Hatchet, and Weoka Creeks. As noted by Robbie Ethridge, some of these tributary settlements were closer to towns on the upper Tallapoosa River than to the Coosa River.[14]

Within the upland Cumberland Plateau, Ridge, and Valley and Piedmont regions, north to south paths, often following watershed divides, connected the Indian towns. Some of these paths were later improved and used for wagon traffic, but this was some of the most rugged terrain faced by the US Army. Supply shortages were pivotal in delaying Jackson's northern campaign for several months. During the first campaign in the fall of 1813, his troops were forced to cut a fifty-five-mile-long supply road from the Tennessee Valley over Sand Mountain to Fort Strother.[15]

In the southern Piedmont of Coosa, Tallapoosa, and Randolph Counties, north of the fall line, local relief is more subdued but still rocky and difficult to traverse. Settlements and fields of the Okfuskee Creek towns lay along the Tallapoosa River and its tributaries from Okfuskee in modern Tallapoosa County to Lutcheepoga in modern Randolph County. The sites of Okfuskee (largest of the Upper Creek towns), Kialigee, and other adjacent towns are now submerged beneath Lake Martin, but upstream, the Hillabee settlements, Tohopeka, Nuyaka, and other towns are still accessible. The Tallapoosa River was bordered by narrow floodplains with fertile soils and browse for livestock. The adjacent slopes were rocky but usually covered by a mast-rich hickory and oak forest, supporting deer and other animals. The river was shallow and rocky but had a well-developed meander belt, producing deep bends such as Horseshoe Bend. Some canoe traffic was possible.[16]

South of the fall line at modern Tallassee and Wetumpka, Alabama, the lower Tallapoosa, lower Coosa, and upper Alabama Rivers were slow-flowing coastal-plain streams with extensive fertile bottomlands and floodplain forests rich in natural resources. Here the talwas immediately adjoined one another with tributary streams serving as boundaries. Historic maps and accounts and archaeological surveys by Greg Waselkov, John Cottier, and others show nearly continuous occupation with towns, houses, and fields along forty miles of the lower Tallapoosa and upper Alabama Rivers, producing some of the densest aboriginal populations in the region. In the eighteen miles between the Creek towns of Tallassee and Tuckabatchee in the east and Mucklassa in the west, there were eight named towns of the Tallapoosa Creeks. On the upper Alabama River, west from the junction of the Tallapoosa and Coosa Rivers, six towns of Alabama or Koasati speakers formed the western part of Creek country. The generally flat terrain of the lower Tallapoosa and upper Alabama river valleys as well as the adjacent Coastal Plain were little impediment to movements of the armies of General John Floyd at Calebee Creek and General Jackson after the Battle of Horseshoe Bend. Barges and small boats hauled army supplies along the lower Tallapoosa River.[17]

Lying south of the Creek settlements, the southernmost and largest physiographic zone was the Coastal Plain, extending from the fall line to the Gulf Coast. Minor physiographic zones—Black Prairie, Southern Red Hills, Pine Hills, and Coastal Strip—crossed the region, going east to west, but all had relatively low relief of less than several hundred feet. Vast fire-climax longleaf and mixed hardwood forests and small patches of prairie covered the area. Embedded within the southern Coastal Plain, at the junction of the Alabama and Tombigbee Rivers, was the Mobile-Tensaw Delta, a large expanse of streams, bayous, islands, fertile bottomlands, the Tensaw settlements, and the plantations of wealthy Creeks of mixed ancestry, called *métis* by some scholars.[18]

Between the present location of Montgomery and the Tensaw settlements in Baldwin and Monroe Counties, there were no Creek settlements in the Coastal Plain, but it was claimed as hunting territory. Although over one hundred miles across, the relatively flat Coastal Plain was the most direct route into the heart of Red Stick territory, far easier than the terrain faced by General Jackson in the north. The area was crossed by the Federal Road and a number of trading paths north from Mobile and Pensacola. The Alabama, Tombigbee, and Chattahoochee Rivers were navigable by flatboats and other small craft. General Claiborne's construction of Fort Claiborne in Monroe County and his attack in December 1813 against Eccanachaca and adjacent settlements on the upper Alabama River removed serious Indian opposition in the Coastal Plain.[19]

The settled heartland of the Upper Creeks was about one hundred miles north to south and sixty miles east to west, encompassing some forty-two hundred square miles. Traditional towns of the Creeks and their allies extended from the Abeika town of Tallushatchee near Jacksonville south down the Coosa River to the Alabama settlement of Autauga on the Alabama River near Prattville. Tallapoosa and Okfuskee settlements extended up the Tallapoosa River to Lutcheepoga in Randolph County. Except for the battles in south Alabama and at Eccanachaca, this was the arena of the Creek War.[20]

During the eighteenth century, broad empty regions surrounded the Creek settlements of central Alabama, separating them from other Indian groups and the southern European colonies. Such zones began in Alabama during the prehistoric Mississippian Period (circa AD 1000–1550) in part due to areas of reduced natural resources but also as defensive strategies. The zones became smaller and less defined during the Protohistoric Period (circa AD 1550–1680) after disruptive Spanish expeditions crossed the region. During the late seventeenth and eighteenth centuries, the areas expanded again as a response to European slave raiding and colonies and the need for more hunting territory. In some directions, the empty lands were larger than the settled areas. In addition to serving for defense, the broad empty zones were used by small parties for hunting, particularly for the important deerskin trade. There were no permanent settlements in these areas, only temporary hunting camps.[21]

The Lower Creeks of the Chattahoochee originally claimed land to the Atlantic Ocean, but by 1803 they had retreated to the Ocmulgee River in Georgia. To the north, an undefined but strongly contested hunting zone lay between the Upper and Lower Creeks on the Coosa, Tallapoosa, and Chattahoochee Rivers and the Cherokee settlements of northern Georgia. On the western side, a broad empty zone extended from the upper Alabama River west and south to the Choctaw and Chickasaw of Mississippi and southern Alabama. Due south lay the pine forests of the Coastal Plain, uninhabited except for the Tensaw and métis settlers near Mobile and the Spanish settlements at Pensacola and along the coast.[22]

During the late eighteenth and early nineteenth centuries, the traditional pattern of nucleated settlements in a core area surrounded by buffer zones began to alter. Some Creeks began to establish out lying "plantations" and "cow pens" within the western and southern buffer zones. Such remote farms were mostly attempts by "wealthy" métis to find space for their increasing livestock herds and to escape the social and political entanglement of traditional Creek talwas. Sam Moniac, William Weatherford, Josiah Francis, Sophia Durant, and others maintained farms along the upper Alabama River between present-day Montgomery and Selma. Far to the south, on Little River and near Claiborne on the Alabama River, William Weatherford, David Tate, and other families had farms and cattle ranches. Immediately downstream and to the west were the expanding American Tensaw settlements.[23]

The Creek War brought drastic changes to traditional settlement patterns. The seminal study by Gregory A. Waselkov and Brian Wood documents widespread population movement, abandonment, consolidation, and destruction of traditional talwas, houses, and fields. Nearly sixty Creek settlements were attacked and burned by US forces and their allies. It would seem that such extensive destruction would be easily detected by archaeology, but routine accidental fires and later agricultural plowing obscure the evidence. Deliberate burning by US forces might be determined by correlating historical records with specific archaeological sites and the presence of standard US .69-caliber lead musket balls and iron grapeshot.[24]

Waselkov and Wood also note the appearance of two new forms of settlements: war camps and refugee camps. War camps, mostly made up of warriors, were set up throughout Creek territory and the surrounding buffer zones. Some were one- to two-day affairs, probably resembling the bark-roofed hunting shelters shown in the eighteenth-century sketches by Philip Georg Friedrich Von Reck. Others may have been even simpler and more makeshift, leaving very little archaeological evidence. Some war camps were larger, more permanent, and included women and children. At the larger camps, we can anticipate mixtures of architectural styles, including traditional rectangular houses, cribbed log houses, and bark lean-tos.

Eccanachaca (or Holy Ground), the nearby smaller camps on the upper Alabama River, and Tohopeka on the Tallapoosa River were new Creek war settlements with no prewar occupation. Holy Ground, whose exact location is only newly discovered, has not been extensively investigated. The 1973 excavations by Roy S. Dickens Jr. in the village area of Tohopeka at the southernmost tip of Horseshoe Bend revealed a number of postholes, pits, and other features, but most of these dated to a much earlier late Woodland Period occupation. Tohopeka contained none of the wealth of structural postholes, storage pits, daub pits, burials, and other features found at Nuyaka, one mile upstream, or at other excavated Creek town sites. This tends to support the suggestion that structures at Tohopeka were mostly temporary shelters and not the traditional wattle-and-daub rectangular houses. An alternative interpretation by Paul A. Ghioto is that structures in Tohopeka were constructed with horizontal, cribbed-log techniques, which would leave very little archaeological evidence. Ghioto's suggestion does not appear feasible as cribbed-log construction takes as much time and energy as wattle-and-daub construction, which continued to be used after the war.[25]

War camps were also set up within the limits of the existing towns of Hoithlewaulee (1EE328) and Autossee (1MC6) on the lower Tallapoosa River. Surface collections and unsystematic excavations of graves at Autossee have not produced definite artifacts or indications of the war camp occupation due to mingling with prewar materials. Excavations by Auburn University students at 1EE328, one of the sites within the historic limits of the Hoithlewaulee talwa, yielded four iron grapeshot, indicative of an US attack, probably in April 1814. The grapeshot, plus the presence of some late British pearlware sherds, suggests that this location was one of the Hoithlewaulee war camps.[26]

Americans and both Creek factions set up varieties of refugee camps. In the south, Americans and some métis fortified houses with wooden stockades, such as Forts Mims, Madison, and Sinquefield. Others fled to Mobile, Fort Stoddard, or west of the Tombigbee River, leaving the Tensaw and métis settlements abandoned. Waselkov and Wood document the burning and abandonment of numerous small, northern, Creek refugee camps by US forces. These camps were located in marginal areas in the Cahaba River valley, in canebrakes along Catoma Creek in Montgomery County, and in more remote locations. In August 1814, over thirty-eight "plantations," "improvements," and "cornfields" were found by Major Howell Tatum along the Alabama River between the mouth of the Cahaba River and the Alabama town of Autauga. Lying well beyond the traditional western Creek settlements, the Cahaba and Alabama river camps may have been attempts by refugees to raise crops to overcome increasing food shortages. By next spring, the inhabitants of the camps left for either the lower Chattahoochee River, Florida, or the remaining Creek lands in eastern Alabama. By war's end, some eight thousand Creek refugees in small camps were receiving US rations at Fort Jackson and other locations. None of these refugee camps have been found or investigated archaeologically.[27]

Architecture

Defensive stockades erected by Americans and Creeks would be clear archaeological evidence of conflict or fear of violence. Frontier American civilian and military forts ranged from light stockades of upright logs to huge, elaborate, bastioned earthworks. Historic archaeological excavations have revealed some of the design and construction techniques of the civilian Fort Mims and the military Fort Montgomery in Baldwin County, Fort Jackson in Elmore County, and Fort Mitchell in Russell County.[28]

A number of Creek communities and individuals also responded by building defensive stockades. These include Forts Leslie and Chinnabee in Talladega County and fortifications at Tuckabatchee, Chattacchufaulee, Tohopeka, Autossee, and Hoithlewaulee on the Tallapoosa River, Eccanachaca on the upper Alabama River, and Coweta, Coweta Tallahassee, and Cussita on the middle Chattahoochee River. Most were probably relatively small, enclosing private residences or the central ceremonial square ground. Little is known of the construction styles and sizes of these indigenous forts. Some, such as those at Eccanachaca, were variously described as a "stockade," "pickets," "stakes and fallen logs," and, at Hoithlewaulee, as "entrenchments." Only one known archaeological example has been investigated. Excavation of a one-hundred-foot section of the defense around the house of Alexander Leslie, a friendly métis trader at Talladega, revealed a stockade of upright, quartered cedar logs enclosing interior buildings of unknown form. The overall shape was probably rectangular, similar to the much larger Fort Mims.[29]

The most famous Creek fortification—the barricade at Horseshoe Bend on the Tallapoosa—is also the most controversial. Erected by warriors from Okfuskee and other nearby towns in two months in 1814, the site was attacked by General Andrew Jackson on March 27, 1814, in the final decisive battle of the Creek War. The Creek barricade effectively withstood two hours of US artillery fire and eventually only fell to a direct frontal charge by infantry. Running across the narrow neck at the northern end of Horseshoe Bend, the over one-thousand-foot-long barricade was variously described in historic accounts as a five- to eight-foot-high breastwork composed of horizontally lain large timbers and tree trunks or five large logs pierced by two rows of firing or port holes. The barricade is shown on historic maps as having a number of zigzag sections, which may have been intended for the military purposes of enfilade or crossfire or as a means of stabilizing the horizontal logs. The four extant historic maps of the battleground give slightly different locations for the defensive wall.[30]

In 1973, Dickens excavated a series of archaeological features in the narrow neck of Horseshoe Bend in the area traditionally thought to be the location of the barricade. Gun Hill, the location of Jackson's three- and six-pounder artillery, lies about 125 yards from the projected western end of the features. Dickens exposed 132 feet of a sub-plow-zone ditch, measuring 4.5 to 7.0 feet wide and 0.5 to 1.5 feet deep. In the ditch he found parallel linear impressions of four logs, 0.6 to 1.5 feet in diameter and an estimated 25 to 40 feet in length. All logs were decayed, but portions of one were tentatively identified as "heart" pine. He interprets these as a foundation for the 1814 barricade. Vertical posts in postholes spaced at approximately 10-foot intervals on the south or interior of the wall served to stabilize the horizontal logs. On the north or outer side, a row of small linear impressions at right angles to the ditch suggest a line of outward-leaning stakes or small poles at angles of about 30 to 40 degrees. Whether these were intended to stabilize the lower row of logs or as defensive obstacles (fascines) is unknown. The archaeological discovery of borrow pits adjacent to the outer edge of the ditch indicates the use of clay either as chinking between the logs or as some form of fill.[31]

Using historic and archaeological data, George Mackenzie and Dickens interpreted the barricade as being two parallel rows of horizontal logs sloping inward with clay fill tamped between them. Spaced vertical posts on both sides held the logs in place. Sharpened stakes extended outward at angles from the outer base of the wall. The portholes or firing holes through the logs and intervening clay fill were kept open by a lining of short logs.[32]

In 1986, Waselkov offered an alternative reconstruction of the barricade. Instead of the log-floored ditch being a foundation for the wall, Waselkov suggested that it was a walkway or defensive platform between two walls. On the inner side, the walkway was bordered by a low retaining wall of horizontal logs supported by spaced vertical posts, which held back an earthen embankment of soil thrown out of the ditch. The northern wall was a single row of stacked horizontal logs held in place by a spaced series of upright and prop logs. Between the props were outward-leaning, sharpened stakes. The gaps between the logs were chinked with clay from the adjacent borrow pits. Although the existing evidence is not conclusive, Waselkov's reconstruction appears more reasonable.[33]

The origin of the design of the Horseshoe Bend barricade is a mystery. Most Creek and US defensive works were based on upright wooden palisades anchored in narrow trenches. Interpretations by Dickens and Waselkov vary somewhat but largely confirm the scale and complexity of the wall. The horizontal log construction, firing holes, fascines, and zigzag construction bespeak a level of sophistication beyond typical Creek and frontier American upright palisades. Waselkov has suggested that some of the Creeks were familiar with the construction techniques of American cribbed-log houses and worm or zigzag rail fences.

While the origin of the design of the barricade remains unknown, the manner of its erection lies clearly within traditional Creek construction techniques. For over 150 years, Creek communities in central Alabama had built superstructures of massive vertical and horizontal logs in the center of their large council houses, or rotundas. Massive pine logs over one foot in diameter and over twenty-four feet long were lifted upwards of twelve to fourteen feet to form pyramidal support structures. The buildings were constructed by communal labor under the direction of an "architect"—a *mico* who specified the size and length of each timber cut from the nearby forest and the placement of each within the structure. The construction of the Horseshoe Bend barricade in two months by the Okfuskee warriors under the direction of such an individual seems reasonable.[34]

Material Culture

By the early nineteenth century, Upper Creek material culture and technology were a blend of items and customs of indigenous, imported European and American, and syncretistic origins. Architecture, subsistence, ceramics, and other traditional crafts continued to evolve but were clearly derived from late prehistoric forms. The trade in deerskins brought in cloth, flintlock muskets and rifles, axes, hoes, knives, kettles, ornaments of glass and silver, and other items of European and American origin. Like many of the southeastern historic Indian groups, the Upper Creeks were adept at innovating new tools, clothing styles, and other items out of indigenous and external materials. Temporal changes in the historic Creek material assemblages were generally gradual, and it is difficult to separate artifacts and occupations of the late eighteenth century from those of the Creek War era.[35]

Limited archaeological testing at the recently discovered site of Eccanachaca, or Holy Ground (1Lo210), on the upper Alabama River in Lowndes County offers a sample of Red Stick material culture. Recovered objects include sherds of Creek pottery, square nails, a stripped flintlock plate, and a British trade axe, all typical of any early nineteenth-century Creek assemblage and suggestive that the inhabitants had not disposed of all things European.[36] In addition, other recovered things that are either seldom or never found on historic Creek sites were also uncovered: evidence of cribbed log houses, British pearlware ceramics, brass arrowheads, a carpenter's chisel, and fragments of cast-iron cooking kettles, further supporting the notion that the Red Stick inhabitants were still using European artifacts and practices. These items may represent loot from Fort Mims or other Tensaw homesteads, which were in turn smashed or burned by the Choctaws in the destruction of the town in December 1813.[37]

Historic accounts are generally consistent about Creek weapons used in the war. George Stiggins wrote, "They go into action with their guns on their shoulders, their knife and tomahawk hanging to their side and war club stuck in their belt."[38]

None of the iconic red-painted wooden war clubs, or atássa —the namesake of the Red Sticks—are known to have survived. Stiggins describes them as "shaped like a small gun about two foot long and at the curve near where the lock would be is a three square piece of iron or steele with a sharp edge drove in to leave a projection of about two inches." There may have been other shapes. All types appear to be revivals or modifications of earlier forms. Red-painted war clubs were secondary to guns in military value, but they remained important in the Creek weapon inventory to the end of the war as readily available and symbolically important. Only the metal parts of the gunstock type would survive in an archaeological context, but none have been identified.[39]

Although Indian knives were often described as "scalping knives" in contemporary reports, there is no evidence of any knives made for or reserved exclusively for this purpose by the Creeks. Most knives were probably common utilitarian types, mass manufactured in Britain and the United States. They included medium-sized wooden-, bone-, or antler-handled sheath or case knives and bone-handled, bolstered dinner knives with re-sharpened points. Blade lengths ranged from four to eight inches. Numerous examples of such knives have been recovered from late eighteenth-century graves and other archaeological contexts at Upper and Lower Creek sites. Presently, late eighteenth-century knives are difficult to separate from those of the Creek War period. Probably, both Red Sticks and Americans were using the same types of knives.[40]

Bayonets were issued to US troops, but none of the Creeks appear to have adopted them. Officers of the US Army and militia carried sabers or swords, but there is little evidence that the Red Sticks ever used them in significant numbers. Swords have been recovered from eighteenth-century Creek sites, but most appear to be of pre–Revolutionary War vintage. Possibly, some of the Creeks may have made or traded for long-handled metal-bladed pikes or spears as ad hoc solutions to the general weapon shortage.[41]

Most historic accounts of the Creek War use the term "tomahawk," but—rather than more elaborate peace-pipe axes, spiked axes, or high-quality presentation axes made expressly for the North American trade—these weapons were most likely small, utilitarian, short-handled iron hatchets. Some were general purpose or carpenter's hatchets of common English patterns. Others were narrow, curve-bladed forms intended for the North American trade. Both forms were forged in large numbers in the industrial midlands of Britain, in France, and in parts of the eastern United States for domestic use and export. It is difficult to distinguish between the iron hatchets of the Creeks and frontier Americans since they tended to acquire them from the same manufacturers. Such small axes have been found in late eighteenth-century graves of both Creek men and women in central Alabama. Those used as weapons of war were the same as those employed in woodworking and other mundane tasks. Only battlefield or similar contexts would identify axes used as weapons.[42]

Prior to trade with Europeans, the principal projectile weapon of southeastern Indians was the bow, with arrows tipped with flaked stone points. In the early eighteenth century, Creeks and other historic groups began making conical Kaskasia-type points of rolled brass or iron from trade kettles and barrel hoops, but by around 1750, bows and arrows were relegated to secondary status. Bows and arrows appear to have been revived in the early nineteenth century, possibly as substitutes for increasingly scarce firearms. Bows and arrows with metal points were used by Red Sticks at Tallushatchee, Talladega, and Calebee. Americans were wounded by arrows at the Battles of Fort Mims and Horseshoe Bend. No wooden bows or arrow shafts from the Creek War are known to have survived, but triangular stemmed and barbed arrowheads of sheet brass or iron recovered from the Fort Mims,

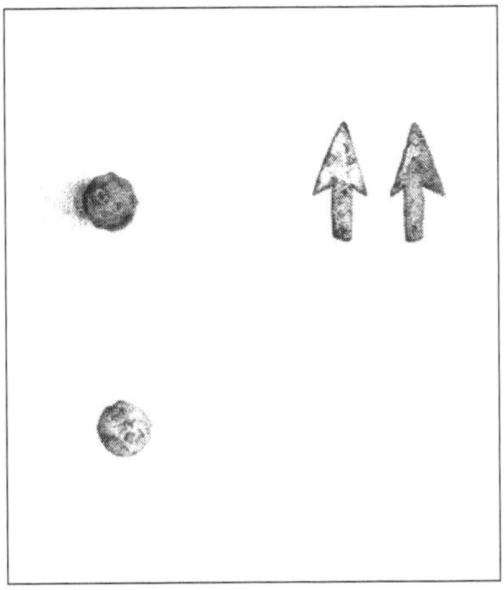

11.2. Signs of war. *Left:* Black ink sketch of iron grapeshot from the historic Creek Indian site of Fusihatchee, Elmore County. From Auburn University Montgomery, Archaeological Collections, Fusihatchee, 1EE191, Surface, F.S. 460. *Right:* Black ink sketch of brass arrowhead from Fort Mims. From the Alabama Historical Commission Archaeological Collections, Fort Mims, 1BA218, Box 6, F.S. 1502. Images courtesy of the Alabama Historical Commission (arrowhead) and Craig Sheldon (grapeshot). Drawn by Stayce Hathorn.

Eccanachaca, Fusihatchee, Autossee, Tohopeka, and Fort Jackson sites are clearly of Red Stick manufacture. Their origin among the Creeks is unknown.[43]

Flintlock muzzle-loading muskets and rifles were the dominant weapons of the Red Sticks and their opponents. Sufficient numbers of serviceable firearms and reliable supplies of gunpowder, flints, and lead balls remained major logistical problems for the Red Sticks throughout the entire war. US troops were mostly armed with variants of the .69-caliber US model 1795 infantry muskets; state militia had some similar muskets but often used rifles from a variety of sources. Pistols in a variety of calibers were carried by officers and, sometimes, enlisted men. Ammunition loads for military muskets came in three types: a single .69-caliber lead ball, buckshot, or a .69-caliber ball and three buckshot of approximately .30-caliber—a combination called "buck and ball." The more varied militia rifles used single lead balls in the .30 to .60 range. At Fort Jackson and Fort Mitchell, archaeological features yielded both French and British gun spalls and prismatic flints, with the former predominating.[44]

No known examples of Red Stick firearms have survived, but it is evident that they were a mixture of muskets and rifles of various calibers, ages, and conditions. During the late eighteenth century, the Creeks used lightweight smoothbore fowlers, in the range of .40 to .55 caliber, but, according to Caleb Swan, preferred rifles, principally of US manufacture. The ratio of muskets to rifles is not known, but the firearms inventory of the Red Sticks must have been eclectic, including commercial muskets, rifles, shotguns, salvaged military muskets, and perhaps some pistols.[45]

Making minor repairs by cannibalizing other obsolete or non-functional guns definitely began in the prewar era. As the conflict wore on and sources of new guns disappeared, many guns became unusable due to wear, forcing the Creeks to strip some broken guns for parts and to repair older guns. The variety of calibers seriously hampered the procurement of ammunition, a problem partially solved by creating bullet molds of soapstone and by using buckshot.[46]

Depending upon their context, lead musket balls can aid in identifying locations of conflicts and the position of different factions. Due to hunting and butchering activities, musket balls in the .40 to .58-caliber range are common artifacts on Upper Creek sites and are not evidence of an attack. Both Red Sticks and the pro-American faction used essentially the same types of European and US guns for hunting and war. US troops and militia were armed with a number of different caliber guns, but according to historic accounts, .69-caliber balls should be the most common sizes. Presence of a significant number of fired .69-caliber balls on a Creek site might indicate an attack by US forces, but they could also represent some of the guns looted from the destruction of Fort Mims and other settlements.[47]

Lead musket balls of a variety of calibers may be the dominant artifacts on remote battlefields such as Burnt Corn, Eccanachaca, Enitachopco Creek, and Calebee Creek. Surveys using metal detectors may be the best way of identifying these sites in the future. Careful plotting of the location of each ball may enable us to identify battle lines. A 2006 metal-detector survey by John Cornelison plotted the location of ninety-one fired and unfired or dropped lead balls in the vicinity of the barricade at the Horseshoe Bend battlefield. Analysis of twenty balls fired by Red Sticks at US troops on Gun Hill, the location of Jackson's artillery, indicate that half were from rifles, one-quarter from either muskets or rifles, and one-quarter from muskets. This tends to confirm the mixed nature of Red Stick firearms. Comparison of the ratio of fired to unfired balls between assemblages found north and south of the barricade indicates that the volume of US fire significantly exceeded that of the Red Sticks.[48]

US Army or militia military items such as clothing, buttons, accoutrements, and even .69-caliber balls found on Creek sites are not necessarily evidence of an attack since they may be Indian souvenirs or loot from other areas. The clearest indications of US attacks would be cast-iron grapeshot. Cloth bags or tin cylinders filled with cast-iron balls, 0.8 to 1.3 inches in diameter, were the major ammunition for the three- and six-pounder artillery of Jackson's army. Grapeshot was a powerful antipersonnel weapon, as demonstrated by its effectiveness in breaking the Red Stick attack at the Battle of Calebee Creek on January 17, 1814. Grapeshot was generally ineffective during two hours of bombardment of the Indian barricade at Horseshoe

Bend. Four of these grapeshot were found in the powder magazine at Fort Jackson; twelve more were recovered during the excavations of the powder magazine and other features at Fort Mitchell in Russell County. Forty-five iron grapeshot were found at Horseshoe Bend in the vicinity of the barricade. Four more were found downstream on the Tallapoosa River at Hoithlewaulee and one at Fusihatchee, both towns attacked by Jackson's troops in early April 1814.[49]

Analysis of the causes of death in human remains at Creek War sites is an unproven approach. Many of the casualties of the Creek War were never recovered from distant battlefields. Many of the attacked communities were abandoned, leaving the dead unburied. A poignant picture of a Creek community after a US attack was given by David Crockett on his way home to Tennessee when he passed by the site of Talladega over a year after the battle: "It looked like a gourd patch; the skulls of the Indians who were killed still lay scattered about."[50]

Even if interred, it would be difficult to distinguish between those killed during the war and victims of numerous earlier conflicts. Due to the Southeast's poor conditions of physical preservation, buried human remains seldom retain sufficient integrity to identify causes of death. A possible but unverified example of a wartime burial was found under the floor of a burned house at Fusihatchee (1EE191) on the lower Tallapoosa River. The intrusion of the grave pit into an older refuse-filled pit and the presence of large chunks of scorched daub or clay plaster in the burial fill above the corpse are indications of a hasty burial. The adult woman in the grave had been severely burned from the waist down. A possible interpretation is that she was killed or wounded during the April 13, 1814, attack by west Tennessee troops and lay partially within the house as it burned. Creek survivors returned after the departure of the Tennessee troops and hurriedly buried her before leaving. It is not possible to date this burial to 1814, but we can expect similar incidents to have occurred.[51]

Archaeology can occasionally identify the presence of historic individuals. Archaeological investigations at the Hickory Ground site on the lower Coosa River near Wetumpka yielded mostly late eighteenth-century Creek Indian and Euro-American trade artifacts. The presence of sherds of English shell-edge, transfer-printed, and annular ware in Creek pits and other features was puzzling since such wares do not usually appear on Creek sites until after the establishment of steamboat traffic to Montgomery in 1821, well after the Treaty of Fort Jackson in 1814. The treaty extinguished traditional Indian claims to this area but contained provisions of land for those "who shall have been friendly to the United States during the War." Tallassee Fixico of Hickory Ground was one of the thirty-five Creek signers of the treaty and was awarded 320 acres centered on Hickory Ground. He and, presumably, some relatives remained here until 1827 or 1828 before leaving for the reserved Creek lands to the east.[52]

The Creek War in central Alabama formally ended on August 9, 1814. We must formulate new questions about this very complex war, particularly, the mostly unknown confrontation between the different Creek factions. No doubt, some primary historic documents await discovery, but researching Creek War sites is an equally promising route for future research. We need to concentrate on finding and investigating major battlefields, war and refugee camps, and Indian and American homesteads. Collections of Creek artifacts existing in archaeological laboratories and museums must be analyzed. Such investigations need to be based on a multidisciplinary approach of archaeology, history, geography, biology, and other disciplines.

Acknowledgments

I am very grateful to my colleagues in the Upper Creek Archaeology Project—John W. Cottier and Gregory A. Waselkov. I have learned much from them.

Notes

1. The restrictions of this study do not ignore the involvement of the Lower Creeks, Choctaws, and Cherokees as US allies. The Creek War in central Alabama formally ended on August 9, 1814, but violence and mop-up operations continued in southern Alabama and Florida, where most of the Red Sticks had fled. This chapter concentrates on the Upper Creeks in central Alabama, and in the specified period, in order to gain clarity and focus.

2. David L. DeJarnette and Asael T. Hansen, *The Archaeology of the Childersburg Site, Alabama,* Notes in Anthropology, no. 6 (Tallahassee: Florida State University, 1960). For the upper Coosa River, see David L. DeJarnette, Edward B. Kurjack, and Bennie C. Keel, "Archaeological Investigations in the Weiss Reservoir of the Coosa River in Alabama," *Journal of Alabama Archaeology* 19 (1973): 1–201; Frederica R. Dimmick, "A Survey of Upper Creek Sites in Central Alabama," *Journal of Alabama Archaeology* 35 (1989): i–86; Gregory A. Waselkov, *Coosa River Archaeology,* 2 vols., Auburn University Archaeological Monograph no. 2 (Auburn: Department of Sociology and Anthropology, Auburn University, 1980); and Vernon James Knight Jr., "Introduction: Archaeological Research in the Middle Coosa Valley," in *Archaeological Survey and Excavations in the Coosa River Valley, Alabama,* ed. Vernon James Knight Jr. (Tuscaloosa: Alabama Museum of Natural History, 1993): 1–5. For the upper Tallapoosa River in Alabama, see Vernon J. Knight Jr. and John O'Hear, *Archaeological Investigations in the Rother L. Harris Reservoir* (Tuscaloosa: Office of Archaeological Research, Uni-

versity of Alabama, 1975); and Vernon J. Knight Jr., "Cultural Complexes of the Alabama Piedmont: An Initial Statement," *Journal of Alabama Archaeology* 16 (1980): 1–27. For the Alabama River, see John W. Cottier and Craig T. Sheldon Jr., *Interim Report of an Archaeological Survey of U.S. Army Corps of Engineers Properties along the Alabama River,* Report to the US Army Corps of Engineers, Mobile District (Auburn, AL: Department of Sociology and Anthropology, Auburn University, 1980); Bennett J. Graham, *A Preliminary Report of Salvage Archaeology in the Claiborne Lock and Dam Reservoir,* report to the National Park Service (Tuscaloosa, AL: Department of Anthropology, University of Alabama, 1967); John W. Cottier, *Archaeological Salvage Investigations in the Millers Ferry Lock and Dam Reservoir,* report to the National Park Service (Tuscaloosa, AL: Department of Anthropology, University of Alabama, 1968); Ned J. Jenkins and Teresa A. Paglione, "An Archaeological Reconnaissance of the Lower Alabama River," manuscript report submitted to the Alabama Historical Commission, Department of Sociology, Auburn University Montgomery, Montgomery, AL, 1980; Roy S. Dickens Jr. et al., "Archaeological Investigations in the Jones Bluff Reservoir of the Alabama River," *Journal of Alabama Archaeology* 17, no. 1 (1971): 1–114; and Carey B. Oakley and G. Michael Watson, *Cultural Resources Inventory of the Jones Bluff Lake, Alabama River, Alabama* (Tuscaloosa: University of Alabama, Office of Archaeological Research, 1977). For the Conecuh River, see Ned J. Jenkins and Cyril B. Mann, "An Archaeological Survey of the Conecuh Drainage," *Florida Anthropologist* 38 (1–2): 136–43; and Tray G. Earnest, McDonald Brooms, and Kate McLaurin-Wright, *A Cultural Resource Reconnaissance of Selected Portions of the Conecuh, Pea, and Choctawhatchee Rivers in Southeast Alabama,* report to the Alabama Historical Commission (Troy, AL: Troy State University, Archaeological Research Center, 1995). The southern Tombigbee River valley is covered in David S. Brose, Ned J. Jenkins, and Russell Weisman, eds., *Cultural Resources Reconnaissance Study of the Black Warrior–Tombigbee System Corridor, Alabama,* vol. 1: *Archaeology,* report to the US Army Corps of Engineers, Mobile District (Mobile: University of South Alabama, Department of Geology and Geography, 1983).

3. Archaeological sites in Alabama and other states are assigned official site numbers; the initial digit stands for Alabama, followed by a two-letter county designation, followed in turn by the individual site number for that county. The official Alabama State Site Files are maintained by the Office of Archaeological Research at the University of Alabama.

The most recent summary of Creek archaeology is by Gregory A. Waselkov and Marvin T. Smith, "Upper Creek Archaeology," in *Indians of the Greater Southeast: Historical Archaeology and Ethnohistory,* ed. Bonnie G. McEwan (Gainesville: University Press of Florida, 2000), 242–64. For the upper Coosa, see DeJarnette, Kurjack, and Keel, "Archaeological Investigations in the Weiss Reservoir";

Knight, "*Archaeological Survey and Excavations*"; Marvin T. Smith, "Seventeenth-Century Aboriginal Settlement on the Coosa River," in *Archaeological Survey and Excavations,* ed. Knight, 63–70; Vernon J. Knight Jr., "Fort Leslie and Upper Creek Ceramics of the Early Nineteenth Century," *Journal of Alabama Archaeology* 43 (1997): 35–47; L. Ross Morrell, *The Woods Island Site in Southeastern Acculturation, 1625–1800,* Notes in Anthropology 11 (Tallahassee: Florida State University, 1965); DeJarnette and Hansen, *The Archaeology of the Childersburg Site;* Harry Holstein, "Excavations at Tallishatchee (1CN 162)," field notes, Jacksonville State University Archaeological Laboratory, Jacksonville, AL. Excavations of the towns on the Tallapoosa River are reported in Roy S. Dickens Jr., *Archaeological Investigations at Horseshoe Bend, National Military Park, Alabama,* Special Publication 3 (Tuscaloosa: Alabama Archaeological Society, 1979); Vernon J. Knight Jr., *Tuckabatchee: Archaeological Investigations at an Historic Creek Town, Elmore County, Alabama* (Tuscaloosa: University of Alabama, Office of Archaeological Research, 1985); Gregory A. Waselkov, ed., *Culture Change on the Creek Frontier,* report to the National Science Foundation (Auburn, AL: Auburn University, 1985); Gregory A. Waselkov, John W. Cottier, and Craig T. Sheldon, *Archaeological Excavations at the Early Historic Creek Town of Fusihatchee, Report to the National Science Foundation, Phase 1, 1988–1989* (Auburn, AL: Auburn University, 1990); and Ned J. Jenkins and Craig T. Sheldon Jr., "Field Records, Excavations at Couloume (1MT3)," Archaeological Laboratory, Auburn University, Montgomery, AL, 1983. Some of the excavations on the lower Coosa River at Ocheaupofau or Hickory Ground (1EE89) are reported in Dianne S. Mueller, "Intrasite Settlement at the Historic Creek Town of Hickory Ground (1EE89), Elmore County, Alabama," *Journal of Alabama Archaeology* 41 (1995): 107–36. The extensive digging at Tuskegee (Taskegee) (1EE1) by the Alabama Anthropological Society is still unreported. Although the middle Chattahoochee River valley lies beyond the area of the Creek War, excavations at historic Creek sites in Alabama and Georgia yielded artifactual and feature data comparable to that found in central Alabama. For a general review of archaeology of the Chattahoochee and Flint Rivers, see H. Thomas Foster II, ed., *Archaeology of the Lower Muskogee Creek Indians, 1715–1836* (Tuscaloosa: University of Alabama Press, 2007).

4. See James W. Parker, "Digging Twice: Camps and Historical Sites Associated with the War of 1812 and the Creek War of 1813–1814," in this volume.

5. Albert J. Pickett, *History of Alabama and Incidently of Georgia and Mississippi from the Earliest Period* (Birmingham: Birmingham Book and Magazine Co., 1962), 545, 561–67; Frank L. Owsley Jr., *Struggle for the Gulf Borderlands: The Creek War and the Battle for New Orleans, 1812–1815* (Gainesville: University Presses of Florida, 1981), 62–64; and Gregory A. Waselkov, *A Conquering Spirit: Fort Mims and the Redstick War of 1813–1814* (Tuscaloosa: University of Alabama Press, 2006), 171–74.

6. Waselkov, *A Conquering Spirit,* 78.

7. Robbie Ethridge, *Creek Country: The Creek Indians and Their World* (Chapel Hill: University of North Carolina Press, 2003), 32–33, 140–57; and Gregory A. Waselkov and Brian M. Wood, "The Creek War of 1813–1814: Effects on Creek Society and Settlement Pattern," *Journal of Alabama Archaeology* 32 (1986): 8–16.

8. For eighteenth-century geographic accounts, see William Bartram, *The Travels of William Bartram, Naturalist's Edition,* ed. Francis Harper (New Haven, CT: Yale University Press, 1967); Major Caleb Swan, "Position and State of Manners and Arts in the Creek or Muskogee Nation in 1791," in *Information Respecting the History, Condition, and Prospects of the Indian Tribes of the Unites States,* 6 vols., ed. Henry R. Schoolcraft (Washington, DC: Government Printing Office, 1928), 5:251-283; and Benjamin Hawkins, *A Sketch of the Creek Country in the Years 1798 and 1799, Collections of the Georgia Historical Society,* vol. 3, part 1 (Americus, GA: Americus Book Company, 1938), 20–80. Modern reconstructions of environmental conditions are found in Ethridge, *Creek Country;* M. Thomas Hatley, "The Tallapoosa River Landscape Revisited," in *Archaeological Excavations at the Early Historic Creek Indian Town of Fusihatchee (Phase 1, 1988–1989),* ed. Gregory A. Waselkov, John W. Cottier, and Craig T. Sheldon Jr., final report to the National Science Foundation (BNS-8718934) (Auburn, AL: Department of Sociology and Anthropology, Auburn University, 1990); and Thomas Foster and Mary Theresa Bonhage-Freund, "Environmental Context," in *Archaeology of the Lower Muskogee Creek Indians,* ed. H. Thomas Foster (Tuscaloosa: University of Alabama Press, 2007), 26–36.

9. Daniel C. Sapp and Jacques Emplaincourt, *Physiographic Map of Alabama: Map 168* (Tuscaloosa: Geological Survey of Alabama, 1975); Ethridge, *Creek County,* 32–53; Harvey H. Jackson III, *Rivers of History: Life on the Coosa, Tallapoosa, Cahaba, and Alabama* (Tuscaloosa: University of Alabama Press, 1995), 1–6; and Henry D. Southerland Jr. and Jerry E. Brown, *The Federal Road through Georgia, the Creek Nation, and Alabama, 1806–1836* (Tuscaloosa: University of Alabama Press, 1989).

10. Morris E. Opler, "The Creek 'Town' and the Problem of Indian Political Reorganization," in *Human Problems of Technological Change: A Casebook,* ed. Edward W. Spicer (New York: Russell Sage Foundation, 1952), 170; Craig T. Sheldon Jr., "Historic Creek 'Summer' Houses of Central Alabama," paper presented at the 64th annual meeting of the Society for American Archaeology, Nashville, TN, 1997, 9–10; Craig T. Sheldon Jr., "Public Architecture of the Historic Upper Creeks," paper presented at the 47th annual Southeastern Archaeological Conference, Mobile, AL, 1991, 14–16; Ethridge, *Creek Country,* 32–53, 93; and Gregory A. Waselkov, "Lower Tallapoosa River Cultural Resources Survey, Phase I," report to the Alabama Historical Commission, Department of Sociology and Anthropology, Auburn University, Auburn, AL, 1981.

11. The contemporary accounts and sketches of late eighteenth-century Creek towns by Swan, Hawkins, and other early visitors are largely confirmed by archaeological investigations at Fusihatchee, Hoithlewaulee, and Tuckabatchee on the lower Tallapoosa River and Hickory Ground on the lower Coosa River. Hawkins's description of the settlements and vegetation along his 1801 trip from the Hickory Ground to Tuckabatchee reveals the mixed landscape. Benjamin Hawkins, "A Viatory or Journal of Distances and Observations," in *The Collected Works of Benjamin Hawkins, 1796–1810,* ed. H. Thomas Foster II (Tuscaloosa: University of Alabama Press, 2003), 80–82. See Swan, "Position and State of Manners," 5:262; Hawkins, *A Sketch of the Creek County;* Ethridge, *Creek Country,* 31–53; Gregory A. Waselkov, "Changing Strategies of Indian Field Location in the Early Historic Southeast," in *People, Plants, and Landscapes: Studies in Paleoethnobotany,* ed. Kristen J. Gremillion (Tuscaloosa: University of Alabama Press, 1997), 179–94; and Waselkov and Smith, "Upper Creek Archaeology."

12. Sapp and Emplaincourt, *Physiographic Map of Alabama: Map 168;* Roland M. Harper, *Forests of Alabama,* Monograph 10 (Tuscaloosa: Geological Survey of Alabama, 1943), 88–95; Roland M. Harper, *Natural Resources of the Tennessee Valley Region in Alabama,* Special Report 17 (Tuscaloosa: Geological Survey of Alabama, 1942).

13. Harper, *Forests of Alabama,* 106–12; Jackson, *Rivers of History,* 1, 99; Ethridge, *Creek County,* 88; Amos J. Wright Jr., *Historic Indian Towns in Alabama, 1540–1838* (Tuscaloosa: University of Alabama Press, 2003), 148; and James Parker, "Fort Strother," in *An Intensive Phase II Cultural Resources Survey of Selected Areas on the Coosa River Navigation Project,* vol. 2, ed. Tim Mistovich (Tuscaloosa: University of Alabama, Office of Archaeological Research, 1981), 51–54. Archaeological surveys indicate that the upper Coosa River valley near Gadsden was originally densely occupied during the prehistoric Mississippian Period of circa AD 1000 to 1540 and the subsequent Protohistoric Period of AD 1540 to 1700. Subsequently, most of the population moved downstream to the region of Childersburg. See DeJarnette, Kurjack, and Keel, "Archaeological Investigations in Weiss Reservoir"; Marvin T. Smith, "Aboriginal Population Movements in the Early Historic Interior Southeast," in *Powhatan's Mantle: Indians in the Colonial Southeast,* ed. Gregory A. Waselkov, Peter H. Wood, and Tom Hatley, rev. ed. (Lincoln: University of Nebraska Press, 2006), 43–56; Dimmick, "A Survey of Upper Creek Sites," 10–13; Vernon J. Knight Jr., Gloria G. Cole, and Richard Walling, *An Archaeological Reconnaissance of the Coosa and Tallapoosa River Valleys, East Alabama* (Tuscaloosa: Office of Archaeological Research, University of Alabama, 1983); and Terry L. Lolley, "Ethnohistory and Archaeology: A Map Method for Locating Upper Creek Towns and Villages," *Journal of Alabama Archaeology* 42 (1996): 64–67.

14. Harper, *Forests of Alabama,* 106–26; George E. Brewer, "History of Coosa

County, Part I," *Alabama Historical Quarterly* 4 (Spring 1942): 34–38; Philip M. Price, "Map of the Coosa River from Lock No. 4, Ala., to Greensport, Ala., 1878," in *Annual Report, U.S. Engineer's Office, Corps of Engineers,* Montgomery, AL, 1890; Philip M. Price, "Map of the Coosa River from Wetumpka, Ala., to Lock No. 4, Ala., 1889," in *Annual Report, U.S. Engineer's Office, Corps of Engineers,* Montgomery, AL, 1889; Craig T. Sheldon Jr., "The Present State of Archaeological Survey and Site File Data for the Alabama River and Adjacent Regions," in *The Search for Mabila: The Decisive Battle between Hernando de Soto and Chief Tascalusa,* ed. Vernon James Knight Jr. (Tuscaloosa: University of Alabama Press, 2006), 117; Morrell, *The Woods Island Site,* 66, DeJarnette and Hansen, *The Archaeology of the Childersburg Site;* Knight, Cole, and Walling, *An Archaeological Reconnaissance;* Dimmick, "A Survey of Upper Creek Sites," 13–21; Lolley, "Ethnohistory and Archaeology," 62; Ethridge, *Creek Country,* 88; and Waselkov, *Coosa River Archaeology.*

15. See Owsley, *Struggle for the Gulf Borderlands,* 68–69; and John Reid and John H. Eaton, *The Life of Andrew Jackson,* ed. Frank L. Owsley Jr. (Tuscaloosa: University of Alabama Press, 1976), 60–61, 66, 69; Benjamin G. W. Griffith Jr., *McIntosh and Weatherford: Creek Indian Leaders* (Tuscaloosa: University of Alabama Press, 1969), 116.

16. Ethridge *Creek County,* 27, 90; Hawkins, *A Sketch of the Creek County,* 72–74; Knight, Cole, and Walling, *An Archaeological Reconnaissance;* and Lolley, "Ethnohistory and Archaeology," 72–73, 75–76. During the major drought of 2007, water levels in Lake Martin fell ten feet, uncovering Creek and early American house sites. A limited survey along Little Kowaliga Creek in Elmore County revealed four typical Creek house sites situated on the ends of low toe ridges above the rich riverine bottomlands. Unfortunately, many sites had been recently looted. The ecological advantages of these locations high above but adjacent to the alluvial bottomlands are indicated by the presence of post-removal US settler house remains on top of the Creek occupations. See Lake Martin survey records, Auburn Montgomery Archaeology Laboratory.

17. Hawkins, *A Sketch of the Creek Country,* 24–34; Ethridge, *Creek Country,* 67–82; Wright, *Historic Indian Towns;* Dimmick, "A Survey of Upper Creek Sites," 21–40; Lolley, "Ethnohistory and Archaeology," 61–62, 67–72; Waselkov, "Lower Tallapoosa River Cultural Resources Survey"; and Oakley and Watson, *Cultural Resources Inventory of the Jones Bluff Lake,* 353–67.

18. Sapp and Emplaincourt, *Physiographic Map of Alabama;* Roland M. Harper, *Resources of Southern Alabama,* Special Report 11 (Tuscaloosa: Geological Survey of Alabama, 1920); Harper, *Forests of Alabama,* 127–209; Lewis H. Larson Jr., "Aboriginal Subsistence Technology on the Southeastern Coastal Plain during the Late Prehistoric Period" (PhD diss., University of Michigan, 1969), 73–103; and Waselkov, *A Conquering Spirit,* 16–23.

19. Archaeological surveys of this region in Alabama show no major historic Indian occupations, only sporadic scattered temporary camps, usually along trading paths. See note 6. The battle at the Holy Ground and subsequent military operations in opening the Alabama River to boat traffic are described by Henry S. Halbert and Timothy H. Ball, *The Creek War of 1813–1814,* ed. Frank L. Owsley Jr. (1895; repr., Tuscaloosa: University of Alabama Press, 1969), 241–66; Owsley, *Struggle for the Gulf Borderlands,* 43–50; and Sean M. O'Brien, *In Bitterness and Tears: Andrew Jackson's Destruction of the Creeks and Seminoles* (Westport, CT: Praeger, 2003), 103–16, 131–32.

20. Wright, *Historic Indian Towns in Alabama;* John R. Swanton, *The Early History of the Creek Indians and Their Neighbors* (Washington, DC: Government Printing Office, 1922); Dimmick, "A Survey of Upper Creek Sites"; Lolley, "Ethnohistory and Archaeology"; Ethridge, *Creek Country,* 26–31.

21. Larson, "Aboriginal Subsistence Strategy," 103–17; Kathryn H. Braund, *Deerskins and Duffels: Creek Indian Trade with Anglo-America, 1685–1815* (Lincoln: University of Nebraska Press, 1993), 31, 62, 132–35, 157; and Sheldon, "The Present State of Archaeological Survey," 120–22. See note 4 for list of archaeological surveys.

22. Robert S. Cotterill, *The Southern Indians: The Story of the Civilized Tribes before Removal* (Norman: University of Oklahoma Press, 1977), 152–52; Ethridge, *Creek Country,* 129, 135–37; Waselkov, *A Conquering Spirit,* 16–32; and Gregory A. Waselkov and Bonnie L. Gums, *Plantation Archaeology at Riviére aux Chiens, ca. 1725–1848* (Mobile: University of South Alabama, 2000).

23. Claudio Saunt, *A New Order of Things: Property, Power, and the Transformation of the Creek Indians: 1733–1816* (Cambridge: Cambridge University Press, 1999); Hawkins, *Sketch of the Creek Country,* 26, 29; and Waselkov, "Changing Strategies of Indian Field Location." See Waselkov, *A Conquering Spirit,* 33–55, for a discussion of the complex relationships of the métis families. Major Howell Tatum, "Topographic Notes and Observations on the Alabama River, August, 1814," in *Transactions of the Alabama Historical Society,* vol. 2: *1897–1898,* ed. Peter J. Hamilton and Thomas M. Owen (N.p., 1898), 130–77, mentions the Durant Plantation on the Alabama River in Dallas County. Very few of the outlying American or métis farms or plantations have been located or archaeologically investigated.

24. Waselkov and Wood, "The Creek War of 1813–1814," 8–15.

25. Ibid., 8–10; Philip Georg Friedrich Von Reck, *Von Reck's Voyage: Drawings and Journal of Philip Georg Friedrich von Reck,* ed. Kristian Hvidt (Savannah, GA: Beehive Press, 1980), 116–17. The Tohopeka and Nuyaka excavations are reported in Dickens, *Archaeological Investigations at Horseshoe Bend,* 47–76. Roy S. Dickens Jr. and James H. Chapman compared a sample of Creek ceramic sherds from Tohopeka village with one from the nearby, more traditional Nuyaka site

just upstream. The Nuyaka materials contained a fuller range of traditional ceramic decoration and vessel forms while the Tohopeka collection was mostly limited to utilitarian "Sofki" cooking jars. This tends to confirm the temporary and expedient nature of war camps. Roy S. Dickens Jr. and James H. Chapman, "Ceramic Patterning and Social Structure at Two Late Historic Creek Sites in Alabama," *American Antiquity* 43, no. 3 (1978): 390–98; Paul A. Ghioto, "Facts, Legends, and Accounts of the Battle of Horseshoe Bend," cited in Waselkov, "A Reinterpretation of the Creek Indian Barricade at Horseshoe Bend," *Journal of Alabama Archaeology* 32 (1986): 99.

26. Archeological collections from Hoithlewaulee (1EE328), Auburn University Archaeology Laboratory: archaeological collections, and Auburn Montgomery Archaeological Laboratory: David W. Chase's and Jack Mitchell's archaeological collections and William Spratling's field notes: Waselkov, *Culture Change on the Creek Frontier;* and Waselkov and Wood, "The Creek War of 1813–1814," 16–18.

27. For descriptions of the refugees and forts in southern Alabama, see Pickett, *History of Alabama,* 528–29; Halbert and Ball, *The Creek War,* 110, 148–49; and Waselkov, *A Conquering Spirit,* 101–6, 116–21. The northern refugee camps and fields are reported in Waselkov and Wood, "The Creek War of 1813–1814," 8–15; Tatum, "Topographic Notes and Observations," 137–46; and, Waselkov, *A Conquering Spirit,* 171–74.

28. The archaeological investigation of Fort Mims is reported in Gregory A. Waselkov, Bonnie L. Gums, and James W. Parker, *Archaeology at Fort Mims: Excavation Contexts and Artifact Catalog* (Mobile: University of South Alabama, 2006), 11–26. Archaeological excavations by James Parker at Fort Montgomery are as yet unreported. The archaeological excavations at Fort Jackson in Elmore County are reported in Donald P. Heldman, "Archaeological Investigations at Fort Toulouse: 1972–1973," report to the Alabama Historical Commission and National Park Service, Montgomery, 1973; Donald P. Heldman, "Archaeological Investigations at Fort Toulouse: 1973–1974," report to the Alabama Historical Commission and National Park Service, Montgomery, 1976; McDonald Brooms and James W. Parker, *Fort Toulouse Phase III Completion Report* (Montgomery: Alabama Historical Commission, 1980); and Gregory A. Waselkov, Brian M. Wood, and Joseph M. Herbert, *Colonization and Conquest: The 1980 Archaeological Excavations at Fort Toulouse and Fort Jackson, Alabama* (Montgomery: Auburn University at Montgomery, 1982), 229–314. For Fort Mitchell, see David W. Chase, *Fort Mitchell: An Archaeological Exploration in Russell Country, Alabama,* Special Publication No. 1. (Moundville: Alabama Archaeological Society, 1974); and John W. Cottier, "An Analysis of the Fort Mitchell Features, Volume 1," draft manuscript, Archaeology Laboratory, Auburn University, 2004.

29. Waselkov and Wood, "Creek War of 1813–1814," 9–10; O'Brien, *In Bitterness and Tears,* 110; Halbert and Ball, *Creek War,* 248–50; and Owsley, *Struggle for the Gulf Borderland,* 47. The modern excavations of the métis fort at Talladega are described in Knight, "Fort Leslie," 1, 4. A "sketch of the Battle of Talladega" in Reid and Eaton, *The Life of Andrew Jackson,* shows the "Fort of the Friendly Creeks" at Talladega as situated on a hill but in a circular form with two gates. The excavations reported by Knight clearly indicate the fort was probably rectangular or square.

30. Owsley, *Struggle for the Gulf Borderlands,* 79–82; Reid and Eaton, *The Life of Andrew Jackson,* 148–55; and Dickens, *Archaeological Investigations at Horseshoe Bend,* 18–23.

31. Dickens, *Archaeological Investigations at Horseshoe Bend,* 23–40.

32. George C. Mackenzie, "The Indian Breastwork in the Battle of Horseshoe Bend," cited in Dickens, *Archaeological Investigations at Horseshoe Bend,* 40–46.

33. Waselkov, "A Reinterpretation of the Creek Indian Barricade," 98–104.

34. Although a post-removal account, Hitchcock's description of the erection of the rotunda at Tuckabatchee in Oklahoma may approximate some of the labor practices used in building the barricade at Horseshoe Bend:

> [Tukabatchee Miko] cut sticks in miniature of every log required in the construction of the building, and distributed them proportionately among the residents [by kin group?] of the town, whose duty it was to cut logs corresponding with their sticks, and deliver them upon the ground appropriated for the building, at a given time. At the raising of the house, not a log was cut or changed from its original destination; all came together in their appropriate places, as intended by the designer. During the planning of this building, which occupied him six days, he did not partake of the least particle of food.

Hitchcock, quoted in John R. Swanton, *Social Organizations and Social Usages of the Indians of the Creek Confederacy* (1928; repr., New York: Johnson Reprint Co., 1970), 179.N8la

35. Braund, *Deerskins and Duffels;* Gregory A. Waselkov, "The Eighteenth-Century Anglo-Indian Trade in Southeastern North America," in *New Faces of the Fur Trade: Selected Papers of the Seventh American Fur Trade Conference,* ed. JoAnn Fiske, Susan Sleeper Smith, and William Wicker (East Lansing: Michigan State University Press, 1998), 193–222; Waselkov and Smith, "Upper Creek Archaeology," 248–49. Unfortunately, very few weapons or related materials of the Creek Indians of the Creek War period have been identified in museum or private collections. One notable exception is the leather frock coat, moccasins,

leggings, finger-woven sash, garters, and shot pouch left by the prophet Josiah Francis in London during his 1815 visit. British Museum, Museum of Mankind, Register Number 7497, London.

36. The artifacts and records of the Eccanachaca excavations are curated at the Center for Archaeological Studies, University of South Alabama. For accounts of the US attack on the site, see Halbert and Ball, *The Creek War,* 241–66; and O'Brien, *In Bitterness and Tears,* 102–16.

37. Similar items of US or European manufacture were found at Fort Mims, suggesting that these items may have been taken from there. Artifacts from Fort Mims and nearby locations are described in Waselkov, Gums, and Parker, *Archaeology at Fort Mims;* and Richard S. Lackey, comp., *Frontier Claims in the Lower South,* with introduction by John S. W. Guice (New Orleans: Polyanthos, 1977), 22–23.

38. George Stiggins narrative in Theron A. Nuñez Jr., "Creek Nativism and the Creek War of 1813–1814," *Ethnohistory* 5, no. 2 (1958): 139.

39. See Marc De Villars, "Extrait d'une lettre de Diron datée de Juin, 1721," in "Documents Concernant L'Histoire des Indiens de la Region Orientale de la Louisiane," *Journal de la Societé des Americanistes de Paris,* n.s., 14 (1922): 136; Kathryn H. Braund, personal communication with author; Stiggins narrative in Nuñez, "Creek Nativism," 139; Waselkov, *A Conquering Spirit,* 88; Waselkov, Gums, and Parker, *Archaeology at Fort Mims,* 66–67.

40. No systematic study of nineteenth-century iron knives used in the North American trade has been made. Some examples of typical iron knives can be seen in Carol I. Mason, *The Archaeology of Ocmulgee Old Field, Macon, Georgia* (Tuscaloosa: University of Alabama Press, 2005), 95–96, plate 16; Robert C. Mainfort Jr., *Indian Social Dynamics in the Period of European Contact: Fletcher Site Cemetery, Bay County,* Publications of the Museum, Michigan State University Anthropological Series, vol. 1, no. 4 (East Lansing: Michigan State University, 1979), 372; Ronald J. Mason, *Rock Island: Historic Indian Archaeology in the Northern Lake Michigan Basin* (Kent, OH: Kent State University Press, 1986), 199–202; Lyle M. Stone, *Fort Michilimackinac: An Archaeological Perspective on the Revolutionary Frontier* (East Lansing: Publications of the Michigan State University Museum, Michigan State University, 1974), 267–73; George C. Neumann and Frank J. Kravic, *Collector's Illustrated Encyclopedia of the American Revolution* (Texarkana, TX: Rebel Press, 1989), 171–72; and Lar Hothem, *Indian Trade Relics* (Paducah, KY: Collector Books, 2005), 50–62.

41. Swords on Creek sites are reported in DeJarnette and Hansen, *The Archaeology of the Childersburg Site,* 46, 49; Morrell, *The Wood Island Site,* 43, plate 17; and John W. Cottier, personal communication with author. For possible pikes, see John W. Cottier, "Selected Preliminary Artifact Descriptions," in *Cataloguing and Documenting the Historic Creek Archaeological Collections of the Alabama*

Department of Archives and History, Report to the National Science Foundation, ed. Gregory A. Waselkov and Craig T. Sheldon Jr. (Auburn, AL: Department of Sociology and Anthropology, 1987), 101–2. A blade-type pike head from a historic Creek site is in the collections of the Alabama Department of Archives and History (Accession No. 85.7.33 and 85.8.773), and a spike-type pike head from a cut and forged section of iron gun barrel was found at Fusihatchee. Unfortunately, none can be dated to the war period, but it is reasonable to suggest that the Red Sticks were forced to resort to such weapons.

42. Tomahawks of the pipe, pontoon, spiked, and other types produced expressly for the North American trade are more common in historic Indian sites in the Northeast and Midwest, but scarce in southern sites. They were generally lightweight and intended for presentation and ceremonial purposes. See Harold L. Peterson, *American Indian Tomahawks* (New York: Heye Foundation, 1971); Hothem, *Indian Trade Relics,* 80–134. Most of the axes found in southern frontier and historic Creek sites are simpler and range from 13.0 to 15.0 centimeters (5.1 to 6.0 inches) in length and from 0.30 to 0.47 kilograms (0.3 to 1.1 pounds) in weight. There are numerous archaeological examples, mostly eighteenth century, in the archaeological collections at the Alabama Department of Archives and History, Auburn University, and the University of Alabama. No systematic modern typological study has been made of iron axes found in southern Indian and frontier sites. There is some speculation that specimens with straight upper sides, curving lower sides, and oval eyes are of eighteenth-century French manufacture. See Jeffrey P. Brain, *Tunica Treasure* (Cambridge, MA: Peabody Museum, Harvard and the Peabody Museum of Salem, 1979), 140–43. The more common forms with straight upper and lower edges, oval to oblong eyes, and, occasionally, square polls are more likely British or American. Some are common full or half hatchets, as illustrated in Henry C. Mercer, *Ancient Carpenters' Tools* (Mineola, NY: Dover Publications, 2000), figure 4, no. 7498; Jay Gaynor, "Mr. Hewlett's Tool Chest—Part II," in *Selections from the Chronicle,* ed. Emil Pollak and Martyl Pollak (Mendham, NJ: Astragal Press, 1991), figure 8; Peterson, *American Indian Tomahawks,* nos. 35, 38. See Gregory A. Waselkov, "Wear and Reuse of European Artifacts," in *Culture Change on the Creek Indian Frontier, Report to the National Science Foundation,* ed. Waselkov (Auburn, AL: Auburn University, 1985), 95–96; Mason, *The Archaeology of Ocmulgee Old Field,* 94; Neumann and Kravic, *Collector's Illustrated Encyclopedia,* 24–27. In reality, there appears to be considerable overlap among the different types. The only known hatchets with definite Creek War provenance were found north of the barricade at Horseshoe Bend by John E. Cornelison, "A Metal Detecting Survey of the Palisade Area at Horseshoe Bend National Military Park," National Park Service, Southeast Archaeological Center, Accession Number 1838, Tallahassee, Florida, 2006, 24, 27, and at the recently discovered site of Eccanachaca.

43. Although a case can be made for the increasing use of bows by the Red Sticks as guns wore out and ammunition became scarce, the wounding of ensign William Chambliss and William Stubblefield by metal-tipped arrows at Fort Mims on August 30, 1813, argues that bows were used at the onset of the war. See Waselkov, *A Conquering Spirit,* 118, 133–35. The subsequent use of bows at Tallushatchee, Talladega, Calebee, and Horseshoe Bend is described in John S. Bassett, *The Life of Andrew Jackson* (1911; repr., Hamden, CT: Archon Books, 1967), 97; O'Brien, *In Bitterness and Tears,* 78, 144; and Thomas S. Woodward, *Woodward's Reminiscences of the Creek or Muscogee Indians* (Mobile, AL: Southern University Press for Graphics, 1965), 89. Ensign Sam Houston was wounded in the thigh with a barbed arrow at the Horseshoe Bend barricade. See Robert V. Remini, *Andrew Jackson and His Indian Wars* (New York: Viking Penguin, 2001), 215; O'Brien, *In Bitterness and Tears,* 147. Stemmed, barbed arrow points of sheet brass or iron were recovered from Fort Mims (two examples), Tohopeka (four), Fusihatchee (one), and Fort Jackson (one). See Waselkov, Gums, and Parker, *Archaeology at Fort Mims,* 32–33; Dickens, *Archaeological Investigations at Horseshoe Bend,* 156, figure 106a–c.; Cornelison, "A Metal Detecting Survey," 23, figure 7f; Waselkov, Wood, and Herbert, *Colonization and Conquest,* 37, 39. Flat sheet-metal arrowheads were rare on Upper Creek sites until the time of the Creek War. Points with similar barbed and stemmed shapes are more common on eighteenth-century historic Indian sites in the midwestern and northeastern United States. A possible line of future research would be to explore the chance that the barbed, stemmed arrow points diffused southward along with the prophets. See George I. Quimby, *Indian Culture and European Trade Goods* (Madison: University of Wisconsin Press, 1966), 72; Mary Elizabeth Good, "Guebert Site: An 18th Century Historic Kaskasia Indian Village," in her *The Central States Archaeological Societies, Memoir II* (St. Louis, MO, 1972), 67, figure 14; Stone, *Fort Michilimackinac,* 276–77; Mainfort, "Indian Social Dynamics," 359, 362; Mason, *Rock Island,* 202–3; and Douglas A. Birk and Jeffrey J. Richner, "Things Left Behind: A Study of Select Fur Trade Sites and Artifacts, Voyageur National Park, Environs, 2001–2002," US National Park Service, Midwestern Archaeological Center, Technical Report No. 84, Lincoln, NE, 2004, 62, 94.

44. Robert M. Reilly, *United States Martial Flintlocks* (Lincoln, RI: Andrew Mobray, 1997), 51–93, Claude E. Fuller, *Springfield Muzzle-Loading Shoulder Arms, 1795–1865* (Glendale, NY: S & S Firearms, 1986), 37–38; Waselkov, Gums, and Parker, *Archaeology at Fort Mims,* 56–61; Carl P. Russell, *Guns on the Early Frontiers* (Lincoln: University of Nebraska Press, 1980), 155; and M. L. Brown, *Firearms in Colonial America: The Impact on History and Technology, 1492–1792* (Washington, DC: Smithsonian Institution Press, 1980), 382–87. For information on military ammunition found in archaeological sites, see Waselkov, Wood, and Herbert, *Colonization and Conquest,* 299–302; Heldman, *Archaeological In-*

vestigations: 1973–1974, 129–30; Cottier, "An Analysis of the Fort Mitchell Features," 77–73; and Cornelison, "A Metal Detecting Survey," 21–22.

45. It is doubtful if many intact or reparable guns were ever left on battlefields or other sites of conflict by the weapon-starved Red Sticks or their opponents. The ratio of rifles to muskets during the Creek War is unknown. In 1791, Caleb Swan wrote: "The Creek Indians are very badly armed. The *chief* has made it a point to furnish them with muskets in preference to rifles . . . [for ease in cleaning]. Their muskets are of the slender, French manufacture . . . but are so slightly made, that they soon become unfit for any service. If the Indians are able to purchase for themselves, they would, however, prefer rifles in all cases, because they find them more sure and lasting." Swan, "Position and State of Manners," 5:263. See T. M. Hamilton, *Colonial Frontier Guns* (Chadron, NE: Fur Press, 1980); Russell, *Guns on the Early Frontiers,* 130–33; Lee Burke, "18th Century English Trade Guns in the South, or the Carolina Gun, Its Time and Place in History," *Bulletin of American Society of Arms Collectors* 65 (September 1991): 2–16; and Cornelison, "A Metal Detecting Survey," 21–22.

46. The typical nineteenth-century musket or rifle contained thirty-eight to fifty-one metal parts that could survive archaeologically. On late eighteenth-century Creek sites, remains of intact or ceremonially "broken" guns are found in graves, and numerous individual gun parts are scattered throughout trash deposits and middens. Without proper forges, tools, and skill, there were limits to the Creeks ability to make major repairs, and many guns became permanently unusable. Cottier, "Selected Preliminary Artifact Descriptions," 103–15; Dickens, *Archaeological Investigations at Horseshoe Bend,* 149–53; Mason, *The Archaeology of Ocmulgee Old Field,* 83–89; and Waselkov, "Wear and Reuse of European Artifacts," 91–95.

Similarly, ammunition was always a major problem for the Red Sticks. While there is ample archaeological evidence that the eighteenth-century Upper Creeks produced lead balls by melting and recasting previously fired balls and other waste lead in small iron or soapstone molds, such production would have become more difficult under wartime conditions. Gunpowder and flints were not produced by the Creeks and had to be acquired elsewhere. The poignancy of the shortage is evident in Thomas Woodward overhearing Red Sticks at the Battle of Calebee saying to one another, "Give me some bullets—give me powder." Woodward, *Woodward's Reminiscences,* 89.

47. A .69 caliber is the nominal ball diameter. Most military balls were .03 to .04 calibers, smaller to allow for "windage" or ease in loading. Surprisingly, .69-caliber lead balls were not common in purely military archaeological contexts at Fort Jackson and Fort Mitchell. Most balls fell into the general range of .49 to .66 calibers, while at Fort Mims they varied from .53 to .54 calibers. At all three locations, buckshot in the range of .30 to .33 calibers exceeded musket and

rifle in number, suggesting that buckshot and buck-and-ball were more common loads than single balls. The high frequency of buckshot on Creek sites may reflect shortages of regular lead balls. Waselkov, Wood, and Herbert, *Colonization and Conquest,* 299–302; Heldman, "Archaeological Investigations: 1972–1973," 172–73; Heldman, "Archaeological Investigations: 1973–1974, 130; Cottier, "An Analysis of the Fort Mitchell Features," 71–73; Waselkov, Gums, and Parker, *Archaeology at Fort Mims,* 56–58.

48. Cornelison, "A Metal Detecting Survey," 20–22, 30–34.

49. Heldman, "Archaeological Investigations: 1972–1973," 172; Heldman, "Archaeological Investigations: 1973–1974," 129; Linda F. Carnes, "European Artifacts," in *Archaeological Investigations at Horseshoe Bend,* ed. Dickens, 149–56; Waselkov and Wood, "The Creek War of 1813–1814," 18–19, 21; Cottier, "An Analysis of the Fort Mitchell Features"; and Cornelison, "A Metal Detecting Survey."

50. Gregory Waselkov discusses the potential information in forensic examination of human remains from battle sites. Waselkov, *A Conquering Spirit,* 331. See also David Crockett, *A Narrative of the Life of David Crockett* (Philadelphia: J. E. Potter, 1834), 100–101.

51. The Fusihatchee burial is recorded in archaeological field records for Fusihatchee (1EE191), Auburn Archaeological Laboratory, Auburn, AL.

52. Archaeological field records for Hickory Ground (1EE89), Auburn University Archaeological Laboratory; Charles Kappler, comp. and ed., *Indian Affairs, Laws, and Treaties* (Washington, DC: Government Printing Office, 1904), 2:107–9; and Land Patent Number 28, Cahaba Land Office, Alabama.

12

Digging Twice

Camps and Historical Sites Associated with the War of 1812 and the Creek War of 1813–1814

James W. Parker

Archaeological sites related to the US war effort in the Creek War during the era of the War of 1812 are scattered across Alabama as well as neighboring states. Beginning in 1996, the US National Park Service, consultants, and state agencies conducted surveys and worked to identify the most important sites of the conflicts (there are two) as part of the American Battlefields Protection Program. Among other things, the survey pointed out the need for additional research to locate the many War of 1812 sites, including the identification of sites associated with Native Americans, such as those associated with the Creek War.[1]

There are a limited number of major sites—preserved and operated either by the state or a federal agency—generally associated with the Creek War and the War of 1812 in Alabama. These include Fort Mims, Fort Mitchell, Fort Stoddert/Mount Vernon Arsenal, Horseshoe Bend National Military Park, and Fort Jackson (now Fort Toulouse/Jackson Park). Other sites have been difficult to locate or, if known, have received little study and are not generally interpreted for the public. This chapter will discuss these lesser-known but important archaeological sites associated with American activities in Alabama during the Creek War: camps.

Essentially, these difficult-to-locate sites must be "dug twice": first, by using historical documentation to help identify and locate the sites; and then, if found, the actual sites could be excavated archaeologically. Maps, letters, and other documentary records provide invaluable information that assists not only in the search for a site, but also in its interpretation. Indeed, the documentary record allows us to flesh out history. But only actual excavation can reveal what actually existed. Thus, digging in written and earth-bound information—digging twice—is essential.[2] The fieldwork on a site must be led by a trained archaeologist familiar with historic sites. Only after such a team is in place should a site be dug, and then only under a defined research goal or mitigation need. Unauthorized excavations by souvenir hunters destroy the integrity of a site. After proper excavations are undertaken, it is the responsibility of the professionals to make sure the important goals of documentation and curation are accomplished. Unless the locale is under immediate threat, large-scale activities should not be undertaken without funding for documentation and curation.

The appendices provide a listing of all identified sites in Alabama associated with the Creek War and War of 1812 and their current conditions. The listing enumerates more than three hundred sites located across state. The archaeological remains from the conflict are extremely varied. Native towns, forts, stockades, blockhouses, supply depots, military camps, destroyed homes, battle sites, and cemeteries are just a few of the types of sites that are associated with the conflict. These sites range from simple to extremely complex. For example, the battlefield at Horseshoe Bend had limited prior use before the establishment of the defensive works and settlement by Red Sticks. Following the war, the site returned to a natural state and later was farmed by American owners and subject to few damaging activities and eventually memorialized and protected as a national military park.[3] Fort Decatur and Fort Burrows were established where earlier occupation was limited and subsequent development was nearly nonexistent. These sites have survived relatively unscathed in the hands of responsible owners. On the other hand, Fort Jackson, also built during the war, provides another level of complexity.

Fort Jackson was built at a site that had been occupied for thousands of years. The fort lay atop remains left by the peoples of the Woodland and Mississippian cultures and their predecessors. In addition at least three French forts were erected at the site and the Alabama-Creek town of Tuskegee (Taskigi) was atop the French remains. After the end of the active warfare the fort was in use for two more years.[4] After abandonment by the military, a town was laid out and lots were sold, but the Fort Jackson Town development was a failure, and the area reverted to fields and woodlands rather than buildings and pavement. The site is now Fort Toulouse/Fort Jackson State Historic Site. Uncovering the complicated history of the site has been challenging.[5] Mobile, the most complex town in the study area, grew into the present-day modern port. With the growth came destruction of archaeological remains. In the case of Fort Charlotte the destruction was intentional, while other sites succumbed or are now covered by modern development.[6] The site of Fort Mims, now owned by the Alabama Historical Commission, was subjected to very haphazard excavations over a fifty-year period and has only recently been systematically reevaluated.[7] The site of one of the most famous battlefields of the Creek War, Holy Ground, was not definitively located until the summer of 2010. Excavations are now ongoing, and the site has been purchased for preservation.[8] The site of Fort

Bowyer was heavily occupied, but few artifacts from the period have been found as the forces of nature and the progression of the complex that became Fort Morgan, the largest settlement in Baldwin County at the turn of the twentieth century, mask the remains. Thousands of objects dating to the 1814–1817 period were excavated at the locale of Fort Montgomery in northern Baldwin County. Much of the material came from the postwar occupation. Other sites that existed only for the 1813–1814 campaigns produce limited material culture. Much of this relates to the nature of the equipment that the army carried.

Fort Jackson, established at the end of Andrew Jackson's military campaign against the Creeks, was the largest and most complex military fortification built by the Americans during the Creek War. The fort served as Jackson's headquarters and, in addition to serving as a base for mopping-up operations after the war, the facility housed Red Stick prisoners. The fort had extensive kitchens (with ovens) as well as impressive bastions. Built and operated during the last phase of the Creek War, it represented a level of sophistication unmatched by the numerous temporary stockades, depots, and fortifications hastily built during the course of the war.[9]

This chapter will concentrate on one broad category of sites: camps and fortifications build by the Americans and their allies during the war. The location of major forts and supply depots is generally known. But by digging twice, we can identify dozens of lesser-known and forgotten sites that, if properly located, excavated, studied, and analyzed, would provide tremendous insight into the life of soldiers during the war. Documentary material provides substantial information about what we might expect to recover archaeologically from US campsites.

A camp can be the simplest of sites or more complex than a major battlefield. Some of the camps were immediately next to or near major forts or depots, usually located along major rivers due to the convenience of transportation. Others were at stops along the roads that were cut or improved by invading armies or, in the later phases of the conflict, troops moving southward to fight along the coast. Many of the routes later became roads used by incoming settlers and through the years have become the county, state, and federal highways of today. By transposing period and later survey maps over present-day maps, it is possible to identify some of these campsites that may have been preserved.[10]

Camps could be of small size and short duration of use. Others were used several times and by several different units. Some were occupied for weeks or months, others for a single day. Natural resources, sanitation, supply, and weather are factors that effect the placement and use of camps. The breaking of a single wagon wheel could also bring about the creation of a camp.[11] For example, Fort Deposit, which was located in what is now the present

Lowndes County, was used a very limited time (less than a week) and then abandoned. It was built in less than two days and was fifty feet square with bastions. Given the temporary nature of the structure, it will no doubt be difficult to locate. On the other hand, some campsites, such as those around Fort Claiborne, had specialized use areas, vaults, and sinks (latrines) and will produce valuable archaeological data when found. Camps at other locations had blockhouses and supply houses.[12]

When the forces of the Mississippi Territory, Tennessee, Georgia, North and South Carolina, and the regular US Army moved during periods of eminent danger, a set of columns and flanks were established so the force could quickly establish a defensive position if attacked. Some of these formations would be three hundred to five hundred yards in width with a length that matched or exceeded. The troops would camp in a square form that mirrored how they marched.[13]

The regular troops were trained in the art of marching and setting camps. The militia, while not as extensively trained, did contain knowledgeable individuals, and veterans of the American Revolution were available for advice. Some, like Joseph Graham of North Carolina, had served in the revolution. Ferdinand Claiborne of Mississippi was an eight-year veteran of the army and fought under General Anthony Wayne at the Battle of Fallen Timbers. There were also published field manuals distributed by the army and for sale in towns. Additionally, experienced engineers and surveyors were also attached to the militia troops.[14]

Camps would have had some desired constants sought by commanders. A good water source, available firewood, and a large and defensible ground were always needed. Commonly, a stopping point would be before or after a watercourse crossing. These requirements were the same whether the army was on the march, at a settlement, at a fort, or in the wilderness. In at least one case, soldiers were sent out to dig wells at a distance of a day's march to provide potable drink for the advancing soldiers.[15]

Because the deposition of waste and trash is important in archaeological searches, the sanitation aspects of the camp are important in locating a site. The topography of the site will dictate usages. Hillsides, away from water sources, were used, and police tubs were placed in camp and were used during the night and then emptied during the day in a watercourse or down slope; and if a vault or sink was dug, it was to be only used primarily in the evenings. Common soldiers were not particular where the waste was placed, as is witnessed by orders forbidding urinating on the pickets, projecting urine from the parapets, or leaving "filth" at guard posts. Use of facilities varied during the day with the formal deposit points reserved for evening as officers did not want men passing outside the lines of camp security to relieve themselves after dark.[16]

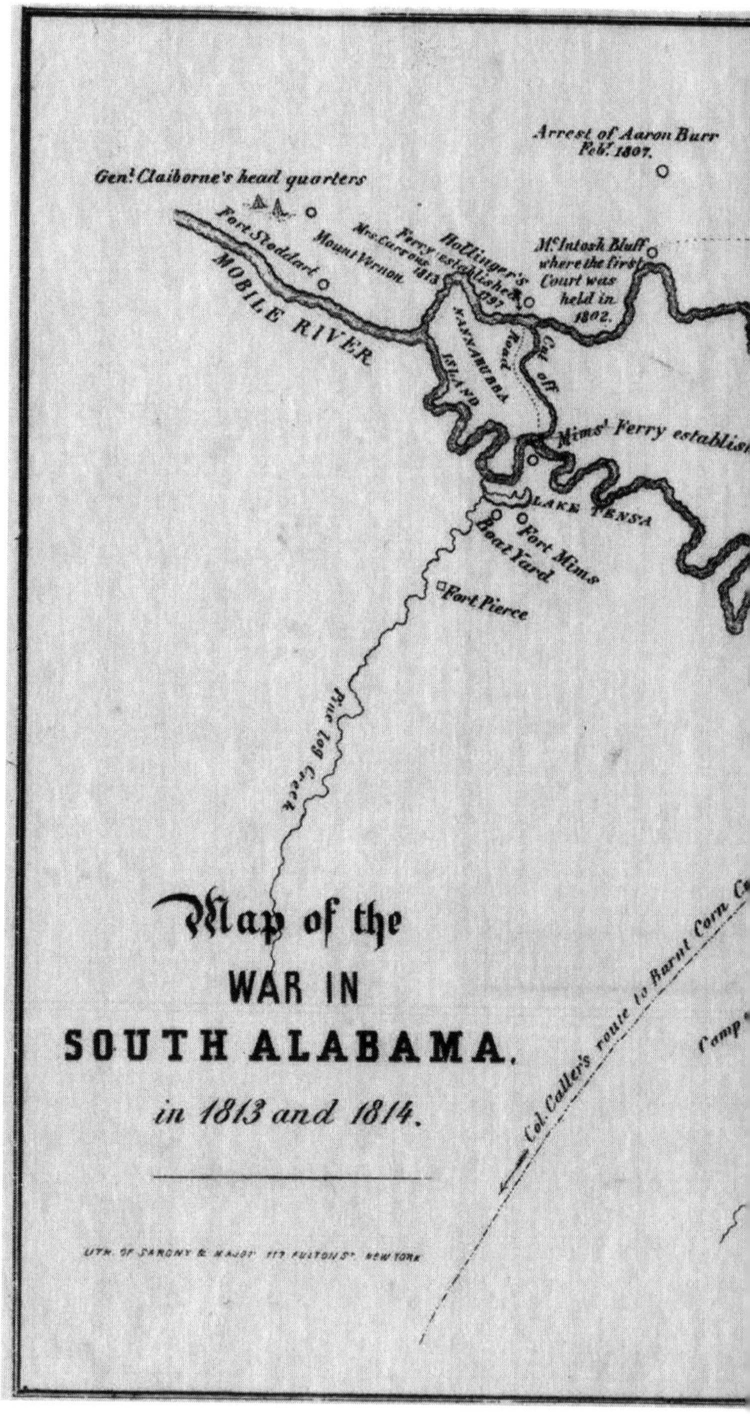

12.1. Map of the war in South Alabama in 1813 and 1814, depicting battle sites, forts, and camps. Courtesy of the

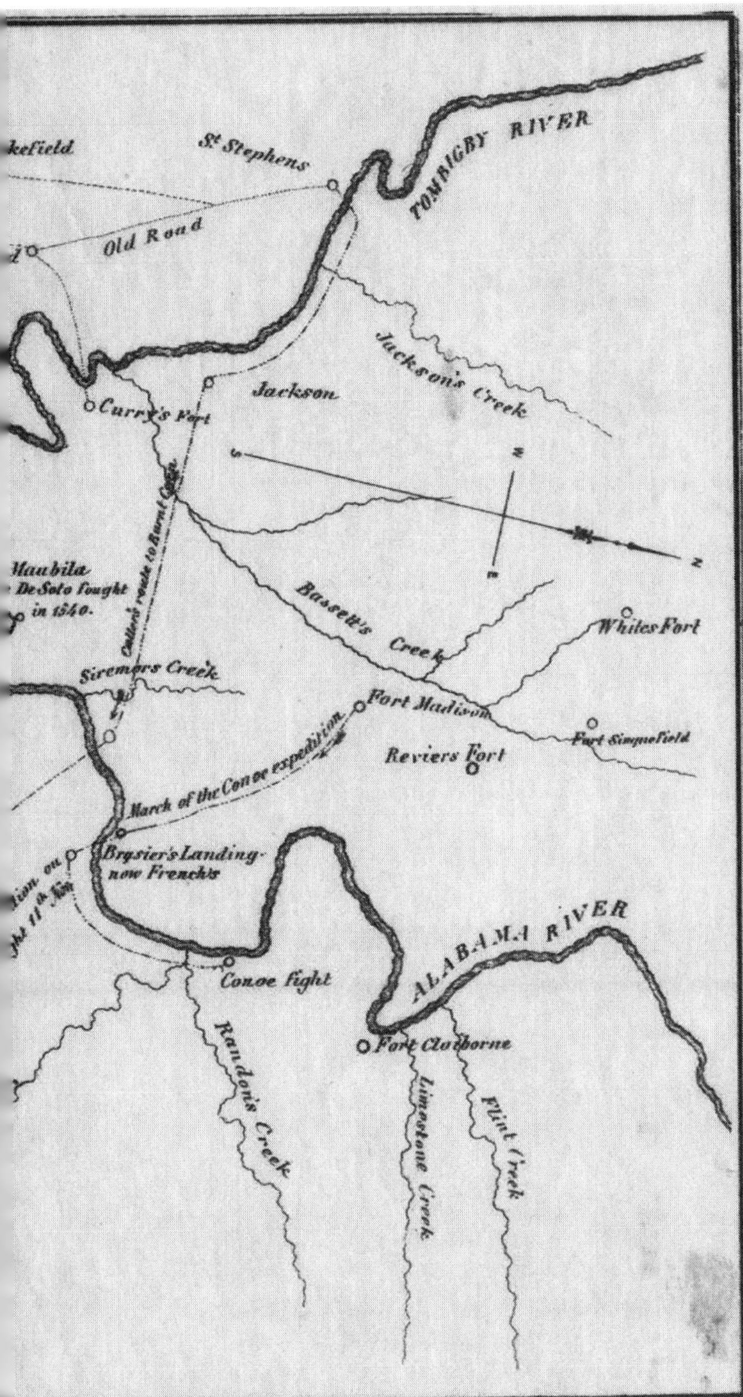

Alabama Department of Archives and History, Montgomery, Alabama.

Wagons and artillery became more common in these formations after roadways were improved. But the wheeled conveyances were there to carry necessary items such as food, tools, ammunition, and sometimes tents.[17] The marching troops were required to carry an additional set of tools when on the move. Shovels, picks, mattocks, and various axes were needed as roads were cut or widened and temporary fortifications erected. These tools are frequently enumerated in inventories. However, the loss of a tool or tools at a campsite would be infrequent as it would have been noted and someone would be held responsible.[18]

US forces included the regular army and militia, as well as Choctaw, Creek, and Cherokee allies. All components of the various US troops found travel difficult. While supplies were moved by wagon later in the war as roads were cut, for the most part, troops were on foot, with some mounted units. The regular army was better equipped than the various militia and volunteer units, but it was usually on the march and this limited what troops could carry. And even under the best of conditions, resupply of units was difficult. Even when a unit was well equipped and on the march, strict controls were in place to keep up with the limited resources. When units of any nature were going on campaign and expecting action, items were left behind at depots and camps as baggage was reduced to what would fit in a knapsack and haversack.

The military trooper carried very little with him. In some cases, equipment and supplies were transported by packhorses or wagons, but most of the things we find archaeologically would have been carried by the soldiers. Regular soldiers would have carried arms, accouterments, ammunition, a knapsack for clothes and blanket, a tin pan/plate, and a few personal items, a cap, maybe a canteen. From an archaeological perspective, cloth and leather do not regularly survive. The flints, gun parts, buckles, and bullets are durable but also dear to soldiers and seldom lost. One group of artifacts was numerous and durable: buttons. A fully equipped regular's kit would have between thirty-five and sixty-four buttons for his outerwear. Another few fasteners would have been on extra clothes.[19]

The regular soldier in the area was not consistently well equipped. The Third US Infantry had been in the field for a lengthy period before it arrived to fight along the Alabama River in late summer 1813. Earlier in the year as the Third prepared to take Mobile, a prize of whiskey was awarded to companies with the most men fully equipped. Later, as General James Wilkinson lined up his troops to impress the Spanish at Fort Carlota (Charlotte), he went through the ranks to find the best equipped and placed them in the forefront.[20]

Following the initial activities around Mobile Bay, the Third began a trek that led to New Orleans and up the Mississippi to Natchez before turning again and crossing present-day Mississippi to Saint Stephens. During the journey, the men and equipment were worn out. They made repairs along the way and even fabricated leggings from deer hides. From there they moved up the Alabama River before receiving supplies as they moved to attack the Holy Ground.[21]

The regulars had gone through hard service and were lacking in uniforms as supplies were limited for the western units through the early years of the war. There were also differences in the uniforms used by the troops, especially within regiments, as newly equipped recruits joined old veterans. For instance, the Third Regiment US Infantry was an old unit with a history of consolidation, movements, and uneven supply and in the later days of the war was infused with fresh men. The Thirty-Ninth US Infantry was at Horseshoe Bend and was later joined by the veteran Twenty-Forth US Infantry, which came from Tennessee with equipment and items purchased in the towns of Nashville and Knoxville.

The receipt of new uniforms or equipment could cause the formation of archaeological anomaly. Old uniforms were cut up and used to make accessories, rags, and fatigue items such as caps to be used when working. A trash midden was partially excavated at Fort Montgomery, where supplies were issued to regular troops and regiments were consolidated in 1815. Hundreds of US Army–issue outerwear buttons were found, even after relic hunters had removed many, in the deposit, and more were left in the unexcavated portions of the feature. It is possible the deposits at Fort Montgomery were the result of reuse of coats and pants. A similar deposit could be found wherever new supplies reached the troops.[22]

Thus, even in regular units, one would expect to see wide variations in equipment and clothing for an individual troop. And this is reflected in inventories. The first inventory below is that of Lieutenant Benjamin Harvey of the Third US Infantry, a well-to-do upper-class officer who was in an established camp and had five years to acquire his kit. He died when the regiment was on the move but had means to transport all of his belongings. At the opposite end of the scale, Ensign Ephraim Thompson of the Twenty-Forth US Infantry died at Fort Montgomery and had just been elevated from the ranks.

Inventory of Goods of Lieutenant Benjamin Harvey of the Third Infantry, September 12, 1813.

1 Full Uniform Coat
1 Undress Uniform Coat
1 Large Coat

1 Sword
1 Chappo (Chapeau) [military style hat]
2 Pr. Boots
10 pr. Pantaloons
1 Roundabout Jacket or Coat [tailless short coat]
3 Shirts
1 Traveling Knife
1 Hammock
2 Blankets
1 Mosquitoe Bar [mosquito net]
2 Mugs
1 Decanter
2 Tumblers
1 Dressing Case
3 Pots
6 Plates
$200 in bank notes[23]

Inventory of Goods of Ensign Ephraim Thompson, 24th Infantry, August 25, 1815.
1 Uniform Coat
1 Homespun Coat
1 Roundabout
1 pr Pantaloons
1 Shirt
1 pr Shoes
2 Blankets & Pack[24]

At the onset of the war, militia equipage varied by status of the unit. In some cases highly uniformed and organized units were present in towns. Volunteers were militia who volunteered to serve and were usually better prepared to go afield. Drafted militia were not as well equipped and in many cases did not have arms.[25]

Inventories of belongings of two militiamen from the Second Regiment West Tennessee Militia provide information of what was carried in that unit, which served in Jackson's campaigns on the Coosa River and the lower Alabama and Mobile Rivers. The common practice was for the most valuable items owned by a deceased soldier to be returned to his family, and other things useful to his compatriots were sold and the cash sent home.

Following the death of Corporal James Jackson, it was decided to give his rifle and accoutrements to a neighbor to take home, but most of his property was sold (see list on page 242).

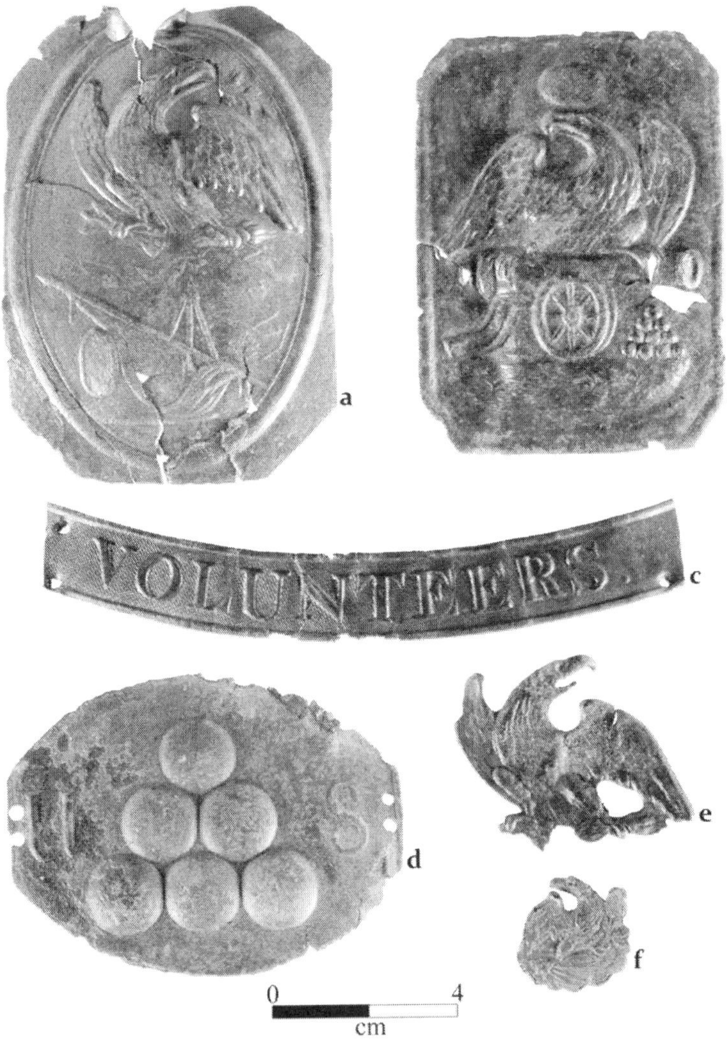

12.2. Military cap insignia from the Creek War and aftermath: (*a*) Infantry cap plate, 1817 design, brass, Cantonment Montpelier; (*b*) Corps of Artillery cap plate, 1815 design, brass, Cantonment Montpelier; (*c*) Volunteers cap plate, brass, Cantonment Montpelier; (*d*) Second Regiment Artillery cap plate, reworked 1812 design, brass, Fort Claiborne; (*e*) Cockade eagle, brass, Cantonment Montpelier; (*f*) Cockade eagle, pewter, Fort Montgomery. Artifact photographs courtesy of Brett McWilliams.

Tomahawk and Butcher knife
Pint Bottle
Pair of Socks
Pair of Mittens
2 pair pantaloons
Knapsack
Westcoat [waistcoat/vest]
Shirt
Hatt [*sic*]
Twist of tobacco

Private Hardy Davis of Captain James Kinkaid's Company left behind these items.

1 Pair of leggings
2 pair shoes
Pair of Mittens
Tomahawk
Knife
Belt
Westcoat
Pantaloons
Shirt
Knapsack
Hatt [*sic*]
Great Coat
Knife
Comb[26]

As can be seen from both the militia and regular army inventory samples, much of what the soldiers carried were soft goods that would not have a probability of surviving archaeologically. Buttons and bullets are the most common items to survive and be found archaeologically at campsites. Other items that one might expect to recover archaeologically include discarded personal items, metal from weapons, tools, equipment, or materials associated with food preparation or consumption.

Common foods distributed to the troops (corn, flour, smoked or pickled meats, and native plants and animals) contribute little that would survive archaeologically. But storage and cooking implements are likely to be found. Food containers were wood, with wooden bands and occasional iron straps. Cooking was done in messes of six men, and usually there was a single sheet-iron kettle on the march. Soldiers carried tin plates if lucky. Forks and knives were a personal responsibility, and it was a common requirement for militiamen to posses a butcher knife. Treen (woodenware) was used in some cases. Heavier items were left behind in preparation for the field. For example, a note from an East Tennessee militiaman points out that the cooking equipment was left behind at a camp near Fort Strother as the move to Horseshoe Bend began.[27]

The surgeon general did not think much of the way the soldiers ate, and he noted that "when a recruit receives his ration, if the meat is fresh he broils it to a cinder on the end of his ramrod; if salt pork he eats it raw; and if salt beef he boils it and with his bread, will make a pretty good meal."[28] A pretty good meal, clean water, firewood, a dry place to sleep, and the companionship of his messmates was all most troops could expect while in camp. On the march in enemy country it was expected that troops would sleep on their firearms, and they did not generally build fires. Food came in spurts, and at times, rawhide was chewed to stave off starvation. Other times flour was plenty, but spoiled flour was also deadly.

The search for the remains left by the marching armies presents many challenges since, frequently, there is little to be found. However, the recording and study of even the smallest of the sites would further our knowledge about daily life of US troops and allies during the war.

Appendix 1 (page 249) is a listing of major Creek War/War of 1812 sites in Alabama that have been identified and studied, along with their current status. Most of these major sites offer visitation and, in many cases, interpretation of the site.

Appendix 2 (page 255) is a compilation from various sources of potential sites and their current status. Some of the sites are recorded in written documents and have yet to be studied. Many of the sites have been flooded by lake development. The Fort Deposit complex on the Tennessee River is probably completely under water. Fort Williams has been flooded. The site of Horseshoe Bend would have been lost if not for awareness at the highest level of Alabama Power Corporation. A few other sites have been victims of construction or urban growth. Some are preserved for the future. Yet many have not been located and will be hard to verify because of the limited remains left behind. The list is divided regionally and includes location by county (where known); type of site, such as fort, camp, or battle site; date of occupation; current status; National Park Service designation; and recommendations, as appropriate.

Notes

1. American Battlefield Protection Program, *Report to Congress on the Historic Preservation of Revolutionary War and War of 1812 Sites in the United States* (Washington, DC: National Park Service, 2007). The report may be accessed

through the National Park Service website at http://www.nps.gov/history/hps/abpp/.

2. Lawrence E. Babits, "Military Records and Historical Archaeology," in *Documentary Archaeology in the New World,* ed. Mary C. Beaudry (Cambridge: Cambridge University Press, 1988), 119–25.

3. Roy S. Dickens Jr., *Archaeological Investigations at Horseshoe Bend, National Military Park, Alabama,* Alabama Archaeological Society, Special Publication 3 (Tuscaloosa: Alabama Archaeological Society, 1979); Gregory A. Waselkov, "A Reinterpretation of the Creek Indian Barricade at Horseshoe Bend," *Journal of Alabama Archaeology* 32 (1989): 94–107.

4. Bascom McDonald Brooms and James W. Parker, *Fort Toulouse Phase III Completion Report* (Montgomery: Alabama Historical Commission, 1980); Gregory A. Waselkov, Brian Wood, and Joseph M. Herbert, *Colonization and Conquest: The 1980 Archaeological Excavations at Fort Toulouse and Fort Jackson, Alabama,* Auburn University Archaeological Monograph 4 (Montgomery: Auburn University at Montgomery, 1982); Gregory A. Waselkov, "Introduction: Recent Archaeological and Historical Research," in *Fort Toulouse: The French Outpost at the Alabamas on the Coosa,* by Daniel H. Thomas (Tuscaloosa: University of Alabama Press, 1989), vii–xlii.

5. James W. Parker, "Fort Jackson after the War of 1812," *Alabama Review* 38 (April 1985): 119–30.

6. Donald A. Harris and Jerry J. Nielsen, *Archaeological Salvage Investigations at the Site of the French Fort Conde, Mobile, Alabama. A Final Report in Fulfillment of Contract No. I-10-1(3) Tunnel Plaza Interchange Archaeological Agreement between the Alabama Highway Department and the University of Alabama* Tuscaloosa: University of Alabama, 1972).

7. See Gregory A. Waselkov, Bonnie L. Gums, and James W. Parker, *Archaeology at Fort Mims: Excavation and Contexts and Artifact Catalog* (Mobile: University of South Alabama Center of Archaeological Studies, 2006), for a history of the site and a complete report of artifact analysis through 2006.

8. Gregory A. Waselkov, "Return to Holy Ground: The Legendary Battle Site Discovered," *Alabama Heritage,* no. 101 (Summer 2011): 28–37.

9. Waselkov, "Introduction: Recent Archaeological and Historical Research," vii–xlii.

10. The study of numerous regular army and militia orderly books as well as personal diaries and letters provides an overview of march activities of the troops. Examples of some of the extant sources are from the Tennessee State Library and Archives: "Diary of Levi Lee," MS. AC. 1549, Pipkin Papers MS. AC. 69-25, McCutchen Collection MS. AC. 1264, Diary of John Reid MS. AC. 72-180; numerous examples from the William C. Cook Collection at the Historic New Orleans Collection include the Orderly Books of John Coffee. Addi-

tional data is found in the Orderly Books of the Second and Third Regiments of the US Infantry, located in Record Group (R.G.) 98, United States Commands, 1784–1821, National Archives and Record Administration (NARA), Washington, DC.

11. Isaac Baker, "Journal of Isaac Baker," *Southwestern Historical Quarterly* 30 (July 1926–April 1927): 272–82.

12. The Dinkins Orderly Book, 1812–1814, contains a description of the construction of Fort Deposit as well as orders describing activities at Fort Claiborne in December 1813 and January 1814. Mary Hardin McCown, ed., "'J. Hartsell Memora': Journal of a Tennessee Captain in the War of 1812," *East Tennessee Historical Society's Publication* 11 (1939): 93–115 and 12 (1940): 118–46, contains descriptions of camp life throughout Hartsell's service along the upper Coosa River region.

13. Orders outlining the manner in which troops were to deploy are frequent in the orderly books of the Second and Third Regiments. Good formation information is also found in the Orderly Books of John Coffee, Historic New Orleans Collection, New Orleans, LA.

14. "Ferdinand L. Claiborne," in *Encyclopedia of the War of 1812,* ed. David S. Heidler and Jeanne T. Heidler (Annapolis, MD: Naval Institute Press, 1989); Francis B. Heitman, *Historical Register and Dictionary of the United States Army, from Its Organization, September 29, 1789, to March 2, 1903,* vol. 1 (Washington, DC: Government Printing Office, 1903), 302; *Nashville Democratic Clarion,* March 22, 1811; *Nashville Clarion and Tennessee State Gazette,* August 10, 1813, and November 8, 1814; Capt William Lawrence Orderly Book, 2nd Infantry, 1812–1815, R.G. 98, NARA. The general order of April 4 directed the use of a manual devised by Friedrich von Steuben during the American Revolution so there would be a common drill and manual. Other popular manuals were by Alexander Smyth and William Duane.

15. Papers of Joseph Graham, Orderly Book, North Carolina Department of Archives and History, Raleigh.

16. Sanitation orders are scattered throughout the Orderly Book of an Unidentified Company of the 7th Infantry, 1812–1814, and the Order Book of Captain James Dinkins, 3rd Infantry, 1812–1815, R.G. 98, NARA.

17. Dinkins Orderly Book, 1812–1815, stated that "hard service was ahead" as they moved toward Fort Claiborne, November 3, 1813.

18. Inventories are wonderful tools for archaeologists. As would be expected, there is an abundance of supply listings associated with the military. A good example is "A return of the Equipage of the 1st Regt. Tennessee Volunteer Infantry Commanded by Col. William Hall . . . 25th March 1813," found in the Alexander Papers, Tennessee State Library and Archives, TSL-VI-6-68-355, Nashville.

19. Ed Gilbert, *Frontier Militiaman in the War of 1812: Southwestern Fron-*

tier (New York: Osprey Publishing Co., 2008), provides a layman's overview of militia arms and accouterments. It is of note that many of the illustrations are of reenactors who participate at events in Alabama. Rene Chartrand, *Uniforms and Equipment of the United States Forces in the War of 1812* (Youngstown, NY: Old Fort Niagara Association, 1992), is the best single source available on that subject.

20. Orderly Book of Captain William Lawrence, 2nd Infantry, April 8, 1813, R.G. 98, NARA.

21. Dinkins Orderly Book, 1812–1815, August 2, 1813.

22. James W. Parker, "Investigations Relative to the 19th Century Tensaw Military Frontier in Southwest Alabama," in *Archaeology in Southwestern Alabama: A Collection of Papers,* ed. Cailup B. Curren (Camden: Alabama Tombigbee Regional Commission, 1982).

23. Inventories can be found among the papers of the secretary of war. The inventory of Benjamin Harvey's belongings was taken after his death near Natchez as the Third Regiment was traversing the Mississippi River. Miller to SW, New Orleans, February 8, 1814, Registers of Letters Received by the Office of the Secretary of War, 1800–1870, Letters Received by the Secretary of War, Unregistered Series, 1789–1861, R.G. 107, NARA, M222, reel 12.

24. "An Inventory of the effects of Late Ens. Thompson of the 24th Regt. Infy, Fort Montgomery," August 25, 1815, R.G. 107, MF 221-A, Reel 59, NARA.

25. C. Edward Skeen provides an excellent look at the many problems faced by militia throughout the nation in *Citizen Soldiers in the War of 1812* (Lexington: University of Kentucky Press, 1999).

26. Notes found in the Record Book of Captain James Craig, held in the Alabama Department of Archives and History and available on its website. The relevant portions were published in *Alabama Historical Quarterly* 19 (Summer 1957): 220–28.

27. Memorandum Book of Joseph Huffmaster, MSS #04-0007, Rosenberg Library, Galveston, TX.

28. The surgeon general of the US Army reported the cooking practices of the War of 1812, as published in *American State Papers, Documents, Legislative and Executive of the Congress of the United States: Military Affairs,* 3 vols. (Washington: Government Printing Office, 1832–1834) See also James W. Parker, "A Study of Supply and Subsistence on the Southern Frontier, at Fort Jackson, 1814–1816," manuscript, Fort Toulouse/Fort Jackson State Historic Site, Wetumpka, AL, 1982.

Afterword

The Western Muscogee (Creek) Perspective

Ted Isham

As a Muscogee (Creek) citizen and member of the Wind clan from the Tulmuchusee tribal town and an adopted member of the Hillabee ceremonial ground, my goal is to present the western Creek perspective of this history that is so important to us. What I did was listen to the people of the Creek Nation. It is an interesting thing to come back to the Creek homeland to talk about these events. Every time I come to the South, to my homeland, there is a very special connection to the area. Before the symposium, I came and revisited some ancient spaces and visited the ancient Hillabee town site. It is always a very special moment and feels like home, and all the Creek names I see on the road signs make perfect sense to me. It is like we never left. And I encourage all tribal members to come back. Creek people are connected to these places where our towns once were, and it gives us our identity. Our history, language, and rituals connect us to our ancestors and the places they lived. The Creek people still have a root to this place, and that is who we are. What I want to bring to the table is their perspective. How do they view these events? What can we bring to the table?

I surveyed a variety of Creek people and collected their thoughts. It was difficult. Ceremonial ground people would not speak on the topic—it wasn't appropriate since the ceremonial ground wasn't a venue to discuss this topic. But even from that we get their perspective. This was a horrific event—a civil war—much like the Trail of Tears. We choose not to bring it out. We gloss over it. We don't want to pass it on to our children. So, collectively, we have these ways of thinking about this that have been handed down generation to generation. First is the idea that the Creek War was a horrific event and many warriors were lost. It is part of our ethos as a people that we see those Red Stick warriors taking a last stand. That piece of information is handed down: we take the last stand. We call ourselves *Este Maskoke Ispo-*

cogees: "the last people." We take "last stands" and pull together. The people pull together in these moments of extreme danger. And that is what they were doing at Horseshoe Bend—pulling together. The tribal towns at Tohopeka were Okfuskee, Hillabee, Nuyaka, Okchai, Fish Ponds, and Eufaula. They came together to make this last stand. What is interesting is that most of us believe that the whole Creek Nation was involved. But at Tohopeka, it was only these six towns. As Muscogees, we strive for peace, first and foremost; that is the ultimate goal, and that is part of our ritual today. But when there was a dire need, the war side came out. There is a mechanism to handle that danger. As the prophets came through and made their war talk and visited war towns, the people who took the war talk came together also. These six are still in existence, and this effect of pulling together is called *etenhvlvtetv.*

Unfortunately, during the war, the Creek towns and people were not all together. They were divided and fighting each other. And it resulted in disaster for the Creek people. But at the end of the war, the survivors came together again. And they rebuilt their towns, only to have them taken again when removal came about fifteen years later. But they stayed together and rebuilt their towns in the West. They survived.

In the Southeast, there were upwards of eighty tribal towns. Forty-four were reconstituted in the West, and now we have fifteen to seventeen today. Okfuskee, Hillabee, Nuyaka, and Fish Ponds still maintain their fires. Okchai and Eufaula have put their fires to sleep—and only in recent times. So that is a testament to who we are as a people. We are survivors. The confederacy pulled together in times of dire need and protected each other. And thus it happened in Tohopeka. Even though we may not know all the details of what the event was about—our elders chose not to pass it on to us—we need to come and ask the feelings and ideas of the Creek people, and we can all learn. We cannot forget the basis of it—the Creek people and the Creek tribal towns. We need to pay attention to the Creek people to glean information to portray a holistic view of what the war was about. People think that history isn't for the vanquished. But the Creek people survived. This is their history.

Appendix 1

Current Preservation Status of Major Creek War/War of 1812 Sites in Alabama

James W. Parker

Autossee (Atasi): This was placed on the National Register of Historic Places as a prehistoric archaeological site on April 18, 1977. The Alabama Historical Commission has listed this as one of the most endangered properties in the state due to severe looting and nearby graveling operations.

Burnt Corn Creek: The location of the battle has yet to be confirmed at the traditional location near a spring close to the creek.

Calebee Creek/Camp Defiance: The general locale of the battle site is known, but field confirmation has not been made. The site is privately owned.

Camp Coffee: A large encampment with fortifications was built in the early stages of the war. The site has not been confirmed, but there is a possibility that part of the site is owned by the Tennessee Valley Authority and the remainder is in private hands. A road and a line of encampments were established between Camp Coffee and Forts Deposit and Strother.

Dauphin Island: Parts of the British camp on Dauphin Island lie within the bounds of the December 12, 1976, National Register of Historic Places boundaries for Fort Gaines. The Dauphin Island Beach and Park Board and Sealab are public entities that probably own parts of the site. Surveys and investigations for French-era sites on the island have not produced artifacts from the War of 1812 occupation. Civil War relic hunting and the construction of Fort Gaines and its associated military complexes have damaged the 1815-era remains.

Emuckfau: A locational study is under way.

Enitachopco: The location of the site has not been confirmed. The identification of this location is part of the study involving Emuckfau.

Fort Armstrong: The Weiss Reservoir on the Coosa River flooded the probable location of the fort in the 1960s. It is possible that associated campsites may exist.

Fort Bainbridge: The fort's location on the Federal Road is known. Though the site is unmarked, relic collectors have damaged the remains.

Fort Bowyer: Any existing remains of the fort located at Mobile Point are within the bounds of Fort Morgan State Historic Site. The locale was designated a National Historic Landmark on October 15, 1966. The Fort Bowyer site was an active military base and subject to extensive land-changing activities for over 120 years. Hurricanes, natural changes, and channel dredging have caused changes in the point shoreline, though the north and south shores have remained more stable. Extensive metal detecting on private property east of the park boundaries has produced artifacts left by British troops.

Fort Claiborne: An important nineteenth-century river port grew around the site of Fort Claiborne. The town of Claiborne is now gone, and the exact location of the defensive works and associated camps is not pinpointed. An archaeological survey is scheduled at the site in the near future.

Fort Decatur and Fort Burrows: These two forts were erected in the later stages of the Indian conflict. The remains of the two earthworks are in remarkable condition, and little relic hunting has taken place. Fort Burrows is privately owned and Fort Decatur is the property of Auburn University.

Fort Deposit: Three locations in Alabama were given the name of Fort Deposit. Two of the sites are near present-day Guntersville and were flooded during the development of the Tennessee Valley Authority lakes. Fort Deposit in Lowndes County was a short-lived post on the Federal Road. A historic marker is placed in the general locale, but actual remains have not been found.

Fort Hull: The post on the Federal Road is presently unmarked and in private ownership. As at many historic sites along the Federal Road, extensive relic collecting has taken place.

Fort Jackson: The original October 15, 1966, listing for the site as a National Historic Landmark was for the remains of the French Fort Toulouse. The listing was amended in the 1980s to include the 1814 fort. Preservation and study have followed with the development of Fort Toulouse/Fort Jackson State Historic Site. Extensive research and excavations have been conducted at the site.

Fort Madison/Fort Glass: The two sites were part of the complex of forts built across "the Forks" region between the Alabama and Tombigbee Rivers. Fort Madison was the most formidable. The locale is marked. Archaeological surveys have been made, but no definitive features or artifacts have been found.

Fort Mims: The site of the Mims stockade is owned by the Alabama Historical Commission and is cared for in cooperation with the Fort Mims

Restoration Association. It is listed on the National Register of Historic Places. The site is subject to development and interpretation efforts. The University of South Alabama has a long history of investigations at Fort Mims. Though the core site is protected, there are many components and nearby sites that are not protected. The Mims slave quarters, boatyard, ferry, and some burial vaults are located in areas subject to disturbance. The nearby Benjamin O'Neal house and Fort Peirce sites are worthy of investigation. Both the house and fort remains are privately owned.

Fort Mitchell: Archaeological investigations at Fort Mitchell were conducted in the 1970s by David Chase and recently by John Cottier of Auburn University. Reports of the second phase of excavations are being prepared. A National Register of Historic Places listing came on June 13, 1972, and the status was upgraded to that of a National Historic Landmark on June 21, 1990. Replication of the 1813-era fort has been undertaken. Russell County maintains a public park at Fort Mitchell.

Fort Montgomery: Located approximately two miles from Fort Mims, this site has undergone extensive relic-collecting efforts. The privately owned locale underwent extensive formal testing in 1981 under a grant from the Alabama Historical Commission to Jefferson Davis College, in Brewton, Alabama. Significant archaeological remains were confirmed, but no definitive location was ascertained for the fort walls. The report of the investigations continues under preparation.

Fort Sinquefield: Listing on the National Register of Historic Places came December 31, 1974. Surveys of the area by archaeological staff from the University of Alabama and the University of South Alabama have been conducted at various times, but no definitive answers relating to the location of the stockade were forthcoming. The property is privately owned and careful commemoration is planned.

Fort Stoddert and Mount Vernon: The two sites comprise a complex that was begun in 1799 with the erection of Fort Stoddert and was expanded when the cantonment at Mount Vernon was begun in 1811. Fort Stoddert is owned by the Alabama Department of Conservation and has been damaged by the continuing use of the river landing at the site over the past two hundred years. Mount Vernon has also suffered from extensive use as a US arsenal, and later a mental health facility used the site. The site was placed on the National Register of Historic Places for Civil War and mental health importance on May 26, 1988.

Fort Strother: The site was placed on the National Register of Historic Places on July 24, 1972. Subsequent investigations have confirmed that the boundaries should be expanded. Extensive disturbance has come through the years from private residences, river navigation lock construction, railroad building, and surface mining. A cemetery and a campsite location have been confirmed, but the exact location of the fort in the extensive complex is not known. Ownership is primarily private. Alabama Power Company is also an owner and has shown responsibility for the historic resources.

Fort Williams: The fort was built as a base for the campaign, including the Battle of Horseshoe Bend. A substantial cemetery became part of the complex. The mouth of Cedar Creek was flooded with the impoundment of Lay Lake. Headstones placed at the cemetery were moved from the flooded area and have been moved a second time. Housing is being constructed along the lake.

Holy Ground: The US Army Corps of Engineers operates a park designated as the site of the Battle of the Holy Ground. An archaeological survey at the area in the 1970s found archaeological sites, but none from the correct era. Gregory A. Waselkov and Craig T. Sheldon Jr., with support from a grant from the American Battlefield Protection Program, led a survey team in 2010 that located the correct site, approximately two miles to the west. The site has been purchased for preservation.

Horseshoe Bend: Preserved as a unit of the National Park Service, Horseshoe Bend National Military Park contains over two thousand acres, including the site of the town of Nuyaka.

Mobile: The taking of this port city in April 1813 was a critical event leading to the Creek War, and the subsequent campaigns along the coast of the Gulf of Mexico brought thousands of troops to Mobile. The aged Fort Charlotte was the center of activities, with camps located south and west of the fort. The growth of the city lead to the demolition of Fort Charlotte, and eventually all of the campsites were urbanized. Parts of the fort site were excavated during the construction of the highway tunnel that destroyed most of the fort site. Portions of the remains lie under the streets and buildings that surround a replica of the fort. The focus of the replica is the French era. Formal surveys and assessments of the campsites have not been accomplished.

Navy Cove: A base for US Navy gunboats was located east of Fort Morgan at Navy Cove. The location was used by maritime interests. Significant damage was done to the ground by the devastating 1906 and 1916 hurricanes.

Talladega: The Battle of Talladega and the location of Fort Leslie are well recorded in nineteenth-century and current literature. Investigations at the fort site found that most of the archaeological remains had been destroyed. The battlefield has undergone urban development. Burials of the soldiers have been marked, and re-internment to the local cemetery was accomplished with an accompanying marker.

Tallushatchee: Researchers from Jacksonville State University conducted excavations at a site in northeastern Alabama that contained remains of burned structures and appropriate period artifacts. Whether this was the location of the main part of the town is still debated.

Currently there are two available guides for those who wish to visit Creek War–era sites: Mike Bunn and Clay Williams, *Battle for the Southern Frontier: The Creek War and the War of 1812* (Charleston: History Press, 2008); and Gregory A. Waselkov, *A Conquering Spirit: Fort Mims and the Redstick War of 1813–1814* (Tuscaloosa: University of Alabama Press, 2006).

Appendix 2

Known and Potential Archaeological Sites in Alabama

James W. Parker

Note: Special thanks to Craig Sheldon, Kathryn Braund, and Greg Waselkov for their assistance with preparation of this chart.

Theater	County	Type/event	Important date	Comments	Citation
NORTHERN					
Battles and skirmishes					
Auchenauulgau/Genalga (Cedar Grove)	Tallapoosa	Talwa/attack	November 1, 1813	Unconfirmed location	1
Emuckfau Creek	Tallapoosa	Talofa/battle	January 22, 1814	Unconfirmed location	1
Enitachopco	Tallapoosa	Talofa/battle	January 20, 1814	Unconfirmed location	1
Hillabee towns	Clay	Talwa/battle	November 18, 1814	Unconfirmed location	1
Horseshoe Bend/Tohopeka	Tallapoosa	Talofa/battle	March 27, 1814	National military park	2
Littafuchee	St. Clair	Talofa*	October 27, 1813	Unconfirmed location	3
Talladega	Talladega	Battle/siege	November 9, 1813	Developed/excavated	1
Tallushatchee	Calhoun	Talwa/battle	November 3, 1813	Excavations and survey	1
Camps, posts, and forts					
Camp 5 mi. from mouth of Cedar Creek	Talladega	Camp	March 21, 1814	Unconfirmed location	5
Camp at Ashburn's	Jackson	Camp	July 28, 1814	Unconfirmed location	5
Camp at Beaver Dam, Flint River	Madison	Camp	November 21, 1813	Unconfirmed location	8
Camp at Cane Creek	Calhoun	Camp	March 16, 1814	Unconfirmed location	5
Camp at Cataula's old fields	Calhoun	Camp	August 4, 1814	Unconfirmed location	5
Camp at Choccolocco Creek	Talladega	Camp	July 1814	Unconfirmed location	5
Camp at John Brown's	Marshall	Camp	October 22, 1813	Unconfirmed location	5
Camp at Paint Rock Creek	Madison	Camp	March 2, 1814	Unconfirmed location	5

Camp Baty	Madison	Camp	November 1813	Unconfirmed location	5
Camp Bradley	Talladega	Camp	November 1813	Unconfirmed location	5
Camp Brownlee	Colbert	Camp	October 7, 1814	Unconfirmed location	5
Camp Carroll	Madison	Camp	Summer 1814	Unconfirmed location	5
Camp Chinnabee	Talladega	Camp	October 29, 1813	Unconfirmed location	5
Camp Coffee/Coffee's Bluff	Morgan	Fortified camp	October 13, 1813	Unconfirmed location	10
Camp Coocey (Coosa)	Cherokee	Camp	November 13, 1813	Adj. to Ft. Armstrong w/houses	5
Camp Desertion	Marshall	Camp	October 25, 1813	Unconfirmed location	5
Camp Gibson	Marshall	Camp	October 20, 1813	Unconfirmed location	10
Camp Hamilton	St. Clair	Camp	March 14, 1814	Unconfirmed location	5
Camp Harrison	St. Clair	Camp	December 11, 1813	Unconfirmed location	5
Camp Johnston	Madison	Camp	February 25, 1814	Urbanized Huntsville	5
Camp near Ft. Williams	Talladega	Camp	March 1814	Unconfirmed location	10
Camp Strother	St. Clair	Camp	November 6, 1813	Unconfirmed location	5
Camp Stuart/Stewart	Calhoun	Camp	November 2, 1814	Unconfirmed location	14
Camp Ten Islands	St. Clair	Camp	November 3, 1813	Unconfirmed location	5
Camp Wahaugee	Talladega	Camp	January 17, 1814	Unconfirmed location	11
Camp Will's Creek	DeKalb	Camp	October 28, 1813	Unconfirmed location	5
Colbert's Ferry	Colbert	Camps	Pre-1813	Natchez Trace Parkway, NPS	1
Ditto's Landing	Madison	Crossing & camp	Pre-1813	Urbanized	1
Fort Armstrong	Cherokee	Fort	November 1813	Flooded by reservoir	1
Fort Deposit "Old"	Marshall	Fort	October 22, 1813	Flooded by reservoir	5
Fort Deposit	Marshall	Fort	November 1813	Flooded by reservoir	5
Fort Hampton	Limestone	Fort	Established 1811	Damaged by relic hunters	1
Fort Leslie	Talladega	Fort	November 9, 1813	Excavations/developed	6

*Abandoned or destroyed

Theater	County	Type/event	Important date	Comments	Citation
Fort Strother	St. Clair	Fort	November 1813	Archaeological surveys	7
Fort Williams	Talladega	Fort	March 1814	Flooded by reservoir	1
Huntsville	Madison	Depot and camp	1813–1815	Urbanized	1
Mountain Camp	Marshall	Camp	October 21, 1813	Unconfirmed location	5
Creek Settlements					
Abicouchee	Coosa	Talwa*	August 1813		12
Auceucaula	Coosa	Talwa	1814		13
Auchenauhatche/Atchinihatchee	Talladega	Talwa	March 1814	Near Ft. Williams	13
Auchenauulga	Randolph	Talofa	1813		12
Cataula/Catawlass village	St. Clair	Talwa	October 1813		13
Chinnabee's	Calhoun	Talofa/fort	Fall 1813		13
Coosa	Talladega	Talwa*	August 1813		12
Eufaula	Talladega	Talwa*	August 1813		12
Fife's Village	Talladega	Unknown	1813		13
Kelly Town	St. Clair	Talwa	1814		13
Kialigee	Tallapoosa	Talwa*	July 1813	Flooded	13
Lathlosulga	Coosa?	Talwa	1814		13
Littafuchee	St. Clair	Talofa*	October 28, 1813		3
Mad Town/Tallavaligau	Jefferson	Talofa*	May 1, 1814	Urbanized	12
Mad Warriors village	Tallapoosa	Talofa*	November 16, 1813		12
Nauchee	Talladega	Talwa*	August 1813		12
Nuyaka	Tallapoosa	Talofa*	November 17, 1813	Location known	1
Okchai	Tallapoosa	Talwa*	July 1814		13

Okfuscooche/Little Okfuskee	Tallapoosa	Talofa*	November 1813		12
Okfuskee	Tallapoosa	Talwa*	November 13, 1813		12
Oschooco	Shelby	Talwa*	ca. May 1, 1814		12
Penootau	Bibb	Talwa	April 25, 1814		13
Socopatoy	Coosa	Talwa	October 1813		13
Sosochuchany	Shelby	Talwa*	April 27, 1814		13
Thlathlagulgau/Fish Ponds	Coosa	Talofa*	July 1813		12
Tootacaugee/Corn House	Randolph	Talofa*	June 1813	Destroyed by Red Sticks	13
Tuscaloosa/Black Warrior's village	Tuscaloosa	Talofa*	October 1813	Surveyed	4
Waccoccee	Talladega	Talwa*	March 21, 1814		12
Weehoofka	Coosa	Talwa*	March 23, 1814		13
Wewokee	Coosa/Elmore	Talwa*	April 11, 1814		12
Cherokee and Mixed					
Black Fox's village	Marshall	Village	Pre-1813	Cherokee on the Creek Path	13
Brown's village	Marshall	Village	Pre-1813	Cherokee on the Creek Path	13
Cornsilk's village	Marshall	Village	Pre-1813	Cherokee on the Creek Path	13
Griffin's village	Marshall	Refugee	1813–1814	Creek on the Creek Path	13
Gunter's village	Marshall	Village	Pre-1813	Cherokee on the Creek Path	13
Melton's village	Marshall	Refugee	1813–1814	Creek on the Creek Path	13
Thompson's village/ferry	Marshall	Village	Pre-1813	Cherokee	13
Turkey Town	Etowah	Town	October 1813	Cherokee	13
Wasa's village	Marshall	Village	Pre-1813	Cherokee on the Creek Path	13
Wills's Town	DeKalb	Town	Pre-1813	Cherokee	13

*Abandoned or destroyed

Theater	County	Type/event	Important date	Comments	Citation
CENTRAL					
Battles and skirmishes					
Autossee	Macon	Talwa/battle	November 29, 1813	Burned	1
Calebee Creek/Camp Defiance	Macon	Battle	January 27, 1814	Unconfirmed location	1
Eccanachaca/Holy Ground	Lowndes	Battle	December 23, 1813	Under investigation	1
Tuckabatchee	Elmore	Talwa/siege	July 20, 1813	Surveyed and investigated	1
Camps, posts, and forts					
Camp Deposit	Lowndes	Camp	December 21, 1813	Rte. from St. Stephens to Holy Ground	10
Camp Jackson	Elmore	Camp	April 17, 1814	Survey and tests	10
Camp near Hoithlewaulee	Elmore	Camp	April 15, 1814	Unconfirmed location	10
Camp at Weatherford's plantation	Lowndes	Camp	December 23, 1813	Between Holy Ground and Pintlala	1
Fort Bainbridge	Macon	Fort	March 1814	Relic-hunting damage	1
Fort Burrows	Elmore	Fort	May 1814	Preserved by owners	1
Fort Decatur	Macon	Fort	March 1814	Owned by Auburn University	1
Fort Deposit	Lowndes	Fort	December 20, 1813	Historic marker	10
Fort Hull	Macon	Fort	March 1814	Damaged by relic hunters	1
Fort Jackson	Elmore	Fort	April 17, 1814	Excavated Nat. Hist. Landmark	15
Fort Mitchell	Russell	Fort	November 1813	Excavated Nat. Hist. Landmark	16
Militia Bluff	Dallas	Fortified camp	May 1814	See Camp Ho-To-Wa, below	10

Creek Sites

Autauga	Autauga	Talwa	May 1814		12
Chattacchufaulee/McQueen's	Macon	Talofa*	November 28, 1813		13
Chooksaputka	Dallas	Talwa*	December 30, 1813		13
Coolome	Montgomery	Talwa*	April 13, 1814	Surveyed	12
Coosada	Elmore	Talwa*	April 1814		12
Coweta	Russell	Talwa	Fall 1813	Marker at site	12
Cussita	Russell	Talwa	Fall 1813		13
Ecunchate	Elmore	Talwa*	April–May 1814		12
Ecunhatke	Montgomery	Talwa*	April 15, 1814		12
Fusihatchee	Elmore	Talwa*	April 13, 1814	Excavated and destroyed	17
Hatchachubba (lower)	Russell	Talwa	April 1814		13
Hatcheechubbee (upper)	Elmore	Talwa	June 1813		12
Halfway House/Hopoithle Mico's	Macon	Talwa*	May 1814		13
Hoithlewaulee/Othlawaulee	Elmore	Talwa*	April 14, 1814	Surveyed	12
Hookchoi	Elmore	Talwa	July 1814		12
Kahaubah	Dallas	Talofa*	May 1814		12
Moniac's Tavern	Montgomery	Tavern	July 1813	Surveyed	1
Mucklassa	Elmore	Talwa*	April 15, 1814		12
Ocheaupofau/Hickory Ground	Elmore	Talwa*	April 16, 1814	Archaeological study made	18
Opilthlucco/Opelika	Macon	Talwa*	July 1814		13
Pauwacta	Montgomery	Talwa*	May 1814		12
Pintlala/Moniac's or Prophet's Town	Lowndes	Talofa*	December 24, 1813		13
Sausanogee	Montgomery	Talwa*	April 14, 1814		12
Tallassee	Macon	Talwa*	August 1813		12

*Abandoned or destroyed

Theater	County	Type/event	Important date	Comments	Citation
Toowassa	Montgomery	Talwa*	May 1814		12
Tuskegee/Taskigi	Elmore	Talwa*	April 17, 1814	Ft. Toulouse/Ft. Jackson NHL	15
Weatherford's Village	Lowndes	Talofa*	December 24, 1813	Location confirmed	13
Yuchi	Russell	Talwa*	October 3, 1814		13
Pearson's Expedition, May–June 1814					
Cabet-Kawher	Dallas		May–June 1814		10
Camp Ho-To-Wa/Camp Pearson	Dallas		May–June 1814		10
Co-ba-bet-ka	Dallas		May 21, 1814		10
Durant's	Autauga		May–June 1814		10
Enonca-ga-ga-la	Lowndes		May–June 1814		10
Lucsouva	Lowndes?		May 28, 1814		10
Pahoose/Pohorew	Autauga		May–June 1814		10
Pintlala Old Fort	Montgomery		May–June 1814		10
Su-suc-e-ma	Lowndes		May–June 1814		10
Waubeguskee Old Town	Autauga	Talwa	August 1814		10
SOUTHERN					
Battles and skirmishes					
Bashi Creek	Clarke	Skirmish	September 1813	Unconfirmed location	1
Bon Secour	Baldwin	Sacked	September 16–17, 1814	Unconfirmed location	20
Burnt Corn 1	Escambia	Skirmish	July 27, 1813	Unconfirmed location	1
Burnt Corn 2	Escambia	Skirmish	November 22–23, 1813	Choctaws attack Red Sticks	1

Canoe Fight/John Randon plantation	Monroe	Battle	November 12, 1813	Confirmed on private property	1
D'Olive plantation	Baldwin	Sacked	September 3, 1814	Urbanized	21
Fish River sites	Baldwin	Sacked	1813–1814	Unconfirmed location	20
Fort Bowyer (1)	Baldwin	Battle	September 15, 1814	Fort Morgan NHL	1
Fort Bowyer (2)	Baldwin	Battle	February 11, 1815	Fort Morgan NHL	1
Fort Mims	Baldwin	Battle	August 30, 1813	State historic park	19
Fort Peirce	Baldwin	Sacked	August 31, 1813	In private hunting camp	1
Fort Sinquefield	Clarke	Attacked	September 2, 1813	Unconfirmed location	1
Josiah Fisher house	Clarke	Attacked	September 6, 1813	Unconfirmed location	1
Kennedy's/Henson's mill	Baldwin	Attacked	August 31, 1813	Historic marker	22
Kimbell-James massacre	Clarke	Attacked	September 1, 1813	Near Fort Madison	1
Surrender of Mobile	Mobile	Surrender	May 15, 1813	Urbanized	1
Camps, posts, and forts					
Battery and camp at Choctaw Point	Mobile	Battery	December 14, 1814	Industrialized	10
Camp at Carson's ferry	Washington	Camp	1813–1814	Unconfirmed location	8
Camp at D'Olive's	Baldwin	Camp	April 22, 1813	Developed	10
Camp at Dupree's	Washington	Camp	October 21, 1814	Coffee's march south	8
Camp at Pleasant Level	Clarke	Camp	November 11, 1813	Rte. from St. Stephens to Holy Ground	10
Camp at Weatherford's ferry	Monroe	Camp	November 1813	West side of Alabama River	10
Camp Beef (Claiborne)	Monroe	Camp	November 22, 1813	Rte. from St. Stephens to Holy Ground	10
Camp Cool Springs	Mobile	Camp	April 22, 1813	Possibly Camp Mandeville	5
Camp Detention	Monroe	Camp	December 13, 1813	Rte. from St. Stephens to Holy Ground	10

*Abandoned or destroyed

Theater	County	Type/event	Important date	Comments	Citation
Camp in the Cut-Off	Baldwin	Camp	November 14, 1814	At Mims' ferry	8
Camp Lance Mandeville	Mobile	Camp	1813–1815	Unconfirmed location	25
Camp near Burnt Corn Springs	Escambia	Camp	December 19, 1813	Rte. from St. Stephens to Holy Ground	10
Camp Portage Cr./Third Regt.	Mobile	Camp	July 1814	Developed	10
Camp Preparation	Monroe	Camp	December 5, 1813	Rte. from St. Stephens to Holy Ground	10
Camp Weatherford	Monroe	Camp	December 6, 1813	Rte. from St. Stephens to Holy Ground	10
Camp West Bank of Alabama	Monroe	Camp	November 21, 1813	Rte. from St. Stephens to Holy Ground	10
Dauphin Island	Mobile	British camp	February 3, 1815	Developed	1
Fort at the Perdido	Baldwin	Fort	May 1813	Burned by Spanish	10
Fort Charlotte/Carlota	Mobile	Fort	May 13, 1813	Excavated and replicated	23
Fort Claiborne	Monroe	Fort	November 1813	Under investigation	1
Fort Montgomery	Baldwin	Fort	August 1814	Surveyed and tested	24
Fort Peirce II	Baldwin	Rebuilt fort	Fall 1813	In private hunting camp	1
Fort Republic	Washington	Civilian fort	July 1813	Under archaeological study	1
Fort St. Stephens	Washington	Old fort	July 1813	Under archaeological study	1
Fort Stoddert	Mobile	Fort	1799	Site of modern boat ramp	1
Mount Vernon	Mobile	Camp	1811	State mental hospital	1
Navy Cove	Baldwin	Naval base	1813–1815	Developed and hurricane damaged	1
St. Stephens Factor's Stockade	Washington	Stockade	July 1813	Under archaeological study	1

Civilian defenses					
Cato's Fort	Washington	Civilian fort	Summer 1813	Unconfirmed location	1
Fort Carney	Clarke	Civilian fort	Summer 1813	Unconfirmed location	1
Fort Easley	Clarke	Civilian fort	Summer 1813	Unconfirmed location	1
Fort Glass	Clarke	Civilian fort	Summer 1813	Archaeologically surveyed	1
Fort Landrum	Clarke	Civilian fort	Summer 1813	Unconfirmed location	1
Fort Madison	Clarke	Civilian fort	Summer 1813	Archaeologically surveyed	1
Fort White	Clarke	Civilian fort	Summer 1813	Unconfirmed location	1
Lavier's Fort	Clarke	Civilian fort	Summer 1813	Unconfirmed location	1
McGrew's Fort	Clarke	Civilian fort	Summer 1813	Unconfirmed location	1
Mott's Fort	Clarke	Civilian fort	Summer 1813	Unconfirmed location	1
Powell's Fort	Clarke	Civilian fort	Summer 1813	Unconfirmed location	1
Rankin's Fort	Washington	Civilian fort	Summer 1813	Unconfirmed location	1
Turner's Fort	Clarke	Civilian fort	Summer 1813	Unconfirmed location	1
Creek sites					
Village below Lower Peach Tree	Monroe	Temporary	September 1813	On eastern side	1
Homes and business					
Bailey, Dixon	Baldwin	House	Summer 1813		20
Boatyard	Baldwin	Boatyard	Pre-1813	Near Fort Mims	1
Bonner, Jourdon	Clarke	House	Summer 1813		20
Cade, William	Clarke	House	September 1813	Lost at Ft. Easley	20
Carson's Ferry/Hollinger's Ferry	Washington	Ferry	Pre-1813		1
Chanto/Fish River	Baldwin	Commercial	September 1814	Developed	20

Theater	County	Type/event	Important date	Comments	Citation
Cochran's cowpens	Escambia	Commercial	October 1814		21
Cole, Richard	Clarke	House	Fall 1813		20
Conway, Charles	Baldwin	House	Summer 1813		20
Cook, John	Baldwin	House	September 1814	Bon Secour	20
Cornells, James	Escambia	House	July 1813	At Burnt Corn Springs	1
Crispoe's cowpens	Escambia	Commercial	October 1814		21
Dunn, Cornelious	Baldwin	House	August 30, 1813	Killed at Ft. Mims	20
Dyer, Mary	Baldwin	House	August 1813		20
Easley, Daniel	Clarke	House	Fall 1813		20
Easley, Warsham	Clarke	House	Fall 1813		20
Griffen, Patsy and Jesse	Clarke	House	Fall 1813	Killed at Bashi	20
Griffen, Susanna and Daniel	Clarke	House	Fall 1813	Killed at Bashi	20
Harrison, Vincent	Clarke	House	Fall 1813		20
Jones, Russell	Clarke	House	Fall 1813		20
Judge Toulmin's place	Mobile	House	October 1814	Developed	21
Kilpatrick, Alex	Clarke	House	Fall 1813		20
Lacoste, Euphrasia	Baldwin	Commercial	September 1813	Bon Secour complex	20
Leach, Dugold	Clarke	House	Fall 1813		20
Matlock, James	Clarke	House	Summer 1813		20
McDavid, John	Clarke	House	Summer 1813		20
McGee, Leonard	Escambia	House	July 1813	Along trail to Pensacola	1
Mims' Ferry	Baldwin	Ferry	Pre-1813	Near Fort Mims	1
Mims, David	Baldwin	House	August 30, 1813	Killed at Ft. Mims	20
Mims, Samuel	Baldwin	House	August 30, 1813	Killed at Ft. Mims	19

Moncrief, Caleb	Clarke	House	Summer 1813		20
O'Neal, Benjamin	Baldwin	House	August 30, 1813	Killed at Ft. Mims	20
Peirce, John and William	Baldwin	House	August 30, 1813	Large complex at site	20
Pogue, David	Clarke	House	Fall 1813		20
Powell, Thomas and Nich. Weeks	Baldwin	Commercial	July 1813	Brick operation at Fish River	20
Randon, Peter	Monroe	House	Summer 1813		
Rodgers, James	Clarke	House	Summer 1813		20
Rosser, Elijah	Clarke	House	Summer 1813		20
Sizemore's Ferry	Monroe	Ferry	Pre-1813		1
Smith, John	Clarke	Buildings	Fall 1813		20
Stedham, Moses	Baldwin	House	August 30, 1813	Killed at Ft. Mims	20
Stiggins, George	Baldwin	House	Fall 1813		20
Suarez, Francisco	Baldwin	Commercial	November 1814	At Perdido Ferry	20
Tormen's Cowpens on Federal Road	Baldwin	Commercial	October 2, 1814		21
Turvin, Ann	Baldwin	House	August 30, 1813		20
Walker, Tandy	Clarke	House	Fall 1813		20
Wells, Joshiah	Clarke	House	Fall 1813		20
Welsh, Dempsey	Clarke	House	Summer 1813		20
White house on Chickasaw Bogue	Mobile	Jackson route	October 1814		21
Wilson, James	Clarke	House	Fall 1813		20
Wood, James (Major)	Clarke	House	Fall 1813		20

*Abandoned or destroyed

Citations

1. For general knowledge about sites related to the Creek War, see Mike Bunn and Clay Williams, *Battle for the Southern Frontier: The Creek War and the War of 1812* (Charleston: History Press, 2008); Daniel T. Elliot, Tracy M. Dean, W. Dean Wood, and Debra J. Wells, *Revolutionary War/War of 1812 Historic Preservation Study,* report submitted to the Cultural Resources GIS Facility, Preservation Initiatives Branch, Heritage Preservation Services, National Park Service (Ellerslie, GA: Southern Research, Historic Preservation Consultants, 2002); Henry S. Halbert and Timothy H. Ball, *The Creek War of 1813 and 1814,* ed. with introduction and notes by Frank L. Owsley Jr. (Tuscaloosa: University of Alabama Press, 1969); David S. Heidler and Jeanne T. Heidler, eds., *Encyclopedia of the War of 1812* (Santa Barbara, CA: ABC-Clio Inc., 1997); Frank L. Owsley Jr., *Struggle for the Gulf Borderlands: The Creek War and the Battle of New Orleans, 1812–1815* (Gainesville: University Presses of Florida, 1981).

2. Roy S. Dickens Jr., *Archaeological Investigations at Horseshoe Bend, National Military Park, Alabama,* Alabama Archaeological Society, Special Publication 3 (Tuscaloosa: Alabama Archaeological Society, 1979); Charles H. Fairbanks, "Excavations at Horseshoe Bend, Alabama," *Florida Anthropologist* 15 (1962): 41–56; Gregory A. Waselkov, "A Reinterpretation of the Creek Indian Barricade at Horseshoe Bend," *Journal of Alabama Archaeology* 8 (1989): 117–33.

3. Andrew Jackson to Willie Blount, Camp Wills, October 28, 1813, in *The Papers of Andrew Jackson,* vol. 2, *1804–1813,* ed. Harold D. Moser, Sharon MacPherson, and Charles Bryan Jr. (Knoxville: University of Tennessee Press, 1984), 442–43.

4. Vernon James Knight Jr., "Black Warrior Town, Phase I," Report of Investigations No. 33, Office of Archaeological Research, Moundville, AL, 1982.

5. Diaries and records from the John Reid Papers, Library of Congress; "Diary of Levi Lee," MS. AC. 1549, Philip Pipkin Papers, MS. AC. 69–25, and McCutchen Collection, MS. AC. 1264, Tennessee State Library and Archives, Nashville, TN; "Journal of Isaac Baker," *Southwestern Historical Quarterly* 30 (July 1926–April 1927): 272–82; Bryan-Leventhorpe Papers, Southern Historical Collection, University of North Carolina Library, Chapel Hill, NC; and "'J. Hartsell Memora': Journal of a Tennessee Captain in the War of 1812," ed. Mary Hardin McCown, *Publications of the East Tennessee Historical Society* 11 (1939): 93–115 and 12 (1940): 118–46.

6. Vernon James Knight Jr., "Fort Leslie and Upper Creek Ceramics of the Early Nineteenth Century," *Journal of Alabama Archaeology* 43, no. 1 (1997): 35–45.

7. Carey B. Oakley and V. Stephen Jones, "Investigations at Fort Strother Cemetery (Site 1Sc 66), St. Clair County, Alabama," report to the Alabama Historical Commission, Office of Archaeological Services, Moundville, AL, 2000; James W. Parker, "Fort Strother," in *An Intensive Phase II Cultural Resources Survey of Selected Areas on the Coosa River Navigation Project,* Report of Investigations No. 32, Office of Archaeological Research, Tuscaloosa, University of Alabama; Robert Earl Perry, "The Historical Significance of the Creek War of 1813–1814, Land Use and Archaeology of Fort Strother in St. Clair County, Alabama" (master's thesis, Jacksonville State University, 2004).

8. Orderly books of John October 1813–May 1815," Historic New Orleans Collection, New Orleans, William C. Cook Collection, Mss 557, fol. 365.

9. *The Clarion,* Nashville, TN, April 5, 1814.

10. National Archives and Records Service Record Groups 98 and 107 provided maps, correspondence, and orderly books. The records of the Third Infantry are in R.G. 98 and the Letters Received by the Sec. of War are found in R.G. 107.

11. Andrew Jackson, "General Orders, Camp Wehougee, Jan. 17, 1814," William C. Cook Collection, Mss 557, 2001-68-L, Folder 54, Historic New Orleans Collection, New Orleans, LA.

12. Gregory A. Waselkov and Brian M. Wood, "The Creek War of 1813–1814: Effects on Creek Society and Settlement Pattern," *Journal of Alabama Archaeology* 32 (June 1986): 1–24.

13. Amos J. Wright, *Historic Indian Towns in Alabama, 1540–1838* (Tuscaloosa: University of Alabama Press, 2003).

14. Nathanial Taylor to James Colbert, November 2, 1814, enclosure in John Rhea to Secretary of War, May 17, 1815, Letters Received, Secretary of War, Registered Series (1801–1870), Record Group 107, Records of the Office of the Secretary of War, National Archives and Records Administration, Washington, DC.

15. Bascom McDonald Brooms and James W. Parker, *Fort Toulouse Phase III Completion Report* (Montgomery: Alabama Historical Commission, 1980); Gregory A. Waselkov, Brian Wood, and Joseph M. Herbert, *Colonization and Conquest: The 1980 Archaeological Excavations at Fort Toulouse and Fort Jackson, Alabama,* Auburn University Archaeological Monograph 4 (Montgomery: Auburn University at Montgomery, 1982); Gregory A. Waselkov, *Fort Toulouse Studies,* Auburn University Archaeological Monograph 9 (Auburn, AL: Auburn University, 1984); and Gregory A. Waselkov, "Introduction: Recent Archaeological and Historical Research," in *Fort Toulouse: The French Outpost at the Alabamas on the Coosa,* by Daniel H. Thomas, vii–xlii (Tuscaloosa: University of Alabama Press, 1989).

16. David W. Chase, "Fort Mitchell: An Archaeological Exploration in

Russell County, Alabama," in *Alabama Archaeological Society Special Publication Number 1* (Tuscaloosa: Alabama Archaeological Society, 1974).

17. Gregory A. Waselkov, John Cottier, and Craig Sheldon Jr., "Archaeological Excavations at the Early Historic Creek Indian Town of Fusihatchee (Phase 1, 1988–1989)," Final Report to the National Science Foundation (BNS-8718934) by Auburn University, Auburn, AL, 1990.

18. Diane S. Mueller, "Intrasite Settlement at the Historic Creek Town of Hickory Ground (1EE89), Elmore County, Alabama (1990–1991)," *Journal of Alabama Archaeology* 41 (December 1995): 107–36; Craig T. Sheldon, John W. Cottier, and Gregory A. Waselkov, "A Preliminary Report on the Subsurface Testing of a Portion of the Creek Indian Property at Hickory," Montgomery, Auburn University at Montgomery, 1988, manuscript on file, Alabama Historical Commission, Montgomery, AL.

19. Susan C. Olsen, Noel R. Stowe, and Marvin Hoyt, eds., *Archaeological Investigations at Fort Mims,* Archaeological Completion Report Series, Number 4, Division of Grants, Office of Archaeology and Historic Preservation (Washington, DC: National Park Service, 1975); Gregory A. Waselkov, Bonnie Gums, and James W. Parker, *Archaeology at Fort Mims: Excavation Contexts and Artifact Catalog,* University of South Alabama Archaeological Monograph 12 (Mobile: University of South Alabama, 2006); Gregory A. Waselkov, *A Conquering Spirit: Fort Mims and the Redstick War of 1813–1814* (Tuscaloosa: University of Alabama Press, 2006).

20. Richard S. Lackey, comp., *Frontier Claims in the Lower South: Records of Claims Filed by the Citizens of the Alabama and Tombigbee River Settlements in the Mississippi Territory for Depredations by the Creek Indians during the War of 1812,* introduction by John D. W. Guice (New Orleans: Polyanthos, 1977).

21. Major Howell Tatum, "Major Howell Tatum's Journal, While Acting Topographical Engineer (1814) To General Jackson, Commanding the Seventh Military District," ed. John Spenser Bassett, *Smith College Studies in History* 7 (October 1921 to April 1922): 5–138.

22. McDonald Brooms, *Archaeological Investigations at the Kennedy Mill Site: 1Ba301 in Baldwin County, Alabama* (Troy, AL: Troy State University, Archaeological Research Center, 1996).

23. Donald A. Harris and Jerry J. Nielsen, *Archaeological Salvage Investigations at the Site of the French Fort Conde, Mobile, Alabama. A final report in fulfillment of Contract No. I-10-1(3) Tunnel Plaza Interchange Archaeological Agreement between the Alabama Highway Department and the University of Alabama* (Tuscaloosa: University of Alabama, 1972).

24. James W. Parker, "Investigations Relative to the 19th-Century Tensaw Military Frontier in Southwest Alabama," in *Archaeology in Southwest-*

ern Alabama: A Collection of Papers, ed. Cailup B. Curren (Camden, AL: Alabama Tombigbee Regional Commission, 1982), 147–54.

25. Peter A. Brannon, "Camp Mandeville," *Arrow Points, Monthly Bulletin of the Alabama Anthropological Society* 8 (March 1924): 48–49; "Monthly Report of A detachment of the M.T. Militia Infantry in the Service to the U.S. for the month of December 1814 Commd. by Major Ross., Camp Lance Mandeville," Historic New Orleans Collection, William C. Cook Collection Mss 557.

Bibliography

Unpublished Primary Sources

Alabama Department of Archives and History, Montgomery, AL

Blount, Richard. Papers.
Halbert, Henry Sale. Papers.
Manac, Samuel. Deposition, August 2, 1813, SPR 26.
Public Information Subject Files—Alabamians at War, War of 1812, and First Creek War.

Archivo General de Indias, Seville, Spain

Papeles de Cuba Legajo 221B, 335, microfilm reel 311. P. K. Yonge Library, University of Florida, Gainesville.

Calvin M. McClung Historical Collection, Knoxville, TN: Sevier, John. Papers

Center for American History, University of Texas, Austin, TX

McCulloch Family Papers.
Smith, James Norman. Memoirs, 1789–1860, 4 vols.

Duke University, Rare Book, Manuscript, and Special Collections Library, Durham, NC

Jackson, Andrew. Letters.
Lafitte, Jean. Papers.

Georgia Department of History and Archives, Morrow, GA

Barnard, Timothy. "Unpublished Letters of Timothy Barnard." Edited by Louise Frederick Hays.
Creek Letters, Talks, and Treaties, 1705–1839
Floyd, John. Papers.
Georgia Military Affairs. 4 vols.

Hargrett Library, University of Georgia, Athens, GA

Butler, Samuel Edward. "Diary of Samuel Edward Butler, 1784–1786." MS 432.
Cuyler, Telamon. Collection.

Historic New Orleans Collection, New Orleans, LA

Cook, William C. Collection.

Horseshoe Bend National Military Park, Daviston, AL

"Bounty Application for Whale."
"Interpretive Prospectus–Current Folder."
"Reports of S. S. Broadus, 1907 and 1911."

Library of Congress, Washington, DC

Jackson, Andrew. Papers. Series 3, vols. A–E. Microfilm. 78 reels. 1961.
Onderdonk, Henry. "Life and Times of Tecumseh."
Reid, John. Papers.

Maryland Historical Society, Baltimore, MD

Military Manuscript Collection, 1783–1888.

Mississippi Department of Archives and History, Jackson, MS

Claiborne, J.H.C. Papers.

National Archives and Records Administration, Washington, DC

Record Group 15. Records of the Veterans Administration.
  Old War Invalid Files.
Record Group 75. United States Bureau of Indian Affairs. Office of Indian Affairs.
  Letters Received, 1824–1881. M234.
  Records of the Cherokee Indian Agency of Tennessee, 1801–1835. 14 rolls. M208.
Record Group 94. United States Adjutant General's Office. Compiled Military Service Records, War of 1812.
  Muster Rolls and Pay Rolls of Colonel Morgan's Regiment of Cherokee Indians, October 7, 1813, to April 11, 1814.
Record Group 98. Records of United States Army Commands, 1784–1821.
Record Group 107. Records of the Office of the Secretary of War.
  Letters Received by the Secretary of War. Registered Series, 1801–1870. M221.
  Letters Received by the Secretary of War. Unregistered Series, 1789–1861. M222.

Newberry Library, Chicago, IL

Ayer, Edward E. Collection.
Payne, John Howard. Papers.

North Carolina Department of Cultural Resources, Division of Archives and History, Raleigh, NC

Graham, Joseph. Papers. 1780–1836.

Rosenberg Library, Galveston, TX

Memorandum Book of Joseph Huffmaster. Mss #04-0007.

Society for Georgia Archaeology, Macon, GA

Letter from Edmund Shackelford to Frances Shackelford. November 26, 1813, MSS 4911.

State Library of Florida, Tallahassee, FL

Journal of Governor Richard K. Call. Fla 921.

Tennessee State Library and Archives, Nashville, TN

Alexander Papers. TSL-VI-6-68-355.
Cherokee Collection. Penelope Johnson Allen Papers. Microfilm #815.
"Diary of Levi Lee." MS. AC. 1549.
Dyas Collection. John Coffee Papers. MS. AC. 38.
Foster, Ephraim Hubbard. Papers. Correspondence. MS. AC. 79–26.
McCutchen Collection. MS. AC. 1264.
Miscellaneous Correspondence.
Morgan, Gideon. Papers. MS. AC. 78–31.
Pipkin, Philip. Papers. MS. AC. 69–25
Reid, John. Memoir and Journal. MS. AC. 72–180.

Thomas Gilcrease Institute of American History and Art, Manuscripts Collection, Tulsa, OK

Cherokee Nation Papers.

University of North Carolina, Library, Southern Historical Collection, Chapel Hill, NC

Bryan-Leventhorpe Papers.

Wisconsin Historical Society, Madison, WI

Draper Manuscript. Tecumseh Papers. Series YY, vol. 10, reel 199, microfilm.
Stiggins, George. "A Historical narration of the Genealogy traditions and downfall of the Ispocaga or Creek tribe of Indians, written by one of the tribe," 60. Lyman Draper Manuscript Collection, vol. 1, series 5: Georgia, Alabama, and South Carolina Papers, Wisconsin Historical Society, Madison, WI.

Published Primary Sources

Acts Passed at the First Session of the Tenth General Assembly of the State of Tennessee. Nashville: T. G. Bradford, 1813.

Adair, James. *History of the American Indians.* Edited and annotated by Kathryn E. Holland Braund. London: Edward and Charles Dilly, 1775. Reprint, Tuscaloosa: University of Alabama Press, 2005.

American Indian Captives. Vol. 33. Edited by Wilcomb E. Washburn. New York: Garland Publishing, 1978.

American State Papers, Class II, Indian Affairs. 2 Vols. Edited by Walter Lowrie. Washington, DC: Gales and Seaton, 1832–1834.

American State Papers, Military Affairs. Vol. 3, *1823–1828.* Edited by Asbury Dickins and John W. Forney. Washington, DC: Gales and Seaton, 1860.

Atkin, Edmond. *The Appalachian Indian Frontier: The Edmond Atkin Report and Plan of 1755.* Edited with an introduction by Wilbur R. Jacobs. Lincoln: University of Nebraska Press, 1967.

Baker, Isaac. "Journal of Isaac Baker." *Southwestern Historical Quarterly* 30 (July 1926–April 1927): 272–82.

Bartram, William. *The Travels of William Bartram: Naturalist's Edition.* Edited by Francis Harper. New Haven, CT: Yale University Press, 1967.

Bassett, John Spencer, ed. *Correspondence of Andrew Jackson.* 7 Vols. Carnegie Institute of Washington series, no. 371. Papers of the Department of Historical Resource. Washington, DC: Carnegie Institute of Washington, 1926–1935.

Boyd, Mark F. "Events at Prospect Bluff on the Apalachicola River, 1808–1818: An Introduction to Twelve Letters of Edmund Doyle, Trader." *Florida Historical Quarterly* 16 (1937): 55–96.

Brannan, John, comp. *Official Letters of the Military and Naval Officers of the United States during the War with Great Britain in the Years 1812, 13, 14, & 15. With Some Additional Letters and Documents Elucidating the History of that Period.* Washington, DC: Way & Gideon, for the editors, 1823.

Brannon, Peter A., ed. "Journal of James A. Tait for the Year 1813." *Georgia Historical Quarterly* 8 (1924): 229–39.

Calendar of Virginia State Papers, 1652-1781. Ed. William P. Palmer. Richmond, 1875. Reprint, New York: Kraus Reprinting Corp., 1968.

Caller, James. *The Declaration of the American citizens, on the Mobile, with relation to British aggressions.* [Wakefield, AL], September 1807.

Carter, Clarence Edwin, comp. and ed. *The Territorial Papers of the United States.* 12 vols. Washington, DC: Government Printing Office, 1934–1945.

Catlin, George. *Letters and Notes on the Manners, Customs, and Condition of the North American Indians.* 2 vols. London, 1841.

Collections of the Illinois State Historical Society. Vol. 10. Springfield, 1915.

Craven, Avery O., ed. "Letters of Andrew Jackson." *Huntington Library Bulletin* No. 3 (February 1933): 109-34.

Crockett, David. *The Autobiography of David Crockett.* Originally printed as *A*

Narrative of the Life of David Crockett, of the State of Tennessee. 1834. Reprint, New York: Charles Scribner's Sons, 1923.

———. *A Narrative of the Life of David Crockett.* Philadelphia: J. E. Potter, 1834.

Davies, Kenneth G., ed. *Documents of the American Revolution, 1770–1783.* 20 vols. Dublin, Ireland: Irish University Press, 1972–1981.

De Villars, Le Baron Marc. "Extract d'une lettre de Diron, datée de Juin, 1721." In "Documents Concernant L'Histoire des Indiens de la Region Orientale de la Louisiane." *Journal de la Societé des Americanistes de Paris,* n.s., 14 (1922): 122–40.

DeWitt, John H., ed. "Letters of General John Coffee to his Wife, 1813–1815, with Introduction and Notes." *Tennessee Historical Magazine* 2 (December 1916): 264–94.

Doster, James F., ed. "Letters Relating to the Tragedy of Fort Mims: August–September, 1813." *Alabama Review* 14 (October 1961): 269–85.

Fisher, Ruth Anna. "The Surrender of Pensacola as Told by the British." *American Historical Review* 54 (1949): 326–29.

Gaines, George S. "Gaines' Reminiscences." *Alabama Historical Quarterly* 26, nos. 3–4 (1964): 133–228.

Gilmer, George Rockingham. *Sketches of Some of the First Settlers of Upper Georgia, of the Cherokees, and the Author.* 1855. Reprint, Americus, GA: Americus Book Company, 1926.

Gleig, George Robert. *A Narrative of the Campaigns of the British Army, At Washington and New Orleans, Under Generals Ross, Pakenham, & Lambert, in the Years 1814 and 1815; with Some Account of the Countries Visited. By an Officer Who served in the Expedition.* Philadelphia: M. Carey, 1821.

Governor's Messages and Letters of William Henry Harrison. ed. Logan Esarey. Indianapolis: Indiana Historical Society, 1922.

Greenslade, Marie, ed. "Letters of John Innerarity: The Seizure of Pensacola by Andrew Jackson, November 7, 1814." *Florida Historical Quarterly* 9 (January 1931): 127–34.

Harris, John. *A Review of the Battle of the Horse Shoe, and of the Facts Relating to the Killing of Sixteen Indians on the Morning after the Battle by the Orders of Gen. Andrew Jackson.* N.p.: 1928.

Hawkins, Benjamin. *Letters, Journals, and Writings of Benjamin Hawkins.* 2 Vols. Edited by C. L. Grant. Savannah: Beehive Press, 1980.

———. *Letters of Benjamin Hawkins: 1796–1806.* Collections of the Georgia Historical Society, Vol. 9. Savannah: Georgia Historical Society, 1916.

———. *A Sketch of the Creek Country in the Years 1798 and 1799.* Collections of the Georgia Historical Society, Vol. 3, Part 1. 1848. Reprint, Americus, GA: Americus Book Company, 1938.

———. "A Viatory or Journal of Distances and Observations." In *The Col-*

lected Works of Benjamin Hawkins, 1796–1810, edited by H. Thomas Foster II, 1–89. Tuscaloosa: University of Alabama Press, 2003.

Heitman, Francis B. *Historical Register and Dictionary of the United States Army, From its Organization, September 29, 1789, to March 2, 1903.* Vol. 1. Washington, DC: Government Printing Office, 1903.

Houston, Sam. *Autobiography of Sam Houston: Compiled from His Writings and Letters.* Edited by Donald Day and Harry Herbert Ullom. Norman: University of Oklahoma Press, 1954.

Jones, Calvin. "Account of the Cherokee Schools, communicated by Gen. Calvin Jones, of Raleigh to the editor of *The Register.*" *American Monthly Magazine* (December 1813): 117–24.

Kappler, Charles J., comp. and ed. *Indian Affairs: Laws and Treaties.* 7 Vols. Washington, DC: Government Printing Office, 1904.

Klink, Carl F., ed. *Tecumseh: Fact and Fiction in Early Records.* 1961. Reprint. Ohawa: Tecumseh Press, 1978.

Lackey, Richard S., comp. *Frontier Claims in the Lower South: Records of Claims Filed by the Citizens of the Alabama and Tombigbee River Settlements in the Mississippi Territory for Depredations by the Creek Indians during the War of 1812.* Introduction by John D. W. Guice. New Orleans: Polyanthos, 1977.

Latour, Arsène Lacarrière. *Historical Memoir of the War in West Florida and Louisiana in 1814–15, with an Atlas.* Edited by Gene A. Smith. 1816. Reprint, Gainesville: University Press of Florida, 1999.

Library of Congress Acquisitions: Manuscript Division. Washington, D.C.: Library of Congress, 1991.

McClinton, Rowena, ed. *Moravian Springplace Mission to the Cherokees.* 2 vols. Lincoln: University of Nebraska Press, 2007.

McCown, Mary Hardin, ed. "'J. Hartsell Memora': Journal of a Tennessee Captain in the War of 1812." *Publications of the East Tennessee Historical Society* 11 (1939): 93–115 and 12 (1940): 118–46.

McFee, Robert B. *History of the Late War in the Western Country (1816).* Readex Microprint, 1966.

McKenney, Thomas L. *Memoirs: Official and personal, with sketches of travels among the Northern and Southern Indians, embracing a war excursion and descriptions of scenes along the Western borders.* New York: Paine and Burgess, 1846.

Milfort, Louis. *Memoirs; or A Quick Glance at My Various Travels and My Sojourn in the Creek Nation.* Edited and translated by Ben C. McCary. Kennesaw, GA: Continental Book Co., 1959.

Mooney, James. *Myths of the Cherokees.* 7th Annual Report. Bureau of American Ethnology. Washington, DC: Government Printing Office, 1900.

Moser, Harold D., et al., eds. *The Papers of Andrew Jackson.* 7 volumes. Knoxville: University of Tennessee Press, 1980–2007.

———. *The Papers of Andrew Jackson, 1770–1845: A Microfilm Supplement.* 39 reels. Wilmington, DE: Scholarly Resources, 1986.

Norton, John. *The Journey of Major John Norton.* ed. by Carl F. Klink and James J. Talman. Vol. 46. Toronto: Champlain Society, 1920.

Nuñez, Theron A., Jr. "Creek Nativism and the Creek War of 1813–1814 [George Stiggins's manuscript]." *Ethnohistory* 5, no. 1 (1958): 1–47; 5, no. 2 (1958): 131–75; 5, no. 3 (1958): 292–301.

O'Callahan, E. B., et al., eds. Documents Relative to the Colonial History of the State of New York. 15 vols. Albany: Weed, Parsons, and Co., 1853–87.

Papers of Sir William Johnson. ed. by James Sullivan, et al. 14 vols. Albany: University of the State of New York, 1921–65.

Payne, John Howard, and Ethan Allen Hitchcock. *A Traveler in Indian Territory: The Journal of Ethan Allen Hitchcock.* Edited by Grant Foreman with a foreword by Michael D. Green. 1930. Reprint, Norman: University of Oklahoma Press, 1996.

Pope, John. *A Tour through the Southern and Western Territories of the United States of North-America.* Facsimile reproduction of the 1792 edition. Bicentennial Floridiana Facsimile Series. Gainesville: University Presses of Florida, 1979.

"Proceedings of Courts-Martial in the Creek War." *American Historical Magazine* 6 (July 1901): 251–59.

Reid, John, and John Henry Eaton. *The Life of Andrew Jackson.* Edited and with introduction by Frank L. Owsley Jr. Tuscaloosa: University of Alabama Press, 1976.

Report of the Committee on Military Affairs. *The Proceedings of a Court Martial Ordered for the Trial of Certain Tennessee Militiamen.* Report No. 140, House of Representatives, 20th Congress, 1st Session. Washington, DC: Gales and Seaton, 1828.

Romans, Bernard. *A Concise Natural History of East and West Florida.* Edited by Kathryn E. Holland Braund. New York, 1775. Reprint, Tuscaloosa: University of Alabama Press, 1999.

Ross, John. *The Papers of Chief John Ross.* Edited by Gary E. Moulton. 2 vols. Norman: University of Oklahoma Press, 1985.

Rowland, Dunbar, ed. *Mississippi Provincial Archives, English Dominion, 1763–1766: Letters and Enclosures to the Secretary of State from Major Robert Farmar and Governor George Johnstone.* Vol. 1. Nashville: Brandon Printing Co., 1911.

"Samuel Bains Letter." *Alabama Historical Quarterly* 19 (Fall/Winter 1957): 405–6.

Swan, Major Caleb. "Position and State of Manners and Arts in the Creek, or Muscogee Nation in 1791." In *Information Respecting the History, Condition, and Prospects of the Indian Tribes of the Unites States.* 6 Vols. Edited by Henry R. Schoolcraft, vol. 5, 251–83 Washington, DC: Government Printing Office, 1928.

Tatum, Major Howell. "Major Howell Tatum's Journal, While Acting Topographical Engineer (1814) To General Jackson, Commanding the Seventh Military District." Edited by John Spenser Bassett. *Smith College Studies in History* 7 (October 1921–April 1922): 5–138.

———. "Topographic Notes and Observations on the Alabama River, August, 1814." In *Transactions of the Alabama Historical Society,* vol. 2: *1897–1898,* edited by Peter J. Hamilton and Thomas M. Owen, 130–77. Tuscaloosa: Alabama Historical Society, 1898.

The Self-Vindication of Colonel William Martin, Against Certain Charges and Aspersions Made against Him by Gen. Andrew Jackson and Others, in Relation to Sundry Transactions if [sic] the Campaign against the Creeks. In the Year 1813. Nashville: John S. Simpson, 1829.

Von Reck, Philip Georg Friedrich. *Von Reck's Voyage: Drawings and Journal of Philip Georg Friedrich von Reck.* Edited by Kristian Hvidt. Savannah, GA: Beehive Press, 1980.

Waselkov, Gregory A., and Kathryn E. Holland Braund, eds. *William Bartram on the Southeastern Indians.* Lincoln: University of Nebraska Press, 1995.

Washburn, Wilcomb E., ed. *Garland Library of Narratives of North American Indian Captives.* 111 vols. New York: Garland Publishing, 1976–1983.

West, Elizabeth Howard, ed. "A Prelude to the Creek War of 1813–1814, in a Letter of John Innerarity to James Innerarity." *Florida Historical Quarterly* 18 (April 1940): 249–53.

White, Robert H., ed. *Messages of the Governors of Tennessee.* Vol. 1, 1796–1821. Nashville: Tennessee Historical Commission, 1952.

Willcox, Joseph Morgan. *A Narrative of the Life and Death of Lieutenant J. M. Willcox.* Marietta, OH: R. Prentise, 1816. Reprinted in *The Garland Library of Narratives of North American Indian Captives,* vol. 33, edited by Wilcomb E. Washburn. New York: Garland Publishing, 1978.

Williams, Samuel Cole, ed. *Early Travels in the Tennessee Country, 1540–1800.* 1928. Reprint, Nashville: Blue and Gray Press, 1972.

Woodward, Thomas S. *Woodward's Reminiscences of the Creek or Muscogee Indians.* American Old West Edition. Montgomery, AL: Barrett and Wimbish, 1859. Reprint, Mobile, AL: Southern University Press, 1965.

Wright, Marcus J. "The Battle of Tohopeka or Horse-Shoe: General Andrew Jackson's Original Report." *Magazine of American History* 19 (1888): 45–49.

Maps and Images

Bonar, William. "A Draught of the Creek Nation, made in 1757 by William Bonar." Great Britain National Archives [Public Record Office], London and Kew, C0700/Carolina 21.

"Caban de Conseille." Département des cartes et des plans, DE DD 2987 (8816) B. Bibliothèque nationale de France, Paris.

Cheatham, John. "Battle Map [of Horseshoe Bend], March 27, 1814." President William H. Harrison Papers, RG 77, Civil Works Map File, Misc. 11–2. National Archives and Records Administration, Washington, DC.

"General Jackson's campaign against the Creek Indians, 1813 & 1814." RG 77, Civil Works Map File, Misc. 11, 1813 & 1814. National Archives, Washington, DC.

Map of the War in South Alabama in 1813 and 1814. New York: Saxony and Major, 1849.

Melish, John. "For General Jackson's 1813–1815 Campaign Against the Creek Indians." In *A Military and Topographical Atlas of the United States; Including the British Possessions & Florida.* New York, 1815.

Price, Captain Philip M. "Map of the Coosa River from Lock No. 4 Ala. to Greensport, Ala." In *Annual Report, U.S. Engineer's Office, Corps of Engineers.* Montgomery, AL, 1890.

———. "Map of the Coosa River from Wetumpka, Ala. to Lock No. 4 Ala." In *Annual Report, U.S. Engineer's Office, Corps of Engineers,* Montgomery, AL, 1889.

Tarrant, Leonard. "Map of the Battle of Horseshoe Bend." Alabama Department of Archives and History, Montgomery, AL.

Newspapers and Periodicals

Augusta Chronicle. Augusta, GA.

Carthage Gazette. Carthage, TN.

Cherokee Advocate. Tahlequah, Cherokee Nation.

Clarion and Tennessee State Gazette. Nashville, TN.

Daily Dispatch. Richmond, VA.

Democratic Clarion. Nashville, TN.

Enquirer. Richmond, VA.

Halcyon Luminary and Theological Repository, New York, NY.

Montgomery Advertiser. Montgomery, AL.

Nashville Whig. Nashville, TN.

National Intelligencer. Washington, DC.

Niles Weekly Register. Baltimore, MD.

Pennsylvania Packet. Philadelphia, PA.

Secondary Sources

Agnew, Brad. "The Whale's Rifle." In "Notes and Documents." *Chronicles of Oklahoma* 56 (Winter 1978–1979): 472–77.

Albert, James Pickett. *History of Alabama, and Incidentally of Georgia and Mississippi, from the Earliest Period.* 1851. Reprint, Birmingham: Birmingham Book and Magazine Co., 1962.

American Battlefield Protection Program. *Report to Congress on the Historic Preservation of Revolutionary War and War of 1812 Sites in the United States.* Washington, DC: National Park Service, 2007.

Anderson, Fred, and Andrew Cayton. *The Dominion of War: Empire and Liberty in North America, 1500–2000.* New York: Viking, 2005.

Anderson, Gary Clayton. *The Indian Southwest, 1580—1830: Ethnogenesis and Reinvention.* Norman: University of Oklahoma. 1999.

———. *The Conquest of Texas: Ethnic Cleansing in the Promised Land, 1820–1875.* Norman: University of Oklahoma Press, 2005.

Babits, Lawrence E. "Military Records and Historical Archaeology." In *Documentary Archaeology in the New World,* ed. Mary C. Beaudry, 119–25. Cambridge: Cambridge University Press, 1988.

Baine, Rodney M. "The Myth of the Creek Pictograph." *Atlanta History* 32 (Summer 1988): 43–52.

Barnard, Susan K., and Grace M. Schwartzman. "Tecumseh and the Creek Indian War of 1813–1814 in North Georgia." *Georgia Historical Quarterly* 82 (Fall 1998): 489–506.

Bassett, John Spenser. *The Life of Andrew Jackson.* 1911. Reprint, Hamden, CT: Archon Books, 1967.

Birk, Douglas A., and Jeffrey J. Richner. "Things Left Behind: A Study of Selected Fur Trade Sites and Artifacts, Voyageur National Park, Environs, 2001–2002." US National Park Service, Midwestern Archaeological Center, Technical Report No. 84. Lincoln, NE, 2004.

Biographical and Historical memoirs of Mississippi, Embracing an Authentic and Comprehensive Account of the Chief Events in the History of the State and a Record of the Lives of Many of the Most Worthy and Illustrious Families and Individuals. 2 Vols. Chicago: Goodspeed Publishing, 1891.

Boom, Aaron M. "John Coffee, Citizen Soldier." *Tennessee Historical Quarterly* 22 (September 1963): 223–37.

Boyd, Mark F. "Events at Prospect Bluff on the Apalachicola River, 1808–1818: An Introduction to Twelve Letters of Edmund Doyle, Trader." *Florida Historical Quarterly* 16 (1937): 55–96.

Brain, Jeffrey P. *Tunica Treasure.* Papers of the Peabody Museum of Archaeology and Ethnology, Harvard University, Vol. 71. Cambridge, MA: Peabody Museum of Archaeology and Ethnology, 1979.

Brannon, Peter A. "Camp Mandaville." *Arrow Points, Monthly Bulletin of the Alabama Anthropological Society* 8 (March 1924): 48–49.

Brantley, W. H., Jr. *Battle of Horseshoe Bend in Tallapoosa County, Alabama, March 27, 1814.* N.p.: Horseshoe Bend Battle Park Association, 1955.

Brasser, Theodore. "War Clubs." *American Indian Tradition* 7 (1961): 77–83.

Braund, Kathryn E. Holland. "The Creek Indians, Blacks, and Slavery." *Journal of Southern History* 57 (November 1991): 601–36.

———. *Deerskins and Duffels: Creek Indian Trade with Anglo-America, 1685–1815.* Lincoln: University of Nebraska Press, 1993.

Brent, Joseph E. "A Visit to Fort Morgan: Mobile's Guardian on the Gulf." *Gulf Coast Historical Review* 3 (1987): 96–102.

Brewer, George E. "History of Coosa County, Part I." *Alabama Historic Quarterly* 4 (Spring 1942): 9–151.

———. "History of Coosa County, Part II." *Alabama Historic Quarterly* 4 (Summer 1942): 157–285.

Brooms, Bascom McDonald. *Archaeological Investigations at the Kennedy Mill Site: 1Ba301 in Baldwin County, Alabama.* Troy, AL: Troy State University, Archaeological Research Center, 1996.

Brooms, Bascom McDonald, and James W. Parker. *Fort Toulouse Phase III Completion Report.* Montgomery: Alabama Historical Commission, 1980.

Brose, David S., Ned J. Jenkins, and Russell Weisman, eds. *Cultural Resources Reconnaissance Study of the Black Warrior–Tombigbee System Corridor, Alabama.* Vol. 1: *Archaeology.* Report to the US Army Corps of Engineers. Mobile: University of South Alabama, Department of Geology and Geography, 1983.

Brown, John P. *Old Frontiers: The Story of the Cherokee Indians from Earliest Times to the Date of Their Removal to the West, 1838.* Kingsport, TN: Southern Publishers, 1938.

Brown, M. L. *Firearms in Colonial America: The Impact on History and Technology, 1492–1792.* Washington, DC: Smithsonian Institution Press, 1980.

Brown, Wilburt S. *The Amphibious Campaign for West Florida and Louisiana, 1814–1815.* Tuscaloosa: University of Alabama Press, 1969.

Bunn, Mike, and Clay Williams. *Battle for the Southern Frontier; The Creek War and the War of 1812.* Charleston: The History Press, 2008.

Burke, Lee. "18th Century English Trade Guns in the South, or the Carolina Gun, Its Time and Place." *Bulletin of American Society of Arms Collectors* 65 (September 1991): 2–16.

Burwick, Frederick. "Continental Sciences: British and Continental Thresholds." In *A Concise Companion to the Romantic Age.* Ed. by Jon Klancher, 168–88. Oxford: Wiley-Blackwell, 2009.

Calloway, Colin G. *The American Revolution in Indian Country: Crisis and Diversity in Native American Communities.* New York: Cambridge University Press, 1995.

Carnes, Linda F. "European Artifacts." In *Archaeological Investigations at Horseshoe Bend National Military Park, Alabama,* edited by Roy S. Dickens Jr., 149–65. Special Publication 3. Tuscaloosa: Alabama Archaeological Society, 1979.

Cave, Alfred A. *Prophets of the Great Spirit: Native American Revitalization Movements in Eastern North America.* Lincoln: University of Nebraska Press, 2006.

Chartrand, Rene. *Uniforms and Equipment of the United States Forces in the War of 1812.* Youngstown, NY.: Old Fort Niagara Association, 1992.

Chase, David W. *Fort Mitchell: An Archaeological Exploration in Russell County, Alabama.* Special Publication No. 1. Alabama Archaeological Society, 1974.

Chaudhuri, Jean, and Joyotpaul Chaudhuri. *A Sacred Path: The Way of the Muscogee Creeks.* Los Angeles: UCLA American Indian Studies Center, 2001.

Claiborne, J.F.H. *Life and Times of Gen. Sam Dale, The Mississippi Partisan.* New York: Harper & Brothers, 1860.

———. *Mississippi as a Province, Territory, and State, with Biographical Notices of Eminent Citizens.* 1880. Reprint, Spartanburg, SC: Reprint Company, 1978.

Coker, William S. "The Last Battle of the War of 1812: New Orleans. No, Fort Bowyer!" *Alabama Historical Quarterly* 43 (1981): 42–63.

Coker, William S., and Thomas D. Watson. *Southeastern Spanish Borderlands: Panton, Leslie & Company, and John Forbes & Company, 1783–1847.* Gainesville: University Press of Florida, 1986.

Coley, C. Jack. "The Battle of Horseshoe Bend." *Alabama Historical Quarterly* 14 (January 1952): 129–34.

Colyar, Arthur S. *Life and Times of Andrew Jackson: Soldier—Statesman—President.* 2 Vols. Nashville, TN: Press of Marshall & Bruce, 1904.

Corn, James F. *Red Clay and Rattlesnake Springs: A History of the Cherokee Indians of Bradley County, Tennessee.* Cleveland, TN: James Franklin Corn, 1984.

Cornelison, John E. "A Metal Detecting Survey of the Palisade Area at Horseshoe Bend National Military Park." National Park Service, Southeast Archaeological Center, Accession Number 1838, Tallahassee, Florida, 2006.

Cotterill, R. S. *The Southern Indians: The Story of the Civilized Tribes before Removal.* Norman: University of Oklahoma Press, 1977.

Cottier, John W. "An Analysis of the Fort Mitchell Features, Volume I." Draft manuscript, Archaeology Laboratory, Auburn University, 2004.

———. *Archaeological Survey Salvage Excavations in the Miller's Ferry Lock and Dam Reservoir.* Report to the National Park Service. Department of Anthropology, University of Alabama, 1968.

———. "Selected Preliminary Artifact Descriptions." In *Cataloguing and Documenting the Historic Creek Archaeological Collections of the Alabama Depart-*

ment of Archives and History, edited by Gregory A. Waselkov and Craig T. Sheldon Jr., 92–136. Report to the National Science Foundation, Grant Award #BNS-8507469, 1987.

Cottier, John W., and Craig T. Sheldon Jr. *Interim Report of an Archaeological Survey of U.S. Army Corps of Engineers Properties along the Alabama River.* Report to the US Army Corps of Engineers. Auburn, AL: Department of Anthropology, Auburn University, 1980.

———. "Last Tango on the Tallapoosa: The Tallassee Phase." Manuscript. Auburn, Archaeological Laboratory, Auburn University, 2007.

Covington, James W. "Migration into Florida of the Seminoles, 1700–1820." *Florida Historical Quarterly* 46 (1968): 340–57.

Cusick, James G. *The Other War of 1812: The Patriot War and the American Invasion of Spanish East Florida.* Gainesville: University Press of Florida, 2003.

Dean, Lewis S. "'Tecumseh's Prophesy': The Great New Madrid Earthquakes of 1811-1812 and 1843 in Alabama." Alabama Review 47 (July 1994): 163–71.

Deppisch, Ludwig M. "Andrew Jackson and American Medical Practice: Old Hickory and His Physicians." *Tennessee Historical Quarterly* 62 (Summer 2003): 131–51.

DeJarnette, David L., and Asael T. Hansen. *The Archaeology of the Childersburg Site.* Notes in Anthropology, No. 6. Tallahassee: Florida State University, 1960.

DeJarnette, David L., Edward B. Kurjack, and Bennie C. Keel. "Archaeological Investigations in the Weiss Reservoir of the Coosa River in Alabama." *Journal of Alabama Archaeology* 19 (1973): 1–201.

Dickens, Roy S., Jr. *Archaeological Investigations at Horseshoe Bend, National Military Park, Alabama.* Alabama Archaeological Society, Special Publication 3. Tuscaloosa: Alabama Archaeological Society, 1979.

Dickens, Roy S., Jr., and James H. Chapman. "Ceramic Patterning and Social Structure at Two Late Historic Upper Creek Sites in Alabama." *American Antiquity* 43, no. 3 (1978): 390–98.

Dickens, Roy S., Jr., Edward L. Prince, and Joseph L. Benthall. "Archaeological Investigations in the Jones Bluff Reservoir of the Alabama River." *Journal of Alabama Archaeology* 17, no. 1 (1971): 1–114.

Dimmick, Frederica R. "A Survey of Upper Creek Sites in Central Alabama." *Journal of Alabama Archaeology* 35 (1989): i–86.

Doherty, Herbert J., Jr. *Richard Keith Call: Southern Unionist.* Gainesville: University of Florida Press, 1961.

Dombhart, John Martin. *History of Walker County: Its Towns and Its Peoples.* Thornton, AR: Cayce Publishing, 1937.

Dowd, Gregory Evans. *A Spirited Resistance: The North American Indian Struggle for Unity, 1745–1815.* Johns Hopkins University Studies in Historical and Political Science. Baltimore: Johns Hopkins University Press, 1992.

Durham, Walter T. *James Winchester, Tennessee Pioneer.* Gallatin, TN: Sumner County Library Board, 1979.

DuVal, Kathleen. *The Native Ground Indians and Colonists in the Heart of the Continent.* Philadelphia: University of Pennsylvania Press, 2006.

Earnest, Tray G., McDonald Brooms, and Kate McLaurin-Wright. *A Cultural Resource Reconnaissance of Selected Portions of the Conecuh, Pea, and Choctawhatchee Rivers in Southeast Alabama.* Report to the Alabama Historical Commission. Troy, AL: Troy State University, Archaeological Research Center, 1995.

Edmunds, R. David. *The Shawnee Prophet.* Lincoln: University of Nebraska Press, 1983.

Elliot, Daniel T., Tracy M. Dean, W. Dean Wood, and Debra J. Wells. *Revolutionary War/War of 1812 Historic Preservation Study.* Report Submitted to the Cultural Resources GIS Facility, Preservation Initiatives Branch, Heritage Preservation Services, National Park Service. Ellerslie, GA: Southern Research, Historic Preservation Consultants, 2002.

Ethridge, Robbie. *Creek Country: The Creek Indians and Their World.* Chapel Hill: University of North Carolina Press, 2003.

Fairbanks, Charles H. "Excavations at Horseshoe Bend, Alabama." *Florida Anthropologist* 15 (1962): 41–55.

———. "The Function of Black Drink among the Creeks." In *Black Drink: A Native American Tea,* edited by Charles M. Hudson, 120–49. Athens: University of Georgia Press, 1979.

Folmsbee, Stanley J., and Anna Grace Catron. "Early Career of David Crockett." In *Houston and Crockett: Heroes of Tennessee and Texas: An Anthology,* edited by Herbert L. Harper, 132–57. Nashville: Tennessee Historical Commission, 1986.

Foster, H. Thomas, and Mary Theresa Bonhage-Freund. "Environmental Context." In *Archaeology of the Lower Muskogee Creek Indians, 1715–1836,* edited by H. Thomas Foster II, 26–36. Tuscaloosa: University of Alabama Press, 2007.

Foster, H. Thomas, II, ed. *Archaeology of the Lower Muskogee Creek Indians, 1715–1836.* Tuscaloosa: University of Alabama Press, 2007.

Frank, Andrew. *Creeks and Southerners: Biculturalism on the Early American Frontier.* Lincoln: University of Nebraska Press, 2005.

Fuller, Claude E. *Springfield Shoulder Arms: 1795–1865.* Glendale, NY: S & S Firearms, 1986.

Fuller, Myron L. *The New Madrid Earthquake.* 1912. Reprint, Washington, D.C.: Government Printing Office, 1992.

Galloway, Patricia. *Choctaw Genesis, 1500–1700.* Lincoln: University of Nebraska Press, 1995.

Gatchet, Albert S. *A Migration Legend of the Creek Indians, with a Linguistic,*

Historic, and Ethnographic Introduction. Vol. 1. Brinton's Library of Aboriginal Literature, Number 4. Philadelphia: D. G. Brinton, 1884.

Gaynor, Jay, "Mr. Hewlett's Tool Chest—Part II." In *Selections from the Chronicle,* edited by Emil Pollak and Martyl Pollak, 293–306. Mendham, NJ: Astragal Press, 1991.

"Georgia Forts: The Fort at Standing Peachtree." *Georgia Magazine* 10 (December 1966–January 1967): 21–23.

Gilbert, Ed. *Frontier Militiaman in the War of 1812: Southwestern Frontier.* New York: Osprey Publishing Co., 2008.

Gipson, L. H., ed. *Moravian Mission on White River.* Indianapolis: Indiana Historical Society, 1938.

Good, Mary Elizabeth. "Guebert Site: An 18th Century Historic Kaskasia Indian Village." In *The Central State Archaeological Societies, Memoir II,* 1972. St. Louis, MO: Central States Archaeological Societies, 1972.

Graham, Bennett. "A Preliminary Report of Salvage Archaeology in the Claiborne Lock and Dam Reservoir." Report to the National Park Service, Department of Anthropology, Tuscaloosa, AL: University of Alabama, 1967.

Green, Michael D. *The Politics of Indian Removal: Creek Government and Society in Crisis.* Lincoln: University of Nebraska Press, 1982.

Grenier, John. *The First Way of War: American War Making on the Frontier, 1607–1814.* New York: Cambridge University Press, 2005.

Griffin, Benjamin W., Jr. *McIntosh and Weatherford: Creek Indian Leaders.* Tuscaloosa: University of Alabama Press, 1969.

Griffin, Patrick. *American Leviathan: Empire, Nation, and Revolutionary Frontier.* New York: Hill & Wang, 2007.

Hahn, Steven C. *The Invention of the Creek Nation, 1670–1763.* Lincoln: University of Nebraska Press, 2004.

Halbert, Henry S. "The Creek Red Stick," *Alabama Historical Reporter* 2 (May 1884): n.p.

———. "Ensign Issac Davis and Hanson's Mill." *Gulf States Historical Magazine* 1 (September 1902): 151.

———. "Some Inaccuracies in Claiborne's History in Regard to Tecumseh." *Publications of the Mississippi Historical Society* 1 (1898): 101–3

Halbert, Henry S., and Timothy H. Ball. *The Creek War of 1813–1814.* Southern Historical Publications 15, edited by Frank L. Owsley Jr. 1895. Reprint, Tuscaloosa: University of Alabama Press, 1969.

Hall, Arthur H. "The Red Stick War: Creek Indian Affairs during the War of 1812." *Chronicles of Oklahoma* 12 (1934): 264–93.

Hämäläinen, Pekka, *The Comanche Empire.* New Haven: Yale University Press, 2008.

Hamilton, T. M. *Colonial Frontier Guns.* Chadron, NE: Fur Press, 1980.

Harper, Roland M. *Forests of Alabama.* Monograph 10. Tuscaloosa: Geological Survey of Alabama, 1943.

———. *Natural Resources of the Tennessee Valley Region in Alabama.* Special Report 17. Tuscaloosa: Geological Survey of Alabama, 1942.

———. *Resources of Southern Alabama.* Special Report 11. Tuscaloosa: Geological Survey of Alabama, 1920.

Harris, Donald A., and Jerry J. Nielsen. *Archaeological Salvage Investigations at the Site of the French Fort Conde, Mobile, Alabama. A final report in fulfillment of Contract No. I-10–1(3) Tunnel Plaza Interchange Archaeological Agreement Between the Alabama Highway Department and the University of Alabama.* University: University of Alabama, 1972.

Hatley, Thomas. "The Eighteenth-Century Tallapoosa Landscape Revisited." In *Archaeological Excavations at the Early Historic Creek Indian Town of Fusihatchee (Phase 1, 1988–1989),* edited by Gregory A. Waselkov, John W. Cottier, and Craig T. Sheldon Jr., 77–107. Final Report to the National Science Foundation (BNS-8718934). Auburn, AL: Auburn University, 1990.

Heidler, David S., and Jeanne T. Heidler. *Encyclopedia of the War of 1812.* Annapolis, MD: Naval Institute Press, 1989.

———. *Old Hickory's War: Andrew Jackson and the Quest for Empire.* Baton Rouge: Louisiana State University Press, 2003.

Heldman, Donald P. "Archaeological Investigations of Fort Toulouse: 1972–1973." Report to the Alabama Historical Commission and National Park Service, Montgomery, 1973.

———. "Archaeological Investigations of Fort Toulouse: 1973–1974." Report to the Alabama Historical Commission and National Park Service, Montgomery, 1976.

Hewitt, J. N. B. "Notes of the Creek Indians." *Smithsonian Institution Bureau of American Ethnology, Bulletin 123* (1939): 123–59.

Holland, James W. "Andrew Jackson and the Creek War: Victory at the Horseshoe." *Alabama Review* 21 (October 1968): 243–75.

Holstein, Harry. "Excavations at Tallishatchee (1CN162)." Field notes. Jacksonville University Archaeological Laboratory.

Hopewell, Clifford. *Sam Houston: Man of Destiny.* Austin, TX: Eakin Press, 1987.

Hothem, Lar. *Indian Trade Relics.* Paducah, KY: Collector Books, 2005.

Howard, James H. *The Southeastern Ceremonial Complex and Its Interpretation.* Memoir of the Missouri Archaeological Society, Number 6. Stillwater: Oklahoma State University, 1968.

Howard, James H., and Willie Lena. *Oklahoma Seminoles: Medicines, Magic, and Religion.* Norman: University of Oklahoma Press, 1984.

Jackson, Harvey H., III. *Rivers of History: Life on the Coosa, Tallapoosa, Cahaba, and Alabama.* Tuscaloosa: University of Alabama Press, 1995.

James, Marquis. *The Raven: A Biography of Sam Houston.* 1929. Reprint, Austin: University of Texas Press, 1994.

Jenkins, Ned J., and Cyril B. Mann. "An Archaeological Survey of the Conecuh Drainage." *Florida Anthropologist* 38 (1–2): 136–43.

Jenkins, Ned J., and Teresa A. Paglione. "An Archaeological Reconnaissance of the Lower Alabama River." Manuscript report to the Alabama Historical Commission, Department of Sociology, Auburn University, Montgomery, 1980.

Jenkins, Ned. J., and Craig T. Sheldon Jr. "Field Records, Excavations at Couloumee (1MT3)." Archaeological Laboratory, Auburn University, Montgomery, 1983.

Jenkins, William H. "Alabama Forts, 1700–1838." *Alabama Review* 12 (July 1959): 163–79.

Jung, Patrick J. *The Black Hawk War of 1832.* Norman: University of Oklahoma Press, 2007.

Kanon, Thomas. "'A Slow, Laborious Slaughter': The Battle of Horseshoe Bend." *Tennessee Historical Quarterly* 58 (Spring 1999): 2–15.

Kanon, Tom. "'Glories in the Field': John Cocke vs. Andrew Jackson during the War of 1812." *Journal of Tennessee History* 71 (1999): 47–65.

———. "The Kidnapping of Martha Crawley and Settler-Indian Relations Prior to the War of 1812." Tennessee Historical Quarterly 64 (Spring 2005): 3–23.

Kennedy, Thomas C. "Sibling Stewards of a Commercial Empire: The Innerarity Brothers in the Floridas." *Florida Historical Quarterly* 67 (1989): 259–89.

Knight, Vernon James, Jr., ed. *Archaeological Survey and Excavations in the Coosa River Valley.* Bulletin no. 15. Tuscaloosa: Alabama Museum of Natural History, 1993.

———. "Black Warrior Town, Phase I." Report of Investigations No. 33, Office of Archaeological Research, Moundville, AL, 1982.

———. "Cultural Complexes of the Alabama Piedmont: An Initial Statement." *Journal of Alabama Archaeology* 16 (1980): 1–27.

———. "Fort Leslie and Upper Creek Ceramics of the Early Nineteenth Century." *Journal of Alabama Archaeology* 43 (1997): 35–47.

———. "Introduction: Archaeological Research in the Middle Coosa Valley, Alabama." In *Archaeological Survey and Excavations in the Coosa River Valley,* edited by Vernon James Knight Jr., 1–5. Bulletin no. 15. Tuscaloosa: Alabama Museum of Natural History, 1993.

———. *Tuckabatchee: Archaeological Investigations at an Historic Creek Town, Elmore County, Alabama.* Report of Investigations no. 45. Tuscaloosa: University of Alabama, Office of Archaeological Research, 1985.

Knight, Vernon J., Jr., Gloria G. Cole, and Richard Walling. *An Archaeological Reconnaissance of the Coosa and Tallapoosa River Valleys, East Alabama.* Report of Investigations 43. Tuscaloosa: Office of Archaeological Research, University of Alabama, 1983.

Knight, Vernon James, Jr., and John O'Hear. *Archaeological Investigations in the Rother L. Harris Reservoir: 1975.* Report to the Alabama Power Company. Tuscaloosa: Office of Archaeological Research, University of Alabama, 1975.

Lackey, Richard S., comp. *Frontier Claims in the Lower South.* Introduction by John S. W. Guice. New Orleans: Polyanthos, 1977.

Lolley, Terry L. "Ethnohistory and Archaeology: A Map Method for Locating Historic Upper Creek Indian Towns and Villages." *Journal of Alabama Archaeology* 42 (June 1996): 1–96.

Lossing, Benson John. "War with the Creek Indians (War of 1812)." *Harper's New Monthly Magazine* 28 (April 1864): 598–616.

Mackenzie, George C. *The Indian Breastwork in the Battle of Horseshoe Bend: Its Size, Location, and Construction.* Washington, DC: US Department of Interior, Office of Archaeology and Historic Preservation, 1969.

Mahon, John K. "British Strategy and Southern Indians, War of 1812." *Florida Historical Quarterly* 44 (April 1965–1966): 285–302.

Maiden, Leota Driver. "Colonel John Williams." *East Tennessee Historical Society Publications* 30 (1958): 7–46.

Mainfort, Robert C., Jr. *Indian Social Dynamics in the Period of European Contact: Fletcher Site Cemetery, Bay County.* Publications of the Museum, Michigan State University, Anthropological Series, vol. 1, no. 4. East Lansing: Michigan State University Press, 1979.

Maltby, William S. *The Rise and Fall of the Spanish Empire.* Basingstoke, Hamps.: Palgrave Macmillan, 2009.

Martin, Joel W. "The Creek Prophetic Movement." *Alabama Heritage,* no. 23 (Winter 1992): 4–13.

———. *Sacred Revolt: The Muskogees' Struggle for a New World.* Boston, MA: Beacon Press, 1991.

Martin, Will I. "Horizons and Festivals of Cherokee County, Alabama." In *Bits and Pieces of the Heritage,* edited by Estell S. Smith. Centre, AL: Coosa Printing, 1976.

Mason, Carol I. *The Archaeology of Ocmulgee Old Field, Macon, Georgia.* Tuscaloosa: University of Alabama Press, 2005.

Mason, Ronald J. *Rock Island: Historic Indian Archaeology in the Northern Lake Michigan Basin.* Midcontinental Journal of Archaeology Special Paper 6. Kent, OH: Kent State University Press, 1986.

McIlwaine, Finley. "The Horse Shoe." *Tennessee Valley Historical Review* 2 (Fall 1973): 2–11.

McKenney, Thomas L., and James Hall. *History of the Indian Tribes of North*

America, with Biographical Sketches and Anecdotes of the Principal Chiefs. 3 Vols. Ed. by Frederick Webb Hodge. Reprint, Edinburgh: John Grant, 1933–34.

———. *History of the Indian Tribes of North America.* 3 vols. 1836–1844. Reprint, Totowa: Rowman and Littlefield, 1972.

McLoughlin, William G. "The Cherokee Ghost Dance Movement." In *The Cherokee Ghost Dance: Essays on the Southeastern Indians, 1789–1861,* ed. William G. McLoughlin, 111–152. Macon: Mercer, 1984.

———. *Cherokee Renascence in the New Republic.* Princeton: Princeton University Press, 1986.

Meek, Alexander Beaufort. *The Red Eagle: A Poem of the South.* New York and Mobile: D. Appleton, S. H. Goetzel, 1855.

———. *Romantic Passages in Southwestern History.* New York: S. H. Goetzel, 1857.

Mercer, Henry C. *Ancient Carpenters' Tools.* Mineola, NY: Dover Publications, 2000.

Miles, Tiya. *Ties That Bind: The Story of an Afro-Cherokee Family in Slavery and Freedom.* Berkeley: University of California Press, 2005.

Monette, John W. *History of the Discovery and Settlement of the Mississippi Valley.* New York: Harper & Brothers, 1848.

Mooney, James . *The Ghost Dance and the Sioux Outbreak of 1890.* Edited by Raymond J. DeMallie. 1896, Reprint. Lincoln: University of Nebraska Press, 1991.

Morrell, L. Ross. *The Woods Island Site in Southeastern Acculturation, 1625–1800.* Notes in Anthropology 11. Tallahassee: Florida State University, 1965.

Mueller, Diane S. "Intrasite Settlement at the Historic Creek Town of Hickory Ground (1EE89), Elmore County, Alabama (1990–1991)." *Journal of Alabama Archaeology* 41 (December 1995): 107–36.

Neumann, George C., and Frank J. Kravic. *Collector's Illustrated Encyclopedia of the American Revolution.* Texarkana, TX: Rebel Press, 1989.

O'Brien, Sean Michael. *In Bitterness and Tears: Andrew Jackson's Destruction of the Creeks and Seminoles.* Westport, CT: Praeger, 2003.

Oakley, Carey B., and V. Stephen Jones. "Investigations at Fort Strother Cemetery (Site 1Sc 66), St. Clair County, Alabama." Report to the Alabama Historical Commission. Office of Archaeological Services, Moundville, AL, 2000.

Oakley, Carey B., and G. Michael Watson. *Cultural Resources Inventory of the Jones Bluff Lake, Alabama River, Alabama.* Report of Investigation No. 4. Tuscaloosa: University of Alabama, Office of Archaeological Research, 1977.

Olsen, Susan C., Noel R. Stowe, and Marvin Hoyt. *Archaeological Investigations at Fort Mims.* Archaeological Completion Report Series, Number 4, Division of Grants, Office of Archaeology and Historic Preservation. Washington, DC: National Park Service, 1975.

Opler, Morris E. "The Creek 'Town' and the Problem of Creek Indian Political Reorganization." In *Human Problems of Technological Change: A Casebook,* edited by Edward W. Spicer, 165–80. New York: Russell Sage Foundation, 1952.

Owsley, Frank L., Jr. "British and Indian Activities in Spanish West Florida during the War of 1812." *Florida Historical Quarterly* 46 (October 1967): 111–23.

———. "The Fort Mims Massacre." *Alabama Review* 24 (1971): 192-204.

———. "Jackson's Capture of Pensacola." *Alabama Review* 19 (July 1966): 175–85.

———. "Prophet of War: Francis and the Creek War." *American Indian Quarterly* 9 (Summer 1985): 273–93.

———. *Struggle for the Gulf Borderlands: The Creek War and the Battle of New Orleans, 1812–1815.* Gainesville: University Presses of Florida, 1981.

Owsley, Frank L., Jr., and Gene A. Smith. *Filibusters and Expansionists: Jeffersonian Manifest Destiny, 1800–1821.* Tuscaloosa: University of Alabama Press, 1997.

Paredes, J. Anthony, Jr. "Creek in the East since Removal." In *Handbook of North American Indians,* vol. 14: *Southeast,* edited by Raymond D. Fogelson, 404–6. Washington, DC: Smithsonian Institution, 2004.

———. ed. "Federal Recognition and the Poarch Creek Indians." *Indians of the Southeastern United States in the Late Twentieth Century.* Tuscaloosa: University of Alabama Press, 1992.

Parker, James W. "Fort Jackson after the War of 1812." *Alabama Review* 38 (April 1985): 119–30.

———. "Fort Strother." In *An Intensive Phase II Cultural Resources Survey of Selected Areas on the Coosa River Navigation Project,* vol. 2, edited by Tim Mistovich, 51–54. Report of Investigation No. 32. Tuscaloosa: University of Alabama, Office of Archaeological Research, 1981.

———. "Investigations Relative to the 19th Century Tensaw Military Frontier in Southwest Alabama." In *Archaeology in Southwestern Alabama: A Collection of Papers,* edited by Cailup B. Curren, 147–54. Camden: Alabama Tombigbee Regional Commission, 1982.

Parkman, Francis. *The Conspiracy of Pontiac and the Indian War after the Conquest of Canada.* 6th Ed. 2 Vols. 1851. Reprint, Boston: Charles C. Little and James Brown, 1870.

Parton, James. *Life of Andrew Jackson.* 3 vols. 1866. Reprint, New York: Johnson Reprint, 1967.

Penick, James L., Jr. "I Will Stamp on the Ground with My Foot and Shake Down Every House," *American Heritage* 27 (1975): 82–87.

———. The New Madrid Earthquakes. 1976. Reprint, Columbia: University of Missouri Press, 1981.

Perdue, Theda. *Mixed-Blood Indians: Racial Construction in the Early South.* Athens: University of Georgia Press, 2003.

Perdue, Theda, and Michael D. Green. *The Columbia Guide to American Indians of the Southeast.* New York: Columbia University Press, 2001.

Peterson, Harold L. *American Indian Tomahawks.* Contributions from the Museum of the American Indian, Heye Foundation, 19. New York: Heye Foundation, 1971.

Pickett, Albert James. *History of Alabama and Incidentally of Georgia and Mississippi from the Earliest Period.* Birmingham: Birmingham and Magazine Co., 1962.

———. *History of Alabama and Incidentally of Georgia and Mississippi from the Earliest Period.* 1851. Reprint, Montgomery, AL: River City Publishing, 2003.

Piker, Joshua. *Okfuskee: A Creek Indian Town in Colonial America.* Cambridge, MA: Harvard University Press, 2004.

Pitcavage, Mark. "Ropes of Sand: Territorial Militias, 1801–1812." *Journal of the Early Republic* 13 (Winter 1993): 481–500.

Quimby, George Irving. *Indian Culture and European Trade Goods.* Madison: University of Wisconsin Press, 1966.

Reid, John, and John Henry Eaton. *The Life of Andrew Jackson: Major General in the Service of the United States: Comprising a History of the War in the South, from the Commencement of the Creek Campaign, to the Termination of Hostilities before New Orleans.* Southern Historical Publications 19. Edited by Frank Lawrence Owsley Jr. 1817. Reprint, Tuscaloosa: University of Alabama Press, 1974.

Reilly, Robert M. *United States Martial Flintlocks.* Lincoln, RI: Andrew Mobray, 1997.

Remini, Robert V. *Andrew Jackson and His Indian Wars.* New York: Viking Penguin, 2001.

———. *Andrew Jackson and the Course of American Empire, 1767–1821.* 3 vols. New York: Harper and Row, 1977–1984.

Ricketts, Robert. "The Men and the Ships of the British Attack on Fort Bowyer—February 1815." *Gulf Coast Historical Review* 5 (1990): 7–17.

Rogin, Michael Paul. *Fathers and Children: Andrew Jackson and the Subjugation of the American Indian.* New York: Alfred A. Knopf, 1975.

Royster, Judith. "Indian Land Claims." In *Handbook of North American Indians,* vol. 2: *Indians in Contemporary Society,* edited by Garrick A. Bailey, 28–37. Washington, DC: Smithsonian Institution, 2008.

Rucker, Brian R. "In the Shadow of Jackson: Uriah Blue's Expedition into West Florida." *Florida Historical Quarterly* 73 (January 1995): 325–38.

Russell, Carl P. *Guns on the Early Frontiers.* Lincoln: University of Nebraska Press, 1980.

Sapp, C. Daniel, and Jacques Emplaincourt. *Physiographic Regions of Alabama, Map 168.* Tuscaloosa: Geological Survey of Alabama, 1975.

Saunt, Claudio. *Black, White, and Indian: Race and the Unmaking of an American Family.* Oxford, UK: Oxford University Press, 2005.

———. *A New Order of Things: Property, Power, and the Transformation of the Creek Indians, 1733–1816.* Cambridge: Cambridge University Press, 1999.

Sayre, Gordon M. *The Indian Chief as Tragic Hero: Native Resistance and the Literatures of America, from Moctezuma to Tecumseh.* Chapel Hill: UNC Press, 2005.

Schwartzman, Grace M., and Susan K. Barnard. "A Trail of Broken Promises: Georgians and Muscogee/Creek Treaties, 1796–1826." *Georgia Historical Quarterly* 75 (Winter 1991): 697–718.

Scott, H. M. *The Birth of a Great Power System, 1740–1815.* Harlow, England: Pearson Longman, 2005.

Sewall, Lewis. *The Miscellaneous Poems of Lewis Sewall.* Mobile, AL, 1833.

Shackford, James Atkins, ed. *David Crockett: The Man, the Legend.* 1956. Reprint, Lincoln, NE: Bison Books, 1994.

Sheldon, Craig T., Jr. "Historic Creek 'Summer' Houses of Central Alabama." Paper presented at the 64th annual meeting of the Society for American Archaeology, Nashville, TN, 1997.

———. "The Present State of Archaeological Survey and Site File Data for the Alabama River and Adjacent Regions." In *The Search for Mabila: The Decisive Battle between Hernando de Soto and Chief Tascalusa,* edited by Vernon James Knight Jr., 107–28. Tuscaloosa: University of Alabama Press, 2006.

———. "Public Architecture of the Historic Upper Creeks." Paper presented at the 47th annual Southeastern Archaeological Conference, Mobile, AL, 1991.

Sheldon, Craig T., Jr., John W. Cottier, and Gregory A. Waselkov. "A Preliminary Report on the Subsurface Testing of a Portion of the Creek Indian Property at Hickory." Auburn University at Montgomery, 1988. Manuscript on file, Alabama Historical Commission, Montgomery, AL.

Silver, Peter. *Our Savage Neighbors: How Indian War Transformed Early America.* New York: W. W. Norton & Company, 2008.

Skeen, C. Edward. *Citizen Soldiers in the War of 1812.* Lexington: University of Kentucky Press, 1999.

Smith, Gene A. "'Our Flag was Display'd within Their Works': The Treaty of Ghent and the Conquest of Mobile." *Alabama Review* 52 (January 1999): 3–20.

Smith, Marvin T. "Aboriginal Population Movements in the Early Historic Interior Southeast." In *Powhatan's Mantle: Indians in the Colonial Southeast,* edited by Gregory A. Waselkov, Peter H. Wood, and Tom Hatley, 43–56. Rev. ed. Lincoln: University of Nebraska Press, 2006.

———. *Archaeology and Aboriginal Culture Change in the Interior Southeast: Depopulation during the Early Historic Period.* Gainesville: University Presses of Florida/Florida State Museum, 1987.

———. "Seventeenth-Century Aboriginal Settlement on the Coosa River." In *Archaeological Survey and Excavations in the Coosa River Valley, Alabama,* edited by Vernon James Knight Jr., 63–70. Bulletin no. 15. Tuscaloosa: Alabama Museum of Natural History, 1993.

———. "Woods Island Revisited." *Journal of Alabama Archaeology* 41 (1995): 93–106.

Snyder, Christina. *Slavery in Indian Country: The Changing Face of Captivity in Early America.* Cambridge, MA: Harvard University Press, 2010.

Southerland, Henry DeLeon, Jr., and Jerry Elijah Brown. *The Federal Road through Georgia, the Creek Nation, and Alabama, 1806–1836.* Tuscaloosa: University of Alabama Press, 1989.

Stanley, John Mix. *Portraits of North American Indians, with Sketches of Scenery. Painted by J. M. Stanley, Deposited with the Smithsonian Institution.* Washington, DC: Smithsonian Institution, 1852.

Starr, Emmet. *History of the Cherokee Indians and Their Legends and Folk Lore.* Edited by Dorothy Tincup Mauldin. 1921. Reprint, Muskogee: Oklahoma Yesterday Publications, 1979. Special Edition, Muskogee, OK: Hoffman Printing, 1984.

Stone, Lyle M. *Fort Michilimackinac, 1715–1781: An Archaeological Perspective on the Revolutionary Frontier.* East Lansing: Publications of the Michigan State University Museum, Michigan State University, 1974.

Sugden, John. "Early Pan-Indianism: Tecumseh's Tour of the Indian Country, 1811–1812." *American Indian Quarterly* 10 (Fall 1986): 273–304.

———. "The Southern Indians in the War of 1812: The Closing Phase." *Florida Historical Quarterly* (January 1982): 273–312.

———. *Tecumseh: A Life.* New York: Henry Holt and Company, 1998.

———. "Tecumseh's Travels Revisited." *Indiana Magazine of History* 96 (June 2000): 151–68.

Swanton, John R. *Early History of the Creek Indians and Their Neighbors.* Bureau of American Ethnology Bulletin no. 73. Washington, DC: Government Printing Office, 1922.

———. *Modern Square Grounds of the Creek Indians.* Smithsonian Miscellaneous Collections, vol. 85, no. 8. Washington, DC: Smithsonian Institution, 1931.

———. *Social Organization and Social Usages of the Indians of the Creek Confederacy.* Bureau of American Ethnology Bulletin no. 42. Washington, DC: Government Printing Office, 1928. Reprint, New York: Johnson Reprint Co., 1970.

Taylor, Colin F. *Native American Weapons.* Norman: University of Oklahoma Press, 2001.

Thomason, Hugh M. "Governor Peter Early and the Creek Indian Frontier, 1813–1815." *Georgia Historical Quarterly* 45 (September 1961): 223–37.

Thornton, Russell. *American Indian Holocaust and Survival: A Population History since 1492.* Norman: University of Oklahoma Press, 1987.

Tucker, Glenn. *Tecumseh: Vision of Glory.* Indianapolis: Bobbs Merrill, 1956.

Vogel, Virgil J. *American Indian Medicine.* Norman: University of Oklahoma Press, 1970.

Walker, Willard B. "Creek Confederacy before Removal." In *Handbook of North American Indians,* edited by William C. Sturtevant. Vol. 14: *Southeast,* edited by Raymond D. Fogelson, 373–92. Washington, DC: Smithsonian Institution, 2004.

Walker, William A., Jr. "Martial Sons: Tennessee Enthusiasm for the War of 1812." *Tennessee Historical Quarterly* 20 (March 1961): 20–37.

Warshauer, Matthew. *Andrew Jackson and the Politics of Martial Law: Nationalism, Civil Liberties, and Partisanship.* Knoxville: University of Tennessee Press, 2006.

Waselkov, Gregory A. "Changing Strategies of Indian Field Location in the Early Historic Southeast." In *People, Plants, and Landscapes: Studies in Paleoethnobotany,* edited by Kristen J. Gremillion, 179–94. Tuscaloosa: University of Alabama Press, 1997.

———. *A Conquering Spirit: Fort Mims and the Redstick War of 1813–1814.* Tuscaloosa: University of Alabama Press, 2006.

———, ed. *Coosa Valley Archaeology.* Vols. 1 and 2. Auburn University Archaeological Monograph 2. Auburn, AL: Auburn University, 1980.

———, ed. *Culture Change on the Creek Indian Frontier.* Final Report to the National Science Foundation (BNS-8305437). Auburn, AL: Auburn University, 1985.

———. "The Eighteenth-Century Anglo-Indian Trade in Southeastern North America." In *New Faces of the Fur Trade: Selected Papers of the Seventh American Fur Trade Conference,* edited by JoAnn Fiske, Susan Sleeper Smith, and William Wicker, 193–222. East Lansing: Michigan State University Press, 1998.

———, ed. *Fort Toulouse Studies.* Auburn University Archaeological Monograph 9. Auburn, AL: Auburn University, 1984.

———. "Introduction: Recent Archaeological and Historical Research." In *Fort Toulouse: The French Outpost at the Alabamas on the Coosa,* by Daniel H. Thomas, vii–xlii. Tuscaloosa: University of Alabama Press. 1989.

———. "Lower Tallapoosa River Cultural Resources Survey, Phase I Survey."

Manuscript report to the Alabama Historical Commission. Auburn University, Auburn, AL, 1981.

———. "A Reinterpretation of the Creek Indian Barricade at Horseshoe Bend." *Journal of Alabama Archaeology* 32 (1986): 94–107.

———. "Return to Holy Ground: The Legendary Battle Site Discovered." *Alabama Heritage*, no. 101 (Summer 2011): 28–37.

———. "Wear and Reuse of European Artifacts." In *Culture Change on the Creek Indian Frontier*, edited by Gregory A. Waselkov, 83–120. Final Report to the National Science Foundation (BNS-8305437). Auburn, AL: Auburn University, 1985.

Waselkov, Gregory A., and John W. Cottier. "European Perceptions of Eastern Creek Ethnicity." In *Proceedings of the Tenth Meeting of the French Colonial Historical Society*, edited by Philip Boucher, 23–45. Lanham, MD: University Press of America, 1985.

Waselkov, Gregory A., John W. Cottier, and Craig T. Sheldon. *Archaeological Excavations at the Early Historic Creek Indian Town of Fusihatchee (Phase 1, 1988–1989).* Final Report to the National Science Foundation (BNS-8718934). Auburn, AL: Auburn University, 1990.

Waselkov, Gregory A., and Bonnie L. Gums. *Plantation Archaeology at Rivière aux Chiens, ca. 1725–1848.* University of South Alabama Archaeological Monograph 7. Mobile: University of South Alabama, 2000.

Waselkov, Gregory A., Bonnie L. Gums, and James W. Parker. *Archaeology at Fort Mims: Excavation Contexts and Artifact Catalog.* University of South Alabama Archaeological Monograph 12. Mobile: University of South Alabama, 2006.

Waselkov, Gregory A., and Marvin T. Smith. "Upper Creek Archaeology." In *Indians of the Greater Southeast: Historical Archaeology and Ethnohistory*, edited by Bonnie G. McEwan, 242–64. Gainesville: University Press of Florida, 2000.

Waselkov, Gregory A., and Brian M. Wood. "The Creek War of 1813–1814: Effects on Creek Society and Settlement Pattern." *Journal of Alabama Archaeology* 32 (June 1986): 1–24.

Waselkov, Gregory A., Brian M. Wood, and Joseph M. Herbert. *Colonization and Conquest: The 1980 Archaeological Excavations at Fort Toulouse and Fort Jackson, Alabama.* Auburn University Archaeological Monograph 4. Montgomery: Auburn University at Montgomery, 1982.

West, Elizabeth Howard. "A Prelude to the Creek War of 1813–1814, in a Letter of John Innerarity to James Innerarity." *Florida Historical Quarterly* 18 (1940): 249–53.

White, Richard. *The Middle Ground: Indians, Empires, and Republics in the Great Lakes Region, 1650–1815*. New York: Cambridge University Press, 1991.

Wilkins, Thurman. *Cherokee Tragedy: The Ridge Family and the Decimation of a People*. Civilization of the American Indian, no. 169. 2nd ed., rev. 1970. Reprint, Norman: University of Oklahoma Press, 1986.

Witgen, Michael. "The Rituals of Possession: Native Identity and the Invention of Empire in Seventeenth-Century Western North America." *Ethnohistory* 54 (2007): 639–68.

Wright, Amos J., Jr. *Historic Indian Towns in Alabama, 1540–1838*. Tuscaloosa: University of Alabama Press, 2003.

Wright, J. Leitch, Jr. *Creeks and Seminoles: The Destruction and Regeneration of the Muscogulge People*. Lincoln: University of Nebraska Press, 1986.

Dissertations and Theses

Akers, Frank H., Jr. "The Unexpected Challenge: The Creek War of 1813–1814." PhD diss., Duke University, 1975.

Larson, Lewis H., Jr. "Aboriginal Subsistence Technology on the Southeastern Coastal Plain during the Late Prehistoric Period." PhD diss., University of Michigan, 1969.

Pate, James P. "The Chickamauga: A Forgotten Segment of Indian Resistance on the Southern Frontier." PhD diss., University of Mississippi, 1969.

Perry, Robert Earl. "The Historical Significance of the Creek War of 1813–1814, Land Use and Archaeology of Fort Strother in St. Clair County, Alabama." MA thesis, Jacksonville State University, Alabama, 2004.

Ruff, Rowena McClinton. "To Ascertain the Mind and Circumstances of the Cherokee Nation: Springplace, Georgia, 1805–1821." MA thesis, Western Carolina University, 1992.

Van Horne, Wayne. "The Warclub: Weapon and Symbol in Southeastern Indian Societies." PhD diss., University of Georgia, 1993.

Internet Sources

Encyclopedia of Alabama. http://www.encyclopediaofalabama.org/face/Home.jsp (accessed May 26, 2011).

Galileo Digital Library of Georgia. Southeastern Native American Documents, 1730–1842. http://neptune3.galib.uga.edu/ssp/cgi-bin/ftaccess.cgi?_id=7f000001&dbs=ZLNA (accessed May 26, 2011).

Kanon, Tom. "Regimental Histories of Tennessee Units during the War of 1812." Tennessee State Library and Archives, Nashville, TN. http://www.tennessee.gov/tsla/history/military/1812reg.htm (accessed February 10, 2007).

Lincoln, Abraham. "House Divided Speech: June 16, 1858." *Abraham Lincoln*

Online. http://showcase.netins.net/web/creative/lincoln/speeches/house.htm (accessed July 14, 2009).

Pulleyn, William. *Etymological Companion* (1853). http://www.worldwidewords.org/qa/qa-thr3.htm (accessed May 26, 2011).

Rabbit, Winter. "144th Anniversary of the Sand Creek Massacre of Nov. 29, 1864." *Native American Netroot.* http://www.nativeamericannetroots.net/showDiary.do?diaryId=194 (accessed July 14, 2009).

Contributors

Susan M. Abram holds a PhD in history from Auburn University, where she wrote her dissertation on Cherokee participation in the Creek War. Her research focuses on southern history with an emphasis on Appalachia and southeastern Indians, particularly the Cherokee. She has also taught courses at Western Carolina University, Southwestern Community College (the Cherokee campus), and Haywood Community College and is active with the North Carolina chapter of the Trail of Tears Association.

Kathryn E. Holland Braund is Hollifield Professor of Southern History at Auburn University, where she specializes in the history of the Creek and Seminole Indians and early exploration in the South. She is the author of *Deerskins and Duffels: Creek Indian Trade with Anglo-America, 1685–1815* and coeditor, with Gregory Waselkov, of *William Bartram and Southeastern Indians*. She is also the editor of recent editions of James Adair's *History of the American Indians* and Bernard Romans's *Concise Natural History of East and West Florida*. She is currently writing a book about the Creek War.

Robert P. Collins earned his BA in German literature at Emory University and worked mainly in journalism and publishing before starting graduate study in history. He is a doctoral candidate at Auburn University, studying early US and, especially, Creek Indian history. His translation of the 1824 diary of a Swiss traveler in the Creek Nation appeared in the *Alabama Review* in 2006.

Gregory Evans Dowd is the author of *A Spirited Resistance: The North American Struggle for Unity, 1745–1815* and *War under Heaven: Pontiac, the Indian Nations, and the British Empire*. His work has won recognition from the American Association of University Publishers, the Western Historical Association, and the Gustavus Myers Center for the Study of Human Rights. He taught as a Fulbright scholar in South Africa, and he has held positions at the University of Notre Dame, Princeton University, and the University of Connecticut. He is currently director of the Program in American

Culture and professor of history and American culture at the University of Michigan, Ann Arbor.

John E. Grenier is the author of *The First Way of War: American War Making on the Frontier, 1607–1814,* which won the Society of Military History's Distinguished Book Award in 2007, and *The Far Reaches of Empire: War in Nova Scotia, 1710–1760,* which won the Wilson Award for the Most Outstanding Contribution to National Defense in the Field of Arts and Letters. Dr. Grenier retired from the US Air Force in 2009 after a twenty-year career. He is currently working on a biography of Robert Rogers. He lives with his wife and daughter in Colorado Springs, Colorado.

David S. Heidler and **Jeanne T. Heidler** met while studying at Auburn University, where both received their PhDs in US history. For the last nineteen years, they have lived in Colorado, where Jeanne is a professor of US History at the US Air Force Academy. As a team, they have written numerous books and articles dealing with the history of the early US republic, the antebellum period, and the Civil War. In addition, they are general editors for several series of monographs examining US civil-military relations, US soldiers' lives, and life on the home front. Random House recently published their book *Henry Clay: The Essential American,* and they are working on a study of the presidency of George Washington.

Ted Isham, a Muscogee (Creek) citizen and member of the Tulmuchusee tribal town and an adopted member of the Hillabee ceremonial ground, has served as the curator of the Creek Council House Museum in Okmulgee, Oklahoma, and the head of the Muscogee (Creek) Nation Preservation Department. He also works with the community as a language preservationist and teacher. He teaches the Creek language at Oklahoma State University in Stillwater, Oklahoma, and develops curricula to aid in teaching the language. Isham has worked on many projects with the Smithsonian Institution's Museum of the Native American Indian and has also worked as exhibit design consultant with Ralph Appelbaum and Associates for the yet-to-be-finished American Indian Cultural Center in Oklahoma City.

Ove Jensen is a park ranger at Horseshoe Bend National Military Park. Before joining the National Park Service in 1996, Jensen attended graduate school at Auburn University, where he specialized in US colonial and revolutionary history, and he served in the US Army for three years as a field artillery officer. During the Gulf War in 1991, Jensen participated in the liberation of Kuwait and earned the Bronze Star medal for combat service.

Tom Kanon is an archivist at the Tennessee State Library and Archives in Nashville, where he has been employed for the past sixteen years. He holds a master's degree in history from Middle Tennessee State University, where he is enrolled in their dissertation program in public history. He has written extensively on the War of 1812, particularly on frontier issues. He is currently working on a book-length treatment of Tennessee's involvement in the War of 1812.

Jay Lamar is director of the Carolyn Marshall Draughon Center for the Arts and Humanities at Pebble Hill, Auburn University. She is coeditor, with Jeanne Thompson, of *The Remembered Gate: Memoirs by Alabama Writers* and copublisher of or contributor to several other volumes, including *In the Path of the Storms: Bayou La Batre, Coden, and the Alabama Coast* and *Albert Murray and the Aesthetic Imagination of a Nation*, both published by The University of Alabama Press.

Marianne Mills served as the superintendent at Horseshoe Bend National Military Park from October 2006 through the fall of 2009. A career employee of the National Park Service, Marianne has worked at national parks from Alaska to the Virgin Islands and consulted with the governments of Hungary, Poland, and the Republic of Georgia on national park planning. She is an alumnus of Northwestern University, Western Illinois University, and the University of Washington.

James W. Parker is the director of Fort Toulouse/Jackson Park, a state historic site managed by the Alabama Historical Commission. An expert on early US forts, he is the author of several works on the War of 1812 in Alabama, including "Fort Jackson after the War of 1812," published in the *Alabama Review*.

Craig T. Sheldon Jr. is Distinguished Research Professor of Anthropology at Auburn University at Montgomery. He specializes in the archaeology and ethnohistory of the late prehistoric and historic periods in Alabama and adjacent regions. He has spent over seventeen years conducting archaeological investigations at Fort Toulouse, Fusihatchee, Hickory Ground, and other Creek Indian sites. His most recent publication was "French Habitations at the Alabama Post, ca. 1720–1763," in *Archéologiques*, coauthored with Ned J. Jenkins and Gregory A. Waselkov.

Robert G. Thrower has served as the tribal historic preservation officer for the Poarch Band of Creek Indians in Alabama for over five years. He is also executive director of the tribe's Calvin McGhee Cultural Authority. In these two positions, he is directly responsible for all aspects of Poarch Creek cultural education, museum development, and historic preservation. He has served as the chairman of the Culture and Heritage Committee for the United South and Eastern Tribes, Inc. This committee represents the culture and heritage concerns of twenty-five federally recognized tribes along the Eastern Seaboard and Gulf Coast. He is the chairman and cofounder of the Southeastern Anthropological Institute and vice president of the Alabama chapter of the Trail of Tears Association. He also serves as a board member of the National Trail of Tears Association. Thrower is a tribal member of the Poarch Creeks and a direct descendant of the Wind Clan of the Upper Creeks of Alabama. An ordained minister and tribal medicine man, he provided traditional spiritual teaching and guidance to participants within the Tribal Drug Court Program. He is also an artist, playwright, filmmaker, and poet.

Gregory A. Waselkov is originally from Cleveland, Ohio. He received a BA in anthropology from the University of Missouri and an MA and a PhD from the University of North Carolina. He served in a research position at Auburn University from 1979 to 1988 and has been on the faculty of the University of South Alabama since that time. Waselkov has directed archaeological research projects at Fort Jackson, Fort Mims, and several historic Creek Indian town sites, as well as at French colonial Old Mobile and numerous other prehistoric and historic sites in Alabama. His latest book, *A Conquering Spirit: Fort Mims and the Redstick War of 1813–1814,* won the Alabama Historical Association's 2008 Clinton Jackson Coley Award for the best work on Alabama local history.

Index

Adair, James, 14, 85–86
African American slaves, 4, 5, 18, 53, 73, 130, 161, 166, 167, 176, at Pensacola: 185, 186, 192, 193
Alba, Pedro de, 67, 70, 82n43
American soldiers. *See* US Army
Arango, Anastacio de, 63
archaeological sites, 200–201; looting of, 201. *See also* Creek Indians
Armstrong, John, 108
Armstrong, Robert, 116
atássa. See war clubs
Austill, Jeremiah, 96
Autossee, 87, 201, *202,* 209, 249; battle of, *xiv,* 5, 78, 96–97, 127, 177, 201, 209, 210, 215, 260

Bailey, Dixon, 16, 18, 20, 21, 96, 265
Bailey, James, 12
Bailey, Mary, 21
Bailey, Ralph, 96
Bains, Samuel, 110
Barnard, Timpoochee, 5
Bartram, William, 13–14, 94
Bean, Jesse, 152, 155
Beasley, Daniel, 61, 96
Benton, Thomas Hart, 165
Big Warrior, 4, 6, 69
black drink, 165
Black Warrior River, *202;* attacks on Creek villages, 111
bloodroot, 89
Blount, Willie, 22, 77, 108, 171
Blue, Uriah, 166, 193, 195
Bonar, William, 89
Braund, Kathryn E. Holland, 32–33, 36, 48n32
Breast Works (Horseshoe Bend). *See* Horseshoe Bend: battle of
Brewer, Willis, 23
broken days, 84–86
Brown, James, 130
Brown, Jerry E., 11–12
Brown, John, 135, 256
Brown, Richard, 123, 124, 125, 126, 130, 132, 137n5
Burnt Corn, battle of, *xiv,* xv, 3, 4, 16, 17–18, 21, 53, 54, 60, 61, 68, 71, *72,* 75, 77, 160, 176, 183, 204, 216, 249, 262; creek, *72, 236–37,* 249; map, *72*
Busk. *See* Green Corn Ceremony

Calebee Creek, battle of, *xiv,* 5, 127, 204, 207, 214, 216, 229n43, 230n46, 249, 260
Call, Richard, 22, 130
Caller, James, 16, 21, 60, 61, 68, 71, 77, 82n38
Camp Coffee, 249, 257
Camp Coosa (Coocey), 123, 257. *See also* Fort Armstrong
Campbell, John, 174
cane, 15; canebreaks, 55, 147, 204, 205, 210; used for "broken days," 84–85, 100n12
Canoe Fight, *xiv,* xv, 5, 86, 96, *236–37,* 263
Caron, 186
Carroll, William, 113, 130
Carson, Joseph, 61, 162
cattle, 15, 128, 184, 208; and origins of the Creek war, 15, 18, 55, 73, 208
Cave, Alfred, 94

Chekelli Mico, 86
Cherokee Indians, *xiv,* 21, 31–32, 33, 43, 65, 74, 238: actions involving, 125–27, 129, 130–35; enlistment period in Creek War, 122–23; guides, spies, and translators, 124, 132; home front, 122, 128, 129; at Horseshoe Bend, 178; organization of troops, 123; supply problems, 128; use of white plumes, 98; weapons, 111, 128, 130
Chickasaw Indians, *xiv,* 33, 88, 100n20, 122, 166, 173, 175, 208
Chinnabee, *152,* 258; Camp Chinnabee, 257; Fort Chinnabee, *xiv,* 210
Chivington, John M., 24
Choctaw Indians, *xiv,* 2, 5, 25, 32, 33, 39, 60, 68, 74, 87, 93, 122, 127, 166, 173, 175, 208, 213, 238
civilization policy, 1, 3, 12–13, 15, 17, 107, 109, 123
Claiborne, Ferdinand L, 5, *19,* 60, 71, 78, 100n6, 127, 176, 177, 207, 235, *236–37*
Claiborne, J. F. H, 44
Cluwallee Camps, 158, 159, 161
Cocke, John, 23, 108, 113, 123, 126, 128, 136, 176, 177
Coffee, John, 22, 23, 111, 112, 113, 116, 124, 125, 129, 130, 133, 134, 148, 149, 152, 153, 177, 178, 203
Colbert, William, 166
Coleman, James, 187
Coley, Clinton Jackson, xii, xiii
comet of 1811, 38, 39, 42
Coneta, 162
Coosada King, 161
Cornells, Alexander, 42, 44, 54, 69
Cornells, James, 63, 71, 75, 76, 77, 266; deposition of, 72–73, 74; wife of, 63, 72, 76, 77
Cotterill, R. S., 12
Coulter, Betsy, 63, 72, 67, 77
Crawley, Martha, 107, 119n7, 125
Creek Indians, *xiv, 164, 202;* building techniques, 226n34; ceremonies, 90–91, 94–95; "civilization" program, 1, 12–15; dances, 94–95, 95; deerskin trade, 14–15, 64, 212–23; encroachment by Americans on Creek lands, 54–55; gender roles, 13, 14; land ownership, 14; modern tribal towns, 248; origin myth, 86–87; regional divisions, 4; towns, 4, 5, 204–8; Tensaw, at, 3, 12, 16–21, 160; war poles, 87; women, 1, 14, 91,92, 214. *See also* Creek National Council; Red Sticks
Creek National Council, 3, 4, 45, 55, 59, 69, 95, 175–76
Creek War, *xiv,* 6, 53, 176, *202,* 210–12; allied (National) Creeks, 5, 6, 124, 126, 148, 151, 153, 154, 155, 178, 238; archaeological sites, 200–201; border violence, 106; border warfare, 107; British "packet from Canada," 53–54, 55, 56–57, 58, 75–76; causes, 3, 10–13, 59, 158; Cherokee view, 122; Creek prisoners of war, 126, 127, 132, 135, 162–63, 178; defensive stockades, 210–11; earthquakes, 41–45; Federal Road, 11–12, 55; military insignia, *241;* post-war devastation, 135, 161; refugee camps, 209, 210; refugees, 159; rumors, impact of, 54–55; surviving historical sites, 232–33; terrain and troop movements, *xiv,* 205–7, 235; towns, destruction of, 208–9, 217; war camps, 209–10; warriors, 97, 98; weapons of allied Creeks, 97–98; women, 4, 17, 22, 125, 126, 127, 128, 132, 135, 151, 153, 159, 161, 162–63, 178, 209. *See also individual battles;* Red Sticks; weapons
Crockett, David, 23, 109–10, 112, 124, 125, 179, 217
Cussetah Mico, 69
Cyrus, 167

Dale, Sam, 5, 86
Dance of the Lakes, 94, 95
Dauphin Island, 182, *190–91,* 195, 249, 264
Dickens, Roy, 209, 211, 212, 224n25
Ditto's Landing, 124, 257
Donelson, Alexander, 116
Donelson, Mary, 120n23
Doyle, Edmund, 184, 185
Duck River, Tennessee, 54, 95, 107

Durant, Sophia, 108
Dyer, Mary, 266
Dyer, Robert, 125

earthquakes, 30, 38–44, 45, 50n42, 50n48, 50n54, 51n58; and Christianity, 43–44, 45. *See also* New Madrid earthquake
Eaton, John H., 25–26, 93
Eccanachaca. *See* Holy Ground (Eccanachaca)
Edmunds, R. David, 49n35
Emuckfau, *202;* Emuckfau Creek, battle of, *xiv,* 5, 116, 127, 130, 132, 147, 178, 249, 256
Enitachopco, *202;* battle of, *xiv,* 5, 116, 130–31, 147–48, 178, 249, 256
Ethridge, Robbie, 36, 80n21, 206, 221n8
Eufaula, 5, *202*

Federal Road, 2, 11–12, 27n4, 55, 59, 73, *164,* 204, 207, 249, 250, 267
First Regiment of Tennessee Volunteer Infantry, 110
Fish Ponds, 5
Florida, Spanish, political situation, 57–58
Flournoy, Thomas, 60, 70, 186
Floyd, John, 5, 127, 176, 177, 207
Forbes and Company, 57, 64, 66, 68, 79, 81, 184, 186, 187
Forbes, John. *See* Forbes and Company
Fort Armstrong, 123, 124, 126, 127, 129, 130, 132, 249, 257
Fort Bainbridge, *xiv,* 249, 260
Fort Barrancas, 66, 193
Fort Bowyer, 8, 163, 165, 182, 186, *190–91,* 194, 233–34, 250, 263; American prisoners from, 195; first British attack on, 186–92; second British offensive, 194–95; weaponry at Fort Bowyer, 188–89, 192
Fort Burrows, *xiv,* 233, 250, 260
Fort Charlotte (or Carlota), 2, 183, 233, 238, 252, 264
Fort Chinnabee, 210
Fort Claiborne, *xiv,* 207, 235, *236–37, 241,* 245n12, 245n17, 250, 264
Fort Dearborn, 174, 176
Fort Decatur, *xiv,* 201, 233, 250, 260
Fort Deposit, *xiv,* 110, 112, 234–35, 243, 245n12, 249, 250, 257, 260
Fort Detroit, 174, 175
Fort Harrison, 173, 174
Fort Hull, *xiv,* 250, 260
Fort Jackson, *xiv,* 159, 163, 215, 217, 233, 250, 260, 262; refugees at, 163, 165; prisoners, 162
Fort Leslie, 210, 252, 257
Fort Madison, 210, 250, 263, 265
Fort Michilimackinac, 174
Fort Mims, 250–51, 263, 265, 266, 267; artifacts from, 227, 229, 230; battle of, *xiv,* xv, 4, 5, 12, 16–18, 21, 23, 36, 53, 61, 78, 88, 96, 159, 160, 107, 167, 176, 213, 214, 233; map, *xiv, 19, 20, 236–37;* propaganda by US following, 21–22, 107–9
Fort Mitchell, *xiv,* 201, 210, 215, 217, 230n47, 232, 251, 260
Fort Montgomery, 166, 201, 210, 225n28, 234, 239, *241,* 251, 264
Fort Morgan, 234, 250, 252, 263
Fort Sinquefield, *xiv,* 53, 210, *236–37,* 251, 263
Fort Stoddert (and Mount Vernon), *xiv, 164,* 210, 232, *236–37,* 251, 264
Fort Strother, *xiv,* 105, 110, 111, 112, 113, 116, 117, 124, 126, 128, 130, 132, 163, 177, 178, 201, 205, 206, 243, 249, 251–52, 258
Fort Toulouse, 159, 233, 250
Fort Toulouse/Fort Jackson State Historical Site, 232, 233, 262
Fort Wayne, 174; Treaty of Fort Wayne, 172, 173
Fort Williams, *xiv,* 132, 139n26, 147, 163, 201, 243, 249, 252, 257, 258
Foster, James, 135
Francis, Josiah, 6, 56, 71, 73, 74, 78, 81n28, 96, 103n58, 160, 162, 163, 166–67, 184, 208, 226n35
Friends of Horseshoe Bend, xiii
Fusihatchee, 201, *202,* 215, 217, 222n11, 227n41, 229n43, 231n51, 261

Gaines, George S., 60
Georgia, 15

Gibson, John H., 124
Graham, Joseph, 159, 162, 165, 235
Gray, John, 162
Great Britain, 31; agents, 55, 59, 159, 184; American prisoners of, 195; artillery, 195, 196; colonists, 33; Indian allies, 166, 175, 185, 193; naval force, 163, 182, 184, 185, 186, 187, 189, 192, 193; rumor of British aid to Red Sticks, 54, 56, 58, 62–63, 71; strategy in War of 1812, 182–83, 187. *See also various British ships*
Green Corn Ceremony, 90–91, 94
Griffith, Benjamin W., Jr., 13, 22
Gun Hill (Horseshoe Bend), 149, 211, 216

Halbert and Ball, *The Creek War,* 11, 17, 18, 23, 24–25, 44, *72,* 82n38, 83n56, 85, 86, 224n19, 227n36
Halbert, Henry S., 11, 17, 18, 23, 24, 44, 82n38, 83n56, 85, 86, 88–89, 96, 100n16
Hambly, William, 184, 185
Harrison, William Henry, 32, 33–34, 38, 52n64, 172–73, 174, 175, 180n8
Hartsell, Jacob, 126, 245n12
Harvey, Benjamin, 239–40, 246n23
Hawkins, Benjamin, 1, 2–3, 9n2, 11, 12–13, 17, 18, 33, 41, 42, 44, 54, 55, 69, 84, 95–96, 97, 98, 103n63, 162, 163, 175, 193, 203, 222n11
Henry, Robert, 189
Hermes, HMS, 163, 185, 187, 189, 192, 195
Hickory Ground, 12, 158, 159, 161, 201, *202,* 217–18, 261
Hicks, Charles, 122
High Head Jim, 65, 70, 71, 73, 74–75, 81
Hillabee, *202;* battle at, *xiv,* 5, 113, 126, 247, 256
Hillabee Massacre. *See* Hillabee: battle at
Hoithlewaulee, 158, *202,* 209, 210, 217, 222, 260, 261
Holmes, J. L., map, *xx–xxi*
Holy Ground (Eccanachaca), *xiv,* xv, 5, 78, 127, 146, 161, 207, 209, 210, 213, 224, 233, 239, 252, 260, 263, 264
Homathle Mico, 184
Hopkins, Samuel, 174
Hopoithle Mico, 162
Horseshoe Bend, 248, 252, 256; American artillery, use of, 148, 149; barricade at, 132–33, 149, 211–12, 216–17; battle of, xiv, xx–xxi, 97, 105, 132–35, 150, 177–78, 214, 233, 239, 243; canoes, 132, 133, 151, 153, 178; captured Creeks, 151, 153; casualty figures, 135, 149, 153; Cherokee rear attack, 133, 150–51; description of battle, 148–49, 150, 151–53; Gun Hill, 149, 211; map, *xx–xxi;* secondary fortifications at, 149–50, 151; significance, xiii, 158, 179, 184; size of Jackson's forces, 148, topography, 146
Horseshoe Bend National Military Park, xi, xii, 146, 154–56, *155,* 232, 233, 243. *See also* Friends of Horseshoe Bend
Houston, Sam, 134, 153, 179, 229n43

Indian countrymen, 62; rumor as a unifying agent, 59–60
Indian removal, 26, 171–72
Innerarity, James, 68, 80n24, 186, 192
Innerarity, John, 64, 65–68, 70–71, 76–77, 80n24, 81n28, 82n43, 186, 187, 192
Isaacs, Sam, 21, 70

Jackson, Andrew, 21, 44, 58, 106, 108, 111–12, 113, 116, 117, 118, 124, *188;* Creek campaign of, 6, 105, *131,* 184; establishes Fort Jackson, 158–59; Horseshoe Bend campaign, 147–53; invasion of Florida, 192–93; Weatherford's surrender, 159–60. *See also* Tennessee militia
James family (attack on), 96
Jim Boy, 66, 69, 81n33, 82n38
John Forbes and Company, 57, 184
Jones, Polly, 159
Junaluska, 153

Kaské, Charlot, 30–31
Kemball family (attack on), 96

Lafitte, Jean, 186
Lashley's Fort, 126
Lawrence, William, 182, 186, 187–88, 189, 192, 194, 195, 196
Lincoln, Abraham, 26
Littafuchee, *202,* 258; battle at, 125, 256
Little Prince, 69

Little Warrior, 53, 54, 56, 58, 59, 62, 74
Lockyer, Nicholas, 186
Louisiana Purchase, 183
Lowry, John, 123, 125, 126, 128, 129, 130, 137n5

Mad Dog's Village, 127
Manac (Moniac), Sam. *See* Moniac (or Maniac, or Manac), Sam
Manrique, Don Mateo González, 56, 58, 63, 64, 67, 68, 76, 78 79, 185, 187, 193
Martin, Joel, 9n7, 39, 40, 41, 50n42, 75, 95
Martin, Thomas, xii, xiii
Master of Breath, 18
McArthur, Archibald, 24
McGhee, Linn, 21
McGhee, Lynn, 21
McGillivray, Alexander, family of, 12
McGirth, Zachariah, 66, 70
McHenry, Francis, 41–42
McIntosh, John, 135
McIntosh, William, 125, 127, 154, 166, 177, 178
McKenney, Thomas L., 38, 49n40, 84, 85, 86, 98, 99n3, 134
McKenzie, George, 211
McLemore, John, 135
McNair, David, 126, 140n29
McQueen, Peter, 18, 62, 63, 64, 66, 71, 74, 162, 166, 184
Meigs, Return J., 122, 123, 126, 128, 129–30, 135–36, 137n5
Menawa, 6, 99, 153–54, *154*
métis, 21, 61, 159, 160, 161, 162, 163, 167, 207, 208, 210, 211, 224n23, 226n29; term described, 18, 168n5
Milfort, Louis LeClerk, 85, 93
militia: discipline of, 164–65, 177; at Enitachopco, 178; equipment of, 110; Georgia, 104, 127, 159, 166, 171; North and South Carolina, 159; in Northwest Indian wars, 171, 174, 175; at Talladega, 113; training, 235; weaponry and equipment, 214–16, 238, 240–43. *See also* Mississippi Territorial militia; Tennessee militia
Miller Covered Bridge, xii
Milton, Homer, 159
Mims, Samuel, 4, 266
Mississippi Territorial militia, 3, 5, 16, 21, 53, 60, 61, 63, 68, 71, 73, 109, 148, 160, 162. *See also* Burnt Corn, battle of
Mississippi Territory, 10, 53, 60–61, 78n1, 107. *See also* Tensaw settlements
Mobile, 2, 20, 58, 62, 63, 64, 68, 70, 75, 78, 159, 160, 161, 163, *164,* 166, 183, 185, 186, 187, 192, 193, 195, 196, 204, 207, 208, 210, 233, 238, 252; seizure by US, 68, 183, 263
Mobile Bay, 41, 163, 182, 187, 195, 238; map of, *190–91*
Mobile Point, 182, 186, 187, 192, 194, 250; map of, *190–91*
Mobile River, 53, 60, 61, 76, 78n1, 240
Mobile-Tensaw Delta, 207
Moniac (or Maniac, or Manac), Sam, 42, 71, 73–75, 76, 77, 94, 167, 208; deposition of, 73–75, 76, 77
Montgomery, Lemuel, 133, 153
Mooney, James, 38, 40, 49n40
Morgan, Gideon, 123, 126, 133
Mortar of Okchai, 14, 33
Mount Vernon cantonment, *xiv,* 71. *See also* Fort Stoddert (and Mount Vernon)

National Park Service, xi, *155,* 232; criteria for a national park, xi; history of Horseshoe Bend National Military Park, xi–xiii, 252
Navy Cove, 182, 252, 264
Neamathla, 167
Negro Fort, 167
New Madrid earthquake, 7, 38, 50n48, 50n50, 51n58
New Orleans, battle of, 166, 193, 194
Nicolls, Edward, 166, 185–87, 192, 193
Nixon, George, 162
Northwest Indian war, 173–75
Norton, John, 33
Nuyaka, xx, 5, 127, 129, 151, 201, *202,* 206, 209, 224n25, 248, 252, 258

Okchai, 5, 151, *202,* 248, 258
Okfuskee, 5, *154, 202,* 206, 258
Opotheleyaholo, 98
Orpheus, HMS, 184
Osage Indians, 33

Osborn, Audley L., 72
Owsley, Frank L., Jr., 11, 16–17, 23, 25–26, 38, 56, 68

Pakenham, Edward, 166, 194, 195
pan-Indian movement, 45, 54, 65–66
Parkman, Francis, 33
Path Killer, 123, 124, 129
Patriot War, 2, 183
Pearson, John, 161
Pensacola, *xiv,* 2, 67, 87, 164, 207; British activities at, 185–87; visited by Red Sticks, 3, 54–67
Perkins, Nicholas, 116
Perryman, Legus F., 91
Pickett, Albert James, 12, 21, 55, 59, 86, 96
Pigeon Roost, 174
Pigot, Hugh, 184
Piker, Joshua, 35, 36, 48n28
Pimartam's Town, 174
Pinckney, Thomas, 109
Pipkin, Philip, 163
"plan of civilization." *See* civilization policy
Poarch Band of Creek Indians, 21, 163
Pontiac, 30, 33, 34, 38; Pontiac's War, 30, 32
Porter, Pleasant, 91
Proctor, Henry, 175
Prophet, The. *See* Tenskwatawa
Prophet's Town, 33, 54, 173
Prospect Bluff, 166, 185, 192, 193
puccoon, 89

Rain Crow, 135
Randon, John: plantation of, 5, 263
Red Pole, 32
Red Stick Society, 99
Red Stick War. *See* Creek War
Red Sticks: captives of, 4, 98, 107; capture of US mail, 64, 75; captured, 125, 126, 132, 153, 177, 234; casualty figures, 111, 125, 135, 177, 178; material culture, 213–14; military objectives, 146–47; Pensacola, visit in 1813, 63–69, 71–77; prophets, 3, 6, 44, 56, 65, 73–74, 75, 84, 133, 158, 161, 203; spies, 129; supply problems, 54, 64, 75, 111; surrender, 161; weapons of, 73, 96, 111, 203, 213–16, 229n43. *See also* Francis, Josiah; High Head Jim; McQueen, Peter; war clubs
Reid, John, 93, 110, 112
Ribbon Dance, 91, *92*
Ridge, Major, 128, 130, *134,* 153
River Raisin, battle of, 54, 175, 176
Ross, John, 127, 132, 153
Russell, William, 174

Sand Creek Massacre, 24
Saunders, Alexander, 127
Saunt, Claudio, 17
Sayre, Gordon, 38, 43
Searcey, Robert, 128
Selocta, *152*
Seminole Indians, 2, 6, 74, 85, 158, 163, 166–67, 184, 188, 193; First Seminole War, 6, 167; Third Seminole War, 167
Sequoyah, 153
Sevier, John, 106, 117–18
Shawnee Indians, 2, 31, 66, 68; medicine sticks, 85
Shoe Boots, 135
Silver, Peter, 59–60, 61
slaves, 36, 53, 62, 71, 73, 96, 127, 130, 145n82, 153, 160, 166, 167, 176, 185, 186, 192, 193, 208, 251. *See also* African American slaves
Smith, Harry, 195
Snodgrass, William, 129
Sophia, HMS, 186
Southerland, Henry D., Jr., 11
Spanish Florida: policy towards Creeks, 78, 183; political situation, 57–58, 63, 183; rumor of aid to Red Sticks, 54, 55, 56, 58, 62–63, 71. *See also* Pensacola
Stiggins, George, 43, 56, 86, 93, 94, 267
Stiggins, Mr. (Joseph?), 42, 50n54
Stump, John, 116
Sugden, John, 39–40, 41, 85

Tait, James, 96–97, 103n64
Taitt, David, 100n12
Talladega, 206, 211; battle at, *xiv,* 5, 110–11, 112–13, *114–15,* 126, 130, 142n54, 147, 177, 201, 214, 217, 226n29, 229n43, 252–53, 256; map of, *114–15, 202*
Tallassee Fixico, 217–18

Tallassee King, 97, 103n64, 162
Tallushatchee, *202,* 253; battle at, *xiv,* 5, 22–23, 112, 125, 129, 147, 177, 201, 205, 207, 214, 229n43, 256
Tarrant, Leonard L.: map, *xx–xxi*
Tate, David, 71; deposition, 68, 75–77
Tatum, Howell, 210
Tecumseh, 2, *37,* 85, 99n7; confused with his brother, 42; early influences, 30–32; meaning of name, 39; pan-Indian confederacy, 34, 36; settlements associated with 35; southern tour, 44; speech at Tuckabatchee, 43–44, 49n40, 203; views of 42n64; visit to Creeks, 12–13
Ten Islands, 112, 124–25, 126, 132
Tennessee militia, 105, 106, 107, 109–10, 119n8; artillery, 116; discipline of, 110–11, 163–65; East Tennessee Militia, 108, 112, 113, 163, 176; engagements, 111–17; First Tennessee Regiment, 163; at Horseshoe Bend, 148–49, 151; problems, 107, 108–10; recruitment of, 113, 117; enlistment period, 111, 120n21, 129, 158; Second Regiment East Tennessee Volunteer Militia, 129; Second Regiment of Volunteer Mounted Riflemen, 125; West Tennessee Militia, 108. *See also* militia; Mississippi Territorial militia
Tennessee settlers, fear of Indian attack, 58, 107–8
Tensaw settlements, 3, 10, 16, 20, 42, 57, 59, 70, 160, 161, 213. *See also* Mississippi Territory
Tenskwatawa, 32, 33, 34, 38, 49, 52, 54, 85, 172; beliefs of, 36
Third US Infantry Regiment, 108, 238–40
Thirty-Ninth Infantry Regiment, 5, 108, 132, 134, 148, 159, 162, 177, 178, 239
Thompson, Ephraim, 239, 240
Thompson, Jack, 124
Tippecanoe, battle of, 33, 35, 173–74
Tohopeka, *xx–xxi,* 24, 48n28; meaning of, 5, 209. *See also* Horseshoe Bend
Tom (enslaved African), 96
Tomathly Micco, 98
Toulmin, Harry, 60, 73, 75, 266
Tourculla. *See* Isaacs, Sam
Treaty of Fort Jackson, 6, 25–26, 163, *164,* 165, 184, 217–18
Treaty of Fort Wayne (1809), 172, 173
Treaty of New York (1790), 59
Tuckabatchee, 38, 95, 96, 164, 172, 177, *202;* siege of, 3, 12, 260
Tukatatchee Miko, 226n34
Turkey Town, 123, 124, 125, 129, *202,* 259
Tuskegee, 159, 233, 261
Tuskenea, 69
Twenty-Forth US Infantry, 239

US Army: artillery, use of: 97, 111, 116, 130, 133, 148, 149, 155, 159, 163, 178, 186, 187, 188, 189, 192, 195, 211, 216, 235, 241; atrocities by, 23, 24–25; attack on Pensacola, 165–66; burning Indian towns, 127, 202–3; Creek War strategy, 108–9; discipline of troops, 110–11; "first way of war," 170–71; grapeshot, use of, 97, 189, 209, 215, 216–17; Indian allies, 5, 6, 25, 124, 125, 148, 151, 152, 153, 154, 155, 162, 178; military camps, 234–35; objectives in Indian wars, 171, 176–77; prisoners of, 125, 126, 132, 135, 177, 234; tactics, 23, 125, 132, 174; soldiers' clothing, 216, 239–40, *241,* 242; soldiers' equipment, 238–43; soldiers' rations, 110, 242–43; supply depots, 159, 205; supply problems, 105–6, 110, 125, 126, 128–29; transportation of supplies, 124, 161–62, 235, 238. *See also* militia; weapons; *specific forts; specific regiments*

Walker, John, 122, 127, 130
Walsh, Paddy, 96
war clubs, 87, 89–90, *90,* 201; burial good, 91–92; ceremonial use, 91, *92,* 98–99; description, types of, 89–90, 93–94; dyes for, 89; Fort Mims, at, 96; manufacture of, 88–89; method employed, 89, 93, 94, 96–97, 213; origin myth, 85–86; painting of, 93; red sticks, known as, 86; symbol of war, 3, 59, 84, 87, 91–95, 98, 101n26. *See also* weapons
war poles, 87, 100n20
Warren, James, 162
Waselkov, Gregory A., 17

weapons, 88–89, *90*, 93, 95, 202, *215*; bayonets, 214; bow and arrows, 23, 93, 97, 112, 214–15, 229n43; knives, 66, 95, 97, 135, 213–14, 227; guns, 213, 215–16, 230n45; hatchets, 31, 66, 89, 91, 99, 127, 214, 228; metal-tipped arrows, 215, 229n43; pistols, 215; swords, 73, 214, 240. *See also* Red Sticks; war clubs
Weatherford, William, 4, 5, 6, 18, 75, 96, 99, 159–61, 162, 208
Webb, Jesse, 97
West Florida. *See* Mobile; Pensacola; Spanish Florida
Whale, The (Tuq-qua, Tucfo, or Tuck Wah), 133, 151
White, James, 126, 177
White, John, 123
White, Richard, 35
white stick (term), 99n2, 101n26
Wilbanks, Warren, 24
Wilkinson, James, 183
Williams, John, 132
Wolf Trail, 160
Woods, John, 111
Wright, J. Leitch, Jr. 17, 21

Yuchi Indians, 5, 6, 262

Zúñiga, Mauricio de, 56